D1567765

The Professional Caterer's Handbook

How to Open and Operate
a Financially Successful
Catering Business

with CD-ROM

Lora Arduser
Douglas Robert Brown

THE PROFESSIONAL CATERER'S HANDBOOK
How to Open and Operate a Financially Successful Catering Business—With CD-ROM

By Lora Arduser and Douglas Robert Brown

Published by **ATLANTIC PUBLISHING GROUP, INC.**

ATLANTIC PUBLISHING GROUP, INC. • 1405 SW 6th Ave • Ocala, FL 34471

800-814-1132 • www.atlantic-pub.com • sales@atlantic-pub.com

SAN Number :268-1250

ISBN-13: 978-0910627-60-3
ISBN-10: 0-910627-60-6

Library of Congress Cataloging-in-Publication Data

Arduser, Lora.
   The professional caterer's handbook : how to open and operate a
financially successful catering business with CD-ROM / Lora Arduser and
Douglas Robert Brown.
      p. cm.
   ISBN 0-910627-60-6 (alk. paper)
   1. Caterers and catering--Management--Handbooks, manuals, etc. I. Brown,
Douglas Robert, 1960- II. Title.

TX921.A74 2005
642'.4068--dc22

                     2005027508

CASE STUDIES & GLOSSARY: Robert Frank
ART DIRECTION, INTERIOR & COVER DESIGN: Meg Buchner • megadesn@mchsi.com

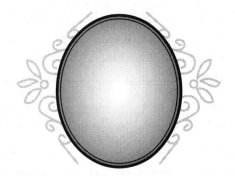

Table of Contents

Chapter 3 Computers and Software 113

Chapter 4   Traditional Marketing   121

Chapter 5   Web Sites   135

Chapter 6   Public Relations   145

Chapter 7   Managing the Event   159

Chapter 8   Setting Up the Event   183

Chapter 9   Beverage Functions   211

Chapter 10 Staffing and Personnel 239

Chapter 11   Pricing and Menus   289

Chapter 12
Food Presentation and Production   319

Chapter 13   Cost Controls   333

Chapter 14
Sanitation and Safety Procedures 375

Chapter 15 Equipment 411

Introduction

If you are looking for one comprehensive book on how to plan, start and operate a successful catering operation, then this is it! No detail is left out of this "encyclopedic" new book explaining the risky but often highly rewarding business of catering. Whether your catering operation is on-premise, off-premise, mobile, inside a hotel, part of a restaurant, or run from your own home kitchen, anyone in the catering field will find this book very useful.

The Professional Caterer's Handbook covers the processes of starting and managing a catering business in an easy-to-understand manner; pointing out methods to increase your chances of success, identifying common mistakes that often doom startups, and showing you how to avoid them!

You will learn how to:

- Find a location designed for success.

- Draw up a winning business plan.

- Buy an existing operation.

- Market your business for success.

- Manage basic cost-control systems.

- Hire, train and keep great employees.

- Plan profitable menus.

- Ensure food safety and follow HACCP principles.

- Layout and plan equipment needs.

To supplement all the valuable information you will learn, we have also created a companion CD-ROM that contains all the forms presented in the book as well as a 100+ page business plan for you to modify for your specific circumstances. Anyone who is in, or wants to be in, the catering business is definitely in for a treat, so let's get started on your way to building a profitable and rewarding catering operation!

From the Experts

I had my first behind-the-scenes glimpse into the world of professional catering when I was a busboy at sixteen. One of our restaurant managers started a catering division as a way to increase sales and profits. It was exciting to see how the events unfolded and the praise he received for being an all-star for the company.

Since then I've always worked around catering: working seasonally for private clubs, owning a bartending/event planning company, running a high-volume restaurant that boasted a third of its sales in catering, and currently I am a consultant and an author in the catering business.

As a student of business, I've always appreciated the catering business model. Startup costs are relatively low, you don't have to invest in an expensive high-visibility location, and you can even bootstrap your operation by renting out kitchen space to start. You have control of your life and your calendar because you can close out dates to meet important family commitments.

The praise and satisfaction of an event done well are rewarding and addictive. Our business is full of successes that started from humble beginnings and became multi-million-dollar operations.

The biggest challenge you'll face is changing your paradigm from caterer to owner of a catering company. Our comfort level tries to keep us wearing our technician's hat. Your profitability will be determined by shedding that hat at times and focusing on those proactive duties that add to your top and bottom line.

Due to the larger transaction size and the almost-unlimited niches one can target for catered events, it gives a caterer an unfair advantage over other food-related business models.

The time is ripe to be in the catering business. Whether you are just beginning your journey or are a seasoned pro, *The Professional Caterer's Handbook* is the perfect catering business primer and guide. This book can almost stand alone as an operations model for you. I wish it had been around when I started my company because it would have taken a lot of pain out of my learning curve!

This book gets to the nitty-gritty and leaves the fluff behind, with information on choosing a location, obtaining financing, staffing, and operational and marketing issues. You'll find many resources to give you an even deeper understanding of the issues that will affect you.

I'm not sure where I heard the quote, "School's never out for the professional," but it is vital to your survival that you and your staff never stop learning and growing. I urge you to invest in extra copies of *The Professional Caterer's Handbook* for your key personnel so you can profit together.

Happy catering!

Michael Attias, President
The Results Group
Brentwood, TN
www.ezRestaurantMarketing.com

Foreward

Hospitality is probably the most diverse industry in the world; it is certainly one of the largest, employing millions of people in a bewildering array of jobs around the globe. Sectors range from the glamorous five-star resort to the less fashionable, but arguably more meaningful, institutional areas such as hospitals, schools and colleges. Yet of these many different sectors, catering has to be the most challenging—and the most rewarding.

Whatever the size of the catering operation, the variety of opportunities available is endless. As one line in this book states, "The sky is the limit with catering." To test the limits, however, requires dedication, innovation, and simple hard work. Whilst the essential skills, both craft and managerial, can be found in other sectors of the industry, it is only in catering that a perfect blend is required if a successful business is to result. And that blend is often required in one person—you!

The scale, complexity and frequency of the demands placed on the caterer would tax the most committed and accomplished military logistician, but you have to do it on your own. This means that competence in cooking, food and wine service, site development, furnishings, transportation, recruitment, training, as well as design, creative flair, a good sales technique, and sound budgetary and planning skills are all fundamental attributes of a good caterer. If this sounds challenging, you're correct, but it is also the gateway to great rewards, where no two functions are the same, where variety comes as standard, and where every day is as fresh and exciting as your very first event.

If you want to accept this challenge, then *The Professional Caterer's Handbook* is the book for you. Each page is full of ideas and sound advice, covering every aspect of a catering operation. Its comprehensive coverage and easy style ensures that the novice caterer will quickly learn not only the fundamentals such as good kitchen management and sound menu planning, but will also be guided on essential business skills such as cost control, accounting and marketing. *The Professional Caterer's Handbook* provides so much information that it is also useful to the more experienced caterer who is perhaps seeking to expand or diversify. Whatever your needs as a caterer, this book has to be your essential companion.

Philippe Rossiter, MBA, FHCIMA
Chief Executive

Catering Basics

Catering has come a long way from the simple chicken and prime rib buffets of the past. "Customers today are looking for the catered experience to be more restaurant-like," says National Restaurant Association Chairman Denise Marie Fugo, who is also president and CEO of Sammy's in Cleveland, Ohio. Fugo and her husband, Ralph DiOrio, started doing small private banquets and off-premise catering in 1988. Sammy's catering eventually became so successful that Fugo closed the restaurant to concentrate solely on catering.

According to the National Restaurant Association's Industry Forecast, social caterers are one of the fastest-growing segments of the restaurant industry. There are over 53,000 caters listed in the Yellow Pages across the United States. According to the online journal catersource®, **www.catersource.com**, the annual sales of these 53,000 caterers are between $7 and $8 billion. This figure includes off-premise and banquet facility caterers but not hotels.

No doubt, catering offers high income potential. Many people leave the worlds of business, law and medicine, to name a few, to begin a second career in catering. While catering can be a lucrative career, it is important to keep all the aspects of the job in perspective. Catering is hard work, and often the easiest part of the job is the cooking. When you're catering an off-premise wedding for 300 people, someone has to load, unload, and load up again the crates of china, silverware and glasses—more often than not, that person is you!

Remember, too, that catering hours are long and the work is done when everyone else in the world is socializing. You don't just work the event, you work hard for many days, weeks, and even months before the event. And when you are working an event, chances are you are forgoing your own social events. For caterers, evenings, weekends and lunchtime are bread and butter times, not down times.

With catering, timing is everything. You need to be able to multi-task, organize your time with military precision, and be prepared for the unexpected. Caterer Bev Goldberg, recalls a time when she encountered the highly unexpected: She was getting ready for a cocktail party in a client's home and double checking her master list: linens, check; plates, check; glassware, check; soft drinks, check; garnishes, check; hors d'oeuvres, check; ice, check. Satisfied that everything needed for the party was ready and loaded into the van, she and two of her staff left for the event location. Upon arrival, she discovered no host and no guests! "The person who had contracted for the party had apparently forgotten and was not at home," she says with a laugh. A veteran caterer with more than 30 years of experience, Goldberg, who co-owns Artistry Catering in Chantilly, Virginia, with her son, Randy, has become used to the frenetic pace and unexpected occurrences of this growing profession. "I love catering," she says. "People still think this is a glamorous job, but it's just plain hard work."

Not yet daunted? Okay, let's see if you've got the skills to back up your enthusiasm.

Skills Needed in the Catering Business

If you are an excellent cook, competent in artistic food presentation, possess some basic business knowledge, and love working with people, you have the basic prerequisites, but there are many skills and competencies that make for successful caterers.

COOKING AND FOOD PRESENTATION

Catered events, unlike restaurant meals, are usually centered around a special event such as a wedding, a product launch, or a special business meeting. As such, people expect more when attending a catered function. The food has to be outstanding and so does the presentation. For some venues (and especially for some clients), you will be told that presentation is the most important factor, but always remember that no matter how artistically food is presented, if it doesn't taste good, it doesn't cut it. Make sure you and your staff are experienced with both aspects of food preparation.

PLANNING AND ORGANIZATION

Whether you cater off-premise or on-premise for business or social functions, you absolutely must have strong planning and organization skills. If you plan smartly, the physical work at the event goes much more smoothly. If you don't, you are likely to find yourself in the middle of a hectic, unsuccessful event with unhappy clients.

Planning is especially important with off-premise catering because you can't just run in the back and grab whatever it is you are missing. You'll need to make plans for how you will keep hot food hot and cold food cold. You need to know exactly what item gets served on which platter so you don't leave behind necessary serving dishes or servingware. You need to ensure that the silverware has been counted and recounted: you don't want to be one fork short with no extra staff to round one up.

While 70 percent of a typical restaurant is food-oriented, with the rest going for service and organization, this figure flip-flops to 30 percent in the catering business. The rest is delivery, transporting the food, lining up rental equipment, and juggling personnel. In restaurants, every day is fairly similar. In the catering world, however, each day and each event is different; this makes organizational skills vital!

EFFICIENCY AND CALM

As with any food industry business, efficiency is important. You need to ask yourself if you can work well under pressure. Because each event is unique, catering can be more stressful than many professions. It's not that most professions do not demand these skills, but in catering you not only have to deal with the stress, you have to make sure your customer never sees the stress. You need to be cool and remain smiling no matter what kind of chaos is tearing at your insides. You may have just finished putting out a fire in the oven after the praline topping for the French toast spilled over the side of the pan, but as soon as you come out to greet your client, you should have your chef jacket on, a smile on your face, and a cool, calm air that reassures your client that his or her event is going to be spectacular.

CRISIS MANAGEMENT

As a caterer a good deal of your time will be spent "putting out fires" literal ones like above, as well as figurative. Expect problems to happen, and be ready to solve them quickly and inventively. You need a great deal of crisis-management and problem-solving skills in catering, particularly with off-premise catering because you are dealing with so many unknown variables. You have to deal with event site problems, serving food at unfamiliar locations, and trying to find delivery entrances and parking spots. You might find, for example, that you planned to bake an egg casserole in hotel pans for a graduation brunch, but once you arrive on-site, the ovens are not wide enough for your pans to fit. The event must go on, so you need to be creative. You either need to find pans on-site or send an extra staff person (if you are so fortunate to have one) with petty cash to go buy one at a nearby kitchen store. With catering you have to learn to recognize that you are in the limelight and there are opportunities for error around every corner.

SALES AND MARKETING

While many caterers get into the industry because they like to cook, anyone who owns their own business knows that a significant portion of your time is spent on sales and marketing. Eventually you may have salespeople working for you, but when you start out in catering, you will be your salesperson. You'll be dealing with corporate executives, party planners, and nervous brides. You'll need to convince these prospective clients that you will not only provide a memorable feast, but that it will be there on time, presented attractively, and served unobtrusively! You will also need to come up with ways to retain business once you've been hired.

With catering it is *you* and not your company that is being hired. You must *personally* impress your client or else you won't have a deal! Make your first impression your best impression. If you have almost all the above-mentioned assets and lack on this one, take some evening courses on public speaking or just rent a couple of books and guides offering techniques on better communication and presentation skills. Regardless of how great a chef you are, how well you work under pressure, and how well you problem solve, without customers there is no business, so you need to be able to sell.

Assess Your Skills Profile

Whether you're a seasoned food service professional or someone changing professions to follow your passion, opening any type of food service establishment can be a daunting task. There are many factors to consider and much research to do in order to decide what type of catering to do—where to locate your business, who to hire, and what kind of food to serve. The most important factor to consider, however, is you. What are your skills and experience, and how prepared are you to start your own catering company?

To be a successful caterer you need to be able to prepare delicious food and be able to present it in an appetizing, mouth-watering way, all the while making a profit. If you are considering starting your own business and you have never worked in the restaurant industry or for a caterer before, you may want to consider looking for a position with a caterer to get a feel for the business before you take off on your own. There are lots of opportunities to pick up work during the busy seasons of late spring, early summer, and the holidays, when catering businesses crank up for graduations, weddings, and entertaining events. This is a great way to get a feel for both the back- and the front-of-the-house work. Make sure to ask lots of questions from where they rent china and tents to what type of accounting software they use.

If you don't have restaurant experience or credentials but you want to get into catering because your friends tell you what a great cook you are or you have helped others host an event and it went really well, you really should consider some formal cooking classes. If nothing else, you will improve your technique and become more efficient. Check out local technical colleges for cooking programs. You may also find cooking classes offered through some specialty food stores and restaurants.

Before you sink your money into the business, ask yourself some questions to see if this really is the direction you want to take. The answers to these questions will help you determine whether or not you are ready to open a catering business and whether you have the resources to do it.

- What are your goals in relation to owning a catering operation?

- What type of personality do you have? Are you an early riser or a night owl? Do you like interacting with people? Do you thrive on activity and crisis?

- Does your family support this decision and are they prepared to sacrifice time spent with you?

- What kind of management experience do you have?

- What kind of restaurant/catering experience do you have?

- How will you finance the operation? Can you live on your profits during those first years or do you have additional income from another source that you can live off of until the business takes off?

Be realistic. If you are a night owl, for instance, you should not consider catering brunches or other morning events. You aren't suddenly going to wake up bright and fresh at dawn simply because you decide to. It's more likely that you'll wake up grumpy and hate going to work every day. The food service industry can be tough even if you love it; don't make your work harder by mismatching your concept and your personality.

Assess Your Finances

Before you start buying pots and pans and searching for a location, take a good, hard look at your finances and determine if you really can afford to start a business. This is particularly important if you are a sole proprietor because your personal finances will come into play when you start looking for business financing.

How much of your own money can you afford to tie up in starting your catering business? If you are looking for financing you will probably have to demonstrate that you can finance a portion of it yourself. Do you have personal equity to invest in your company, and can you afford the monthly loan payments you'll need to make?

Make sure to check your personal credit before going out to find financing. To check on your personal credit record, call one of the three major credit unions: Equifax at 1-800-685-1111, Experian at 1-888-397-3742 or TransUnion at 1-800-888-4213.

The Fair and Accurate Credit Transactions Act allows you to get one report from each of these three credit unions for free once per year.

Many people dream of starting their own business, but you have to be realistic and take a good, long look at whether you have, or can get access to, the financing needed to create and sustain a business.

While your current finances are very important, just as important are the potential profits your catering company can earn. You don't want to invest your money, or expect others to finance or invest, in a business that doesn't have a high likelihood of profitability.

Catering and Profits

Whether you plan to cater small intimate affairs every day, or huge extravaganzas for thousands a people once a year, the profit margin potential in the catering business is extremely high. Some caterers manage to walk away with 66 percent pre-tax profits. This figure may seem hard to believe, but when you stop and think about all the ways that caterers can keep their overhead costs at practically nothing, it becomes a more credible figure. About 70 percent of caterers report that they have been profitable each and every year of their last five years in business.

If you are working out of your own kitchen, you can start out with an investment as low as $1,000, but outlay can be as high as $100,000 if you want to outfit a professional kitchen. Despite the scale of operation, your pre-tax profit remains high and revenues of between $200,000 and $2,000,000 often yield pre-tax profits of between $50,000 and $1,000,000.

There is no doubt that successful caterers can be very profitable, but there are many different ways to earn those profits within the catering industry. It is important to choose the type or types of catering that fit best with your skills and expectations.

Types of Catering

The sky is the limit with catering. You'll find caterers in the catering departments of restaurants or large hotels, and then there are the private caterers who do traditional off-premise catering, offer gourmet to-go dinners, or have a personal chef business.

Many people who start out in catering want to immediately own their own business, so many will start out doing off-premise catering out of home kitchens. Others are interested in joining a large hospitality company and will look for work in a major hotel or at a large restaurant. These types of organizations generally provide on-premise catering. Catering is also segmented by what type of event is being hosted. Caterers work for both business and social events. It is not necessary to specialize in any event type because they are usually scheduled differently. Social events are likely to occur at night and on weekends, while business events happen more often during regular business hours.

If you are a business owner, the types of events you take on are dictated by your own interest or your own schedule. Many people who start catering businesses do so while they are still employed, so they limit their catering work to nights and weekends. Of course, "limited" isn't really the right word here because there is no shortage of events occurring in these hours!

For you to get a good understanding of what is involved with the different types of catering, let's take a closer look at each one.

Off-Premise Catering

Off-premise catering refers to a business that has a central kitchen but no separate facilities for dining. Off-premise caterers transport the food and various other items to different locations. They might provide service for events in people's homes, at other banquet facilities that have no kitchens, at parks for outdoor weddings, at offices for business meetings, etc. In many ways, off-premise catering is more challenging than on-premise because each situation is new. When engaged in on-premise catering, you always know the particulars of your space, and transportation, traffic and weather are rarely a factor. With off-premise catering, each event is unique and so are the problems that might arise!

Many people who start their own businesses will engage in off-premise catering because it takes less startup cash than on-premise catering. All you need to start is a kitchen facility—coined as a commissary—that will be used exclusively for preparation of foods to be served at other locations. Because of their low overhead, small off-premise caterers have the advantage of greater flexibility when it comes to price structures.

Off-premise catering has other advantages over on-premise catering as well. The experience can be more exciting and rewarding, especially if you're the type of caterer who enjoys the challenge of working in unusual and unique locations and dealing with new people who you'll probably never meet again.

One interesting specialization of off-premise catering is called Mobile Catering. This is where a caterer specializes in feeding a basic menu to a large group of people, such as forest firefighters, disaster relief workers, construction-site workers, and people taking camping trips or excursions. The caterer develops a seasonal menu and a picnic table concept on the back of a properly equipped truck. The fare is usually hot or cold sandwiches, beverages, soup, coffee, bagels, burritos, etc. Certainly this type of work is less glamorous than catering a gala ball, but it is profitable just the same and provides a little less stress on a day-to-day basis.

Regardless of the exact type of off-premise catering you do, there are several important considerations you'll need to keep in mind.

TEAMWORK

Build a strong team with strong leadership. Remember, the teamwork required in an off-premise-type catering operation can make your company stronger. Your staff will learn to handle just about everything that can go wrong, and most importantly, you'll have the potential to make six-figure incomes, each year!

SUBCONTRACTORS

As the overall operating costs for off-premise catering are generally lower than for on-premise catering, you may find it within your budget to engage subcontractors for certain aspects of the event; for example, floral design, music, and entertainment. This can often prove more cost effective than doing it yourself. Many cities have agencies that provide these services; check the Yellow Pages under "entertainment" for such agencies. Often the best source of information is other caterers. Ask them which companies they use for flowers or music. Network with the people in your community to learn where to find sources of talent and expertise.

FIVE KEYS TO SUCCESS IN OFF-PREMISE CATERING

Here are five important things to look out for when involved with off-premise catering:

1. **Be ready for surprises.** There are literally thousands of potential sources for disaster that can ruin an otherwise successful affair. For example, you are catering a bar mitzvah. Your cook does not know there is a difference between kosher hot dogs and regular hot dogs, but you don't realize this until you are unpacking at the event site. Now what do you do? Always have a Plan B. In the case of the non-kosher dogs, Plan B would be to send a runner to the nearest grocery store and purchase the promised product.

2. **Be prepared.** You need to be organized, plan ahead, and visualize in advance all of the aspects of a catered event. As a catering professional, you'll find that you make many lists. Be sure to check these lists four times before an event, and then check them again! Have someone else check them as well; they may catch something you missed.

3. **Do a site visit.** If you are catering an event off-premises, be sure you visit the site. This should be done in the early planning stages, and you should visit the site again as the day approaches. Compare what you see to your lists, and make sure you bring everything you need to make the event a success.

4. **Be involved.** Understand that you can only be successful in off-site catering by running your company from the center of the action and getting involved in all of the details of the business. Ask for feedback from the client and guests. Oversee the catering staff to make sure that they are performing to required standards. This also means jumping in and helping out when a table needs to be bussed or coffee needs to be refilled.

5. **Keep cool.** The customer is screaming, the brioche is burning, and one of your staff members just cut himself. The result: stress. Learn how to deal with it! A step in the right direction is to manage your time effectively. Set realistic goals—for a lifetime, for five years, for each year, month, week and each day.

On-Premise Catering

On-premise catering is defined as catering for an event held on the physical premises of the facility that is organizing the function. It is estimated that on-premise catering accounts for about two-thirds of all catering sales in the United States. On-premise catering operations range from large profit-oriented and "not-for-profit" operations to smaller, startup enterprises, but it generally takes place at hotels, clubs and conference and convention centers. Some restaurants also have their own banquet facilities and engage in on-premise catering. Other restaurants choose to close their operations to the public for a night and rent the space for a private function.

On-premise catering often offers an advantage to clients because it is a type of "one-stop-shopping." Potential clients do not have the added stress of finding and securing a site to hold the function, and typically the on-premise site is already nicely decorated and well laid-out for parties and similar events.

FOUR TIPS FOR ON-PREMISE CATERING

1. **Specialize.** If you're looking for a niche in the on-premise catering business, explore the possibility of catering weddings. Weddings can yield high profits, largely because of all the extra purchases that are incorporated into a single event. A word of caution, though, is to be sure to include a bridal consultant on your staff. This person will help with all the nuances and expectations that brides have and they are also versed in cultural differences and customs that you will encounter. Don't rely solely on your bridal consultant, though. You need to become familiar with the rituals of traditional weddings and the types of concerns bridal couples and their parents will have. There are many Web sites devoted to people planning weddings; visit any of these to see the types of concerns couples will have. One such Web site is at **www.usabride.com**.

2. **Streamline.** Make sure that the layout of your premises works with you rather than against you. The convenience factor is important when you're working under pressure. Remember, the distinct advantage of catering on-premises is that everything can be positioned pretty much within reach. If, for example, a customer receives a steak they do not like, another one can be prepared without serious difficulty. This may not be an alternative when serving at an off-premise location.

3. **Comfort.** With on-premise catering, you need to make sure you know how many people can be comfortably seated in your facility. Are you able to provide entertainment? Can you prepare a wide variety of menu items at the last minute?

4. **Clubs.** If you run a private club, promote your catering services amongst your members. Offer special deals for private parties and celebrations. Country clubs are better off concentrating on catering for weddings, dances, etc. City clubs are advised to target the business sector. Consider specializing in catering for corporate meetings, board luncheons, civic events, etc. There are many marketing opportunities to help develop this clientele. Join your local chamber of commerce and become involved in your city. These alliances will provide you with rich networking opportunities and new business!

CATERING FOR BUSINESSES

Corporate sales make up approximately 75 percent of the total catering sales in the United States. Typical business events that require catering include the following:

- Meetings/Conventions
- New product introductions
- Recognition events
- Anniversaries
- Team meetings

- Incentive events
- Building openings
- Training sessions
- Annual meetings
- Employee appreciation events

As you can see, the types of business events are quite varied, and the corporate catering market is thus divided into three segments: shallow, midlevel and deep.

The shallow market refers to the segment of low-budget functions such as employee-appreciation lunches. These events have limited budgets and resources and often they do not include a great deal of lead-time. This segment usually includes businesses that are nonprofit, the educational sector, and the military sector. While these events may be less profitable than others, they do fill a certain niche for the caterer. These types of events can be used to fill in for lag time between larger and more resource-intensive events. After all, some money coming in is better than no money at all. In addition, the number of resources required is limited, so the expense of catering such an event is limited as well.

The midlevel market includes clients such as local associations that host regular training meetings. Price is important in this sector, but the resources are not as limited as in the shallow market. Therefore, the client is willing to spend a little more to make the event more impressive. Business at this level often leads to repeat business and word-of-mouth advertising.

The deep market involves more elegant, upscale events such as university presidential inaugurations or board of director dinners. Cost is usually not a factor in this segment of the market. The client is interested in providing an excellent and memorable event and is willing to spend what is required for this.

SOCIAL EVENT CATERING

Individuals rather than businesses usually book social events. They are set up around occasions that take place in people's life cycle and include such events as:

- Weddings
- Anniversaries
- Bar mitzvahs
- Birthdays
- Holiday parties
- Births
- Reunions
- Graduations
- Fundraising events

Social catering is the first thing that comes to mind when people think of the catering business. Even though it is the smaller industry sector, caterers are drawn to this type of event because they are fun and lively and most everyone can relate to a birthday or anniversary as opposed to the launch of new product or a new building opening.

There are many different facets to the business of catering. It is up to you to decide which combination of catering segments most appeals to you and fits best with your skill set and objectives. Once you have a fairly clear idea of the direction you would like to take your catering career, it is time to get started and get into the business. The next chapter details how to start your own catering company. Even if you intend to get experience working for an existing caterer, this is valuable information for planning ahead in your career and exploring, or preparing for, the factors involved in launching a catering business.

LOCATION: Located in Boothwy, PA, off I-95, Exit I, Thyme Catering is accessible to Delaware, Philadelphia and suburbs of Philadelphia.

SERVICES: Catering for weddings, funerals, corporate events, bar and bat mitzvahs, reunions, anniversaries, and fundraisers. Menus can be found on the Internet at **www. thymecatering.com**, or call 610-494-0450 for an appointment.

Thyme Catering is a full-service catering company established in 1980. Jan Cohen, owner and operator along with her partner chef John Feeley, Jr., recently moved the operations into a beautiful banquet facility that can accommodate up to 300 guests for dining and dancing. Attention to detail is a point on which Thyme Catering focuses.

When our servers are carrying dishes on small trays, we tell them to keep them stacked in the center and to not carry with glasses. On a large football tray, they know their capacity for weight. One thing every server learns is that it is harder to put them down then to pick them up.

We look for a lot in our employees. They must be fun to work with, self-motivators, confident, neat, clean, and hard workers.

We never turn business away. We do home parties of 30 or more and corporate parties of 10 or more. We also plan weddings for 300 in our banquet facility. The biggest party we are doing is in the near future for a holiday party for 800 people.

Getting Started

You have done the requisite soul searching and self-analysis and decided to go ahead and start a catering business. Now the real work begins. Preparing to start a business is as hard as actually running a business so you must be fully aware of all the elements that go into planning a new business. The following chapters are designed to do just that.

Planning Your Business

Before you can start any business and be successful, you need to formulate a concept of vision for the company. What exactly do you want to accomplish with your catering company? To come up with a concept, think about your interests. If you're going to open a catering operation, you really need to enjoy what you do because it can be a 24-hour-a-day, 7-day-a-week job. Do you like a particular type of cuisine? If you like gourmet cooking, you won't be happy running a mobile sandwich catering operation, for example. Do you have children at home that you need to watch during the day? Better stick to social events that are usually hosted during the evening rather than concentrating on corporate business.

Don't forget that while your interests should drive your concept decision, you are going to have to sell it to the public. Consider whether or not you think clients will be interested in buying the product you want to sell. If there is no interest, there are no sales. If there are no sales, there is no profit! By balancing your interests and clients' needs, you should be able to come up with an innovative idea that will keep you happy in your new occupation and location.

DEVELOP A MISSION STATEMENT

If you want to open a catering operation but are unsure of your concept, developing a mission statement can provide the clarity you need. Your mission statement should tell you and others what your company values, who your customers are, what your economic objectives are, what your goals are, what your products are, and what your market looks like.

Condense those ideas into a one or two sentences that define your overall mission. See the example below:

MISSION STATEMENT DEVELOPMENT	
Goals	• Establish an upscale catering operation • Specialize in corporate events
Beliefs	• Clients will pay for superior food and presentation
Values	• Quality • Service • Excellence • Integrity
Product	• Catered meals with all the extras
Customers	• Corporations with more than 500 employees
Market	• Corporate, off-premise catering
Mission Statement	To be the premier provider of catering services to organizations that require top-quality food and service and appreciate the finest attention to detail.

Your mission statement doesn't have to contain much detail at this stage; it is simply a device that will help you focus your direction and help formulate your idea of what type of operation you want to run.

DEFINE YOUR INDUSTRY

To know whether or not your idea has market potential you need to be knowledgeable about the catering industry. There are many good sources from which to gather information on the industry. Here are some tips:

- Become a member of The National Restaurant Association. This is the leading business association for the restaurant industry, and membership in the association gives you access to catering resources. You can contact the organization by writing to:

National Restaurant Association
1200 17th St NW
Washington, D.C. 20036
(202) 331-5960
www.restaurant.org

- For great resources on everything from creative food presentation ideas to lighting and themed event ideas, you should subscribe to and read industry trade magazines such as:

  - *catersource* Magazine: **www.catersource.com**

  - *Art Culinaire:* **www.getartc.com**

  - *Special Events Magazine:* **www.specialevents.com**

  - *Event Solutions:* **www.event-solutions.com**

- The American Culinary Federation's magazine, *The National Culinary Review,* is an excellent source for current food and dining trends as well. The publication is available to members. You can find membership information on the Web at **www.acfchefs.org**.

- The Web site for CateringWeb.com (**www.cateringWeb.com**) is also a good resource.

CONDUCT A FEASIBILITY STUDY

In conjunction with defining your industry, you need to look at your business idea and determine whether it has the ability to be a success and to be profitable. When developing your feasibility study, you need information concerning costs such as linens, employee uniforms, equipment, china, insurance, utility bills, rent or mortgage, office supplies, payroll expenses, taxes, advertising expenses, repair and maintenance expenses, food cost, wages, health insurance, and workers' compensation expenses. You will use this detailed information later in the process to develop financial projections, and look at those along with projected sales forecasts to draw a good picture of your operation's health and to help you determine what prices you will need to charge to remain in operation at a profit. The National Restaurant Association has sample feasibility studies that may be helpful in creating your own.

BUILD A NETWORK

Because catering is highly competitive, networking is not always the easiest feat. Contact your local American Culinary Federation at **www.acfchefs.org**. You should also get in touch with the National Association of Catering Executives (**www.nace.net**) and the National Caterers Association **www.ncacater.org**. These organizations will keep you in touch and current with events and other relevant information that you need to know to be successful.

Other networking ideas include the following:

- **Enroll in a culinary program.** Many of the students in a culinary program will be starting out in the restaurant business, but other students will be entrepreneurs and food service professionals brushing up on their skills. Get to know some of these people.

- **Join the chamber of commerce.** This affiliation offers an excellent opportunity for networking and meeting business professionals in the restaurant industry as well as other industries.

- **Visit the local farmers' market.** Chefs frequent many area farmers' markets. Strike up conversations with people; you never know whom you might be talking to.

- **Take initiative.** Form your own organization! Contact area restaurateurs and see if they would be interested in forming a local organization.

KEEP UP WITH FOOD TRENDS

If you are going to start a catering operation, you'll need to keep up with the industry. Make sure you are aware of current food trends so you aren't left behind.

- **Take a look at the *Restaurant Industry Forecast*.** This report is available from the National Restaurant Association. The document provides information concerning forecasted restaurant industry sales and forecasted trends.

- **Eat out often.** See what restaurants are doing. These food trends and themes are often echoed in the catering industry.

- **Subscribe to magazines such as *Gourmet* and *Bon Appetite*.** These magazines are designed for the general public and will help you define your clients' expectations regarding current food and dining trends.

KNOW YOUR COMPETITION

Starting any type of business requires a great deal of preparation and research. The first thing you'll want to do is assess the potential for catering business in your community.

A careful analysis of your potential customer base is vital. This task goes beyond estimating whether you have enough events to cater in your area and whether you have the necessary drive and flair to stay the course. You need to explore the competition. Find out who your competitors are and what market share they already cover. Without this information, you simply cannot be successful in the catering business. Take a long, hard look at the competition. Here are some suggestions:

- **Contact your local Bureau of Vital Statistics and Bureau of Records.** Find out the number of births, marriages and deaths in your community. This will help to indicate to you the potential number of events catered in your area.

- **Check the local newspaper's society column.** This resource will provide you with wedding announcements and other social events in your area. It will also provide you with some of the names of key players in the social world. Jot down these names and add them to your list of marketing contacts.

- **Organizations.** Check with some nonprofit organizations and fraternal clubs, as well as your area's clubs, churches, etc. Ask them how many catered events take place in their function rooms.

- **Gather the necessary data.** Don't forget to ask for relevant data from the local chamber of commerce and your local Small Business Administration office. You can find contact information for local small business associations at **www.sba.gov**.

- **Yellow Pages.** Check your local Yellow Pages to get a sense of the competition. Keep in mind, however, that many small operations probably are not listed due to the expense. You should also do a Web search to find area competition; these days many, if not most, businesses have a Web site. When assessing the competition, you will want to find out how many catering operations are in your locality and what their main target audiences are.

CHOOSE A LEGAL BUSINESS FORM

Once you have determined your concept, you'll need to start thinking about the legal aspects of your business. What type of business do you want to be? In order to answer that question, you need to research the different forms available and the pros and cons of each. Be sure to seek legal and accounting advice before making a final decision.

Factors that will influence your decision regarding your business form include:

- Legal restrictions
- Type of business operation
- Capital needs
- Tax advantages or disadvantages
- Liabilities assumed
- Earnings distribution
- Number of employees
- Length of business operation

The major forms of business organizations are sole proprietorship, partnership, corporation, and the new hybrid limited liability company. The advantages and disadvantages of each are listed below.

Sole Proprietorship

This is the easiest and least costly way to start a business. A sole proprietorship is formed by simply finding a location and opening the door for business. There are likely to be fees to obtain a business name, registration, fictitious name certificate, and other necessary licenses. Attorney fees for starting a sole proprietorship are minimal, and as the sole owner, you have absolute authority over all business decisions. You also have sole responsibility for the financial obligations of the company; that is why many people choose other, more complex, forms of business.

Partnership

There are several types of partnerships. The two most common types are general and limited partnerships. A general partnership can be formed simply by an oral agreement between two or more persons, but a legal partnership agreement drawn up by an attorney is highly recommended. Legal fees for drawing up a partnership agreement are higher than those for a sole proprietorship, but may be lower than incorporating. A partnership agreement can be helpful in solving any disputes, but partners are responsible for the other partner's business actions, as well as their own.

To remedy this, a limited partnership agreement can be arranged whereby only one partner must remain wholly responsible and the other partners can limit their liability as well as their participation.

Any partnership agreement should include the following:

- Type of business

- Amount of equity invested by each partner

- Division of profit or loss

- Partners' compensation

- Distribution of assets on dissolution

- Duration of partnership

- Provisions for changes or dissolving the partnership

- Dispute settlement clause

- Restrictions of authority and expenditures

- Settlement in case of death or incapacitation

Corporation

The corporate structure is usually the most complex and costly form of business to organize, but it is the one that limits the owners' legal liability by legally separating the owners from the business. A business may incorporate without an attorney, but legal advice is highly recommended. Control of a corporation depends on stock ownership. Persons with the largest stock ownership, not the total number of shareholders, control the corporation. With control of stock shares (51 percent of stock outstanding) a person or group is able to make policy decisions and run the company.

Control is exercised through regular meetings of the board of directors' and annual stockholders' meetings. Records must be kept to document decisions made by the board of directors, and there are many legal obligations and regulations governing the management of corporations. Small, closely held corporations can operate more informally, but recordkeeping cannot be eliminated entirely. Officers of a corporation can be liable to stockholders for improper actions. Liability is generally limited to stock ownership, except where fraud is involved. There are both "C" and "S" corporations, and you should consult a lawyer to figure out which one is best for you.

Incorporating gives you maximum protection from creditors and from the possibility of a client lawsuit, but you should check with your attorney and accountant about other legal and tax issues that will affect you as a corporation.

Limited Liability Company (LLC)

An LLC is not a corporation, but it offers many of the same advantages. Many small business owners and entrepreneurs prefer LLCs because they combine the limited liability protection of a corporation with the "pass-through" taxation of a sole proprietorship or partnership. With an LLC you are taxed similar to a sole proprietor, yet your personal assets are not liable if you run into any credit or insurance problems.

LLCs have the following additional advantages over corporations:

- LLCs allow greater flexibility in management and business organization.

- LLCs do not have the ownership restrictions of "S" corporations, making them ideal business structures for foreign investors.

- LLCs accomplish these aims without the IRS's restrictions for an "S" corporation.

- LLCs are now available in all 50 states and Washington, D.C.

If you have other questions regarding LLCs, be sure to speak with a qualified legal and financial advisor.

CHOOSE A NAME

This is one of the most exciting pre-opening activities you'll do—naming your business! Catering is a creative venture, so you can be as creative as you want with your name; use your mission statement as a guide to come up with a name that fits with what you are trying to accomplish and that will appeal to your target market.

You want the image of your catering business to be inherent in its name so as soon as potential clients hear it, they will be attracted to it. Think about the image you want to create. What makes your company special? What type of ambiance do you want to create at events? What kind of food do you prepare? Are you an upscale social caterer? Do you specialize in picnics and other outdoor events? Are you exclusively a wedding caterer?

Your business name is your identity; it shows your clients your idea about where you position yourself in the world of catering. Here are a few guidelines:

- **Experiment.** Don't be afraid to experiment with names by choosing, for instance, the one that is most likely to become imprinted in the prospective client's mind, "Beyond A Mouthful," maybe? Or, for example, you could name your business after your services' characteristics, perhaps "A Moveable Feast." Alternatively, your name may represent a personal touch, such as "Catering by Daphne." If you are a known persona or chef within your community, naming your business after yourself can help create business opportunities.

- **Let your name sell your services.** Remember that your name must serve first and foremost as a selling tool. Be wise. Find a name that reflects the mouth-watering food you're capable of preparing for your guests.

- **Choose a name that is pronounceable.** Usually short business names are best because they are more likely to be remembered by potential customers. You also can use alliteration or a play on words for this same effect. A customer is likely to remember "The Moveable Feast" because it is based on the name of a novel by Ernest Hemingway. "A Forkable Feast" is also memorable because of the alliteration in the phrase. Both of these names suggest the kind of catering the establishment does. "A Moveable Feast," for instance, would specialize in off-premise catering; "A Forkable Feast" would likely specialize in tapas or cocktail receptions.

- **Consider alphabetical order.** This is especially important if you will be relying on sales generated from the phone book. We've all seen the "AAA" listings for everything from exterminators to event planners. People do tend to pick from the top of the list when faced with many choices, so having your business start with a letter at the beginning of the alphabet is a good idea.

After you have selected the name, you'll want to look into having it registered. After all the work and attention you've given to this detail, you don't want to have someone else come along and use the same name later on.

In general, if you are going to do business in a state under a name other than your own personal name, you'll need to check with the state Attorney General's office to see if you need to register. You can find these offices online. They often provide a good deal of information concerning how to register for a name. If you need some help finding this office, visit State and Local Government on the Internet at **www.statelocalgov.net/index.cfm**. You may also need to run a fictitious business name statement, four times, in a local, legally qualified (weekly) newspaper. If no one protests, the name is officially yours.

Another option to consider is to trademark your name to protect it. You can trademark on a national or statewide level. To register your operation as a local trademark, contact the Secretary of State's office in your state. To register as a national trademark, you will need to contact the United States Patent and Trademark Office (**www.uspto.gov**). They also have a search engine, TESS, that can help you determine if the name has already been trademarked.

Now, armed with a mission statement and name, you are ready to formalize your idea and expand upon it by writing a business plan. It sounds daunting, and many people try to skip lightly over this part or avoid it completely, but it really is an essential tool for creating and maintaining a profitable and long-term viable catering operation.

The Business Plan

Perhaps the most important tasks you will need to undertake before trying to execute or seek financing is writing the formal business plan. This plan will be your road map for success. Every business needs to have a business or strategic plan in place. Having a formal plan will help you keep your goals in focus and guide you through the tough decisions.

So what specific information goes into a business plan? This is an excellent question, and it is one that many new and potential small business owners should ask, but oftentimes don't. The body of the business plan can be divided into four distinct sections: 1) the description of the business, 2) the marketing plan, 3) the management plan, and 4) the financial management plan. Addenda to the business plan should include the executive summary, supporting documents and financial projections. Let's look at these sections in detail.

DESCRIPTION OF THE BUSINESS

In this section you provide a detailed description of your business. An excellent question to ask yourself is: "What business am I in?" When answering this question, include your products, market and services, as well as a thorough description of what makes your catering operation unique. Remember, however, that as you develop your business plan, you may have to modify or revise your initial questions.

The business description section is divided into three primary sections. Section 1 actually describes your business, Section 2 describes the product or service you will be offering, and Section 3 talks about the location of your business and why that location is desirable. When describing your business you should explain the following:

1. Legalities—Include the type of business (proprietorship, partnership, or corporation). Indicate what licenses or permits you will need.

2. Business type—Catering, restaurant, retail, etc.

3. What your product or service is—Include a sample menu.

4. Business character—Is it a new independent business, a takeover, an expansion?

5. Why your business will be profitable—What are the growth opportunities? Will franchising impact on growth opportunities?

6. When your business will be open—What days and hours?

7. What you have learned about your kind of business from outside sources (trade suppliers, bankers, publications).

A cover sheet goes before the description. It includes the name, address and telephone number of the business and the names of all principals. In the description of your business, describe the unique aspects and how or why they will appeal to consumers. Emphasize any special features that you feel will appeal to customers, and explain how and why these features are appealing.

The description of your business should clearly identify goals and objectives, and it should clarify why you are, or why you want to be, in business.

Product/Service

Try to describe the benefits of your goods and services from your customers' perspective. Successful business owners know, or at least have an idea of, what their customers want or expect from them. This type of anticipation can be helpful for building customer satisfaction and loyalty, and it certainly is a good strategy for beating the competition or retaining your competitiveness. In this section describe:

1. What you are selling—Include your menu here.

2. How your product or service will benefit the customer.

3. Which products/services are in demand—Will there be a steady flow of cash?

4. What is different about the product or service your business is offering.

Location

The location of your business can play a decisive role in its success or failure. Remember the old maxim, "Location, location, location." Your location should be built around your customers, it should be accessible, and it should provide a sense of security. Consider these questions when addressing this section of your business plan:

1. What are your location needs?

2. What kind of space will you need?

3. Why is the area desirable? Why is the building desirable?

4. Is it easily accessible? Is public transportation available? Is street lighting adequate?

5. Are market or demographic shifts occurring?

It may be a good idea to make a checklist of questions you identify when developing your business plan. Categorize your questions and, as you answer each question, remove it from your list.

Once you have defined your business, it is necessary to develop a plan to market it and attract customers. This is called the marketing plan.

The Marketing Plan

Marketing plays a vital role in successful business ventures. How well you market your business, along with a few other considerations, will ultimately determine your degree of success or failure. The key element of a successful marketing plan is to know your customers—their likes, dislikes and expectations. By identifying these factors, you can develop a marketing strategy that will allow you to arouse and fulfill their needs.

Start by identifying your customers by their age, sex, income/educational level and residence. At first, target only those customers who are more likely to purchase your product or service. As your customer base expands, you may need to consider modifying the marketing plan to include other customers.

Your marketing plan is really a plan within a plan and should include answers to the following questions:

1. Who are your customers? Define your target market(s).

2. Are your markets growing? steady? declining?

3. Is your market share growing? steady? declining?

4. Are your markets large enough to expand?

5. How will you attract/hold/increase your market share? How will you promote your sales?

6. What pricing strategy have you devised?

COMPETITION

Competition is a way of life. We compete for jobs, promotions, scholarships to institutes of higher learning, in sports, and in almost every aspect of our lives. Nations compete for the consumer in the global marketplace, as do individual business owners. Advances in technology can send the profit margins of a successful business into a tailspin, causing them to plummet overnight or within a few hours. When considering these and other factors, we can conclude that business is a highly competitive, volatile arena. Because of this volatility and competitiveness, it is important to know your competitors.

Questions like these can help you:

1. Who are your five nearest direct competitors?

2. Who are your indirect competitors?

3. Are their businesses steady? increasing? decreasing?

4. What have you learned from their operations? from their advertising?

5. What are their strengths and weaknesses?

6. How does their service differ from yours?

Start a file on each of your competitors. Keep manila envelopes of their advertising and promotional materials and their pricing strategy techniques. Review these files periodically, determining when and how often they advertise, sponsor promotions, and offer sales. Study the copy used in the advertising and promotional materials and their sales strategy. For example, is their copy short? descriptive? catchy? How much do they reduce prices for sales? Using this technique can help you to better understand your competitors and how they operate their businesses.

PRICING AND SALES

Your pricing strategy is another marketing technique you can use to improve your overall competitiveness. Get a feel for the pricing strategy your competitors are using. That way you can determine if your prices are in line with competitors in your market area and if they are in line with industry averages. Some pricing considerations are:

1. Menu cost and pricing
2. Pricing below competition
3. Price lining
4. Service components
5. Labor costs

6. Competitive position
7. Pricing above competition
8. Multiple pricing
9. Material costs
10. Overhead costs

The keys to success are to have a well-planned strategy, to establish your policies, and to constantly monitor prices and operating costs to ensure profits. It is a good policy to keep abreast of the changes in the marketplace because these changes can affect your competitiveness and profit margins.

ADVERTISING AND PUBLIC RELATIONS

How you advertise and promote your catering operation may make or break your business. Having a good product or service and not advertising and promoting it, is like not having any business at all. Many business owners operate under the mistaken concept that the business will promote itself, and channel money that should be used for advertising and promotions into other areas of the business. Advertising and promotions, however, are the lifeline of a business and should be treated as such. Because it is so important, we have devoted a whole chapter to marketing and promoting your catering operation in this handbook.

Your marketing plan should also use advertising and networking as a means to promote your business. Develop short, descriptive copy (text material) that clearly identifies your goods or services, its location and price. Use catchy phrases to arouse the interest of your readers, listeners or viewers. Remember, the more care and attention you devote to your marketing program, the more successful your business will be.

Business success, however, is not dependent on marketing success alone. You can have all the potential customers in the world, but if you don't know how to manage your business effectively, those customers will notice and they will go somewhere else. To ensure this does not happen, you must prepare a management plan.

The Management Plan

Managing a business requires more than just the desire to be your own boss. It demands dedication, persistence, the ability to make decisions, and the ability to manage both employees and finances. Your management plan, along with your marketing and financial management plans, sets the foundation for and facilitates the success of your business.

MANAGING EMPLOYEES

Like plants and equipment, people are resources—they are the most valuable assets a business has. You will soon discover that employees and staff play an important role in the total operation of your business. Consequently, it's imperative that you know the skills you possess and know where you need help. You can't be expected to know and do everything, and that is where hiring the right personnel to complement your business comes in.

Hiring the right people is just the first step, though. Equally important are the knowledge and skills needed to manage and treat your employees right. If you treat them right, they will stay with you longer and your business will be more stable and reliable. To accomplish this, make your employees part of the team. Keep them informed of changes, and get their feedback. Employees oftentimes have excellent ideas that can lead to new market areas, innovations to existing products or services, or new product lines or services that can improve your overall competitiveness.

When developing your management plan, you should answer questions such as:

1. How does your background/business experience help you in this business?

2. What are your weaknesses and how can you compensate for them?

3. Who will be on the management team?

4. What are their strengths/weaknesses?

5. What are their duties?

6. Are these duties clearly defined?

7. Will this assistance be ongoing?

8. What are your current personnel needs?

9. What are your plans for hiring and training personnel?

10. What salaries, benefits, vacations and holidays will you offer?

11. What benefits, if any, can you afford at this point?

Managing your business is hard work and it is not always intuitive. While you may not have to really work at becoming an excellent caterer, you will probably need to work very hard at becoming an excellent manager. Make sure you take the time to prepare yourself for the responsibilities of managing your business as well as the people that help make your business successful.

Despite solid marketing and management, a business relies on sound financial planning to remain profitable. Crunching numbers and analyzing financial statements may not be at the top of your interests list, but they need to be at the top of your priority list. Let's take a closer look at the financial aspect of your business plan.

Sales Forecasting

Once you have chosen your market area you need to do sales forecasting in order to see whether you can generate enough sales for you to open and to stay in business. Your sales forecast is very important to developing your overall business plan as it forms the basis for your financial planning and determination of viability.

An effective way to forecast your sales is to use comparative information from similar stores. These similar stores are sometimes called analogue stores. These operations will be in the same or similar area as your potential location and will attract the same type of customer. If you are an on-premise social caterer, for instance, you will want to use other on-premise social caterers in the area for comparison. These operations do not have to be in the immediate area of your proposed location, but the demographics of their location should be similar.

COMPARE AND CONTRAST

Do a simple comparison and contrast of specific similarities or differences such as physical appearance, size of facility, and menu. This comparison is a simple matter of research and observation. Write down the criteria you want to look at in a list beforehand, then go out and observe the operations. Check off how similar or dissimilar they are to your proposed operation. This will give you the most appropriate stores with which to compare sales.

RATING

Another method to gain competitive information is to rate similar establishments and discover those that are the most similar to yours. To use this method, create a table with factors that can contribute to sales. Rate those factors on a scale of 1 to 10 (1 being the lowest, and 10 being the highest) by rating how much each factor contributes to sales. The information you glean from this comparison is a picture of operations that are similar to yours. In this method, not only do you have this list, but you also have information on what factors influence sales the most.

DETERMINING MARKET SHARE

Another way to forecast sales for your location is to determine your market share. Market share is the ratio of money spent in your industry within a standard metropolitan area versus your total business sales. These figures can be obtained from the U.S. Department of Labor's Bureau of Labor Statistics' *Consumer Expenditure Survey*, which can be found at **www.bls.gov/cex**. Another source for information is the U.S. Department of Commerce's *Census of Business*, which is conducted every five years (**www.doc.gov** or **www.census.gov**). The census includes the Census of Retail Trade, which presents information pertaining to sales, profits and employment of retail companies. These characteristics are represented according to geographic area, type and size of market, merchandise line, SIC (Standard Industrial Classification) code, and type and size of company.

Also keep in mind that the figures from the Bureau of Labor Statistics are taken at the regional level and we are applying them at the market area level. Further, theory and reality are not the same: each caterer is not going to see the exact same amount in sales. Remember, this is an estimate that can help you make decisions regarding your business, but it is not a guarantee of your future sales.

STATISTICAL METHODS OF SALES FORECASTING

A great deal of sales research includes the use of statistical forecasting models. We will not go into the specifics of these models in this book, but we will introduce them. We suggest that if you want to use these models as a part of your business research or even for a specific site search, you work with a consultant that has expertise in these statistical concepts.

- **Creating an analog database.** The analog database is created from customer, demographic and competitor information. This information is used to determine sales and trade areas. After this information is added, statistical methods are used to determine how the various items in the database are related to sales. Does driving distance have an impact? What effect does the population's education level have on sales? Finally, sales of the analog stores are averaged to forecast the sales for your operation. A word of caution is appropriate in averaging. If all of your database stores are similar, averaging will work. If, however, you have analog stores that greatly vary from most of the others in the database, your average will be skewed and you will want to use the mean of the outlying stores.

- **Regression method.** This model is basically an equation that relates an operation's sales to specific variables. It is similar to the analogue database, but it goes a step further and rates the variables at which you are looking. An advantage of using the regression system in forecasting is that it can break down complicated situations such as the different sets of customers; corporate versus social clients, for example.

- **Gravity model.** This method builds a model with which to forecast your sales. Rather than using real data, the method creates a model based on the assumption that people tend to gravitate to locations nearest to them. The reasons for choosing a specific caterer are more complex than simple proximity to a service provider, but these gravity models do look at relationships between stores in a trade area in terms of size, distance from competitors, distance from centers of population, operational procedures and sales estimates. Advantages of using a gravity model for sales predictions are that it can offer many what-if scenarios and it is good if you are looking at a large market.

To perform the analyses required to develop a reasonable sales forecast, there are many different resources available including:

STATISTICAL SOFTWARE PACKAGES

There are software statistical packages available such as SYSTAT. Their Web site (**www.systat.com**) has a variety of statistical software packages you can purchase for this analysis.

If you have a knack for math, you may want to undertake this analysis yourself. Otherwise, it is wise to hire someone who can manipulate the data correctly.

MARKET RESEARCH FIRMS

Many market research firms will also provide this service; check your local Yellow Pages for firms in your area. You also can find many of these firms on the Web. Here are a list of a few with their services:

- CTS—**www.cts.com**. This company offers marketing databases, maps, data analysis, and analysis planning.

- Claritas—**www.claritas.com**. This site provides census-based data and a GIS system that lets you map and analyze a specific geographic area.

MAGAZINES

Magazines such as *American Demographics*, which can be found online, also provide market research information that can be useful in your research.

The Financial Plan

Sound financial management is one of the best ways for your business to remain profitable and solvent. How well you manage the finances of your business is the cornerstone of a successful business venture.

Each year thousands of potentially successful businesses fail because of poor financial management. As a business owner you need to identify and implement policies that will lead to and ensure that you can meet your financial obligations.

To effectively manage your finances, you must first start with a sound and realistic budget. You do this by determining the actual amount of money needed to open your business (startup costs) and the amount needed to keep it open (operating costs). Your startup budget will usually include such one-time-only costs such as major equipment, utility deposits and down payments. A typical startup budget allows for these expenses:

- Personnel (costs prior to opening)
- Occupancy
- Equipment
- Supplies
- Salaries/Wages
- Income
- Payroll expenses

- Legal/Professional fees
- Licenses/Permits
- Insurance
- Advertising/Promotions
- Accounting
- Utilities

An operating budget is prepared when you are actually ready to open for business. The operating budget reflects your priorities in terms of how you spend your money, the expenses you will incur, and how you will meet those expenses. Your operating budget should also include enough money to cover the first three to six months of operation, or the amount of time you estimate it will take you to generate enough business income to cover your business expenses. An operating budget usually includes the following list of expenses, but you should work with an accountant to determine your actual expense accounts.

- Personnel
- Rent
- Loan payments
- Legal/Accounting
- Supplies
- Salaries/Wages
- Dues/Subscriptions/Fees
- Repairs/Maintenance

- Insurance
- Depreciation
- Advertising/Promotions
- Miscellaneous expenses
- Payroll expenses
- Utilities
- Taxes

The financial section of your business plan should include loan applications you've filed, a list of capital equipment and supplies, a balance sheet, a break-even analysis, pro-forma income projections (profit and loss statement), and a pro-forma cash flow. The income statement and cash flow projections should include a three-year summary, a detailed month-by-month breakdown for the first year, and a detailed quarter-by-quarter breakdown for the second and third years. Depending on your level of experience with financial statements and projections, you may want to consider using a professional business advisor or accountant to help you with this section of your plan.

Other financial questions that you need to consider:

1. What type of accounting system will you use? Is it a single-entry or dual-entry system?

2. What are your sales goals and profit goals for the coming year?

3. What financial projections will you need to include in your business plan?

4. What kind of inventory-control system will you use?

Your financial plan needs to include an explanation of all projections, and all assumptions used to develop those projections need to be explained as well. Unless you are thoroughly familiar with financial statements, get help in preparing your cash flow and income statements and your balance sheet. Your aim is not to become a financial wizard, but to understand the financial tools well enough to capitalize on the benefits they provide you in terms of overall business management.

The following is an outline of a typical business plan, but, again, work with an advisor or accountant to prepare a formal plan that will meet your needs today and be useful for future planning and consideration. The next section provides a list of business plan resources that you can consult to prepare your formal plan.

Business Plan Outline

ELEMENTS OF A BUSINESS PLAN

I. Cover sheet

II. Statement of purpose

III. Table of contents

A. The Business

1. Description of business

2. Marketing

3. Competition

4. Operating procedures

5. Personnel

6. Business insurance

B. Financial Data

1. Loan applications

2. Capital equipment and supply list

3. Balance sheet

4. Break-even analysis

5. Pro-forma income projections (profit and loss statements)

    a. Three-year summary

    b. Detail by month, first year

    c. Detail by quarters, second and third years

    d. Assumptions upon which projections were based

6. Pro-forma cash flow

    a. Follow guidelines for number 5.

C. Supporting Documents

1. Tax returns of principals for last three years

2. Personal financial statement (all banks have these forms)

3. Copy of proposed lease or purchase agreement for building space

4. Copy of licenses and other legal documents

5. Copy of résumés of all principals

6. Copies of letters of intent from suppliers, etc

BUSINESS PLAN RESOURCES

There are many sources to consult when writing your business plan. This is an extremely important document for your business; you can't afford to "wing-it." While the cost of obtaining expert advice is well worth it, you may want to do the preliminary work yourself. This forces you to consider all the aspects of running a business and you gain a deeper understanding and appreciation for the complexities involved in business management. The following resources will help guide you along the process.

Small Business Administration (SBA). The SBA offers a *"Resource Directory for Small Business Management"* that includes a wealth of information including how to write business plans. For a free copy, contact your nearest SBA office or log onto **www.sba.gov**.

Service Corps of Retired Executives (SCORE) offers workshops and free counseling.

Business Information Centers (BICs) offer resources and on-site counseling for businesses. For more information about SBA business development programs and services, call the SBA Small Business Answer Desk at 1-800-U-ASK-SBA (827-5722) or log onto **www.sba.gov/bi/bics**.

U.S. Government Resources. The Government Printing Office (GPO) offers resources to business owners as well. GPO bookstores are located in 24 major cities and listed in the Yellow Pages under the "bookstore" heading. You can write to Government Printing Office, Superintendent of Documents, Washington, D.C. 20402-9328 to request a list of materials they publish, or you can purchase items from the bookstore online.

U.S. Department of Treasury Internal Revenue Service (IRS). The IRS offers information on tax requirements for small businesses. You can write them at P.O. Box 25866 Richmond, VA 23260, or call 1-800-424-3676.

The National Restaurant Association also has publications that can help you write a business plan. You can purchase these at a discounted price if you are a member.

How to Write a Great Business Plan for Your Small Business in 60 Minutes or Less is an excellent resource guide that outlines how to create a business plan step by step. It can be purchased directly from Atlantic Publishing for $39.95. Another good business plan resource targeted specifically towards food service operations is *Opening a Restaurant or Other Food Business Starter Kit: How to Prepare a Restaurant Business Plan & Feasibility Study.* This valuable resource is also available from Atlantic Publishing for $39.95. To order call 1-800-814-1132 or visit **www.atlantic-pub.com**.

Acquiring Startup Capital

One of your first challenges with starting a new business is securing enough capital so that you will be able to run your business and still pay your own bills. Many small catering operations require little startup cash, so you may be able to secure a small loan, use your own savings, or rely on family and friends for small personal loans to get yourself started. If you are planning to open a larger operation, however, you will most likely need to rely on more traditional types of funding, such as a loan from a bank.

The following is a summary of where and how to access the funding you need to start your catering business.

TRADITIONAL LOANS

Borrow From Yourself

Inventory your assets, including real property, retirement funds, vehicles, savings accounts, stock funds, and other investments. You may elect to use some of these assets as cash, or you may be able to use them for loan collateral. While you need to be sure you don't strap yourself, it is always good to at least use some of your own money to start your business. By not borrowing the full amount, your loan payments will be smaller and you may enhance your ability to borrow in the future if you need to.

Borrow From Family and Friends

While it may be good advice to never loan a friend money, many businesses have been started on just such a loan. Getting loans from friends and family is often the only way to secure financing when the banks turn you down. Often money is loaned interest-free or at a low interest rate, which can be quite beneficial when getting started. If you do decide to go this route, make sure you have sufficient contracts in place and put everything in writing. If your business goes south, you don't want your relationships to do the same.

Borrow From Banks and Credit Unions

These institutions are the most common sources of funding, and they will provide a loan if you can show that your business proposal is sound. While it is true that small business people are known to have a difficult time borrowing money this way, it is more often because the business owner is unprepared or inexperienced and not just because the loan is for a small business.

Banks make money by lending money, so if you do your homework and come ready with the answers the bank will ask, then you are more than likely going to be able to secure a loan. Requesting a loan when you are not properly prepared sends a signal to your lender; that message is: high risk!

To be successful in obtaining a loan, you must be prepared and organized. You must know exactly how much money you need, why you need it, and how you will pay it back. You must be able to convince your lender that you are a good credit risk.

We've provided the following guidelines for borrowing money from lending institutions to prepare yourself for the loan-approval process.

FINDING A BANK AND BANKER

Entering into a loan relationship is not something to take lightly. You should compare it to a marriage rather than a lunch date. When you go looking for a bank to give you a loan to secure your business location, talk to friends and associates. Find out what banks they have dealt with and what types of dealings they have had. Remember, knowing that someone makes deposits and withdrawals from an existing account without incident does not qualify as a recommendation for working with that bank to secure a loan.

If you are unable to get reliable recommendations, go to several banks and interview the loan managers. Compare rates, services, and customer service. How easy was it to get an appointment with the appropriate person? Did they seem genuinely interested in your business? How well did they explain their services and loan requirements?

Keep in mind other factors when you are looking at banks. It probably makes sense to do your regular banking with the institution you get your business loan through. How convenient is this bank and its branches to your location? This is an important consideration, especially if you need to do night drops or get change during the day.

What the Banker Wants From You

Getting a commercial loan to open or run a small business is not easy because these types of loans represent a significant risk to the lender. To compensate them for this risk, you will be required to give more than other types of borrowers. Here's the scoop on what will be expected from you.

Higher Rates

In general, small business owners will pay higher interest rates than other types of commercial loans. If you have good credit, however, you may have a little more negotiation power.

More Personal Financing

Banks will ask you for a second and possibly third income source to back up your loan.

Greater Ratio Of Assets To Debt

These days bankers are looking for you to have three to five times as much equity in your business as you are carrying in loans.

More Collateral

If you are applying for a loan, you are going to have to show the loan officer some collateral, or evidence that the bank will be able to collect the money from you whether you succeed or fail. The general trend is that banks are asking for more collateral than they used to. Nowadays they may want as much as three times the amount of the loan.

The following are common forms of collateral the bank may be willing to accept.

- **Your signature and credit reputation.** This is called an unsecured loan, and it is probably not a situation you will find yourself in. Most banks are gong to require more than good credit to shell out a substantial loan amount.

- **Real estate.** Real estate, such as your house, is a form of collateral used for long-term loans. You may be able to secure a loan and still keep some of the equity in your home. Check with your loan officer about these options.

- **Savings accounts and certificates of deposit.** These can be signed over to the lending bank. The account stays open, but you assign the account to the bank and give them your passbook.

- **Cash value of a life insurance policy.** Again, with these policies you would assign the policy to the lending bank. You could also borrow against a life insurance policy, but you will probably get a lower interest rate from the bank, so using it for collateral may be a better option.

- **Stocks and bonds.** Banks will usually lend a percentage of the market value of stocks and bonds in order to account for market fluctuations. The percentage is usually higher on the less risky stocks and bonds because these will see less fluctuation.

- **Co-signer.** If all else fails you may be able to have someone co-sign for your loan. This means that if you can't repay the loan, the co-signer is responsible for it. This situation would occur if you had nothing else to offer for collateral. You would want a co-signer that did have something to offer, such as real estate or stocks.

NEGOTIATING YOUR LOAN

You have on your best suit and you have an excellent business plan in hand. You feel prepared to face the bank, but when you walk through that door your legs turn to jelly and you feel like you are groveling for any scraps you might be given. You feel like whatever magic numbers the bankers pull out of their hat are the numbers you have to accept or risk losing the loan altogether.

Do you want in on a secret? That isn't true. Loan rates and terms are negotiable. Up to 60 percent of businesses could get lower rates if they simply asked for them rather than accepting the rates quoted.

Loan rates consist of the actual rate and the term (or maturity) of the loan. Either of these factors may be negotiated. The best time to try to negotiate a rate is after the loan officer has made an offer, but before the final papers are drawn. Bankers look at several factors when determining whether or not to approve a loan. These factors include their assessment of risk (are you likely to pay the loan back?), the amount being borrowed, and administrative costs.

If you want to ask your loan officer for a lower interest rate, try one of the following strategies:

- Take a shorter loan period. The shorter the loan, period the less risk there is to the bank.

- Improve your collateral. Again, this helps to eliminate the risk involved with your loan.

WRITE A LOAN PROPOSAL

Approval of your loan request depends on how well you present yourself, your business, and your financial needs to a lender. Remember, lenders want to make loans, but they must make loans they know will be repaid. The best way to improve your chances of obtaining a loan is to prepare a written proposal. A well-written loan proposal is much like a business plan, and it contains the following sections.

- **Cover Letter**
  - This is equivalent to an executive summary. It is where you sell the bank on approving your loan. Make it compelling but keep it succinct. Always personalize your proposal and relate the cover letter to any discussions you have had prior to the proposal being submitted.

- **General Information**
  - Business name, names of principals, Social Security number for each principal, and business address.

- **Purpose of the Loan**
  - Exactly what the loan will be used for and why it is needed.

- **Amount Required**
  - The exact amount you need to achieve your purpose.

- **Business Description**
  - History and nature of the business including what kind of business it is, its age, number of employees, and current business assets.

- **Ownership Structure**
  - Details of your company's legal structure.

- **Management Profile**
  - Provide a short statement about each principal in your business. Include background, education, experience, skills, and accomplishments.

- **Market Information**
  - Clearly define your company's products as well as your markets.

  - Identify your competition and explain how your business competes in the marketplace.

– Profile your customers and explain how your business can satisfy their needs.

- **Financial Information**
  – Provide balance sheets and income statements for the past three years. If you are starting out, provide a projected balance sheet and income statement.

  – Personal financial statements for yourself and other principal owners of the business.

  – Collateral you are willing to pledge as security for the loan.

REVIEW OF THE LOAN REQUEST

When reviewing a loan request, the lender is primarily concerned about repayment. To help determine your ability to repay, many loan officers will order a copy of your business credit report from a credit reporting agency. Therefore, you should work with these agencies to help them present an accurate picture of your business. Using the credit report and the information you have provided, the lending officer will consider the following issues:

- Have you invested savings or personal equity in your business totaling at least 25 to 50 percent of the loan you are requesting? (Remember, a lender or investor will not finance 100 percent of your business.)

- Do you have a sound record of credit?

- What is your worthiness as indicated by your credit report, work history, and letters of recommendation?

- Do you have sufficient experience and training to operate a successful business?

- Have you prepared a loan proposal and business plan that demonstrate your understanding and commitment to the success of the business?

- Does the business have sufficient cash flow to make the monthly payments?

HOW MUCH MONEY DO YOU NEED?

To help you estimate the amount of financing you will need to get your venture off the ground, use the following checklist. Keep in mind, however, that not every category may apply. You should estimate monthly amounts.

EXPENSE	
Operating Expenses	
Salary of Owner/Manager (if applicable)	
All Other Salaries and Wages	
Mortgage/Property Taxes	
Advertising	
Delivery Expenses	
Supplies	
Telephone	
Utilities	
Insurance	
Taxes, Including Social Security	
Interest	
Maintenance (Facilities/Equipment)	
Legal and Other Professional Fees	
Dues/Subscriptions	
Leases (Equipment/Furniture/Etc.)	
Inventory Purchases	
Miscellaneous	
One-Time Startup Costs	
Fixtures/Equipment/Furniture	
Remodeling	
Installation of Fixtures/Equipment/Furniture	
Starting Inventory	
Deposits with Public Utilities	

EXPENSE	
Legal and Other Professional Fees	
Licenses and Permits	
Advertising and Promotion for Opening	
Accounts Receivable	
Cash Reserve/Operating Capital	
Other	
TOTAL*	

*Your total amount will depend upon how many months of preparation you want to allow for before actually beginning operations.

FINANCING FOR PROPERTY

Appraisals If you are trying to secure a loan to buy property, you will need to get an appraisal done before the loan can go through. Your real estate agent can set up an appraiser. If you do not use a real estate agent, you can check with your local real estate board or your bank for a list of appraisers. You can also find a listing of brokers and appraisers at **www.commercialcentral.com**.

The Web site **www.appraisersource.com** is also an online resource for appraisers.

Surveys and Inspections You will also need to get a survey and building inspection done if you are buying an existing building. If you are buying a piece of property to build on, there may also be environmental inspections you need to do. While all these inspections cost money up front, it protects you in the long run. If you have a survey done now, you avoid problems down the road when you want to expand the parking lot and find out you are pouring asphalt onto the neighbor's property!

Inspections may also give you some negotiating leverage. If inspections turn up some hidden problems, you may have ammunition for lowering the purchase price.

The Deal Whatever else you do, make sure you get everything in writing!

If you've never bought real estate before, the deal can be intimidating, and you should expect something to go wrong up to the last second. When the signing occurs for a real estate transaction, the people in the room may include you, the seller, both real estate agents, your lawyer, the seller's lawyer, and the loan officer. It's a good idea to have your lawyer with you in case there are any last-minute snags, plus, as they are pushing pieces of paper in front of you to sign and whisking them away, it's nice to have someone who has done it a hundred times before. While it is a very ritualistic transaction to the other people in the room, your head will likely be reeling.

Closing the Sale. Once you and the seller have agreed on the particulars, you are committed to a binding sales contract and ownership is transferred. There are often lawyers, brokers, accountants, lenders, escrow agents, government officials, trade unions, family members, and other people involved in this transaction. Because of this medley of interested parties, the process usually takes 30–60 days to finish.

The close of escrow happens when all the documents are recorded at the County Recorder's Office; this usually happens the morning after the closing date.

Documents to record include:

- Deed
- Promissory note
- Mortgage or deed of trust
- Other security agreements
- Sales contract

- Options
- Bill of sale
- Assignments
- Request for notice
- Notice of completion of work

WHAT IF YOU GET TURNED DOWN?

If your loan application is rejected, you do have options:

Ask why. Find out specifically why your loan was refused. It may be a simple thing you can fix. Perhaps you left a key component out of your business plan. If this is the case, rework the plan and go back to the bank. Perhaps you don't have enough collateral for the size of loan you want. Can you make it work with a smaller loan amount?

Shop for another bank. Banks have specific requirements as to what types of loans they can make and how many they can approve. It may be that your type of loan or the amount of your loan did not fit into their criteria. If this is the case, shop for another bank.

If you go through the traditional loan process but are still turned down, there are other alternatives to explore before giving up, the main one being the government-sponsored Small Business Administration (SBA). After you have been turned down twice for a loan, you can contact the SBA to see if you can get a loan through them.

SMALL BUSINESS ADMINISTRATION LOAN PROGRAMS

The SBA offers a variety of financing options for small businesses and is the largest source of long-term small business financing in the nation. Whether you are looking for a long-term loan for machinery and equipment, a general working capital loan, a revolving line of credit, or a micro-loan, the SBA has a financing program to fit your needs. These programs are discussed in detail on the SBA's Web site at **www.sba.gov**.

The SBA program is set up to help people start businesses. It does this by guaranteeing bank loans. The loan programs are designed to help people gain access to capital that they cannot obtain through regular banking channels. Although the SBA can make direct loans to businesses, they encourage new business owners to establish a relationship with their bank and use the SBA as a last resort. To be eligible to have your loan guaranteed by the SBA, your business must be independently owned, must not dominate the field, and not exceed their size standards.

There are many loan options available through the SBA. The following provides the essentials on loans that can be used for startup and real estate purchases.

Basic 7(a) Loan Guaranty

This is the SBA's primary loan program that helps businesses obtain financing they would normally be ineligible for. Proceeds of these loans can be used for working capital, purchasing machinery and equipment or land and buildings, performing leasehold improvements, and refinancing existing debt. The maximum loan amount is $2 million, and the SBA's exposure is limited to 75 percent of that, or $1.5 million. Loans for working capital under this program need to be repaid within 10 years, and equipment or capital expenditure loans can be amortized over up to 25 years.

504 Loan Program

This program, also known as the Certified Development Company Loan Program, provides long-term, fixed-rate loans that can be used by growing small businesses to acquire land and buildings as well as machinery and equipment. The purpose of this program is to stimulate economic development within a community. The small business must contribute at least 10 percent of the total loan amount. The advantages of the 504 loan over a conventional loan are a lower down payment, below-market financing, and a longer repayment term.

SBAExpress

The SBAExpress enables business owners to obtain capital from a lending institution without having to go through the SBA process. The bank's existing documentation and process are used, and the SBA can guarantee up to 50 percent of the total amount loaned (total amount of the loan cannot exceed $350,000). SBAExpress loans for working capital mature in five to seven years, and real estate loans have an amortization of up to 25 years.

SBALowDoc

SBALowDoc loans further streamline the process of obtaining a small business loan, and responses are made within 36 hours of receiving an application. Borrowers complete the front side of a one-page application and the lender completes the back, making the process quick and efficient. Under the SBALowDoc program the maximum loan amount is $150,000, with loan maturity dates of five to seven years for working capital and, again, up to 25 years for fixed assets.

CommunityExpress

This pilot loan program is designed to stimulate economic development in low to moderate income areas and to help New Market business owners access capital within new markets. To be eligible for CommunityExpress, small businesses must be part of the SBA's New Markets, which are defined as small businesses owned by minorities, women and veterans who are underrepresented in the population of business owners compared to their representation in the overall population, and businesses located or locating in low and moderate income urban and rural areas. The maximum loan amount is $250,000.

Minority/Women Pre-qualification Loan Program

These programs assist woman and minorities to secure business loans. The maximum loan amount under both of these programs is $250,000.

The SBA also works in conjunction with other organizations to offer loan financing as follows:

- **Small Business Investment Companies (SBIC).** SBICs, investment companies licensed by the SBA, put venture capital into small businesses in venture capital investments and long-term loans.

- **Specialized Small Business Investment Companies (SSBIC).** SSBICs make smaller investments than SBICs. They only invest in small businesses owned by socially and economically disadvantaged individuals.

- **The Angel Capital Electronic Network.** This network is a service that gives so-called "angel" investors information on small businesses.

- More information on these financing opportunities can be found at **www.sbasmallbusinessloans.com**.

Economic Development Administration

The Department of Commerce makes and guarantees loans to businesses in redevelopment areas. To find out more, visit **www.osec.doc.gov/eda**.

Other Government Programs

Check the Catalog of Federal Domestic Assistance at **www.cfda.gov**. If you are a minority, such as a woman-owned business, there may be additional funds available to you. You can access information online concerning government grants at **www.sbasmallbusinessloans.com/finnif.htm**. This link will take you to a secured link where you can purchase the access for $49.95.

Equity Investment

Equity investment means that you give someone a share of your business in return for his or her investment dollars. The investor normally shares in your profits, but only shares in your losses up to the amount of their initial investment. There are three levels of ownership an investor generally participates in: general partner, limited partner, and shareholder.

A general partner shares in profits and losses in proportion to the investment. This type of partnership generally exists when both parties are willing to work full-time in the business. If an investor becomes a limited partner, he or she does not share in the responsibility of managing the business, and their risk is limited to the initial investment. An investor becomes a shareholder if you decide to incorporate your business and sell stock; the investor receives stock shares for his or her investment.

Equity investments may be a good way for you to get the necessary funds to purchase your location and start your business. This may also be a way for you to bring in people who have skills in areas you may lack. You should be careful about selling more than 49 percent of your business; if you sell more than half of your business interest, you also sell your right to make decisions.

The following are the most common sources of equity funds:

Personal equity. These are ventures that are funded entirely with personal equity or with a combination of personal equity and lease and debt financing.

Partnerships. Some caterers solicit funds by getting partners to invest. Typical partnership arrangements are general or limited. General partnerships usually mean both parties will be involved in the operation. In limited partnerships there is usually a general partner and one or more inactive, limited partners, with the general partner acting as manager and the limited partners as passive investors.

Corporation. Corporate ownership can be a great way to raise capital. Generally it is done through a stock offering—in the case of a large corporation, to the public, and in a small company, to private investors.

Venture capital

Venture capitalists normally do not fund a venture unless it has expansion potential and is proven to be well managed. Venture capitalists are interested in long-term financial gain and are less interested in the net operating profits of a new establishment. Buyers intending to purchase chain catering operations might be able to obtain venture capital because of the high earning potential.

There are lots of ways to access the financing your require—you just need to be resourceful and prepared. Lenders and investors need to feel confident they will be repaid or rewarded for helping you finance your company—champion your effort, come with a well-thought-out business plan, and chances are you will get the cash needed to start your business.

Location, Location, Location

Another important choice you must consider is the location of your business. If you are a small, home-based caterer, you've already made that decision for now, but this section will still be of interest to you if you plan to expand your business in the future. If you are an off-premise caterer, you go to the customer; therefore, you won't have to rely on business location as much as on-premise caterers. You location decisions will center more on cost and economy than style and ambiance. Obviously. the decision about location is critical for those planning to go into on-premise catering, The following information is especially relevant.

RESEARCH SOURCES

When undertaking the task of finding and opening a new catering location, you need to take your time, do a great deal of research, and then do some more. There are four research segments to look into when trying to find a location. Depending on your particular situation, you may need to go through all four steps of research, or you may only need to do two or three.

1. **National research.** This type of research is mainly undertaken by chains and large operations. At this stage you are looking at the entire nation as a prospective market.

2. **Market area research.** A market is a city or a metropolitan statistical area (MSA). Once you have chosen a city in which to locate your business, you need to begin looking at the districts within the city and focus on one that will be good for your operation.

3. **Trade area research.** Trade area refers to the area from which most of your customers come. For example, you may have defined your market as corporations in the downtown area of Anyville. Within this area the majority of your business comes from an area of three blocks. These three blocks are then considered your trade area. While there are no hard and fast rules

about what percentage of your business makes up a trade area, location experts generally say around 80 percent.

4. **Site research.** Finally you go and take a look at the actual sites. At this stage you will have narrowed your search to a few potential sites and you are comparing characteristics to find the best location for your business.

The software company Oracle offers a product called Workspace Manager What-If Analysis, which walks you through the process of site selection. It may be a good idea to purchase this and give yourself a "dry run." The program provides a detailed example of a seafood restaurant opening a new location. You must have an account with Oracle to use the software. You can find information at **http://otn. oracle.com/sample_code/products/workspace_mgr/htdocs/what_if.html**.

POPULATION AND DEMOGRAPHICS SOURCES

Market research information will help you choose the best location for your business. This information can be obtained from various resources and will be used at all levels of your site search.

The U.S. Census Bureau. This organization is an excellent source of information on population density statistics as well as population characteristics, or demographics. Some of the typical categories of information you can find for particular areas or cities include:

- Population

- Population density

- Demographic characteristics of the population

  - Age
  - Number of households
  - Household size
  - Education levels

  - Marital status
  - Homeowners
  - Income levels

- Information on the competition in the area

- Site characteristics

- Market characteristics

- Average money spent on catering per customer in your target market

The Census Bureau's Web site is **www.census.gov**. Three areas on the Census Bureau's Web site are of particular interest: the American Community Survey, CenStats, and County Business Patterns.

The American Community Survey. This survey can provide you with information from the census supplemental survey. This information includes tables with demographic information by county and

MSAs (an area made up of at least one major city—over 50,000 people—including the county or counties located within the MSA). The American Community Survey is a new survey that is replacing the Census Bureau's long survey. It provides economic, social, demographic, and housing information for communities every year instead of every ten years.

CenStats. This portion of the Web site gives you economic and demographic information that you can compare by county. The information is updated every two years. This section also includes information on residential building permits, which are updated every month.

County Business Patterns. County Business Patterns gives you economic information arranged by industry and it is updated every year. It includes data on the total number of establishments, employment, and payroll for over 40,000 zip codes across the country. Metro Business Patterns provides the same data for MSAs.

The drawback to much of the census information available is that it is collected infrequently—some information can be up to ten years old. If you are looking in an area that has changed a great deal in the last decade, you may want to supplement the information you get from the U.S. Census Bureau with information from demographic research firms. These firms typically use census data to generate information on population and demographics between census years.

Other Demographic Information Web Sites

While the U.S. Census Bureau can provide you with a great deal of demographic information, the following Web sites are worth exploring as well.

American FactFinder. This Web site, located at **http://factfinder.census.gov/servlet/BasicFactsServle**, lets you search, browse and map U.S. Census data, including economic, population, geographical, and housing statistics.

CACI Information Decision Systems. This site allows you to order demographic information by zip code. Pricing is by subscription or information can be priced per requested report. Log on to **www. infods.com** for a free sample of reports and a free zip code search.

FedStats. This Web site, at **www.fedstats.gov**, lets you track economic and population trends. The statistics are collected by more than 70 federal agencies.

Service Annual Survey. This part of the U.S. Census Web site offers annual estimates of receipts for some service industries. This information can be found at **www.census.gov/svsd/www/sas.html**.

Statistical Abstract of the U.S. Section 27, Domestic Trade and Services This Web page, located at **www.census.gov/prod/2001pubs/statab/sec27.pdf**, provides information on sales employees, payrolls and other business statistics.

Statistical Resources on the Web. This Web site, located at **www.lib.umich.edu/govdocs/stats. html**, is an index to statistical information available on the Internet. It lists over 200 topics.

Statistics of Income. Hosted by the Internal Revenue Service, this site contains financial information concerning businesses in the retail and service industries. You can find it by logging on to **www.irs. gov/taxstats/display/0,,i1=40&genericId=16810,00.html**.

U.S. Bureau of Economic Analysis, U.S. Department of Commerce. This agency hosts a Web site at **www.bea.gov**, which provides publications and data on businesses by industry.

Industry research. You'll also want to investigate your industry's market research. Again, the National Restaurant Association and National Association of Catering Executives are good sources for this type of information.

NARROWING YOUR SEARCH

As you begin researching your location, you'll probably find that you need some help. It's a big undertaking; you should use all the resources available to you. Of course, some resources are more expensive than others, but the following list includes many free resources you can use to help you find the best location for your catering operation.

Area Development Magazine

This magazine is devoted to site and facility planning. While it appears to be geared more toward industry and manufacturing, it is worth a trip to their Web site at **www.areadevelopment.com** Along with looking at site listings, you can get some general information about states such as population figures, leading industries, emerging industries, number of college graduates, taxes, and tax incentives.

Economic development organizations

Most states have economic development organizations that can provide you with a wealth of information, such as an overview of the area, the business climate, and a list of available sites and buildings. A list of such organizations can be found in the October issue of *Area Development Magazine*. You can also do a Web search on "economic development organizations" to locate these associations. An example of one can be seen at **www.pittsyecondev.com**.

Location-finding team

If you work for a company already, you can put together a team of individuals to work on the location process. Select people who have been involved in locating property before. At the same time, try to make the team diverse enough to bring up as many issues or questions as possible. For instance, it would be good to include someone from the production side of the operation as well as the financial side so the interests of both of these groups will be taken into consideration.

If you are going out alone or even with a partner, you should form a "team" to help you with your search as well. The team may simply consist of you and your spouse or you and your best friend from college who has a business degree. At some point, however, your team should include the services of an accountant and a lawyer. You will always need the services of a good accountant and a good lawyer in your years as a business owner, so you might as well find people you trust and bring them onboard early. The expense of their services in the location process will be worth the money they can save you by protecting you from a bad deal.

Utility companies

Utility companies often offer economic development services. These services include community development planning assistance, financial assistance, computerized databases of commercial sites and buildings, site plans, topographic maps, labor demographic information, utility information, and community profiles. To see an example of what types of information can be found at utility companies, log on to **www.cinergy.com**.

Web sites

An excellent research tool, **www.bizsites.com/Webxtras/locationconsul-tants.html** houses a wealth of information. For instance, you can find typical electrical costs for different states, crime rates, labor information, corporate tax rates in each state, a state tax comparison, regional business reviews, and case studies that you can read and learn from other people's mistakes!

The site **www.listsnow.com** can provide you with consumer lists and demographics with details such as specific as names and phone numbers. Prices vary and can range from $30 to several hundred dollars. This Web site also can provide you with lists of businesses in particular zip codes. These lists include information on the type and size so it is a good resource when you are assessing the competition.

Another site offered by American Business Information is found at **www.abii.com**. You can set up your own consumer or business demographic list requests. The prices for these lists vary with the amount of information you are requesting. Prices for information regarding market areas generally run $2,000 to $4,000.

Another helpful location Web site is **www.geodezix.com**. Their services include initial trade area analyses and consumer demographic information.

Two other helpful sites are **www.pwcglobal.com**, which offers site selection services to business owners looking for a location, and **www.geovue.com**, which provides geographic, demographic, and business data for site selection.

Software packages

There are software packages that do market analyses and site analysis. Prices can range anywhere from a couple hundred dollars to a few thousand. You can view some software products on **www.easidemographics. com**. Offered by Easy Analytic Software, Inc., this site also provides some free demographics reports online.

The Right Site, software offered through RealEstate.com, has a demographic database to use for site selection and market analysis. The Right Site comes in two editions, one for $250 and a more extensive addition for $500. Both editions offer customized demographic reports. They also offer The Site Kit: Field Guide and Software for Commercial Real Estate Evaluation for $89. This software program provides quick answers to site evaluation questions. All three products can be ordered online at **www.commercial.realestate.com /mesahouse/site_evaluation.asp**.

Nonprofit organizations

Many cities and counties have nonprofit economic development groups that also provide information. You can find these by searching on the Internet. An example of one such organization is the Hamilton County Development Company, Inc., which can be found at **www.hcdc.com**.

Map sources

If you are a member of AAA, you have access to free roadmaps that will help you in your research. Other map sources include TIGER from the U.S. Census Bureau, MapBlast and MapQuest. TIGER lets you view cities, regions, and MSAs. You are able to add information layers pertaining to census boundaries, highways, MSAs, census tracts, streets, zip codes, family size, household size, percentage of age groups in particular areas, ethnicity, and home ownership rates.

The Census Bureau also offers county block maps and census tract maps. GIS mapping programs may also be available through many county and city offices. For example, in Cincinnati a group of agencies put together a map program called CAGIS (Cincinnati Area Geographic Information System). This computerized mapping system allows users to view area maps that contain information on land records, sewers, streets, electrical systems, and drainage among other things. These maps are easily accessible through the Internet; you can view them at **www.cagis.hamilton-co.org**. An internet search of the area in which you are interested should tell you if this type of map is available.

Geographic Information Systems (GIS)

There are also many companies offering GIS and other mapping services on the Web. For example, Caliper Corporation at **www.caliper.com** offers a product called Mapitude, which is used for developing maps and other graphics. Geographic Data Technology at **www.geographic.com** sells digital street databases. Sites USA, Inc., at **www.sitesusa.com** offers mapping services, demographics for site analysis, and custom store modeling.

The advantages of using GIS are many. If you can use the software yourself, you'll cut out the middleman! Maps can be layered to show information such as population density, traffic flow, and property costs, along with other information. The mapping software also can pinpoint locations and help determine property availability and zoning. You can find GIS products on the Web from **www. gazelle.com**.

Real estate investment firms

Many of the larger chains follow real estate investment firms such as RealtiCorp. These groups have begun using siting applications that you may find useful. You can find one such application at **www. extendthereach.com**.

Chamber of Commerce

Your local chamber of commerce is a good spot for networking. They also may have resources for financing and research.

Small Business Associations

Many cities have small business associations. Again, this type of group gives you networking opportunities as well as possible sources of funding. Small business associations often offer loans with low interest rates. There are several publications that are available on the online library at **www.sba. gov**.

Financial institutions

You probably will be looking for funding for your operation, so start dealing with banks early on in the process. They can be a source of information as well as money. The Beige Book is a publication that includes information gathered by each Federal Reserve Bank on current economic conditions in its district in categories such as consumer spending, manufacturing, real estate, and construction.

Commercial real estate brokers

Real estate agents may best be used when the search has been narrowed to a few communities. Look on the Internet for sources of commercial real estate brokers at **www.realtor.com www.vandema.com** or **www.anysite.com**. Cohen-Esrey is a broker specializing in restaurant sites and they may have information on catering sites as well. They can be found on the Web at **www.cohenesrey.com**.

You can also check your area multiple listings service on the Web; they have commercial real estate listings. Check with friends and associates as well. Real estate is a word-of-mouth business, and this is often the best avenue for finding a good realtor. The Web site **www.mesahouse.com** can lead you to information on commercial real estate agents and other commercial real estate resources.

S.C.O.R.E. Association

S.C.O.R.E. (Service Corps of Retired Executives) is a nonprofit association with over 300 chapters in locations throughout the United States. The organization consists of working and retired executives and business owners who donate their time to help new small business owners. This organization offers workshops and free counseling; contact your local chapter for more information (**www.score.org**).

Location consultant

You may want to seek the services of a site-finding consultant. This can be an expensive way to narrow your search, so be sure you are clear about exactly what the consultant is being hired to do. This may be a good option for someone looking for a location as an individual. A consultant can give you an unbiased opinion on information and can help you with the legwork.

If you decide to use a consultant, keep in mind that market and location consultants can be expensive. It's worth shopping around and getting references to be sure the consultant you choose has experience in the tasks you want him or her to undertake and experience in working with the food service industry.

There are a number of professional organizations you can contact to find a consultant:

- Independent Real Estate Consultant (**www.fastighetsstrategi.se/english**)

- National Association of Corporate Real Estate Executives (**www.nacore.com**)

- American Management Consultants (**www.americanmc.com**)

- Qualified Solutions Consulting (**www.restaurantexperts.com**)

- Vectiv Corp. (**www.vectiv.com**)

- *Area Development* and other trade magazines

Be sure to look at more than one consultant, and hire the one that best fits your needs. If you are looking in the Midwest, select a consultant that has experience finding locations in the Midwest. When you have targeted a list of potential candidates, request a statement of qualifications, references, and a plan for how they will service you.

MARKET SURVEYS

A market survey is a good tool to use to supplement your census research. Remember, the census does not provide the most current information. The following is an example of a market survey. The information you need to complete these sheets usually can be found in records at the public library, city offices, and the chamber of commerce. Small business associations can also provide you with a wealth of information.

SAMPLE MARKET SURVEY								
Market (City)								
1. Approximate total population of target market area								%
2. Number of households								%
3. Average household size								%
4. Ages	19–24	%	25–34	%	35–50	%	50–65	%	65–Up	%
5. Household Annual Incomes					Below $11,000		%
$12,000–$24,000		%	$25,000–$36,000		%	$37,000–$50,000		%
$50,000–$80,000		%	$80,000–$100,000		%	Above $100,000		%

Use your own customer profile to help you decide which categories are appropriate for your market survey.

COMPETITOR SURVEY

When it comes to assessing the competition, you'll be wise to do some field work. Visit competitors and see what they offer. Using a simple survey like the following one can help you track competitor information.

SAMPLE COMPETITION SURVEY

Competitor Name	
Location	
What are the major roads in the vicinity?	
Is there a sign?	
How much parking?	
What are the operating hours?	
Is it a freestanding building? In a mall?	
What is the general appearance of the building exterior?	
What is the estimated square footage?	
What is the general appearance of the building interior?	
Describe the type of events catered.	

Number of weekly events					Mon
Tues	Wed	Thurs	Fri	Sat	Sun

What's the seating capacity of on-premise catering?	
What type of cuisine do they serve?	
What would you guess the average event booking revenue is?	
Do they offer entertainment or other additional services beyond food?	
What are the price ranges of appetizers?	
What are the price ranges of entrées?	
What are the price ranges of desserts?	

Analyze the competitor survey results and look for ways in which you can add value through your location or product and service offerings.

FACILITY REQUIREMENTS

When selecting a location, you also need to think about the type of space and the design requirements for your site. If you are doing on-premise catering, break up the operation into front-of-the-house and back-of-the-house to figure out what you need in both areas. If you are looking for a location for an off-premise catering operation, you'll just need to worry about production facilities.

How much space you will need

According to facility experts, dining takes up the majority of space. This is followed by kitchen and prep space, and then storage space. For a restaurant, space breaks down as follows: dining space is 40 to 60 percent of total facility; kitchen space is 30 percent, storage and administrative office take up the remaining space. About 12 percent should be allotted for actual food preparation; the remainder of the production space will be for dishwashing, trash, and receiving. Catering operations will probably want more production and storage space since you will be preparing food in larger quantities than most restaurants do. If you are providing on-premise catering, you will need to determine how much room you need for dining. Your sales forecast information can provide you with some information on how much dining space you will need.

If you are starting from scratch, you may want to engage the services of an architect or restaurant design consultant to help you design your space, but the services of these professionals can be several thousand dollars.

SITE CHARACTERISTICS

Let's say you have narrowed your search down to three locations. Now you need to compare these locations to determine which one is the best.

If you provide on-premise catering, here are some factors you should consider in the comparison:

Parking. How much parking is there? The Urban Land Institute (**www.uli.org**) and International Council of Shopping Centers (**www.icsc.org**) lists standard ratios of parking needed for shopping centers. They suggest that there should be at least 2.2 square feet of parking for every square foot of shopping center space. For supermarkets they suggest at least 3 square feet of parking for every square foot of supermarket space. These standards will help you make some estimates on the amount of parking you need. In areas with little parking or areas with higher crime rates, you may want to consider using valet parking.

Ingress/Egress. How easily is it to get into and leave the parking lot? Look at the roads in front of your possible location. Are there medians? These can make turning into your parking lot a problem. What about traffic lights? If you are on a busy road and your site is located on a corner without a light, customers may find it difficult to get into your parking lot as well.

Accessibility. How easy is it for your customers to get to the location from their homes and businesses? One of the things you'll want to do is drive within the trade area. Get in your car and drive from various points to your potential location. How long does it take you to get there?

Security. How safe is the location perceived? Check with the local police department to see what types of security problems exist in the neighborhood. Be sure to make your specific site safe with outside lighting as well.

After much analysis and some soul searching you will need to make a location decision. It is an exciting time as this is one of the first really tangible steps you take in the process of taking your dream to reality. You can't let the excitement take over because negotiating for the purchase or lease of a commercial property is serious business. The following section provides tips, tricks of the trade, and advice for making the process efficient and hopefully painless.

SECURING AND NEGOTIATING A LOCATION

Now that we've looked at how to find the right spot, we must focus on actually securing that spot. The process of buying a commercial location is very much like securing real estate for your home. You'll make an offer on the property and then you have to go through financing, inspections, appraisals, and permitting.

When you are looking at specific sites in a market area, you should think about getting a commercial real estate agent to help you. An agent will be able to provide you with neighborhood, site, and market information you might not otherwise have. Not only can he or she help negotiate the deal, but realtors can also connect you with appraisers and inspectors that they use and trust. To find a commercial realtor, contact the local real estate board. If you begin working with one and you don't like that realtor, get another one. Negotiating your location property is too big of a job to leave in the hands of someone you do not like or trust.

LEASE VERSUS OWN

Should you lease a building or purchase one? The decision isn't easy, and you should apprise yourself of the advantages and disadvantages of both and how these factors impact your situation specifically. We've compiled some of the most important factors for consideration below.

Leasing

Oftentimes you can lease a building with less money upfront than is required for an outright purchase. For this and other reasons you may consider leasing rather than buying a location for your business. Leasing can make it easier to start your new business, and there may be certain tax advantages to leasing. Additionally, if the time ever comes when you want to move, you will not have all the costs associated with selling the building.

Analyze the following items in a typical commercial lease to help you make your decision.

- Length of lease. Many commercial leases go for five or ten years rather than a single year.

- Rent and rate and timing of rent increases.

- Whether the rent includes insurance, property taxes and maintenance costs (called a gross lease), or whether you will be charged for these items separately (called a net lease).

- The amount of the security deposit and conditions for its return.

- The square footage of the space you are renting.

- How improvements and modifications will be handled and who will pay for them. Pay specific attention to sign specifications.

- Who will maintain and repair the premise.

- Whether there's an option to renew the lease or expand the space.

- How the lease may be terminated, including notice requirements, and penalties for early termination.

Commercial leases are different from residential leases. If you've rented an apartment, that doesn't mean you know what you're getting into. Commercial leases do not fall under most consumer protection laws. For example, there are no caps on security deposits or rules protecting a tenant's privacy. Commercial leases are usually customized to the landlord's needs, but they can be subject to more negotiation between the business owner and the landlord. Because there is no standard lease form, you must be sure to read each lease agreement you look at carefully. It is probably wise to have your lawyer look at these as well.

The following are common lease issues you need to be aware of.

Lease breaking. Unlike a residential lease where if you break the lease, you simply forfeit your security deposit, commercial leases are contracts. If you break it, more than your security deposit may be at stake. Pay close attention to these terms in the lease agreement.

Future growth. Think before you enter into a lease agreement. Make sure it fits your business needs now and in the future. Especially consider where you think your business will be in the future if you are entering into a long-term lease agreement. Make sure the lease covers your ability to make the necessary modifications your building may need now as well as five years down the road.

Signage and competition. Make sure you are able to put up a sign. If you lease in a large commercial complex, make sure the lease includes some competition safeguards for you. You don't want to open your catering business and then have the landlord rent the space next door to another catering company two months later!

Leasing broker. You may want to engage a leasing broker to help you locate business leases. A leasing broker works much the same way as a real estate broker, they charge a fee but they will do a great deal of the legwork, and you benefit from their knowledge and expertise.

Buying

If you are considering buying a building, you have a few options. You can buy an existing building, build a new facility, or you can buy an existing operation and make it your own. All three options have merit; you need to decide which is best for your company and what best fits with your current situation.

Buy an existing building. This is an obvious choice if you want to be in a certain location and are not afraid of the work involved in transforming a space into what you envision. When thinking about a building to buy, older buildings often have more character than new buildings, and you may also be able to benefit from a tax break with some older buildings. Since 1976 there have been provisions in the federal tax code to benefit taxpayers who own historic commercial buildings. (More information on this is available in the section Building and Construction Permits.) If this is the option you choose, make sure you engage the services of an experienced commercial real estate broker.

Build a new facility. If you really want to make your entire operation your own, you might want to start from the ground up. This is a complicated endeavor and not recommended for someone starting their first venture. For experienced caterers who know exactly what they want, do not want to compromise on anything, and who have the required fund, this is an excellent option.

If you are buying a site to build a structure, you may find this Web address useful: **www. CMDFirstSource.com/means/index.asp**. After registering as a user, you can enter information on the type of structure you want to build, the gross square feet you need, and the zip code. The program will then provide you with an itemized cost estimate. You can find a database for building codes for most major cities on this same Web site.

This, again, is not a process you want to enter into without the assistance of qualified professionals. From buying the land to finding a contractor for construction, you need to rely on professionals for advice and assistance.

Buying an Existing Operation

Buying an existing operation requires less capital at the start of your venture because, in many cases, when someone sells an existing operation, the purchase price includes all the equipment as well. You need to be careful if you are considering buying an existing operation; you want to know why the owner is selling. Also make sure your business plan will be successful within the operation you are buying.

- **Check the financial records.** You'll want to take a look at the company's financial records from the past several years to get a good sense of the company's financial health. While you may be able to breathe some life back into the business, don't expect miracles.

- **Why are they selling?** Do some sleuthing and find out why they are selling and what the word on the street is about the location. Be on-site for a few days and see what happens at the operation currently. Finally, make sure the location is a good one for your operation.

STRATEGIES FOR BUYING AN EXISTING BUSINESS

Buying and selling a business is a complicated process. Before you contact any sellers, you should prepare a document that outlines your desired sales price, terms and conditions. With careful preparation you will be able to take your desired sales price, terms, conditions, initial investment and revenue goals from the page to a signed contract for the purchase of a business that has a high probability of meeting your business objectives.

During the process of buying an existing operation, you must determine the type of catering operation that is right for you. Consider the operation's investment yield, taxes, and the effect the business will have on you personal life. Basically, you need to find a catering operation that will meet your income requirements and that will provide you with a great deal of job satisfaction: when you're working a 12–14 hour day, you better be enjoying it!

OBJECTIVES FOR PURCHASING AN EXISTING OPERATION

- **Obtain the best possible sales price.** Sales price should never exceed the company's replacement cost.

- **Make a reasonable down payment.** Ultimately you want a 1:1 debt-to-equity ratio, so your down payment should not exceed an amount that when added to other investment charges is more than 50 percent. Remember that even though a lower down payment reduces your investment risk, it also increases your finance charges. If you can't support your debt load, you will lose your business anyway.

- **Make a reasonable initial investment.** You should aim to match your debt-to-equity so you don't want all of your equity going towards making a down payment.

- **Maximize future profits.** Assess the operation's future performance against past performance. You only want to purchase a company that has high potential to be a revenue-generating business.

- **Reduce the possibility of failure.** Only one out of five established businesses that are purchased go under. That is much better than the four out of five failure rate for new businesses.

- **Enhance borrowing power.** Most lenders prefer financing an existing, profitable operation to a new venture.

- **Minimize liabilities.** Both you and seller should work at minimizing taxes. The only way to ensure that this happens is for both parties to hire accountants.

When buying a business you want to research the seller's motivation. Figuring out why the seller wants to sell is crucial because you don't want to be left with a business that can't be profitable. The following is a list of six major seller motivations:

1. **Owners who want to retire.** These folks usually want to move out of the area and receive a retirement income. They usually seek acceptable seller financing or an annuity arrangement.

2. **Disillusioned owners.** The neophyte or absentee owner often decides to get out of the business when it starts doing poorly. Often the business is not as profitable or fun as they had thought, and they don't know what to do to remedy those problems.

3. **Owners with tax problems.** Once depreciation expenses and interest expenses have evaporated, owners often sell in order to move into a larger operation and to reinstate these tax shelters.

4. **Owners with other investment opportunities.** Often owners want to use the money received from the sale of their catering companies for investments elsewhere or, if the market is favorable, just to cash out at a very good price.

5. **Owners with distressed properties.** Struggling properties often do not throw off enough profit to fund necessary remodeling or overhaul.

6. **Distressed owners.** Often profitable operations are run by people having troubled relationships with their business or marital partners or their shareholders. In some cases, one of these parties has died. These can give serious cause for an owner to leave a profitable operation.

Once you respond to a sales solicitation, you will receive enough information to determine if the catering company meets or exceeds your investment requirements, but you need to dig deeper than that to find out whether a catering company is or is not a good opportunity.

INVESTIGATING AN EXISTING OPERATION

Experienced buyers know almost immediately from the sales brochure if the catering company will meet their needs. One of the ways to determine this is through the real-property lease payment. If it is less than or equals 6 percent of the catering company's total sales volume, it is worth further investigation. You should also consider future sales volume and profit-generating capacity.

To find out more about the company, you should tour the facility; learn the lease highlights, and find out about other purchase options. It is also important to evaluate the neighborhood, the competition, the customer viewpoint, and history of ownership.

MAKING THE PURCHASE

Once you are satisfied with your analysis and you have determined that a business meets your requirements, you need to enter into a sales agreement. This is not an area that you want to navigate without professional assistance from your lawyer and perhaps a broker specializing in putting commercial buyers and sellers together.

Terms, Conditions and Price

Terms. The terms of sale are the procedures you will use to pay the seller. In most cases, sellers receive a minimal down payment and the remainder of the purchase price over a three- to five-year period. All-cash offers are rare, and seller financing is often used to make their operations more attractive to you and other potential purchasers. If you want to have more of the terms go in your favor, then it is a good strategy to make a substantial cash down payment.

Rather than cash, your may want to pay with property or corporate stock instead. This is a negotiating point that may or may not work in your favor, and here you need to rely on expert financial advice to make the best decision.

A very common practice, especially with catering companies, is for the seller to finance a portion of the sale price. They do this so that they can get high sales prices in exchange for the consideration. You can negotiate these terms, but typically they are tied to the marketplace.

Conditions. There are several conditions that both you and the seller will attach to most sales contracts. Sometimes they are separate agreements, but most of the time they are part of the sales contract itself. The following lists conditions that you should be aware of:

- **Conclusion of sale.** Sellers typically want to finish the transaction as fast as possible because delays give you time to second-guess. Don't get pressured into taking over before you are prepared.

- **Buyer access.** Sellers generally want minimal contact with you while waiting for the transaction to close, but it always good to have the seller provide needed assistance and training for a length of time after the possession transfer.

- **Guarantees.** Sellers usually have to guarantee the condition of assets and sometimes they guarantee that you can assume some of the catering company's current contracts. Sellers should never guarantee things they don't have total control over and imprecise language in these clauses should be avoided.

- **Indemnification.** Sellers will want to be compensated if you back out of the deal. These clauses spell out the recourse they have should that happen.

- **Escrow agent.** Independent escrow agents are usually hired to supervise transactions. These agents see that all terms and conditions are met and that ownership is transferred. Having an independent third party ensures that the many details of the transaction are handled well and legally.

- **Legal requirements.** Both you and the seller must agree to comply with all pertinent laws and statutes. Escrow agents ensure that all current creditors are notified of the catering company's sale and that all legal requirements are met. This ensures that the buyer can begin with a clean slate, without any of the seller's responsibilities to creditors.

- **Buyer's credit history.** Before agreeing to seller financing, the seller will investigate your credit history. It is standard for you to have to give personal financial statements, résumés, references, and permission to run a credit report. Serious buyers have no problem with this because it secures the seller's respect and encourages the sharing of confidential information.

- **Security for seller financing.** Many deals go bad because the buyer and seller can't agree on financing. If a seller agrees to hold paper, the buyer must sign a promissory note and security agreement. The note represents the buyer's promise to pay, and the security agreement is the collateral pledged to secure the loan. If the seller is the only lender, a clause should be added that requires his or her approval before the new owner can obtain additional financing. The promissory note should contain a default provision that the lender can foreclose if loan payments are not met. Other specific provisions pertinent to the business might be that the seller can foreclose if the new owner doesn't maintain a required balance sheet, or if he or she does not produce previously agreed-upon menu items.

- **Assumable loans and leases.** Part of purchasing an established organization is assuming conditions that are already in place. This is advantageous to you because often these contracts are below what you would pay if you were to enter into an agreement today. If this is the case, be sure to make a condition of sale that you are able to assume the business's loans and leases.

- **Collection of receivables.** It is reasonable for the owner to receive a modest fee for the collection of receivables. This can be true for business booked prior to the change of ownership.

- **Inventory sale.** This is usually handled at the close of escrow. Physical inventory of all food, beverages and supplies should be taken by an independent service and a separate bill of sale prepared for the agreed-upon price of this merchandise.

- **Non-compete clause.** This is quite common in the sale of an ongoing business, because the new owner doesn't want the seller to open a competing business nearby. Sellers try to avoid these, but they understand they're inevitable.

- **Repurchase agreement.** Sellers often include agreements that grant them the option to buy back the catering company within a certain time period. This usually notes the purchase price and terms of the sale. Be wary of these because if the company becomes incredibly valuable all of a sudden, the former owner can buy it back or sell the repurchase agreement to someone else.

- **Employment contract.** If a seller agrees to remain as an employee of the new company, a very specific contract should be drafted. Most sellers have no interest in these contracts and just want out. However, by offering to stay, the seller can increase his or her potential for selling the company.

- **Consulting contract.** This is often a more acceptable employment contract that gives the new owner a tax-deductible expense but doesn't burden the former owner, either.

- **Conditions not met.** Sometimes buyers and sellers cannot meet every sales condition. Sellers can use this as a way to back out of the deal. Make sure you reserve the right to proceed with the sale even if certain conditions are not met.

Price

As a potential buyer you must do a thorough financial analysis of the company including carefully studying current profitability and using this information to determine potential capacity for generating revenue. Because there is a very close relationship between a company's current profitability and its likely sales price, you should examine this income very carefully. Understandably, sellers are not particularly eager to divulge their financial records to buyers. However, if a seller is forthcoming with this information, it signals to you that he or she has nothing to hide.

It's a good idea to hire an accountant to assist in this financial analysis. This will help determine whether the deal meets your investment requirements. You should also complete at least a rough market and competition survey before performing your financial evaluation. This will ensure your familiarity with the company's location and will help you estimate future revenues and expenses.

The seller expects a written offer with price, terms, conditions and an earnest money deposit before he or she will allow a potential buyer to review confidential financial information. You must agree beforehand that you can withdraw if you are unhappy with the financial records. If you don't do this, your earnest deposit is at risk.

You'll probably need to reconstruct historical financial statements to show what they could have been had you been operating the business. This is usually done for only the previous year's statement. This is a time-consuming process, and if errors are made, the estimate of the company's sales price may be inaccurate. Sellers will tend to overestimate customer counts and check averages and underestimate utilities and other expenses. Be wary when evaluating these numbers, and hire professional counsel as needed.

It is also important to be aware that sellers will initially include only the financial details they want to reveal. These numbers are usually pretty optimistic, but can give you a good idea of whether the operation matches your investment needs. The typical listing agreement contains the asking price, financing possibilities, current sales volume, current expenses, and age and size of the operation. Make sure to evaluate this information carefully, with special attention to the apparent net cash flow, before spending a lot of time and money on a detailed analysis.

When you gain access to the financial statements, you should analyze balance sheets and income statements carefully. Balance sheets can reveal the anxiety level of a seller, and can indicate the current management's ability. If this ability is in question, this could predict greater earnings under your sound management. Use the income statements likewise to determine whether the operation could have satisfied salary demands and provided a return on the initial investment, had it been under your management for the previous 12 months.

Ultimately you will base your offer price on the current income, but sellers realize that you are buying more than just the current operations—you are buying the operation's potential revenue generation as well. You need to make sure you have spent sufficient time and energy preparing your pro forma statements to represent, as best you can, the earning potential of the company. You don't want to pay too much and the seller will also want to make sure you don't pay too little; much of that estimation comes from the pro forma statements.

INITIAL INVESTMENT

Equally as important as price, terms and conditions is the total amount of money required to begin operating. Catering operations can require large amounts of cash when starting up and you must estimate as accurately as possible the total initial investment needed to get your business up and running the way you envision it. It is easy to assume that when purchasing an existing business you will avoid most startup costs, but there are, however, a number of costs associated with purchasing an existing business that you need to be aware of.

- **Investigation costs.** You must be willing to spend time and money to thoroughly examine the opportunities that are available. Many investors falsely believe that once initial development work is complete, the startup costs are eliminated. While they are reduced considerably, startup costs still exist, and wise investors calculate them in their analyses.

- **Down payment.** A standard down payment is approximately a quarter of the sales price. If you offer this down payment, you can usually expect below-market financing for the remainder of the sales price. The down payment may also affect the sales price itself, and many sellers will accept a lower sales price with a larger down payment and vice versa.

- **Transaction costs.** Escrow agents will prorate insurance, payroll, vacation pay, license renewal fees, advertising costs, etc., on the close-of-escrow date. This will leave you, the buyer, with a debit balance that the escrow agent will transfer to the seller. The fees paid to the escrow company and for the drawing of documents needed to close the transaction constitute the closing costs.

- **Working capital.** You must budget necessary amounts of money to ensure sufficient supplies are on hand to run the catering operation.

- **Deposits.** Most creditors require cash deposits as assurance they will be paid for their products and services. Utility, telephone, sales tax, payroll tax and lease deposits all must be factored in.

- **Licenses and permits.** Most food operations will have permits that need to be acquired. Be sure to include the cost of these in your startup budget.

- **Legal fees.** Competent legal advice is a necessity. Escrow agents should not be counted on to draw papers correctly and to make sure that the interests of various parties have been represented. As a buyer you should have your own counsel looking out solely for your interests. Subsequently, the fees for these services should be budgeted.

- **Renovations, furniture and equipment.** There may be building code violations to rectify or large renovations necessary to bring the operation into a competitive position. It may also be necessary to purchase new china, tables, etc., to replace worn older ones.

- **Advertising.** Promoting an opening or reopening, rebuilding signage, and offering promotional discounts or other incentives are good ways to build patronage for a new establishment.

- **Fictitious name registration.** If the name of a catering operation is fictitious, the name must usually be registered at the local courthouse or County Recorder's Office.

- **Loan fees.** If you are not acquiring seller financing, you will accrue loan fees from the lending parties.

- **Equity fees.** If you want to sell common stock to a few investors, you will incur attorney, document preparation and registration fees.

- **Insurance.** A lender will require a borrower to have appropriate life and disability insurance and that the borrower name the lender as sole beneficiary.

- **Pre-opening labor.** This is one of the expenses that is greatly minimized by purchasing an existing operation instead of starting one from scratch. You can usually plan to make some personnel changes, and a portion of current staff members should be expected to leave during the change of management. It costs money to replace these workers, so make room in the budget for it.

- **Accounting and other consulting fees.** Fees for assistance in the evaluation of a catering operation purchase need to be budgeted for.

- **Other prepaid expenses.** When new ownership takes over an existing business, it is not uncommon for creditors to demand a form of prepayment.

- **Sales taxes.** Property may be subject to a transfer tax, and non-food supplies are often subject to sales tax.

- **Locksmith.** If you're like most buyers, you will change all the locks after the sale is concluded.

- **Security.** You will likely transfer the current security service into your business. If one doesn't exist, you should invest in one to protect your new business.

- **Contingency.** It may be a good idea to have a contingency fund large enough for the first six months' operating expenses.

FINANCING

The typical offer and acceptance agreement includes several conditions necessary for the deal's completion. Most of these are met easily, but there are two that are difficult to meet. You must qualify for financing and you must attain all necessary permits. There is little you as a buyer can do if you don't qualify for permits, unless you need to fix only simple code violations to qualify. In the financing realm, you and the seller can often work together to adjust the final sales contract to ensure you can receive funding. Before you do this, though, you need to realize that there is no bigger threat to your success than inadequate or inappropriate financing.

Excessive debt burden is one of the most consistent reasons catering operations go under. Do your homework first, and make sure you qualify to receive a loan or can access the required funds some other way. There are costs involved in the preliminary steps to purchasing a business; you don't want to wait until the very end to find out you won't be able to make your dream come true at this time after all.

Laws, Regulations and Licenses

When you start a business, you need to learn about the federal, state, and local regulations affecting that business. There may be zoning laws to consider, licenses to purchase, and inspections to pass. The federal government has many resources that a new business owner may find helpful. The U.S. Business Advisor Web site at **www.business.gov**, for example, offers resources such as:

- A business resource library

- The Small Business Administration's startup advisor

- Online counseling

- Information on financial resources

- Links to laws that affect various industries

- **Business.gov**, an online resource guide with legal and regulatory information for small businesses

Other federal Web sites that have information you might find useful:

- The Small Business Administration's Web site has information about laws and regulations that affect small businesses at **www.sba.gov**.

- The IRS also offers information for small business owners on their Web site at **www.irs.gov/businesses**.

- The U.S. Department of Labor has a Web page **www.dol.gov/osbp/sbrefa/main.htm** that focuses on helping small business owners comply with that department's rules. Their Elaws Web page also provides employment laws assistance to small business owners at **www.dol.gov/elaws**.

Many states' Departments of Development offer one-stop shopping for new entrepreneurs. An example is Ohio's 1st Stop Business Connection, **www.odod.state.oh.us/onestop/index.cfm**. This site takes you through the steps to create a business information kit that contains all the forms and copies of the state regulations you'll need for your business enterprise for free. You can find out whether your state has an agency such as the Ohio's 1st Stop by contacting your local economic development center, chamber of commerce, or small business development center.

For any local regulations that may affect your business, you should check with your chamber of commerce and your local Equal Employment Opportunity Commission (EEOC) office for information. You can contact the U.S. EEOC for help in finding your local office. They can be reached at 1-800-669-4000 or log on to **www.eeoc.gov/contact.html** for a list of field offices.

STATE REGISTRATION

Contact the Secretary of State's office as early as possible to discuss your plans for opening a new business. All states have different regulations. This office will be able to describe all of the state's legal requirements and direct you to local and county offices for further registration. There is generally a fee required for registering a new business; most often it is less than one hundred dollars.

The city, county and state agency will most likely run a check to make certain no other businesses are currently using your particular business name. As mentioned earlier, you may also be required to file and publish a fictitious name statement in a newspaper of general circulation in the area. You must renew this fictitious name periodically in order to legally protect it.

Should your state have an income tax on wages, be sure to request all pertinent information from the State Department of Labor or Taxation. This includes all required forms, tax tables, and tax guides. Also contact the State Department of Employee Compensation for their regulations and filing procedures.

CITY BUSINESS LICENSE

Almost all cities and most counties require a permit to operate a business, so you need to contact your city business department. Your application will be checked by the zoning board to make certain that the business conforms to all local regulations. If you purchase an existing catering operation, you will eliminate most of these clearances.

SALES TAX

In many states, you may also be required to obtain a vendor's license if you collect sales taxes on your food. These taxes may be state, county and local. Check your state's Department of Taxation Web site for information concerning these taxes in your state.

You also need to contact the State Revenue or Taxation Agency concerning registry and collection procedures. Each state has its own methods of taxation on the sale of lodging and food products. Most states that require collection on food and beverage sales also require an advance deposit or bond to be posted against future taxes to be collected. The State Revenue Agency will often waive the deposit and accept instead a surety bond from your insurance company. The cost of this insurance is usually around 5 percent of the bond.

To further complicate the matter, sales tax is only collected on the retail price purchased by the end user. Thus, when purchasing raw food products to produce menu items, it will not be necessary to pay sales tax on the wholesale amount. However, you must present the wholesaler with your sales tax permit or number when placing orders, and sign a tax release card for their files. You need to thoroughly investigate your state's particular requirements.

HEALTH DEPARTMENT LICENSE

Most state health departments classify catering operations along with restaurants and other food service establishments such as food delivery operations, vending machine locations, and temporary food locations. In order to serve food, you may need to get a food service license. Since every state is different, you will need to contact the local or state Department of Health for information on how to obtain a food service license.

The health department should be contacted as early as possible for a personal visit to discuss your plans. It is to your advantage to show cooperation and compliance from the very beginning. The health department can, and will, close your facility until you comply with its regulations. A catering operation shut down by the health department will almost surely be ruined if the closure becomes public knowledge.

Prior to opening, the health department will inspect the catering operation. If the facility passes the thorough inspection, they will issue a license enabling you to open your catering operation. The cost of the license is usually less than $50. Should they find faults in your facility, however, you will be required to have them corrected before a license will be issued.

Periodically during the year, the health department will make unannounced inspections of your catering operation. An examination form will be filled out, outlining their findings. You must have all violations rectified before their next inspection. You can be certain that they will be back to see if you have complied.

Once your commercial kitchen has passed the inspection based on health department regulations, you can operate legitimately from your kitchen. Your establishment might be considered a commissary, a restaurant, or a food processing plant. You're better off applying for the type of license that will allow maximum flexibility and permits broader privileges such as retailing, for example.

Many health inspections are brought about by customer complaints. The health department will investigate every call they receive. Depending upon the number of calls and the similarity among the complaints, a pattern will be formulated. They will then trace the health problem to its source. Usually the problem is a result of some mishandling of a food product by a member of the staff. However, the problem can sometimes be traced to your supplier.

Although the health department can at times seem like a terrific nuisance, they really are on your side; their goals and yours are the same. Cooperation between both sides will resolve all the catering operation's health conditions and make it a safe environment.

Many states now have laws requiring that the manager—and in some states the entire staff—goes through and passes an approved health and sanitation program. Check with your state catering association to see if this applies to your location. The most common approved program is the ServSafe program developed by the National Retaurant Association's Educational Foundation.

Even if you are operating from home, you require a license from the local health board. Before setting up a home-based catering operation, be sure to contact your local health department to make sure this is legal. Many localities will not allow it. Of course, if your particular city or county does not, and your heart is set on catering, you may want to consider moving the operation to a nearby area that does allow for home-based catering operations. Be sure to do your research early and thoroughly in this area!

FIRE DEPARTMENT PERMIT

A permit from the fire department, also referred to as an occupational permit, is also required prior to opening. As with the health department, contact the fire department as early as possible, preferably in person, to learn about their regulations and needs. The fire department inspectors will be interested in checking fire exits, extinguisher placements and the hood and sprinkler systems. Many city fire departments do not permit the use of open-flame candles, flaming foods or flaming liquor in the building. If you intend to use some of these methods, it is best to ask about the regulations in advance.

Based upon the size of the building, the local and national fire code, and the number of exits, the fire inspectors will establish a "capacity number" of people permitted in the building at one time. Follow their guidelines strictly, even if this means turning away customers because you've reached capacity.

Check with your local fire department to find out the specific fire regulations that will affect your business.

BUILDING AND CONSTRUCTION PERMIT

Should you plan on doing any renovating to the your catering operation that will change the structural nature of the building, you may need a local building permit.

Building permits are generally issued from the local building and zoning board, and the fee is usually around $100, but it may be based on a percentage of the total cost of the project. You will need to approach the building inspector with your blueprints or plans to initially determine if a permit is required. Should a permit be required, the building and zoning board will inspect your plans to ensure that they meet all the local and federal ordinances and codes. Once the plans are approved, a building permit will be issued. The building inspector will make periodic inspections of your work at various stages of completion to ensure that the actual construction is conforming to the approved plans.

Most states have building codes in place that provide standards for new construction and renovations. The areas included in the codes are structural standards, plumbing and electric. Most states will require you to get a permit for any new building or renovation as well, especially if there is a change in use, such as changing a private home into a catering operation.

Again, check with local authorities in your area to determine how local building codes will affect you.

SIGN PERMITS

Many local city governments are beginning to institute sign ordinances and restrictions. These ordinances restrict the sign's size, type, location, lighting, and the proximity to the business. This is especially true if there is a particular neighborhood atmosphere the local government may be trying to keep intact or if the neighborhood is designated as a historic district.

Even if there aren't any regulations, if your business is in a residential area it's unlikely your neighbors will appreciate a neon sign announcing your presence. Keep your business's ambiance and your neighbors' expectations in mind when choosing signage for your business.

ZONING

Zoning laws prohibit certain activities from being conducted in particular areas; for example, a factory can't operate in areas zoned for residential use. Often some mix of land use is allowed; one area of a county may allow mixed commercial and residential use, for example. Zoning laws also affect elements such as parking, signage, noise and appearance. In historic districts, you'll find fairly heavy restrictions on what type of signage you can use and many laws concerning the appearance of your building, including acceptable remodeling plans.

Some cities also restrict the number of particular types of businesses in a certain area; these cities may only allow three food service establishments in an area, for instance. There may be particular commercial areas not zoned for restaurant operations or there may be ordinances concerning permits, parking, or liquor licenses that make a location unusable for you. Do a thorough check with the local zoning office before you purchase property.

You'll need a Certificate of Use and Occupancy from your municipality before the business can be conducted legally. Off-premise caterers who construct a new facility or convert an existing building previously used for other purposes will have to check zoning regulations carefully. To operate a business on land not zoned for that purpose, a conditional-use permit may be required.

HISTORIC BUILDINGS AND DISTRICTS

As discussed in the "Buying an Existing Building" section of this handbook, if you are operating out of an older home or building, it may be eligible for the National Historic Register. Since 1976 there have been provisions in the federal tax code to benefit tax payers who own historic commercial buildings. These buildings are structures that are listed on the National Register of Historic Places, in national historic districts, in local historic districts, or are national historic landmarks. This tax credit has gone a long way in helping cities revitalize historic areas. Currently the tax benefit to the owner is a 20 percent tax credit, for properties listed on the federal list. For more information on this tax credit, contact the Internal Revenue Service's Web site at **www.irs.gov** or write to: Federal Historic Preservation Tax Incentives, Heritage Preservation Services (2255), National Park Service, 1849 C St NW, Washington, D.C. 20240. They can be reached by e-mail at **hps-info@nps.gov** or by phone at 202-343-9594.

If your business is in a historic district, you will be required to follow any zoning and construction regulations the local government, state government, or federal government has in place for national historic districts. Which guidelines you will need to follow depend on whether your property is within the boundaries of a local historic district, state-defined historic district, or federally recognized historic district. In general these regulations are set up to preserve the character of the properties within the boundaries of the district. Your local historic preservation office can be very helpful in uncovering the rules and figuring out how to work with them. If you search on Google.com for your state historic preservation office, you'll be able to find contact information. Check your local and state guidelines for information on local or state historic district tax credits.

STATE LIQUOR LICENSE

A state liquor license requires extensive investigation because of its complexity. Certain states vary the restrictions on sales of alcoholic beverages by county. A license to sell liquor in some states may cost but a few hundred dollars; in others, a license can cost upwards of $100,000. Several states are on quota systems, and licenses are not even available. Certain counties in some states prohibit liquor sales entirely. In conjunction with your lawyer, you should conduct a thorough investigation concerning the rules in your particular state.

Once you obtain a license, it is imperative that you adhere to its laws and regulations. Most states have several thousand rules, so many in fact that they must be put into book form to contain them all. Most are just based on common sense, but they all have a designated purpose. You can easily lose the license due to an infraction; obviously this would be disastrous and could ruin your organization.

If you have other employees, make certain they are thoroughly familiar with all the liquor laws. Carefully train new employees; test them if necessary. Constantly reiterate the laws. Employees will become lax if they are not reminded often of this big responsibility.

Get to know the liquor commissioner or inspector for your area. Demonstrate your wish to cooperate and understand the responsibility of having a license.

To find out more about your state's liquor laws, visit the National Conference of State Liquor Administrators' directory at **www.ncsla.org/states.htm** and choose your state from the drop-down menu.

INTERNAL REVENUE SERVICE REGISTRATION

In conjunction with the liquor license, you may also need to obtain tax stamps from the Internal Revenue Service. Simply call the local IRS office and have them send you application Form #11 or download the form at **www.irs.gov** Based on the information about the catering operation you supply on the form, the IRS will assess a fee. This application informs the IRS that you are engaging in the retail sale of liquor.

FEDERAL TAX IDENTIFICATION NUMBER

All employers, partnerships and corporations must have a federal identification number. For most sole proprietors, this number is usually their Social Security number. This number will be used to identify the business on all tax forms and other licenses. To obtain a federal identification number (other than your Social Security number), fill out Form #SS-4, obtainable from the IRS. There is no charge. Also at this time request from the IRS the following publications, or you can download them via the Internet at **www.irs.gov**.

- Publication #15, circular *"Employer's Tax Guide."*

- Several copies of Form W-4, "Employer Withholding Allowance Certificate." Each new employee must fill out one of these forms.

- Publication #334, *"Tax Guide for Small Businesses."*

From the Occupational Safety and Health Administration (OSHA), request free copies of "All About OSHA" and "OSHA Handbook for Small Businesses." Depending upon the number of employees you have, you will be subject to certain regulations from this agency. Their address is: OSHA, U.S. Department of Labor, Washington, D.C. 20210

From the Department of Labor, request a free copy of "Handy Reference Guide to the Fair Labor Act." Department of Labor, Washington, D.C. 20210, **www.dol.gov**.

STATE TAX ASSISTANCE

Many states offer tax assistance to small business owners through their Department of Revenue. To find a list of all the state Department of Revenue Web addresses, go to **www.aicpa.org/yellow/ yptsgus.htm**.

Insurance Requirements

Properly insuring a catering business is similar to the coverage for any business enterprise where members of the public are in frequent attendance. Liability protection is of the utmost concern. Product liability is also desirable, as the consumption of food and beverages always presents a hazard. Described in this section are all the different types of insurance coverage applicable to a standalone catering operation. By no means is it recommended that you should obtain all of this insurance, for you would probably be grossly over-insured, but armed with this information, you and your insurance agent can determine which combination of insurance coverage you should have.

Regardless of your final choice, make sure that you have the basic business coverage package of fire/ theft/liability/workers' compensation.

Many caterers who operate out of their house are under the impression that their home insurance offers sufficient coverage for the business. Nothing, in fact, could be further from the truth, as it is highly unlikely that this type of insurance will extend to cover your business. Check with your insurance agent to find out. You can contact the Insurance Information Institute (**www.iii.org**) regarding specific insurance questions or you can Google "catering insurance" and be directed to a number of companies that provide insurance to catering companies.

Kornreich/NIA Insurance Services, for example, has developed a program exclusively for caterers that will fit the needs of a small business owner. It is advisable, however, to check with other owners or with professional catering associations, such as the National Association of Catering Executives, to make sure you get the right amount and kinds of insurance from a reputable agency. Below is a list the different types of insurance you may need to consider.

Fire

Fire insurance covers the buildings and all permanent fixtures belonging to and constituting a part of the business structures. Coverage usually includes machinery used in building services such as air-conditioning systems, boilers, and elevators. Personal property may also be covered. Comprehensive coverage including, for example, wind, storm, smoke, explosion, malicious mischief, etc., is recommended.

Replacement Cost Endorsement

This type of insurance provides for full reimbursement of the actual cost of repair or replacement of an insured building.

Extended Coverage Endorsement

This type of insurance covers property for the same amount as the fire policy against damage caused by wind, hail, explosion, riot, aircraft, vehicles and smoke.

Vandalism

Insurance coverage for loss or damage caused by vandalism or malicious mischief.

Glass Insurance

Covers replacement to show windows, glass counters, mirrors, and structural interior glass broken accidentally or maliciously.

Sprinkler Damage

Insures against all direct loss to buildings or contents as a result of leakage, freezing, or breaking of sprinkler installations.

Flood Insurance

Flood insurance is written in areas declared eligible by the Federal Insurance Administration. Federally subsidized flood insurance is available under the National Flood Insurance Program.

Earthquake Insurance

Covers losses caused by earthquakes.

Contents and Personal Property Damage

This insurance may cover any or all of the following:

- General property
- Improvements and betterments
- Replacement cost
- Extended coverage

- Direct damage
- Business interruption
- Vandalism
- Consequential damage

Business Operations Insurance

Business operations insurance may cover:

- Valuable papers
- Transportation policy
- Endorsement extending period of indemnity
- General liability
- Earnings insurance
- Contractual liability
- Owner's protective liability
- Personal injury vehicle insurance
- Fidelity bonds
- License bonds
- Liquor liability
- Fiduciary liability
- Group life insurance
- Travel/Accident
- Health insurance
- Electrical signs
- Business interruption
- Comprehensive general liability
- Product liability
- Rental value insurance
- Leasehold interest
- Umbrella liability
- Crime
- Dishonesty, destruction and disappearance
- Business legal expense
- Life insurance
- Partnership
- Key man insurance
- Major medical

Liquor Liability

This coverage is part of business operations insurance, but you need to check into your state's specific liquor laws to ensure that the coverage is appropriate. For example, even if you are offering liquor free rather than selling it, you will probably want some form of liquor liability insurance to cover you in case a guest is involved in an accident after consuming alcohol on your premise.

Workers' Compensation Insurance

Most states require employers to carry workers' compensation insurance if they have one or more workers. Catering is a high-risk business, and chances of accidents are greater than in many other businesses. Providing a safe place to work, safe tools and training, as well as warning employees of existing dangers, are great policies to have. These types of procedures are a good start to keeping your employees safe, but you still need insurance protection for those times when even the safest system fails.

Workers' compensation insurance covers loss due to statutory liability as a result of personal injury or death suffered by an employee in the course of his or her employment. This insurance coverage pays all medical treatment and costs plus a percentage of the employee's salary due to missed time resulting from the injury. Workers' compensation insurance is highly regulated by both state and federal agencies, particularly OSHA. Be certain to obtain all the information that pertains to your particular state.

Product Liability Insurance

Product liability insurance is designed to protect consumers from damage or injury caused by use of a particular product. In the case of catering, what you are most worried about is the safety of the food you serve. Accidents happen: What if a customer finds a foreign object in his food? He might choose to sue you for damages. And product liability issues surface all the time: At the bride's request you serve cake at a wedding that was prepared by her best friend, in her home kitchen. There are no licenses and no permit from the board of health—what if the cake is somehow contaminated? A common practice among off-premise caterers is to leave the leftover food for the client. You have no control over how the food is stored or for how long, but if the food causes some sort of illness, you may still be liable. These are the types of incidents where you need to have product liability insurance.

Liability Insurance

A potential client, while touring the caterer's premise, slips and falls on a wet floor and becomes injured. An employee, while serving hot gravy, spills it, damaging a guest's evening gown and severely burning her leg. Liability insurance will protect you against claims that surface from circumstances like these. Rather than insuring yourself against problems with the food, this type of insurance is meant for harm caused because of equipment or employees.

Auto Insurance

You need to insure your own car if you are using it for business purposes, but you should also be aware that when an employee uses his or her own car on your behalf, you could be legally liable for any accidents that occur. Auto insurance helps protect against losses arising from the use or misuse of a car. Depending on the size of your operation and how employees transport food, low-cost fleet policies are available when insuring five or more vehicles. Check with your insurance agent for other discounts they may offer.

Employee Benefit Insurance Coverage

Insurance benefits for employees such as health, dental and disability insurance can be very expensive for a small business. Regardless, you may want to consider offering basic coverage like health, group life insurance, disability insurance and retirement. By offering your employees these benefits, you will gain more loyal, reliable employees. Check your local Yellow Pages for insurance agents, and make sure you get several quotes before making a decision!

Cancellation Insurance

This type of insurance protects you and the party host from loss of deposit and profit. Usually there is a negotiable cap that insurers dictate, and many will insure you on a per-event basis.

Insurance is a complex subject. There are so many nuances that you really need to discuss your needs with a trusted agent. Together you will be able to put together just the right package to cover your assets and strike a correct balance between the cost of premiums and the cost of not being covered.

Pre-Opening Activities

Planning to open a business is requires a lot of planning. The time you spend up front preparing yourself and organizing your operational needs, the more smooth the entry into actual business mode. In this section we'll talk about the activities you need to take care of before your actual opening date. Make yourself a checklist and check off the items as you complete them.

OPEN THE BUSINESS BANK ACCOUNT

One of the first business-related things you need to do is separate your private funds from your business funds. Opening a business checking account is a good way to start. Opening a business bank account is a great deal more important than at first it may appear. If you received your financing through a local commercial bank, you should probably use this bank for your business account as well. You'll be in a better position to negotiate monthly fees, overdraft protection, etc.

Whichever bank you decide to use, it is important that it can provide you with the following services:

- Night deposits
- All credit card services (if you will be using them)
- Change service (coins, small bills)
- A line of credit for certain suppliers
- Nearby location for daily transactions

It is very important that you get to know all the bank personnel on a first-name basis, particularly the manager. You will be in the bank every day. Make an effort to meet them and introduce yourself. Their assistance in obtaining future loans and gaining credit references will be invaluable. It is suggested that you use a smaller bank so long as it can provide all of your needs. Typically, you get more personalized service as your account means more to them than a larger bank.

Take plenty of time to shop around for the bank that will serve you the best. When you go into a prospective bank, ask to see the bank manager, tell him or her of your plans and what your needs are. All banks specialize in certain services. Look at what they charge for each transaction and all other service charges. Compare very closely the handling charges on charge card deposits. A small percentage over thousands of dollars every year adds up to a great deal of money. Look at the whole picture very carefully and then make a decision.

Once you have selected a bank, you need to order banking supplies including:

- Checks
- Deposit book
- Coin wrappers for all change
- Deposit slips
- Night deposit bags and keys
- Small bank envelopes

CONTACT PURVEYORS AND SUPPLIERS

If you are operating a larger catering operation, you want suppliers to come to you. Approximately six to eight weeks prior to your scheduled opening date, contact all the local suppliers and meet with their sales representatives. Make certain each sales representative understands that quality products are your top consideration. Competition is fierce among both sales representatives and suppliers. Let each one know you are considering all companies equally. Never become locked into using only one supplier. Shop around, so to speak, and always be willing to talk with new sales representatives.

Consider these points when choosing a supplier:

- Quality of products. Accept nothing but A-1.
- Reliability.
- Delivery days. All deliveries should arrive at a designated time.
- Is the salesperson really interested in your business?
- Does he seem to believe in what he sells?
- Billing terms (interest, credit, etc.).
- Is the company local (for emergencies)?
- From the first meeting with the sales representative you should obtain:
  - Credit applications to be filled out and returned.

- Product lists or catalogs describing all the products.

- References. Check them out!

You should supply them with a list of the products you will be purchasing regularly as well as estimates of the amount of each item you will be using every week.

Emphasize to the sales representative that when selecting a supplier, price is certainly an important consideration, but not your only one. Point out to the sales representative the other concerns you have about using their company. Indicate that you do intend to compare prices among the various companies but wouldn't necessarily switch suppliers due to a one-time price undercutting. Loyalty is important to sales representatives; they need to expect and count on your order each week. At the same time, let them know they must be on their toes and earn your business.

Most companies offer a discount once you purchase a certain number of cases of something. Find out what each company offers as a discount and keep this in mind as well when comparing prices and suppliers. Choosing a supplier is often very difficult because there are so many variables to consider. Begin by analyzing these factors in terms of the overall picture and gradually work your way down to the smallest of details: your purchasing decisions will become consistently more accurate this way.

If you are a very small business, you probably won't be able to find many suppliers willing to deliver small amounts. In this case your best bet as far cost goes is to buy at a discount house such as Sam's Club or Costco. For a yearly membership fee you can get access to smaller quantities of bulk items including food, toilet paper, facial tissue, and soap. Visit theses stores' Web sites at **www.samsclub.com** and **www.costco.com**. You can also call larger area suppliers and see about setting up an account where you can use their "will call" system. While you will have to pick these items up, it does make things easier if you can purchase the items on credit.

ORGANIZE PAYROLL AND EMPLOYEES

If you are operating a large catering company, you will have a payroll because you are likely to have staff for cleaning, cooking, serving, or performing maintenance duties. You may also have the need for casual employees to assemble chairs, do odd painting, hang pictures, and anything else required before you open for business. The time clock should certainly be used during this period—it will give you much better control and you can monitor the overtime and avoid it wherever possible.

Remember that many of these casual jobs will be boring and tedious. Compensate these employees well for their efforts. Having a free lunch or dinner available will certainly be appreciated, and these small tokens on your behalf will be returned in gratitude and productivity. Everyone needs to feel appreciated, and though it is easy to get caught up in your work and responsibilities, acknowledging everyone's contribution is very important. The small amount of time spent doing it will pay off in terms of loyalty, production and service.

To organize your actual payroll system we highly recommend the use of Quickbooks computer software, Peachtree or other competing software for payroll processing. In addition, Quickbooks is very useful in other parts of your business and in your business planning. You can find more information about Quickbooks at **www.quickbooks.com**.

CONTACT UTILITY COMPANIES

Notify public utility companies of your intention to be in operation by a certain date. Allow plenty of lead time for completion. Don't lose valuable time because your utilities are not hooked up yet. Some of these companies may require a deposit before they will issue service. Every company and city has different policies, so be sure to investigate yours thoroughly.

Phone

You can get by with just one phone, especially if you are operating a small catering operation, but we recommend at least two phone lines: one for business and one for personal; don't lose customers because they can't get through. Don't forget about data and fax lines. Place local emergency numbers at all phones.

Gas and Electric Companies

All major kitchen equipment will need special hookups that can only be completed by trained technicians from either the gas or electric company or by authorized representatives. These people should be contacted as early as possible to come evaluate the amount of work required. In many cases they will need to schedule the work several weeks ahead of time.

Many gas and electric companies have service contracts that can be purchased. If available, it is highly recommended that you purchase one because equipment that is maintained to the manufacturer's specifications will last longer and operate more effectively and efficiently.

Set up a loose-leaf binder to contain all the information on your equipment and its maintenance schedules. Included in this binder should be warranties, brochures, equipment schematics, operating instructions, maintenance schedules, part lists, order forms, past service records, manufacturers' phone numbers, a chart showing which circuit breaker operates each piece of equipment, etc. Keep this manual up to date from the very beginning. Be aware of your equipment service needs and be proactive—downtime due to equipment failure is expensive: you lose business and you pay a premium for emergency service. Train your employees thoroughly in the proper use of all equipment and it will serve the catering operation well for many years.

Water

Water is different in all parts of the country due to the type of chemical particles it contains. Water that has been subjected to a chemical treatment plant may contain a high level of chlorine. Water taken directly from the water table will contain any number of additives depending upon the geological makeup of the soil from where it came. Different types of water can give different results when used in cooking. The Department of Natural Resources can give you information concerning the water's chemical makeup in your local area.

Chemical particles in the water can have a particularly bad effect on the brewing of fresh coffee. Food recipes and cocktails made with water will also be affected.

Several companies now have filtering devices that attach directly to your water lines. If prescribed, filters need only be connected to the water lines that are used for drinking/cooking water. Bathroom and dishwasher lines would not require a filter. Filtering devices are usually tube-shaped canisters that contain charcoal or a special filtering paper. Discuss your particular situation with the Department of Natural Resources and the sales representative for your coffee supplier.

Sanitation Service

In most counties, a private business must provide its own garbage pickup. A catering operation of any size has a great deal of waste. In order to preserve a proper health environment, the services of a trash removal or sanitation service company will be required.

Receive quotes from all the sanitation companies in the area. Prices may vary considerably depending upon who purchases the dumpsters. You may wish to get advice from your health department for the selection. Any service contract should contain provisions for the following:

- Dumpsters with locking tops.
- Periodic steam cleaning of the dumpsters.
- Fly pesticide sprayed on the inside of the dumpster.
- Number of days for pickup.
- Extra pickups for holidays and weekends.

Manufacturers in the area may actually use some waste from the catering operation. Soap manufacturers would be interested in purchasing all the meat and fat scraps for a few cents a pound. Pig farmers may buy all the food scraps. These companies will provide special containers to store the products. Scrap glass from empty liquor bottles may also be sold or donated to the local recycling or ecology project.

SET UP SECURITY MEASURES

You need to protect your property from theft, fire and vandalism. Talk to a locksmith and look into security systems to decide what measures you need to take.

Locksmith

A registered or certified locksmith must be contacted to change over the locks as soon as you occupy the building. Keys to locked areas should be issued on a "need to have" basis. Only employees that need to have access to a locked area to perform their jobs should have a key to that lock. The locksmith can set door locks so that certain keys may open some doors, but not others. Only the owner and manager should have a master key to open every door. Each key will have its own identification number and "Do Not Duplicate" stamped on it. Should there be a security breach, you can easily see who had access to that particular area. The catering operation should be entirely re-keyed when key-holding personnel leave or someone loses their keys. The locksmith should also change safe combinations periodically.

Fire and Intrusion Alarms

Every business should have two separate alarm systems. A system for fire, smoke and heat detection and one for intrusion and holdup.

The fire-detection system consists of smoke monitors and heat sensors, strategically placed around the building. This system must be audible for evacuations and directly connected to either the fire department or a private company with 24-hour monitoring service. In newer buildings, the sensors also activate the sprinkler system.

Most cities and states also require catering operations to install a hood system in the kitchen area. This consists of a sprinkler-type system situated above equipment with an exposed cooking surface or flame. The system may be operated either automatically or manually. When released, a chemical foam is immediately sprayed out over the area. This is particularly effective in stopping grease fires. Once activated, the system will automatically shut off the gas or electric service to the equipment. In order to regain service, the company that installed the system must reset it. As previously indicated, check with the local fire department for further recommendations. They may also direct you to a reputable fire and safety service company.

An intrusion alarm system is also recommended. Begin to research this subject by initially contacting the police department and advising them of your intentions. Contact several of the recommended companies and ask for a survey and proposal (usually at no charge) of the building and your needs.

The security system should contain magnetic contact switches on the main doors, windows, internal doors, and other places of entry such as trapdoors and roof hatches. Don't overlook the air-conditioner vents. The interior of the building should be monitored by strategically placed motion detectors that are zoned so that if one fails, the entire system will continue to function. The safe and the area around the safe should most definitely be monitored. The locking-type holdup buttons, which may only be released with a key, are an excellent option and should be placed in the cashier area, bar and office. Most alarm companies can also provide video monitors.

As previously indicated, the installation of an alarm system in a catering operation is a necessity. The loss of business and profits due to burglary, vandalism or arson is not a gamble you want to take. An added benefit is that the installation of an alarm system will increase the value of the property. A 24-hour monitored system may make you eligible for reduction of 5 to 10 percent on your insurance premiums.

ARRANGE FOR REGULAR SERVICES

There are many services that your business needs to remain operating. Some will be scheduled regularly (landscaping) and some will be on an as-needed or preventative basis (electricians and plumbers). Rather than having to contact these service providers after you have encountered a problem, it is best to set up a working relationship before you start operating.

Plumber

A local plumber will be needed to handle any miscellaneous work and emergencies that may come up. The plumber must have 24-hour emergency service. Make every effort possible to retain the plumber that did the original work on the building. He or she will be thoroughly familiar with the plumbing and know why certain procedures were performed. This can be a terrific advantage.

Clogs and backups can be major problems for a catering business. Extra-wide pipes should be fitted to the dishwasher and sink drains. Grease will collect in the elbows and fittings along the plumbing. When cold water is put through the drain, the grease will solidify, closing the inside diameter of the pipe. Food products or paper may then lodge into these areas causing a clog, which will result in a backup. The plumber must have an electric snake and the necessary acids to remove the clog. A hand snake and plunger should always be on hand in the kitchen.

Electrician

As with the plumber, it would be a great advantage to retain the original electrician who worked on the building. An electrician will be needed when equipment is moved or installed. If it has not been done already, the electrician should check out and label all the circuits and breakers in the building. The electrician should also provide 24-hour emergency service.

Refrigeration Service

The most important consideration when choosing a refrigeration company is how fast they can respond to emergencies. At any given time the refrigeration systems and freezer could fail, resulting in the loss of potentially several thousand dollars of food. Make certain any prospective company understands this crucial point. They must have 24-hour service.

In some situations, there may be no hope of getting the refrigeration units back to work in time; usually because of a broken part that must be replaced. Short of losing all the food, there are some possible solutions. You might contact the purveyors you use who have large refrigeration units. They may be able to store the food temporarily. Call tractor-trailer companies in the area; they may have an empty refrigeration truck that could be rented. Simply transfer the perishables into it for storage.

A fully loaded freezer will usually stay cold enough to keep frozen foods frozen for two days if the cabinet is not opened. In a cabinet with less than half a load, food may not stay frozen for more than a day.

If normal operation cannot be resumed before the food starts to thaw, use dry ice. If dry ice is placed in the freezer soon after the power is off, 125 pounds should keep the temperature below freezing for two to three days in a half-loaded 10-cubic-foot cabinet; three to four days in a fully loaded cabinet.

Place dry ice on cardboard or small boards on top of the packages. Do not open the freezer again except to put in more dry ice or to remove it when normal operation is resumed. Monitor the temperature with an accurate recording device.

Exterminator

Exterminators must be licensed professionals. Get references from the other catering operations or restaurants they service. You may wish to consult the health department for their recommendations, as only certain pest-control products can be used in food service establishments. Exterminators can eliminate any pest-control problems, such as rats, cockroaches, ants, termites and flies. Have several companies come in to appraise the building. They are experts and can read the "tell-tale" signs that might otherwise be missed. Take their suggestions. The company selected should be signed to a service contract as soon as possible. This is not an area to cut corners or try to do yourself—it won't pay in the long run.

Outside Landscaping

You may choose to have the exterior areas of your operation professionally designed and landscaped, especially if you provide on-premise catering. An appealing exterior is at least as important as the interior. You may have little room to work with, but a landscaper can put together a design that can be very appealing. Contact local landscapers and get their opinions, designs, quotes and references.

Exhaust Hood Cleaning Service

If you have a large kitchen, you'll want to get an exhaust hood cleaning service. Contact a company that specializes in the cleaning of exhaust hoods and ventilation systems. They should appraise and inspect the whole ventilation system prior to opening. Depending upon the amount and type of cooking performed, they will recommend a service that will keep the system free from grease and carbon buildup.

Usually twice-a-year cleaning is required. Without this service, the exhaust hoods and vents become saturated with grease, causing a dangerous fire hazard. In such a case, all that is necessary to ignite a fire would be a hot spark landing on the grease-saturated hood. Most of these companies also offer grease and fat (deep fryer oil) removal as well.

Heating and Air-Conditioning

You will need the services of a company that can respond 24 hours a day at a moment's notice. Losing the heating system in the winter or the air-conditioning in the summer will force the catering operation to close. Make certain the company is reliable and has many references.

Heating and air-conditioning systems need regular service and preventative maintenance to ensure they function at maximum efficiency. Energy and money will be wasted if the system is not operating correctly. A service contract should be developed with these companies to ensure the machines are being serviced to the manufacturer's schedule. Keep the contract and all additional information in the equipment binder we discussed previously.

ORGANIZE YOUR OFFICE

You need to have a well-organized and well-planned system for keeping records and staying on top of paperwork. You don't need a fancy office with cherry furniture and conference tables, but you will need a space for office-related paperwork, such as accounting records and catering contracts, and a place to work on all this paperwork. This may just be a room in your house, or it may be a room in your catering operation itself. You can also explore the possibility of renting a separate office if you don't currently have space. Many office buildings rent out office space to individual business owners.

Keeping Records

You got into catering because you love it, but the bottom line is that you can't stay in business unless you make a profit. One of the most important tasks as a business owner is keeping records so that you can keep track of your costs and your revenues. These records will help you determine what does and does not work, and they will help you in your day-to-day activities. Many of the costs associated with recordkeeping may be written off your taxes, and not only will it help you in an IRS audit situation, it will also help you to track such things as which advertising is paying off and which supplier is charging too much.

The successful caterers are those who can balance the sale of the event with its cost. It's as simple as that. Accounting procedures, however, can appear daunting to the uninitiated so it is important to emphasize that records must be kept on a daily basis: record revenues and expenses immediately. Don't make the mistake of not keeping your records up to date. There can be government penalties if you fall behind with your accounts.

A popular tax method used by many small businesses was not to pay taxes on money received until the following tax year. In 1987, however, Congress closed this loophole. Small businesses are now obliged to use cash-accounting on a calendar basis. So unless your accountant devises some means of circumvention, you'll have to declare all income when you receive it. You'll also have to deduct expenses when you pay them. At the same time, the tax year for your business will be the same as your personal tax year.

Here are some terms you might find helpful for preparing your recordingkeeping system:

Cash versus accrual-basis accounting. Accrual-based accounting accounts for income and expenses according to the job to which they are allocated, not as these expenses are paid for or received. With this system, for example, you are able to shift out a deposit and if your event is postponed/cancelled more than 10 days before January 14, say, you can still get your money back. You won't have to bear the tax expense on your deposit either.

Gross versus net profit. This is a very important accounting concept! Your gross profit is what you make on an event after paying the expenses allocated specifically to that event. When you deduct the operating costs from the gross profit, you get the net profit before tax.

Overhead. It is vital to know what the overhead is for your business; for example, rent, equipment lease payments, labor costs, insurance, purchased equipment, etc. Calculating a "pro rata" share of overhead can be done in one of two ways. Note, however, that these methods assume regular future business and do not take into account your startup costs:

Calendar Based
> Add up your entire overhead for the year (including your taxes and living expenses). Divide the total by twelve.

Dollar Percentage
> Add to each dollar of direct-event expense, a markup percentage that includes your margin for overheads, plus taxes, plus net profit.

Certified public accounts. Your accounting system does not replace a certified public accountants (CPA). It only provides you with figures that will enable you to manage your business more effectively.

Assets. Assets include cash, accounts receivable, inventory, buildings and equipment. Consider a tactic called factoring where the caterer "sells" his or her current debts (accounts receivable) to a collection agency in return for cash.

If you have not had much exposure to accounting, you should take a bookkeeping course at a local college. You will learn the fundamentals and be able to hand your accountant a fairly understandable package from which to generate financial statements and tax returns.

For some business owners, recordkeeping is not their strong suit. Consider hiring affordable part-time help; many people working as bookkeepers do so on a freelance basis. As with hiring anyone, make sure you check references!

Understanding Cash Flow

Many businesses fail due to poor cash flow management. It is important to understand ready cash and day-to-day cash flow. Ready cash flow is money in the bank or in the business. This is cash on hand; the cash needed to pay the rent and meet payroll. It does not include inventory, accounts receivable or property.

Profit, on the other hand, is the amount of money you expect to make if all customers pay on time and your expenses are spread out evenly over the time period being measured. Payment isn't received right after a job is finished, and sometimes you don't receive any payment at all, yet you are required to pay your expenses regardless of whether you have been paid. This is what contributes to the cash flow mystery.

The bottom line is that you must have cash in order to keep the doors of your business open. Learn the basics about how to manage your cash flow. It can mean the difference between the success and failure of your catering operation.

- **Cash flow.** This term refers to the flow of cash in and out of a business over a certain period of time. If the cash coming in to the business is more than the cash going out of the business, your company has a positive cash flow. If the opposite is the case, consider selling obsolete inventory to remedy the cash flow imbalance.

- **Annual cash flow projection.** This should be on the "must do" list for all small businesses. In fact, most equity investors or lenders will want you to show them a long-term cash flow projection. So how do you prepare a cash flow projection?

  1. Start the projection with budgeted net profit or loss.

  2. Adjust for non-cash items, such as depreciation expense.

3. Next, adjust for timing differences (insurance premiums, property taxes charged to expenses each month, but paid once per year). It is important at this stage to make sure that your income statement, balance sheet and cash flow statement reconcile, especially if you're preparing projections for a loan package or other financing.

Strategic cash flow statements are prepared on either a quarterly or annual basis. For example, you may want to include a monthly cash flow projection for year one, quarterly projections for years two and three, and annual projections for years four and five. It is best to follow the format of separating operating cash flow from investing and financing activities.

- **Operating cash flow.** Often referred to as working capital, this refers to the cash generated from the sales of your catering services—the lifeblood of your business.

- **Investing cash flow.** This is generated, internally, from non-operating activities. It includes investments in equipment or other fixed assets as well as investments in stocks, bonds, etc.

- **Financing cash flow.** This refers to the cash flow to and from external sources; for example, lenders, investors and shareholders. Include in this section new loans, the repayment of loans, issuance of stock, and dividends paid.

Payment Policy

The longer the period you allow your clients to pay their bills, the more your cash flow will suffer. Take a lesson from the past. Many years ago it was common practice to invoice the client for the food and services two to four weeks after the event. As corporate catering grew, many caterer's payment policies evolved to accommodate their clients' financial payment policies. These clients would disburse their final payment between 45 and 90 days after the event. If you want to avoid such cash flow problems, be a smart caterer—create a formal, written payment policy based on the financial needs and the mission of your catering operation.

Request payment of one-third of the total bill at the point when the contract is signed, with the next third due immediately before or on the day of the event, and the final third due within 30 days after the event. This type of payment schedule is flexible and can be adapted depending upon the type of function and the client.

Accounting Systems

Devise a recordkeeping system that has clearly defined categories and separate columns for recording individual items of income and expense. Include in this chart a separate category for the cost of staple foods; for example, poultry, fish, etc. This chart will enable you to track your various costs to determine which items are the most profitable.

Accounts used for recording revenues and expenses may include the following:

Revenue accounts:

- Food revenues
- Equipment revenue
- Music and entertainment revenue
- Sales tax collected
- Mixers, bar setup revenue
- Floral and décor revenue
- Revenues from other services

Expense accounts:

Cost of Sales Accounts:

- Cost of sales—food
- Cost of sales—equipment
- Cost of sales—other services
- Cost of sales—mixers, setups
- Cost of sales—floral and décor
- Cost of sales—music and entertainment

Payroll and related costs (direct operating costs):

- Uniforms
- Replacement costs
- Transportation
- Miscellaneous
- Utilities
- Laundry
- Supplies
- Licenses and permits
- Advertising and promotion
- Sales tax reimbursement to state

Administrative and general expenses:

- Office supplies, printing and postage
- Data processing costs
- Insurance
- Professional fees
- Rent and lease expense
- Telephone/Internet
- Dues and subscriptions
- Fees to credit organizations
- Repairs and maintenance

Tracking Expenses

When tracking your expenses, keep your receipts. You may need them if you are audited. You should also create a monthly expense record and record each expense on this. After you record the expense on your spreadsheet, file all your receipts by month and year. At the end of the year, file the receipts by month in case you need them for a tax audit.

You can use any money software program to track your monthly expenses such as Quicken or Microsoft's money. You can also just create your own Microsoft Excel spreadsheet. Quicken offers money management software for small businesses at affordable prices. Log on to **www.quicken.com/ small_business** to find out more about their services and products.

Following is an example of what a monthly expense sheet might look like.

MONTHLY EXPENSE SHEET								
Entry No.	Date	Daily Expense Total	Legal Fee	Food	Phone	Office Supplies	Internet	Utilities
101	11/2	$553	$400	$25		$16	$112	
102	11/2	$400		$32	$66			$302
103	11/6	$102		$102				
104	11/18	$84		$14		$5		$65
105	11/18	$22				$22		
106	11/31	$55		$55				

Tracking Revenue

Your revenue paperwork should be similar to your expense paperwork. You should have a monthly summary sheet of all the income you have made. File your catering contracts and invoices as you do your receipts—by the month.

An income summary sheet might look something like the following:

INCOME SUMMARY SHEET						
Entry No.	Date	Client Name	Event Source	No. of Guests	Tax	Payment
101	11/2	Adams	Brochure	20	$100	$800
102	11/2	Jones	Area Hotel	80	$300	$4,000
103	11/6	Anderson	Web Site	120	$280	$3,200
104	11/18	Coates	Web Site	150	$1100	$11,000

INCOME SUMMARY SHEET						
Entry No.	Date	Client Name	Event Source	No. of Guests	Tax	Payment
105	11/18	Thompson	Web Site	50	$80	$600
106	11/31	Thiedman	Brochure	60	$100	$800

Income Statement and Balance Sheet

The income statement and balance sheet show the financial status of your business. The income statement shows the net profit (or loss) for a certain accounting period. The balance sheet is a snapshot of the financial health of your business operations on a given date. It depicts the assets and liabilities, as well as the net worth of your company, which is the figure you get if you deduct total liabilities from total assets.

Income Statement

To understand the basics about calculating your income statement, start by understanding the terminology.

Operating revenues are payments received from clients.

Operating expenses represent running costs; for example, wages and salaries.

Expenses incurred represents the cost of goods used to serve the client.

The basic formula for calculating an income statement is as follows:

Operating Revenue - Operating Expenses = Net Income/Loss

The Balance Sheet

There are four important factors that affect your balance sheet:

- The personal investment you have made in the business.

- Your ability to obtain credit or borrowed capital.

- Your ability to compete in the market.

- The location (as well as local economic conditions) of the place where your business operates.

A balance sheet, in general, has three main categories.

- **Assets**—What your business owns

- **Liabilities**—What your business owes its creditors.

- **Equity**—Your market value, on a given date, either historical or projected. Owner's equity is the owner's right to the assests of the business after total liabilities are deducted.

The balance sheet is a representation of the basic accounting equation:

Total Assets - Total Liabilities = Owner's Equity

Essentially, what the company owns is equal to the combination of what it owes to creditors and investors.

CASE STUDY: WORD FROM THE EXPERTS

BACCHUS BARTENDING

LOCATION: Salt Lake City, UT

SERVICES: Bacchus Bartending provides professional, experienced bartenders and beverage service at affordable prices for all of your private functions. From weddings to corporate functions and birthdays to holidays, we can take care of all of the details for beverage service at your event. Based in Salt Lake City, Bacchus Bartending serves the Wasatch Front and Summit County.

Your staff can be your best resource. Our current employees recommend other bartenders that they have worked with and feel would be a good fit for us when we are looking for new employees.

We pride ourselves on being unique. Many times we will create drinks that are the bride's colors or the business's colors. We're also versatile—we have done as small of a group as four adults and we have done as large as 4,500. Most of our bartenders have a wine key that is unique to their style.

Be prepared for the unexpected. We were once going to an event and the ice delivery was scheduled for the wrong day. Our bartenders had to run and grab ice from stores. The important thing is the guests weren't aware of any problems. Remain professional!

LOCATION: Carmel, NY

Charlotte feels that if everything is treated special, then everything is special. Her guests, business, employees and food are all the most important factors in her business. Nothing gets unnoticed.

Charlotte Berwind
Fine Foods & Party Planning
~
845/228-4905
fax: 845/228-9469

2 Rosedale Drive,
Carmel, NY 10512
~
www.cbfinefoods.com

We once had a client leave the food from a party in the trunk of their car. It was winter and I guess they thought it would be fine; and it might have if they didn't park their car in a heated indoor garage. They called furious the next day that the food was bad. If the client does not sign the waiver and the food has been held at proper temps and cooled down properly, we donate to local soup kitchens.

To save money, we teach our employees that each sheet of paper has monetary value, that half of a lemon has monetary value, every wasted move has monetary value. We share that saved money with our employees when they discover how to save money as if it were their own.

We try not to overload trays or the person washing dishes. Having places for the waiters to land with their full trays and personnel to scrape and stack for the dishwasher is helpful. Have appropriate racks ready. Personnel are the key to everything.

I go to trade shows, eat out, read all the magazines, buy books, window shop, and anything else to get new ideas. Inspiration for trends comes from some unlikely places. You just have to look at the world around you and think, "How can I put that on a plate, a skewer, on a table?"

Above all, Charlotte wishes she had a Magic 8 Ball that really worked!

Computers and Software

These days virtually no business runs without the help of a computer. While there are two general choices, PC and Macintosh, most businesses use a PC. Macs are generally used by artists and other people performing design-intensive tasks.

When deciding what type of system to buy, some common questions include:

- What kind of computer should I get?

- How much RAM do I need?

- How fast should the central processing unit (CPU) be?

- Should I get a Pentium or Athlon processor?

- What brand and what size monitor should I get?

- What type of video card should I get?

- Should I get a dial-up connection, DSL or cable modem?

- Will I need to form a network?

- What are the best accounting packages for the computer?

These are difficult questions, and today's answer will be out of date in six months. The best advice on what type of computer system to purchase for your business is, simply: Get the most powerful computer system within your budget. Here are some considerations:

CPU speed. The CPU is the engine of your computer. In general, the faster the engine, the greater its performance. Get a processor built for future capacity growth. Therefore, the fastest in your budget is recommended.

RAM. RAM is the temporary storage place for all information on your computer. The fastest RAM is the best to get. You should at least get 256 megabytes (MB) of RAM on each computer, though 512 MB of RAM per workstation is preferable.

Operating system. The most common operating system in use today is Microsoft Windows XP Professional Edition. This system provides a stable operating platform and superior networking capabilities.

Monitor. A 17" or larger monitor is recommended. You have lots of choices in brands, as well as flat-panel and LCD-screen varieties. Popular styles are a 17" flat-panel or a 17" or larger LCD monitor.

Video card. For business applications, a graphics accelerator card with a minimum of 32 MB of RAM is recommended. There are dozens to choose from depending on the application, with chipsets from various manufacturers.

Athlon versus Pentium. Both are world-class processors. There are diehard fans of each.

Dial-up, DSL or cable. If you need high-speed connections, you want DSL or cable (if they are available in your area). Dial-up is the least costly but slowest type of connection. For the average Web browser, dial-up is usually sufficient. If you use a broadband connection, invest in a DSL/cable router or a good firewall software application.

Networking. If you have more than one computer, you will want to network your computers. This will allow you to share programs, files, printers, Internet connections and more. There are dozens of networking systems available, including standard wired networking, phone-line networks and wireless networks. There are advantages to each:

- Standard wired networking is fast, but requires extensive cable installation in your building.

- Phone-line networks offer good performance, low cost and use the existing phone lines in your business to make network connections. You can still talk on your phone while your network is being used.

- Wireless networking is the most costly, but it's highly versatile, requires no cable installation and is very effective. One major advantage of wireless is you are not limited by phone lines or network cable. You can take your wireless laptop anywhere in your business and maintain your network connection.

Computer Systems and the Catering Industry

While the above is true for all business applications, businesses in the catering industry have need for specialized functions. Computers can be used to book events, advertise, track sales and purchases, keep track of inventory, compare prices, maintain the ledger and payroll, and develop menus.

Let's take a closer look at how computer hardware and software will serve and benefit the catering industry, and take a glance at what options and features you might have.

POINT-OF-SALE SYSTEMS

The most widely used technology in the food service industry is the touch-screen POS (point-of-sale), system. The POS system is basically an offshoot of the electronic cash register.

A POS system comprises two parts: the hardware, or equipment, and the software, the computer program that runs the system. This system allows you to key in a booked event as soon as the client books one.

Some benefits of using a POS system:

- Customer tracking
- Tracks credit card purchases
- Reports sales forecasting
- Records employee timekeeping

- Increases sales and accounting information
- Accurate addition
- Prevents incorrect dates from being entered
- Reports possible theft of money and inventory

Many POS systems have been greatly enhanced to include comprehensive home delivery, guest books, online reservations, frequent-diner modules, and fully integrated systems with real-time inventory, integrated caller ID, accounting, labor scheduling, payroll, menu analysis, purchasing and receiving, cash management and reports. Up-and-coming enhancements and add-ons include improved functionality across the Internet, centralized functionality enabling "alerts" to be issued to managers and voice-recognition POS technology.

Software

There are many software packages available to assist business owners in the catering business. The following are some of the most commonly used systems.

BACK-OFFICE SOFTWARE

There several other types of software you might find useful in your daily operations:

- **General ledger accounting.** This software basically tracks accounts receivable and payable (what is owed to you and what you owe).

- **Financial reporting software.** This software can help you develop a chart of accounts so you can create balance sheets and income statements.

- **Inventory-control software.** Again, this may be especially helpful if you run a larger operation and have employees. It can help you track inventory so you can see when you are running low on items.

- **QuickBooks**® is another good choice for back office software. The QuickBooks's 2002 version is rich in features, including built-in remote-access capabilities and Web interfaces. QuickBooks is available at **www.quickbooks.com**. Another popular account package is Peachtree®, available at **www.peachtree.com**.

KITCHEN SOFTWARE

ChefTec is an integrated software program with recipe and menu costing, inventory control, and nutritional analysis.

- **Recipe and menu costing.** Store, scale and size an unlimited number of recipes. Write recipe procedures with culinary spell-checker. Instantly analyze recipe and menu costs by portion or yield. Update prices and change ingredients in every recipe with the touch of a button. Cost out bids for catering functions. Attach photos, diagrams and videos to bids, or add pictures of plate layout for recipe consistency.

- **Nutritional analysis.** Preloaded USDA information with an option to add your own items. Calculate nutritional value for recipes and menus. Provide accurate, legal information on "low-fat," "low salt," etc. The nutritional-analysis module will get a quick and accurate analysis of nutritional values for up to 5,000 most-commonly used ingredients. Allows you to add your own specialty items. Calculate nutritional values for your recipes and menu items. See at a glance which menu items are low-fat, low-calorie, etc. Print a "Nutrition Facts" label.

- **Inventory control.** Preloaded inventory list of 1,900 commonly used ingredients with unlimited capacity for adding additional ingredients. Import purchases from online vendors' ordering systems. See impact of price increases on recipes. Automate ordering with par values. Use handheld devices for inventory. The inventory-control module allows you to track rising food costs automatically. Compare vendor pricing at the touch of a button, from purchases or bids. Enter invoices quickly using the "Auto-Populate" feature. Generate customized reports on purchases, price variances, bids and credits. Takes the pain out of physical inventory, ordering and maintenance of par levels.

MenuPro allows you to quickly create your own professional menus at a fraction of the cost of print-shop menus. Whether you need "Daily Specials" or an elaborate dining room menu, MenuPro gives you quick, top-quality designs and artwork without the expense or hassle of using a graphic artist or desktop publisher.

CATERING SOFTWARE

There are a wide variety of software programs available specifically for the catering industry. Check out the following options:

- **Caterease™** software has many useful tools. Visit **www.caterease.com** for a virtual tour and online demo. The program has data-entry tools such as customizable drop-down quickpick lists that let you pick common terms and drop-down calendars and calculators. The event scheduler shows a graphic calendar of all of your events, much like Microsoft's Outlook program does. The New Event Wizard makes booking events easy by walking you through the process of entering information.

- **EATEC** from Eatec Corporation **www.eatec.com**, provides a software solution specifically designed for the food service industry provides a particular plan for caterers. The main menu of the catering system lets you enter an order, update it, perform event cost analysis, and keep track of equipment and recipes suitable for off-premise use. It also has accounting functions, keeps track of suppliers, and generates menus and nutritional information for food items. Its features also let you break events into components, so when you are negotiating with a client on event details, you can easily add and subtract items to see how things affect cost.

- **Costguard®** is another software option, **www.costguard.com**. It lets you scale recipes and cost them in a consistent manner. You can also track inventory and suppliers from a food list and generate recipes as well as shopping lists.

- **ESHA Research's Food Processor** programs are designed to help you with nutritional aspects of food. It has a database of over 29,000 foods and will track allergies, organize nutritional requirements by day and meal, and create recipes with nutritional information. If your client list is interested in nutrition or you are involved in any type of industrial catering, you'll want to check it out.

- **Caterware's Caterplus™** Catering and Event Management Software is another good software option. Features include account management functions, such as contacts, billing and invoicing; performance tracking functions, such as accounts receivable, account statistics, and events calendar; event-management features, such as cost and price tracking per selection, notes, tasks, location, charge summary, and payment summary; and list-management functions, such as contacts, reports, staff information, tasks, and venues.

EMPLOYEES SOFTWARE

- **Employee Schedule Partner.** Employee Schedule Partner is a complete software package for employee scheduling that allows you to make a schedule without touching the keyboard. Click a button and the software will fill your schedule with employees automatically. Click another button to replace absent employees, and a list of available employees with phone numbers will appear. The online coach will give helpful hints to new users. Other features include an unlimited number of employees and positions that can be tracked, you can manually override selections at any time, you can track employees' availability restrictions, schedule employees to work multiple shifts per day, and you can track payroll and hourly schedule totals for easy budget management. The software is even password protected to prevent unauthorized use.

- **Employee Time Clock Partner**—Our hands-down favorite time clock software is Employee Time Clock. This is a complete employee time clock software package. It is very powerful yet simple to use. Automatically clock in and out (just enter your employee number). Employees can view their time cards to verify information. It is password protected so only management may edit time card information, and it even calculates overtime both daily and weekly.

DESKTOP PUBLISHING APPLICATIONS AND IDEAS

Computers can also be used for desktop publishing tasks. For example, you can print your own customer and employee newsletters, menus, business cards, employee-of-the-month certificates, customer gift certificates, advertising posters, employee manuals, wine lists, and office stationery. Some popular desktop publishing software programs are Adobe InDesign, QuarkXPress, Greenstreet Publisher and Microsoft Publisher. You can find out more about these programs at **http://desktoppub. about.com/cs/win/index.htm**.

E-Mail and the Internet

E-mail is a system that enables a computer user to exchange messages with other computer users within a communications network (Internet). To use e-mail, you must have access to a computer that is linked to the Internet via a modem and phone line, cable modem, DSL connection or other network connection. E-mail services are typically provided at no cost from your Internet service provider, and they come with any domain names you purchase for Web sites.

ADVANTAGES OF E-MAIL

Convenience. One advantage of using e-mail is you send your message when it's convenient for you, even if it's four o'clock in the morning. Your recipient responds at his or her convenience as well.

Cost. No more toll telephone calls! No more "telephone tag"! You can send dozens of e-mails throughout the world, simultaneously; they will be delivered in mere seconds; and it costs nothing. Communicate with all your purveyors or employees with one written message, for free.

Written record. Unlike a phone call, an e-mail is a record of any items discussed. This is an avenue of communication when confirming details or booking with clients so you have a record of what was agreed.

Proper e-mail etiquette:

- **Avoid flaming.** A flame is a nasty, personal attack on somebody for something he or she has written, said or done.

- **Be very clear.** If you are responding to a message, include only the relevant part of the original message. Make sure you clearly refer to the original message's contents. Always include a descriptive subject line for your message. If responding, your subject line should be the same as the original's, preceded by "RE."

- **Write clearly and carefully.** Written communication is much more apt to cause miscommunication because there are no nonverbal clues to the intent or tone of the message you are sending; your words may come back to haunt you. Read carefully what you receive to make sure that you are not misunderstanding the message. Read carefully what you send to make sure that your message will not be misunderstood.

- **Don't use excessive emphases.** Avoid cluttering your messages with tons of exclamation marks and quotation marks around words or phrases you want to emphasize.

- **DO NOT USE ALL CAPS!** Capital letters are considered the e-mail equivalent of shouting.

Internet

The Internet is a global network enabling computers of all kinds to directly and transparently communicate and share services throughout much of the world. Because the Internet enables so many people and organizations to communicate and share information, it is a shared global resource and is very important to our economy and how we do business.

The most widely used part of the Internet is the World Wide Web. A Web browser reads and interprets the underlying programming of a site and what you see is a Web page. Using the Web, you have access to millions of pages of information. The most popular Web browsers are Microsoft Internet Explorer and Netscape Navigator.

When setting up your e-mail and Web accounts, you should give careful consideration to your choice of domain names and e-mail addresses. These become a main part of your company's representation to your customers. It is also a good idea to think about your need for a domain name to put up a Web site. In the marketing section we talk in more detail about the importance of a Web Site in the catering business.

Although we can't go into the details of Web site creation and hosting, be aware that you might not always be able to use your company name as part of your e-mail address or as your Web domain. You have to make sure your Internet service provider does not have a customer already using your name and you also need to check to see if another Web site (anywhere in the world) is using the domain name you want. There are many print and electronic resources available to help you navigate this technical world as well as Internet hosting consultants. *Chapter 5: Web Sites* covers this in depth

Traditional Marketing

Catering is a customer-driven, often seasonal market. Unlike an everyday dining-out experience, catering clients always expect exceptional quality and excellent value. People comparison shop when they look for caterers, and your marketing plan must keep the competitive nature of the business in mind. When developing an overall plan, you must keep in mind that there are three life cycle stages in marketing:

- **Getting the job.** Before you can get catering jobs, you need to define your market. If you have finished your business plan you already know who your target clients are. If you haven't finished your plan, or haven't even started it yet, get busy! Getting clients takes time, a lot of marketing, and a little bit of luck. This section is devoted to helping you learn about, and use, the many marketing tools available, especially the ones more critical to catering.

- **Performing well.** Once you've gotten the job, you have to make sure the event is a success. Be sure that service is punctual, food and beverage meet your quality standards, all details are attended to, the host has a good time, and all fires are handled with professionalism on event day.

- **Following up.** Follow up is something many caterers do poorly. Once the event is over, it is out of their mind. The follow-up step is what will get you repeat business and outstanding word-of-mouth advertising. Be sure to make a thank-you call the day after the event to be sure the host thought everything went well.

The Four P's of Marketing

An effective marketing plan accounts for **p**lace, **p**roducts (and services), **p**rice, and **p**romotion.

Place refers to location and amount of space available as well as the ambiance of a functional space. A top concern of every client is whether or not there will be enough space for guests. They may also have concerns about parking, accessibility and the neighborhood.

Products refer to the goods you provide the client. With a catering business the most obvious product you sell is food, but there are other products you provide as well. Catering is often a full-package deal, and that means you will also sell beverages and other services such as floral arrangements, decorations, photography and entertainment. Some components of your food products include portion size, presentation, and the placement of the item on your menu.

Price is one of the most important pieces of your marketing plan. It is also one of the greatest concerns of your clients. Make sure to read the section on pricing, and make careful consideration of all the factors involved with it before offering your potential client a quote.

Promotion includes the cost of developing and maintaining a Web site, creating business cards and brochures, radio and print advertisement, dues for professional groups, etc. Basically, you can think of promotion as a full-time function that spreads into every aspect of how you do business—it is the overt messages you send potential and existing clients as well as all the subtle things you do (how you answer the phone, how quickly you respond to requests, how you handle crises).

Marketing Strategy

Marketing is mandatory, not only when setting up your catering business, but on a continuing basis. In fact, it's absolutely essential in order to ensure the long-term success of your enterprise. Your goal as a smart caterer is to find new markets for your products and services. This involves clearly identifying your target market and then selecting the advertising medium that is best able to reach your target audience. Use the following marketing approach as a guide for developing your marketing strategy.

TARGET MARKET

The first step in any marketing program is to undertake a full and detailed analysis of your potential clients in the local marketplace. First, decide what kinds of clients appeal to you. Do you want to cater small, intimate parties or large-scale events? Understand that when you market your business, you should keep in mind why your clients are buying catering services from you. Clients who demand elaborate cuisine often want to compete with their friends and relatives. They want to show that they can afford the luxury of hiring your catering services. Market your services to them in such a way as to satisfy their vanity.

Think about what types of events you want to pursue. At what types of events do you excel? Where is your competitive advantage over the competition? For example, if you can't handle large functions profitably (in the 500-person range), then you may want to eliminate these clients from your target list. On the other hand, if your business has the facilities and expertise to put on elegant wedding receptions, then that segment of the market should be targeted for an appropriate amount of sales resources.

If you are not sure exactly who you want to target or you are considering new target markets, here is a list of a few potential markets to investigate. Remember, you don't have to focus on only one. You may end up targeting several.

- Corporate business
- Political groups
- Trade shows
- Religious organizations
- High schools and colleges
- Charities

- Financial institutions
- Wedding planners
- Travel-related businesses
- Social and ethnic clubs
- Civic organizations
- New businesses in the area (check with the chamber of commerce)

If you're interested in catering weddings, for example, you may want to develop a relationship with florists, department-store heads, musicians, and personnel in charge of venues that book weddings. You also can list your company on Web sites set up for people planning weddings. At **www.usabride. com** and **www.wedfind.com** you can be included in their list of local vendors.

If you are more interested in corporate catering, contact all corporations in your area, big and small. The chamber of commerce should be able to supply you with a list of local names. Bear in mind that corporate clients buy first and foremost out of necessity and convenience, so your marketing should convey that message.

Once you have defined the type of catering operation you want to own and the markets you want to pursue, you can start analyzing your potential customers. To define your niche, you need to know your area's demographics. You can find a great deal of demographic information on the U.S. Census Bureau's Web site at **www.census.gov**. See the discussion in the "Location, Location, Location" section for detailed information about and resources for researching demographics.

Demographics provide a place to start defining your target market. To further narrow or zero-in on specific needs in the market, you can try one or all of the following approaches.

- **Interview potential customers.** Once you have a concept and target market in mind, interview people who would likely be your customers. These people may be friends, or people that live in particular neighborhoods.

- **Go to catered events whenever possible.** If there is an art show opening or fundraiser, try to go. By attending events that are catered, you can learn about your competition and about potential events for your own business.

- **Talk to caterers.** In general, the food industry is pretty competitive, but if you are not in direct competition with a particular catering operation, the owner or manager may be willing to be interviewed and would be an excellent source of information.

- **Read trade magazines.** Trade magazines such as *Restaurant Hospitality* and *Restaurant and Institutions* are good sources for general customer information. *Restaurant Hospitality* can be found at **www.restauranthospitality.com** and *Restaurant and Institutions* is located at **www.rimag.com**. There are also Web sites and magazines targeted specifically to the catering industry. The site **www.catersource.com** is one such site. The site offers business support for caters including their online bimonthly *CaterSource Journal*. *Catering Magazine* is a magazine for professional caterers and can be found at **www.cateringmagazine.com**.

- **Consult the National Restaurant Association.** The National Restaurant Association can also provide you with some customer research. You can log onto the association's Web site at **www.restaurant.org**.

Marketing Tools

Although a good party goes a long way toward garnering new customers, you need to develop other marketing tools to increase your customer reach and expand your business. Press releases, media placement, mail campaigns, and telephone solicitation are just some of the ways you can reach your target markets. A Web site is also a must for any catering business today. Your advertising budget will vary from season to season and your budget will be different than your competitors', but what matters is not the dollar value of the marketing but the effect it has on your bottom line.

LOW-COST MARKETING IDEAS

Very few firms have the budget to spend large amounts of money on traditional advertising in local periodicals, on billboards, or in other media. You must make use of marketing approaches that are innovative and less costly. Many marketing concepts exist that can be implemented for a reasonable cost, but realize that advertising is an ongoing expense if you are to give your business the best possible exposure in the local marketplace. The following is a list of some low-cost yet highly effective marketing tools.

Develop a portfolio. Purchase a high-quality camera and take shots of every unique or distinctive event that you host. You may even find a staff member whose hobby is photography. Pay him or her to do the work for you. Photos should show your staff in uniform, some of your food displays, and guests munching away enthusiastically. Select your best photos and use them in brochures or mailings (be sure to obtain signed photo releases if using photos of guests).

This elegant photo is a good example of a portfolio image. The event was a community fundraiser. Submitted by Charlotte Berwind, Fine Foods & Party Planning.

Develop a catalog. Catalogs should include bios of your chef and management team, along with a selection of your showpiece menus. Letters of recommendation are also good additions. Be careful not to make the catalog and/or portfolio appear overwhelming.

Market your fine reputation. This is especially important in the beginning. Don't cut corners. Invest in quality advertising for your establishment. Make sure that you spend every marketing dollar effectively and productively. Remember, your compensation will not always come in the form of dollars and cents—reputation is equally as valuable, perhaps more so in the long run.

Develop a brochure. A first-class brochure should include color photos and enticing text. Establish credibility by first telling your readers about the number of years in business, prominent clients, awards received, etc. Include information about your food and services, and offer a guarantee. Make your brochure easy to read. Deliver the message in as few words as possible.

Print business cards. Business cards and stationery should reflect your image. Get staff to carry business cards in their uniform shirt or jacket pocket so that they can retrieve them quickly. Encourage them to hand them out to as many people as possible.

Use direct mail. Direct-mail campaigns still bring in customers. If your target is the corporate client, mail fliers to nearby corporate offices. Check periodically with the local chamber of commerce for updated business listings. If you are specializing in social events, send fliers to people who fit your typical customer demographic. Watch the papers for upcoming high-profile happenings. In your direct mail, be sure to include your catering menus, brochures, newsletters, and other promotional literature that prospective clients will be interested in.

Word-of-mouth. By far the most important marketing tool you have is the power of word-of-mouth. The key to developing leads is through connections. Whenever you do a large or distinctive function for a trade or business group or a social event, send an account of the event to relevant publications along with photos and a few comments from your very satisfied customers. Ask to use these customer comments in your sales catalogs or brochures as well. Most brides and corporations will not risk trying an unknown caterer. In fact, many caterer's complete marketing plans are based on the favorable feedback of satisfied clients and guests. You've undoubtedly heard the adage, "You're only as good as your last party"; it holds more than a ring of truth.

Word-of-mouth advertising is so important. We have some specific tips to cultivate positive client feedback and referral and develop a deliberate, creative and authentic plan to create great word-of-mouth advertising.

Clients don't talk about you unless they're thinking about you. You want them thinking about you in the right way, which means you have to educate your guests on why they come to you. To do this, you must create points of difference between you and your competitors. Then people can tell their friends specifics about why they should hire you.

An effective word-of-mouth program has five main goals:

1. Inform and educate your patrons.

2. Make the guest a salesperson for your business.

3. Give guests reasons to return.

4. Make your service unique and personal.

5. Distinguish your business from the competition.

The personal touches that ooze "quality service" and that are unique to your catering service are in themselves your best form of marketing. A satisfied client is likely to pass on, by word-of-mouth, what superb service they received. Make every effort to go that one step further to satisfy each and every client. It will certainly pay dividends in the long run. Thoughtfulness for your client is always remembered favorably and can be demonstrated in the simplest of ways: If you are catering a dinner party at a client's home, prepare some breakfast muffins to leave as an extra treat. The next morning and for days and months after, the client will remember those muffins and speak highly of your services.

Networking. Use this popular marketing tool to keep in touch with potential clients. Join and become active in certain groups such as the chamber of commerce, civic clubs (Rotary, Lions, Elks), church and synagogue groups, special-interest groups, NACE, and NCA. But remember, you're not asking them to buy catering; you're goal is to establish relationships with these people first. When they're ready to buy, they'll contact you.

Contact the NACE (National Association of Catering Executives) at **www.nace.org**. The NACE also offers a certification program, Achievement of the Certified Professional Catering Executive (CPCE) designation, which is another good marketing device.

Write effective press releases. Write at least six press releases per year. Read the local newspapers and listen to local radio stations to get a feel for what they cover. Keep it short and to the point. Place the most important information at the beginning of the press release and make sure your message is clear. Top the release with a headline that summarizes the story. Include photos of the event. Think of yourself as a reporter for the media when writing the press release: be objective. Give the who, what, when, where, why and how. A great resource to help you with press releases and ad copy is at **www .weddingandeventmarketing.com**. You can download a publication entitled "How to Write Catering Ads that Sell," which gives tips on how to write sales and advertising copy. The site also offers a Wedding and Event Business Builder Toolkit Home Study Course (561-776-1603), which costs about $800.

When deciding which media to target with your press release, don't neglect small weekly papers. Such newspapers might be hungrier for stories than major publications or television stations.

Work with the media. Call newspapers and find out who the business or food reporters are and the best times to reach them. Next, call the appropriate person—at the appropriate time. Be brief, friendly and to the point. Don't mention that your business advertises in the newspaper, because editors don't run stories to help advertisers. Don't send gifts to editors or reporters, because they may see it as a form of bribery. Don't become hostile and never repeat a negative accusation made against your business.

Cause-related marketing. Investigate the possibilities of "cause-related" marketing as it allows you to help charitable organizations within your community while, at the same time, reaping the rewards from the publicity surrounding these charitable events. Every city has public radio fund drives, fundraising walks, and other similar events. Consider providing lunch for the phone volunteers or setting up a booth with snacks for the walkers at the next event in your town.

Perform community service. Establish a connection with a community-service organization and you will galvanize positive public perception about your business. Starbuck's is a master at advertising their good deeds work with employees wearing T-shirts advertising the company's involvement with causes such as fighting breast cancer. You may want to work with a local homeless group to organize a used-clothing drive. Enlist customers and employees to take part in walk-a-thons. Donate your space and staff for a charity fundraiser, etc. Network your business's good deeds through your contacts in the community—the chamber of commerce, local clergy, alumni organizations or other civic groups.

Web marketing. There are several online sources for marketing your catering business. Some sites to review are **www.leadingcaterers.com**, **www.partyleads.com** and **www.localcatering.com**. These sites are used by people looking for catering services. Potential clients plug in information about the event—the date, number of guests, type of event, food preferences—and they receive a list of caterers who can fulfill the requirements.

Yellow Pages. Think twice before paying for expensive advertising space in the Yellow Pages. This is something of a controversial issue amongst caterers. Some aren't convinced that this type of advertising is a sure way of developing new business. The general rule of thumb seems to be the more "up-market" the caterer, the smaller the Yellow Pages ad should be. On the other hand, low-end and medium-quality caterers who need volume will benefit more from the traditional-style, large-display ads. Also, names that begin with "A" are generally favored as Yellow Pages listings, as lists of recommended caterers for specific locations, are presented in alphabetical order.

Create signs and use a logo. Logos are memorable, and it is well worth it to pay for one to be designed professionally. Use your logo on all your communication, not just marketing material. Use prominent signs and display your logo. Make sure they are large enough and that they are easily seen but make sure they are professional—no 8 ½" x 11" sheets of colored paper tacked to utility poles.

Offer tasting sessions. Consider offering your prospective clients a sample of your food. The main advantage is that once you actually sit down with a prospective client and spend time discussing the menu, you are creating a relationship and thus more likely to get that customer's business than an unknown company.

Offer cooking classes. Another possible marketing strategy is to offer cooking classes. You may be interested in doing a class at your facility, or just doing a demo at a mall kiosk to increase your public exposure.

Participate in wine tasting events. Pair with a local wine shop and offer free appetizers at their wine-tasting events. Be sure to leave plenty of your business cards for people take home with them!

Marketing Literature

Here we are talking about business cards, brochures and promotional folders. Although these items require an initial investment, they are definitely worth producing. Limit yourself to items that you can afford to have created to exacting and impeccable standards.

Most caterers use brochures and promotional folders for selling their services to potential clients. These folders typically contain a business card, sample menus, letters of recommendation, lists of additional services, and photographs. These folders should look professional; clients are comparing yours against the other caterers they are selecting from, so you want your information to stand out from the crowd. Make sure your literature is eye catching and inviting.

There are many good design programs out now so that you could try to design these by yourself. You do want to make sure they look professional, though, so even if you do most of the work yourself, you will probably want to employ a graphic designer for artistic input.

Whether you use a designer only as a consultant or for the whole project, there are many sources for finding these artistic individuals. If you have an area college with an art program, you might try contacting the school to see if anyone is interested in bulking up their portfolio. Many of these students are entirely capable of producing professional designs even though they haven't had much on-the-job experience.

There are many designers who also do freelance work. Contact one of the professional design organizations, such as the American Institute of Graphic Arts (AIGA), to see if they can provide you with a directory of freelancers. The AIGA can be contacted at AIGA, 164 Fifth Avenue New York, NY 10010; telephone 212-807-1990, fax 212-807-1799. Their Web site is **www.aiga.org**. Also look at **www.sologig.com** and **www.elance.com** for freelancers.

DESIGN FACTORS

If you are designing your own business card or brochures, be sure to keep the following design principles in mind:

- Alignment
- Contrast
- Repetition
- Proximity

Alignment communicates connection between the elements of your design. When designing a business card or brochure (or any other promotional piece), think about the paper as a grid. Place your elements on the grid, trying to balance them and create a pleasing design for the eye. Don't be too constricted by the grid, however; be bold and place some elements outside of it (angle a picture of an event or plate of food on a brochure, for example) to create visual interest.

Contrast needs to be obvious or it might look like a mistake. For instance, you can bold all your headers in a brochure and keep all the other text as regular text.

You can also unify a design and create contrast with **repetition**. The most common example of this is bullet lists. If you are designing a brochure, for instance, you may want to repeat elements to tie the brochure together. For example, you will want to use the same font for all your headers. If you have a line drawing of your business on the front, you may want to consider repeating that image on the back of the brochure in a smaller size. Also remember that you don't have to fill up all the white space; leave your design a little breathing room.

Proximity creates a focus for your brochure or business card by creating relationships between elements. After you've designed a brochure, try the squint test. Hold the piece at about arm's length. If all you see is gray, you need to work on proximity!

Try to use these four elements in all your graphic designs. Also think about color. Two- and four- color jobs are more expensive to print, and a nice, clean black and white design might serve just as well.

BROCHURES

A simple design for a brochure is a tri-fold, or letter fold, or six-panel like the example below:

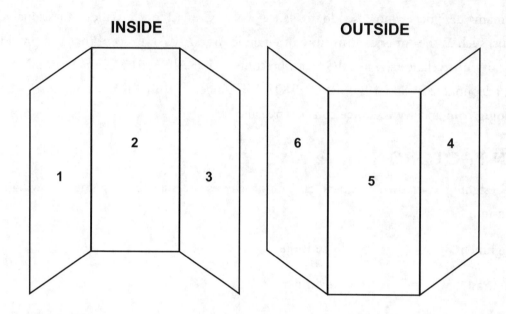

With a brochure like this, you want to put your logo and a photo or line drawing on the front cover (Panel # 4). For the inside (Panels # 1, 2, and 3), you might want to write some copy about the types of events you cater or your menus. You may also want to include photos of the rooms and a list of room amenities. On Panel # 6 you could include more information on the rooms or area and on Panel # 5 you could put a map with directions, your address, phone number, and associations of which you are a member. You could also put this contact information on Panel # 6 and save Panel # 5 for mailing addresses and stamps if you want to mail out your brochure.

BUSINESS CARDS

While there is less space to fill on a business card, it is often more difficult to design. Because a business card is so small, you want to make sure you don't try to include too much information. It is also very important for it to be eye catching, otherwise the person you hand your card to is just going to throw it to the back of their desk drawer with all the other

Sample business card from Decadence Catering. This card is printed on glossy black stock to reflect Decadence's sophisticated image. The black and white imagery is used consistently on all marketing materials.

business cards in there. Remember that less is more, and that simplicity is often best. Use an image for the focal point of your card, and make sure to include pertinent information such as the business name, address, phone and fax numbers, and Web site address. Once you get all this information on the card, there is little room for anything else!

The same design principles apply to a business card for your business. While many people prefer the simplicity of a 3.5 x 2-inch card because it fits easily into people's card holders, others prefer a folded card because it draws people's attention and seems a little more sophisticated.

Poynteronline, **www.poynter.org**, has several helpful design pages you might want to investigate. There is a page on color, typography and one that discusses using a grid for design.

TAKE-AWAY MENUS

It is a good idea to have a take-away menu printed to send to prospective clients along with other marketing materials. It can be a simple sampling of the types of foods you offer, or a complete price list. Menu design and presentation will be discussed in depth in a later chapter.

PAPER AND COLOR CONSIDERATIONS

Different colors evoke different emotions, so choose the colors for your marketing literature with careful consideration. For example, if you cater upscale, formal events, you might want to limit the colors to black and white.

There are probably thousands of choices of paper when you consider all the variables. There are colored papers, textured papers and coated papers, and different weights of paper. When designing a brochure or business card, use a weight heavier than regular writing paper, probably something in the 60-pound range. While coated papers are more expensive than uncoated, use a coated paper because the ink does not seep into the paper when printed and colors are much brighter and crisper since they don't bleed at the edges.

Also keep in mind that heavier paper and colored ink are more expensive than letter-weight paper and black ink. But when it comes to these key advertising pieces, you should not skimp; you want to catch your potential client's eye and attract them to your business.

When it comes to printing your cards and brochures, check out local printers and compare prices. You will probably find a wide range of prices for the same service. You might find that a particular printer already has the paper or ink you want in stock from another job. In that case, you might be able to get a discount. There are also a number of printing companies on the Internet that offer affordable printing as well as design services. Check out the following:

- **www.printingforless.com**
- **www.psprint.com**
- **www.vistaprint.com**
- **www.48hourprint.com**

There are also many software programs you can use to design your own business cards and brochures. Here is a list of just a few along with the Web site addresses where you can get more details. Many are easy to use, professional looking, and could save you a quite a bit on printing costs.

- RKS Software: **www.rkssoftware.com**

- CAM Development: **www.camdevelopment.com/designer/business_card/default.htm**

- PARABEN Software: **www.paraben.com/html/pbcb.html**

- BVRP Software USA: **www.bvrpusa.com**

ILLUSTRATIONS

You will likely use a photo or original drawing for the main artwork or logo on printed materials, but there are also times you will want to use other illustrations. How do you find them and what are the rules about using someone else's original material?

Most prepared artwork is copyrighted and you cannot use it without permission. Many times you will see the copyright (©) or trademark (™) symbols, indicating that the work is copyrighted. Even in the absence of these symbols you need to track down the person who created the piece (owns the copyright) and ask permission to use it. It's always a good idea to have this permission in writing in case of any future misunderstandings.

A good place to start looking for copyright ownership is the U.S. Copyright Office at **www.loc.gov/copyright**. The Copyright Clearance Center, Inc., **www.copyright.com**, is another good resource. You may be able to easily acquire permission through the service offered on this site. You can also go to the United States Patent and Trademark Office's Web site at **www.uspto.gov** to look for images that have been trademarked.

Finally, if the image is in a published source, you can contact the publisher to inquire about permission. When acquiring permission, keep in mind that there is often a fee for usage. This fee can be as low as $10 or as high as several thousand depending on the image. If this seems like too much of a hassle or you are concerned you won't get permission, there are some good free sources of images as well. Clipart are copyright-free illustrations that anyone can use. Dover Publications publishes clipart books. They offer everything from books of Victorian house designs to herbs and plants. You can order any of their publications from their Web site at **http://store.doverpublications.com**. These books are generally in the $20 price range.

Using Your Marketing Literature

Now that you have all these beautiful marketing pieces, what do you do with them? Get creative when thinking about distributing your cards and brochures. Are there any local small hotels that would let you drop off a stack? What about people you work with or people at church? Check with the alumni association and local universities and businesses, as well as wedding planners and bridal shops if you cater weddings. If you're a member of the chamber of commerce or a local tourist office, try them as well. Area event planners and music venues may be other good sources.

Also be sure to have a stack of your promotional material with you whenever you cater an event. It's hard to determine how much business is lost by the simple fact that a caterer did not have a card to give a guest who loved the food at the last party you catered!

TRACKING YOUR MARKETING SOURCES

When clients call to hire you or get information, be sure to ask them where they heard about you. By tracking this information you'll be able to assess the effectiveness of your marketing tools. At the end of the year you'll want to compare the cost of your advertising to the revenue you received in bookings for each source.

For example, let's say you placed an ad in a local magazine for $300. You were hired for two events because of that ad. Deduct the cost of the ad from the event revenue. If each event generated $400; $800 − $300 = $500—$500 is your total revenue.

You can track your sources on a spreadsheet for each month. Then you will have an easy reference at year's end to look at and assess how your advertising is working. A sample spreadsheet is shown below.

	RADIO ADVERTISEMENT	CHAMBER OF COMMERCE	WEB SITE	BROCHURES
Jan	0	4	10	2
Feb	0	2	2	0
March	4	6	15	6
April	0	0	0	0
May	1	6	1	3
June	4	4	10	6
July	2	2	2	0
Aug	4	6	15	6
Sep	1	1	4	10
Oct	4	8	8	1
Nov	3	8	6	0
Dec	2	8	7	0
TOTAL	25	55	80	34

You'll then need to track the costs of each of these advertising sources as well. By totaling the cost compared to the number of event bookings, you can determine which is your most successful and which is your cheapest forms of advertising. These figures can help you decide which types of advertising are working and which ones you can fit into your budget for the coming year.

Marketing is a substantial and crucial function that requires lots or planning and preparation as well as flawless and professional execution. It's a tall order, but those companies that do it successfully are the ones that have lots of business and consequently have the opportunity to remain in the game.

CASE STUDY: WORD FROM THE EXPERTS

THE SHELDON CASINO

LOCATION: Sheldon Fairgrounds Sheldon, Vermont

SERVICES: The owner and head chef of The Sheldon Casino, Earl Ballard, provides catering services for all event sizes with two beautifully decorated indoor halls, a large covered outdoor pavilion, and a smaller room perfect for showers or meetings. The Sheldon Casino provides catering in the traditional Vermont fashion with prices for everyone!

We are a very down-to-earth, family business. We have a great team of employees, and we strive to offer affordable services to working-class people in a beautiful atmosphere. We want to make their occasions as special and memorable as possible.

We invite prospective customers to eat with us either in the diner we run on Friday and Saturday nights or in our main hall where we serve Sunday brunch every Sunday from 9-1. Customers can also request to have the chef make a sample of something that they're interested in for a menu.

We are now starting to offer special packages to our potential customers including photographers, DJs, bakers (for cakes), etc., for a "one-stop" wedding shopping experience. We hope to take some of the pressure off customers who are overwhelmed with the details of planning.

We like to get an accurate head count two weeks prior to an event so that we don't have an overabundance of food left over. What food is left over is offered to the customers to take home with them. Anything left after that is offered to our employees to take home with them.

Web Sites

$\mathcal{E}$ ach day the Internet reaches millions of people who use it for work, play and research. The Internet is the best marketing tool in the world; it allows you to be visible to anyone, anywhere. The list below highlights the potential advantages of a Web presence. Place a checkmark next to each advantage that would serve your business:

- ❑ Additional marketing tool.

- ❑ Gather marketing information.

- ❑ Analyze and evaluate marketing information.

- ❑ Generate events.

- ❑ Lower your phone expenses.

- ❑ Improve communication.

- ❑ Establish more frequent communications with customers.

- ❑ Establish more meaningful communications with customers.

- ❑ Reduce fax costs.

- ❑ Reduce courier costs.

- ❑ Deliver electronically encoded resources around the world.

- ❑ Supplement employee training through electronic updates and bulletins.

- ❑ Broadcast press releases.

- ❑ Communicate to people who are not available right now.

- ❑ Submit invoices and expenses more quickly.

- ❑ Reduce international communications costs and improve response time.

❑ Ease of collaboration with colleagues.

❑ Establish contact with potential "strategic partners."

❑ Identify and solicit prospective employees.

❑ Provide immediate access to your catalog.

❑ Permit customers to place orders electronically.

❑ Reduce costs of goods sold through reduced personnel.

The Internet is everywhere. You see Web sites promoted in the mass media—on commercials, on billboards, in magazines, and in this book. You even hear them on the radio and see them on TV. The reason for this proliferation is simple: The Internet is the most economical way to communicate with a worldwide audience. Can you think of any other tool that lets you advertise or sell products to a worldwide market, 24 hours a day, for a minimal monetary investment? The possibilities are endless—the return on investment, enormous. If you are not already convinced, here is a brief list of why you need to have a presence on the World Wide Web:

- **The world's largest communications medium.** The World Wide Web provides maximum exposure and maximum potential to communicate with a worldwide audience, 24 hours a day. There are an estimated 285 million people online, from nearly every country. Forty-eight percent of users access the net one to four times a day; 39 percent use it more. One in five Web users access their browsers more than 35 hours a week.

- **Instantaneous access to information.** A Web site can be browsed at any time—day or night. Information can be downloaded, e-mails transmitted, supplies and services bought and sold.

- **Virtually unlimited potential.** There are no time constraints or physical or geographical limits in cyberspace, and over 62 percent of Web users have bought something online.

- **The user is in control.** Web users choose where they want to go, when they want to go there, and can stay for as little or as long as they choose.

- **Visual marketing.** Technology provides incredible ways to convey information about your business, products and services.

So, how do you get started with developing your company's presence on the Web? Here are the basics.

Select a Domain Name

This is a very important first step in creating a Web site. Usually you will want your domain name to be similar to, if not identical to, your business name. If your catering company is called The Moveable

Chef, your Web site could be **www.moveablechef.com**. Of course, you'll need to confirm that no one else is currently using this domain name. A free service that will search for domain names is **www.domainit.com**.

Once you find a name that is not taken, you need to register it. This usually involves a fee of approximately $70. This fee usually buys you rights to the name for a certain period of time (normally two years); then you will be required to pay an annual fee to keep the name registered. Make sure to take full advantage of your domain name once it is secured—put it on your letterhead, business cards and brochures.

Decide What to Put on Your Web Site

Take some time and explore other caterer's Web sites. What do they typically contain? Most will include menus, photos of events, pricing information, location, and some general information about the business. Make a list of what you like and don't like about these sites.

Next, look at your brochure. The items you included in it are likely the same, or similar, things you will want to include on your Web site. Here is a list of items that you should consider.

- **Pictures.** A picture is truly worth a thousand words. Select high-quality images and photos to "sell" the beauty of your food and presentation.

- **News, events and specials.** You can even develop a Web-based distribution list from your list of loyal customers and use e-mail to promote a new high-profile chef, new menus, or events for which you'll be providing food.

- **Menus.** Use only your best items, but try to show the full range of your options. Also think about using full-color photographs of each entrée!

- **Directions.** Use a link into Mapquest.com on your site, especially if you do on-premise catering. In this way, customers enter their home address and get door-to-door directions from their home to your business.

- **Contact information.** Make sure you include an e-mail address and phone number for potential clients to contact you.

- **Products for sale.** If you sell your salad dressing retail, be sure to provide information on the product and provide a way for customers to purchase it online.

- **History.** Sometimes a history is truly unique—a story worth telling. Your Web site can do this for you.

The opportunities are endless. Be imaginative!

Create Your Web Site

There are endless choices of Web site designs and there are thousands of Web development companies throughout the world. Consider companies specializing in the hospitality industry. Gizmo Graphics Web Design of Land O' Lakes, Florida, **www.gizwebs.com**, is one of those choices. They have put together a solid, high-quality, low-cost package. They offer a comprehensive cradle-to-grave cost approach, which includes all annual hosting fees, domain registrations, and annual support. You should also check with catering association Web sites. They usually have a list of products and services featuring companies that specialize in work for caterers.

Check out Blizzard Internet Marketing at **www.blizzardinternet.com** for tips on ways to improve your Web site. It also shows you how to put information onto your Web site.

Some words of caution:

- **Don't overlook the little details.** A Web site can be a significant investment. Hire a professional if you want professional results.

- **Keep in mind the "hidden costs."** Most developers don't include Web site hosting, domain-name registration and renewal, support, and continued development services after site completion.

- **Make sure you promote your site.** A site is worthless if no one knows it exists. Search engine registration is a critical part of a successful Web site, so be sure when someone in your town is looking for catering and types "Caterers, [your town, state]" into Google.com, yours is one of the first listings that pop up! Check with your Web designer for strategies for achieving this.

If you are particularly creative, like to exercise a great deal of control over all business activities, or just plain like learning new skills, you might want to try your hand at developing your own Web site.

Today it is possible for someone with little experience to create a Web site. Programs such as DreamWeaver make it easy for non-designers and people who don't know HTML coding to create a visually pleasing Web page that works.

If you want a bit of guidance and instruction using these types of programs, check into classes at a local community college or your local university's community classes. These courses are usually offered at reasonable rates and are often offered online.

If you do decide to create your own site, keep some basic principles in mind:

- **Remember that many different people with different hardware, platforms, connection speeds, and software will be accessing your site.** If your main guest is a leisure traveler, you may want to limit the amount of fancy doodles on your site such as animation, Flash, and rotating images. These items take a long time to load onto the guest's computer and you don't want to lose potential customers due to impatience. If you cater to the corporate section, this may not be as big of an issue, but in general you want to make sure that the load time is no longer than ten seconds.

- **Keep basic design principles in mind.** Keep the page simple and uncluttered. Remember to think about contrast, focus, proximity, alignment, and repetition as discussed with brochure design.

- **Consider accessibility issues.** Log onto **www.access-board.gov** for accessibility information concerning the Web. You can also log onto **www.w3.org/wai** for a checklist of recommendations or log onto **www.cast.org/bobby** for a free test of your Web site's accessibility.

- **There are also general conventions that are used when designing a Web site,** and Web users expect to find certain things in certain places. For instance, link buttons generally run down the left side of the screen, and the bottom of the screen contains the legal disclaimers and other non-marketing information. Browse various sites on the Internet to get an idea of these unspoken conventions.

Once your site is built, you need to get a Web site host—sometimes this is part of the package when you have your designed professionally. If it is not, or if you want to do some independent research, check out Web hosting services at **www.tophosts.com**. This site focuses on the top 25 hosts each month.

Some ISP providers offer their subscribers customized Web site hosting as well; your domain name will have the ISP address in it but the cost of this type of hosting is often significantly cheaper. Check with your current ISP provider to see if they offer this service and what limits there are on the amount of information you can upload to the site. The ISPs usually limit the size of Web site that they host so if your site is graphic intensive, then this is not the option for you.

A Web site is an investment, not an expense. In the current marketplace, every caterer must have a Web presence. Clients expect it, and if you don't have one, you have already put yourself at a disadvantage. The Internet is the wave of the future; jump aboard now and ride it to your success!

Catering Resources on the Web

Once you have developed your Web site, it maybe worthwhile to contact other vendors and ask them to link to your site (you can do the same for them); for example, contact a wedding planner or photographer. Many community Web sites also have commercial sections listing types of business by categories.

There are also national sites, such as **www.partypop.com**. This site allows users to find party and wedding vendors in their local area. Vendors can add their business to the database and make it accessible to millions of brides and party/wedding planners every month. Another event planning resource is **www.gatheringguide.com**. At this site, users can search for the right caterer for their event. It also has a section of tips to help users find the right caterer. For weddings, **www.theknot.com** also has list of area-specific caterers.

Local Catering, **www.localcatering.com**, is a catering-specific national site. It was started in 2001 to bridge the technology gap in the catering industry. Customers complete a simple, online form and event details are instantly submitted to qualified merchants. In addition to providing customers with quotes for catering, photography, floral services, limousines, event planning, and more, Local Catering boasts extras like star-rated customer reviews and event financing assistance.

Sample Catering Web Sites

One of the best ways to determine how to build your own Web site is to review similar sites. Following are some examples of catering Web sites:

- **www.food-evolution.com.** To achieve an upscale image, this site uses Flash animation. Users have the option to watch a short introduction or navigate through the site with the simple left-hand menu. Delectable food imagery is used throughout. Users may also subscribe to an e-newsletter—a great way to keep prospective clients and keep in touch with past customers.

- **www.intentionsevents.com.** This elegantly simple site focuses on "exquisite offerings for exquisite tastes," featuring cakes, specialty items, and wedding planning. The photo gallery showcases a selection of wedding and specialty cake designs.

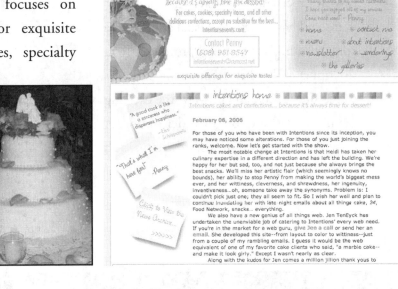

- **www.lancercatering.com.** A highly visual site, the Welcome page of Lancer Catering has four specific catering areas (meetings and events, weddings, on-the-go, and picnics) from which the user can select. Other highlights include a detailed narrative of Lancer's history and a download-able employment application.

- **www.orangecountycatering.com.** Boasting "a fresh approach to entertaining," this site utilizes bright colors, illustrated oranges and high-quality photography. Menus are available online, and there is an extensive section of testimonials from satisfied customers.

- **www.spicedright.com.** Based in Atlanta, this site focuses on smokehouse barbecue items and has a friendly, casual appeal. The contact number is featured prominently in the upper right- hand corner on all areas of the site. Users can also view the catering menu, request a quote or order online. A detailed form covers meats, side items, and dessert choices.

CASE STUDY: WORD FROM THE EXPERTS

LAFOND CATERING

SERVICES: Cindy LaFond and her husband run a small catering business. They provide a food service program to UCSB sorority students Monday-Friday and cater upscale weddings on the weekends. They have four chefs that work 30-40 hours per week, several dishwashers, head waiters—one of which hires and organizes the waiters, captains, bartenders and student waiters. They have a mobile kitchen unit with wolf range, convection oven, refrigeration and sinks. The commissary kitchen is located on campus.

Training is a big thing for us. We have a handbook, a one-page cheat sheet, an annual meeting, a one-hour staff mini training session prior to weddings, and chef training on a daily basis.

We use tons of designs such as Urban Look-Linear, square plates, square cocktail tables, station tables with various heights of square and diamond shapes, clear laminate and white passing trays, towers of colorful cocktails on laminate trays, simple fabric backdrops behind bars and stations, and natural hedging to cover service areas (no lattice).

LOCATION: Virginia

SERVICES: Jason Ingram is the owner of Hill City BBQ, which specializes in barbeque. Jason feels that having a small business and being able to adapt to each individual event helps him be a better caterer *Hill City BBQ specializes in old-fashioned whole-hog pig pickings. We are a full-service catering company that provides all the delicious side items that we all associate with BBQ. All of our meats are smoked fresh on-site the day of the event and never brought out already cooked and just dropped off. We are a small company so we can alter our menus as well as our serv ice to fit each event. Our business is specialized, and we aim to cook for those who want true BBQ and not just any warmed meats.*

One hour before dinner we take the meat off the smoker and chop it fresh in front of the guest the old-fashioned way. People are always welcome to help "Mop the Hog" during the cooking process; kids love it!

SERVICES: Penny Rego is the owner of Intentions, a gourmet cake and confectionery caterer; **www.IntentionsEvents.com**

I left the corporate world to pursue something I love—baking and pastry art. I try to be professional (shades of my former life), but I get excited when someone calls to discuss an order. We make plans and talk specifics, and when I hang up, I happy dance.

I always thought I'd be able to be the crazy, disheveled pastry chef, but in order to run a successful business, I have to be extremely professional. I keep a detailed calendar and plan an event months in advance, right down to the details like, "Call client and get name of florist," marked on a specific date. Planning ahead is super important. I have to make sure I have all the ingredients necessary for a variety of upcoming commissions; I can't just assume I have enough sugar or baking powder. As a result, I have to make sure I keep a detailed inventory. We also make sure our clients are satisfied, and often receive thank-you cards after the event. Professionalism guarantees that clients will recommend us to friends.

To save money, we look for sales and shop at a variety of sources for the best prices without sacrificing quality. Whenever possible, I use locally grown products, especially for the homemade jams used as cake fillings.

The best way to sell a certain food is to love it yourself; your client or customer will see your enthusiasm. Offer samples if possible. Show, don't tell. At a bridal show, I can go on all day telling potential clients how good our vanilla cake is. Or I could offer them a taste. That's going to sell a lot more cake and provide opportunity for many more happy dances.

Everything from Intentions is made with good intentions—crabbiness and crankiness are not allowed during production, design or delivery. This is supposed to be fun—the reason I left the corporate world—and fun for the client, whereby I show up and their work is done!

Public Relations

*P*ublic relations is really the sum of its definitions: It's the message a person, company or organization sends to the public. It's a planned effort to build positive opinions about your business through actions, and communications about those actions.

Public relations (PR) is any contact your organization has with another human being, and the resulting opinion. This opinion may or may not be accurate, but it comes from everything the public reads, sees, hears and thinks about you. Effective PR has been described as becoming a positive member of your community and getting credit for it. Basically, good PR sends a positive message to the public about your establishment.

Because PR is so pervasive, you should incorporate its use in your overall marketing communications program. This includes advertising, internal communications, and sales promotion. Speeches, contests, promotions, personal appearances and publicity are typical PR events, but really, the results generated from all of these parts—including acquiring unpaid-for media space and time—are PR. It's who the public thinks you are, and you need to take active steps to nurture that opinion and ensure it remains positive.

What Public Relations Does and Doesn't Do

If done well, PR distinguishes you from the pack in the eyes of your customers. It leaves them with a favorable impression of you and great tidbits of information to pass on to their friends about your establishment. It makes you newsworthy in a great way and can help save your reputation and standing in your community during an emergency.

Good PR improves sales by creating an environment in which people choose to spend their time and money. As mentioned before, PR is about getting credit for being an upstanding member of your community. But if you don't really live up to that expectation, even the best PR can't make you look like you do. PR accentuates the positive and creates lasting value by highlighting what makes your establishment special. PR cannot create lasting value if none is there to begin with. What it can do is communicate existing value effectively and leave that message in your customers' minds.

PR can make a good story great, and a bad story seem not as bad. But PR is not just the public's opinion of your business, it's also the physical state of your establishment. People aren't just interacting with your staff, they're interacting with your facility. If the media are reporting on something wonderful that happened at your business and the place is in a state of disrepair, what message is really being communicated? PR is invasive; you need to be aware of your image at all times.

The key to implementing an effective PR campaign is determining what you want your business image to be and then determining how best to create that image in the eyes of the public. You need to clearly define your objectives and create a plan to implement them. PR is not a way to gloss over a tarnished image or to keep the press at a safe distance; it's an organized and ongoing campaign to accentuate the positives of what your business intends to do and how you intend to go about doing it.

Public Relations and Marketing

PR is one of the many marketing tools you have in your arsenal. As a result, most catering operations keep these two departments, or functions, close together. This is because PR is one of the crucial aspects of a successful marketing plan. In fact, in many instances, the two have been combined and are referred to as marketing public relations, corporate public relations, relationship marketing, or mega-marketing. All of these terms reflect the symbiotic relationship between PR and marketing.

On a practical level, this close relationship obtains and retains customers, which is the obvious goal of any marketing plan. When management is communicating effectively with guests, employees, and community leaders, it is implementing an effective marketing plan.

Fundamentally, all marketing is integrated. Consumers don't distinguish between one message from your business and another—all the messages are yours. In that light, since it's your job to communicate as well as possible, understanding that all your marketing is integrated allows you to focus on an overall approach to building good PR.

Applying Your PR Plan

Once you have established the objectives of your PR campaign and integrated them into your marketing plan, it is time to execute. These questions can help you do just that.

- What's the right medium for this strategy?

- Who are the key contacts?

- How strong are the necessary personal relationships required for this plan? Do any need to be established or re-established?

- Is this plan thorough? Have we considered all the risks?

- Are we prepared to deliver a package to the media?

The delivery package is key to your PR campaign; you must attend to this very carefully and diligently. This delivery package is an essential part of your plan. It contains descriptions, plots, contacts, phone numbers—all the pertinent information that will inform the media and direct them to you. The press may not use one word of your material, but there is a much greater likelihood they'll describe you the way you want them to if you've given them the resources to do just that. Following is a list of practical factors that will help you gain recognition.

- **Be honest.** The media wants credible, honest material and relationships. Your message should be genuine and factual. This doesn't mean you have to reveal confidential data; it just means that materials should be thorough and truthful.

- **Respond.** Don't lie, dodge or cover up. If you don't have an answer to every question—and you might not—don't say "No comment," or "that information is unavailable." Simply respond that you don't have that information, but will provide it as soon as humanly possible. Then provide it as soon as humanly possible.

- **Give the facts, and follow up.** If you supply the media with a printed handout of key facts, it significantly decreases the chances of getting misquoted. Make a concentrated effort to follow up and go over information with the media. Again, if you don't have a requested piece of information, get it and follow up with a note and call to make sure the correct data reaches the media.

- **Be concise.** Usually the media will burn you for what you do say, not what you don't. Be deliberate about providing the facts without editorializing, exaggerating, or pulling things out of thin air.

- **Nurture relationships.** If you follow the above steps, you're on your way to building a strong and lasting relationship with the press. These relationships can sour instantly if you are reactionary, hostile, aloof, hypersensitive or argumentative in any way. No matter what you think of an interviewer, treat him or her with respect, courtesy and professionalism. Causing negative reactions from the press will deny you print space and airtime.

How you interact with the press is crucial, but it's only half the process. The quality of the content of your communication; that is, having a clear and deliberate focus about how you are going to tell your story, is the other side of press relations. The following list will help you identify your purpose and communicate it effectively to the press.

- **Be clear about your purpose.** Why do you want public exposure? To what are you specifically trying to draw attention? If you are selling your new high-profile chef from New York, then don't go on about your homemade raspberry pie. Be sure your message conveys your purpose.

- **Identify your target.** Who are you targeting? Prospective customers? Your employees? The local business community? Civic leaders? Lay out whom you want to reach, and then determine who in the media will speak to them most effectively.

- **Think as they're thinking.** Why would this be interesting to the media? Figure out how your interests can be packaged in a way that directly matches the interests of the press. Make your story one they want to print—one that will help them sell papers and gain listeners.

- **Customize your materials.** Once you have identified your purpose, who your target is, and the media's angle, tailor your materials to include all three. Give the press everything they need to tell the story—photos and copy—and be sure it's in exactly the style and medium they're using.

- **Know where to send your materials.** Is this a news story or a feature story? Do you know the difference? A news story goes to a newspaper's city desk. Feature stories go to the appropriate editor, such as the food editor. It's a very good idea to cultivate relationships with these editors beforehand so that when the time arises, they are thinking well of you and would like to help.

- **Make their jobs easy.** Do not ask the media for the ground rules for getting press and building relationships—learn these on your own and then meet them. Spending valuable time and resources building a relationship with a reporter, only to then submit materials at the last minute or provide insufficient or inaccurate information, burns bridges quickly. Do as much of their work for them as possible: give them something that is ready to go, answers all their questions, and is interesting. This is the difference between staying in the middle and rising to the top of a busy person's in-box. Also, be available immediately to answer questions.

If a reporter calls and you aren't there or don't return the call immediately, your great story—prepared at considerable expense—may end up in the trash.

Media Relations and Campaigns

Media relations is one of the most important aspects of PR because effective media relations generates publicity. Effective media relations opens the channels for your public to receive the messages you want them to receive. Media relations is how you build your relationships with the press and it determines how they respond when you want them to report on a story.

The first goal in building strong media relations is to determine who your target media are. News media should be classified by the audiences they reach and the means they use to carry their messages.

Your target media will change according to the type of message you wish to send and the type of audience you wish to reach. Your advertising agency can supply you with contact information for the newspapers, radio and television stations in your area. In addition, you may want to target national media, as well as specialized trade and business publications.

It may be a good idea to hire a part-time PR consultant, former reporter, or editor who can help you present your materials to the press. If this is beyond your budgetary limits, the following is a list of essentials you should have on hand to building a good relationship with the press:

- **Fact sheet.** One of the most helpful items of media information is the fact sheet as it provides the information a reporter would otherwise have to research. It also shortens the length of interviews because it answers questions in advance. It should describe your business and what you are trying to get press for. At a glance it tells where you are located, when you opened, your cuisine, the types of events you cater, your capacity, and number of employees.

- **Staff biographies.** You will need to write biographies for all of your key people (which may only be you and your spouse). In your biographies list work experience, education, professional memberships, honors, and awards.

- **Good photography.** Do not take chances with an amateur photographer. Space is very limited in the print media, and editors go through thousands of photographs to choose just a few. This is true even for local editors. Don't give them any reason to ignore your pictures. Have them taken by a pro. Ask for references and check them thoroughly. When the photos are done, write an explanatory caption for each picture in your collection. This gives editors an easy understanding of what they're looking at. Then, before sending photos to the media, be sure you find out whether they prefer black and white, slides or transparencies, and send them in the desired format.

- **Press kit folder.** Put all of these materials into a single folder with your company's name and logo on the cover. You might also include brochures, rate cards, package offers, a brief on your involvement with local charities, etc. Don't over stuff it, but give the press a solid idea of what distinguishes you from the competition.

Before you begin your media campaign, you should get to know the media as much as possible. This may mean inviting them—one at a time—to have a brief tour or visit of your establishment and, perhaps, lunch. This gives them a sense of you and your business and begins to build a relationship. These visits are not the time to sell them on doing a story on you. It's a time for you to get to know each other and to build a relationship. If the reporters trust you, they will help you, and vice versa. They need article ideas as much as you need press, and getting to know them will give you insight into how you can help them do their job.

Once you've built this relationship, and your friends in the media trust you won't be barraging them with endless story ideas, you can begin your media campaign. It is important to remember that having a positive rapport with a reporter doesn't mean he'll do a story on you. Your relationship with the reporter will help get a newsworthy story printed, but you won't get a boring story to press just because the reporter likes you. Your story needs to be newsworthy on its own. Also, reporters are always working against time. The more you can give them pertinent, accurate, concise information, the better your chances of getting their attention.

If you've built a respectful relationship with the media, a reporter who gets a story from an interview or news conference at your establishment will mention your place in her story. These are the "freebies" that come from developing strong relationships with the media and learning to think in their terms.

TAKING YOUR MEDIA CAMPAIGN TO THE NEXT LEVEL

- **News releases.** Many businesses go one step further and give their media contacts news releases that are written in a journalistic style. A news release describes the newsworthy developments in your business in a ready-to-print article. Editors can then change it or print it as is. These can be immensely valuable for getting your message out there.

- **Tip sheets.** If writing journalistic articles is beyond your reach or budget, tip sheets can be very effective in getting your story across. A tip sheet gets the message to the media by simply outlining the who, what, when, where, why and how of your story. It's basically an outline of the story the reporter will then write. Tip sheets give the spine of the story and, because they are so concise, they often get more attention from busy editors.

Here are a few more tips on how to work effectively with the media:

- Earn a reputation for dealing with the facts and nothing else.

- Never ask to review a reporter's article before publication.

- Never ask after a visit or an interview if an article will appear.

- Follow up by phone to see if your fact sheet or press release has arrived, if the reporter is interested, and if she needs anything else.

- Provide requested information—photos, plans, etc.—ASAP.

What's News?

Once you have identified your target media and begun your media relations program, you need to learn what makes news. To do this, pick up the paper, and turn on the TV. The media is looking for the strange, volatile, controversial and unusual. It's not newsworthy that you run a nice catering company that provides great food at a reasonable price. It's newsworthy when a customer gets food poisoning, or when a group's convention booking gets cancelled.

This is not the type of news you want to make, but it's news. Obviously, you want to be making great news. One of the foundations for accomplishing this is to take proactive steps to avoid negative articles: make sure your reservations system works, your staff treat guests courteously, etc. Not only will these practices keep you out of the negative press, they are good business practices that will keep the clients coming in.

Once you've taken all the steps you can think of to avoid negative press, you are ready to generate positive stories in the media. Here is a list of basic newsworthiness criteria:

- Is it local?

- Is it timely?

- Is it unique, unusual, strange?

- Does it involve and affect people?

- Will it evoke human emotion?

Think in terms of what it is that sets your establishment apart from the competition and what is newsworthy about those qualities. When this is done, again, target your media. When you've got a story, be smart about who would be interested in writing about it and whose audience would love to read about it. Here is a short list of possible newsworthy ideas:

- A new manager or chef.

- Visits by well-known politicians, entertainers, authors or local heroes.

- Private parties, conventions or meetings of unique organizations: antique car enthusiasts, baseball card collectors, scientific organizations, etc.

- Your building's historical significance.

- A new menu.

- Hosting a charitable event.

- Reduced rates, special menus, promotions.

- Personal stories about the staff: the cook who returned a doctor's medical bag, helped a patron stop choking, returned a tip that was too big.

How Is PR Different from Advertising?

PR is not advertising; PR uses advertising as one of its tools. A good PR campaign is almost always coordinated with advertising, but PR is not paid-for time and space. With advertising, clients pay the media to carry a message, and the client has complete control over this message. With PR, the media receives no money. Because of this, your story about the medical dinner meeting you catered with a noted speaker may end up on the 5 o'clock news, in the paper, or nowhere at all.

The success of a PR story often depends on how timely it is or whether a newspaper editor feels it's worth reporting on. Furthermore, only a portion of your intended message may be used. The media may not even use your business's name. Because they are choosing to write about your topic, and you've basically given them only a potential idea for a story, the story could end up in a very different form than you initially presented or hoped.

Basically, with PR you have none of the control that you do with advertising. But when done well, PR garners positive attention for your establishment, is hugely cost-effective, and is more credible than advertising. This is because the public is getting its information from a third party—not directly from your business. Customers assume that advertising is self-serving, but a positive message delivered by a third party is determined to be authentic and trustworthy. Therefore, third-party messages are infinitely more persuasive than advertising.

Seeing the differences between PR and advertising, one sees differences both in guarantees of space and in the effectiveness of the different types of media. The enormous value of securing unpaid media space through your PR campaign becomes clear.

Launching a PR Campaign

In a small catering operation the owner is typically solely responsible for public relations. When you launch your campaign, it's important to remember that you will be competing with professionals for a very limited amount of airtime and editorial space. You may be able to get PR from your local chamber of commerce or convention/visitors' bureau. And if you work within a larger corporation, you often will have access to PR departments who guide you or manage your PR campaign.

Most states also have a Business/Economic Development Department that will be happy to help you, since their goal is to create new business in your state. Hotel and catering associations can also prove to be valuable allies since they either have PR people on staff or use national PR agencies.

To launch a campaign, you need a media list. This list includes the names of appropriate editors, reporters, news directors, assignment editors, media outlets, addresses, and contact numbers. From this list you call, visit or otherwise contact the media who are crucial to your campaign. If you want to mail fact sheets, press releases, press kits, etc., you can hire a company that sells media mailing lists, and you can pay them or another firm to do your mailing for you. If that is beyond your budget, call the editorial department of a newspaper or a newsroom and get the contact numbers of the people you seek to reach. It's more work, but from there you can put together your own media list.

SPECIAL EVENTS

Special events are a very effective way to generate publicity and community interest. You may be opening a new property or celebrating a renovation or an anniversary. Any such occasion is an opportunity to plan a special event that will support or improve your PR program. There are usually two kinds of special events: one-time and ongoing. Obviously you're not going to have a groundbreaking ceremony annually, but you might host a famous Fourth of July party every year.

The key question to ask when designing a special event is "why?" Clearly defining your objectives before you start is crucial. Is your goal to improve community opinion of your business? to present yourself as a good employer? to show off a renovation? Once your purpose has been clearly defined, a timetable and schedule of events can be made. Ample time is necessary, since contractors, inspection agencies, and civil officials may be involved. If you are planning an anniversary celebration, research what events were going on in your community when you opened: Was there a huge fire? Did Dwight Eisenhower speak at the local college? Once you have this information, send it to the press. They will see your event as part of the historical landscape, as opposed to a commercial endeavor that benefits only you, and they'll appreciate your community focus.

Special events require preparation to ensure everything is ready when the spotlight of attention is turned on you. Be certain the day you have chosen does not conflict with another potentially competing event or fall on an inappropriate holiday.

With a groundbreaking or opening of a new property, you should invite the developer, architect, interior designer, civic officials and the media. You should prepare brief remarks and ask the architect to comment on the property. In your remarks, remind your listeners that the addition of your business does not boost school taxes or increase the need for police and fire protection; it adds new jobs and new tax revenues.

If you are celebrating an opening, tours of the property are a must and should be led by you. Refreshments should be served, and in many cases, lunch or dinner is provided. Whatever your occasion, you should provide press kits to the attending media and mail them to all media that were invited. Souvenirs are a good idea—they can be simple or elaborate, but should always be creative, fun and useful to your guests.

CUSTOMER LOYALTY

Public relations is all about perception, and we all know first impressions last. Obviously how you relate to your clients affects their opinion of you. That opinion then translates into potential loyalty, and loyalty boosts your bottom line. Furthermore, it costs about five times as much to attract a new customer as it does to retain an existing one. This is another huge reason you should commit to establishing lots of repeat customers. While this may not seem to be a public relations issue (there are no media involved), it certainly does apply because PR is all about creating a positive impression with the public.

Use PR to focus on your repeat customers—your most profitable clients—and encourage them to keep coming back. Two things to focus on for retaining clients:

- Pay attention to your most profitable clients. Listen. Keep in touch. Find out what they want and need and why they've chosen you.

- If they go to the competition, find out why.

Comment cards where clients rate your service and facilities can be a great way to find out what they think of you. You can offer discounts or promotional items for the return of these cards. If you do use a comment card, the one question that must be there is "Would you hire us for a future event?" If you get "no's, take immediate action to determine why and then fix the situation.

There are many things you can do to build loyalty. Here are a few:

- Build a database or a mailing list of your customers.

- Track purchases and behavior: food preferences, table preferences, entertainment needs, special needs.

- Constantly update your information based on interactions with your customers.

- Recognize birthdays, anniversaries and special occasions.

- Show your appreciation through holiday greetings, discounts, and other forms of recognition.

- Thank your customers for their business.

- Whenever you can, individualize your communications.

- Listen to and act on customer suggestions.

- Inform guests on new or improved services.

- Tell guests of potential inconveniences like renovations, and stress their future benefits.

- Answer every inquiry, including complaints.

- Accommodate all reasonable requests for meal substitutions, table changes, etc.

- Empower employees to solve problems.

- Talk to your customers and employees so you can let them know you're listening and find out what's going on.

This last point—communication between guests, employees and you—is enormously important. Just as you need to focus on getting your message to your guests, you also need to focus on getting their messages to you. If they think their opinions are important to you, they will think they are important to you—and they'll come back. People have more choices than ever about where to spend their money. If they know you will attend to their individual needs and you will take care of them, then their choice will be to spend their money with you.

COMMUNITY RELATIONS

Your local community supports the bulk of your business. It means your business needs to be a leader in its community. In practice this means building bridges between your company and your community to maintain and foster your environment in a way that benefits both parties.

Your goal is to make your immediate world a better place in which everybody can thrive. The following are a few ideas that can be part of an effective community relations program.

- Fill a community need—create something that wasn't there before.

- Remove something that causes a community problem.

- Include "have-nots" in something that usually excludes them.

- Share your space, equipment or expertise.

- Offer tutoring, or otherwise mobilize your workforce as a helping hand.

- Promote your community elsewhere.

Being a good citizen is, of course, crucial, but you also need to convince your community of the value of your business as a business. These are real benefits, and they should be integrated into the message you send by being a good citizen. Designing this message is a straightforward but remarkably effective process.

1. List the things your establishment brings to the community: jobs, taxes, well-maintained architecture.

2. List what your business receives from its community: employees, fire and police protection, trash removal, utilities.

3. List your business's complaints about your community: high taxes, air pollution, noise pollution, narrow roads.

Once you have outlined these items, look for ways your business can lead the way to improve what doesn't work. As you do this, consult with your local Chamber of Commerce or Visitors' Bureau. They may be able to integrate you into existing community betterment programs aimed at your objectives.

If done well, your community relations program will create positive opinions in your community. In turn, this will cause local residents to recommend you as the place to work; will encourage people to apply for jobs; and may encourage suppliers to seek to do business with you. Also, if there is an emergency at your establishment, having a positive standing in the community will enable your property to be treated fairly.

An effective community relations program is a win-win situation because it gives you the opportunity to be a deep and abiding member of your community—improving the quality of life and opportunities around you—and, at the same time, contributes significantly to your bottom line.

REMEDY BAD PR

Bad things can happen and emergencies make the news. Bad news stories are bad PR, and they can destroy the image you've worked so hard to build. They can wipe away years of hard-won customer relations. There are numerous kinds of emergencies—earthquakes, fires, floods, political protests, crime and more—and any of these events, if not managed properly, can destroy your public image.

In order to meet a PR emergency, you must prepare now. If you have a strategy developed in advance, when something bad does happen, you assure the most accurate, objective, media coverage of the event. It's important that all your employees are aware of this plan and that they are reminded of it regularly. Since your employees generate a huge amount of your PR, it's crucial for them to know how to act and what to say—and not say—during a crisis. This simple detail can make all the difference in the world. Here are three basic aspects to an emergency press relations plan:

- **You should be the only spokesperson** during the time of the emergency. Make sure your employees know not to talk to the press and to refer all inquiries to you. Make sure you are available at all times, day or night.

- **Know the facts of the situation** before answering questions from the media.

- **Initiate contact.** Once the story is out, don't wait for the media to call you. This way you will ensure that they get accurate information. Plus, the media will appreciate your forthcoming attitude, and your cooperation will reflect in their reporting.

In times of crisis it's crucial to put a positive slant on the news. Try to focus press attention on the diligent efforts of management to handle the emergency, or on employees whose compassion and assistance made a difference. If something happens in your establishment that is not your fault and your establishment handles it well, it's an opportunity to showcase your heart and responsiveness.

The importance of a crisis-public relations plan cannot be overstated. When an employee is injured or killed in your establishment or a guest suffers from food poisoning, the public assumes you're guilty. Whether or not you're even mildly at fault, people assume you are. Therefore, how you handle public relations during this time means the difference between a temporary loss of public support and the permanent loss of a great deal of your business.

One always hopes that a crisis-PR plan remains unnecessary, but being prepared for the worst is the best policy. Furthermore, while the entire establishment suffers during an emergency, the owner who is caught unprepared suffers the most. Therefore, after calling the police, fire department, or other authorities, it is your job to immediately find out what happened and take corrective actions.

Having built strong media relations pays off during an emergency. A reporter you have a good relationship with may report an incident at a "local catering facility," while one less acquainted with you—or downright hostile—will mention you specifically and push for the story to be on the front page. This is a crucial difference. It means that the person who will be the media liaison during an emergency should be building and nurturing strong media relations now, in case anything does happen.

Essentially, if you don't guide the flow of information around your news event, somebody else will misguide it for you. With proper PR, a story that could be presented as a case of a business that didn't have its new computer running on time can be authentically retold by you to show how the business was the victim of a software glitch and the staff acting heroically—and always in great humor—averted what could have been a disaster. Your ability to work with the media can shift the public from viewing you as incompetent to them having more faith than ever in your establishment. Public opinion depends on how effectively you manage information and how well you get your story across.

Marketing is a substantial and crucial function that requires lots or planning and preparation as well as flawless and professional execution. It's a tall order, but those companies that do it successfully are the ones that have lots of business and consequently have the opportunity to remain in the game.

LOCATION: Nashville, Tennessee

SERVICES: Michael Attias operates a restaurant in Nashville, Tennessee, and helps restaurant owners add or expand a catering profit center through his company, The Results Group. You can download his FREE Report: Tapping Into Your Hidden Catering Profit$ at www.ezRestaurantMarketing.com.

YOUR TOP 100 By Michael Attias

When asked, a majority of restaurant owners said they believe they are in the "food business," when in reality they are in the business of selling food. As wonderful as your food may be, nothing happens until it is sold.

Successful salespeople maintain a "Top 100" list of the 100 prospects that they want as clients. Developing your "Top 100" list can be done in an afternoon. Ask yourself what type of companies you would like to have as clients. You might decide you want to do business with medium-sized employers or focus on a niche or two. Armed with your target, you must now develop that list; use a chamber directory or do some research at your local library.

Once you have your list, have one of your key employees call each company to get the decision-maker's name. Completed, you now have your strongest marketing weapon.

Mail your "Top 100" monthly with specials, menus and offers of menu sampling. Also, pass around your list to clients and friends to see if there is a referral you can tap into.

Concentrating on your "Top 100" for an hour or two a week could add 10 percent or more to your bottom line and will ensure you stay profitably on top.

Managing the Event

Selling runs parallel to marketing, and both are essential to the continued success of your catering operation. With your marketing plan in place, you know who your target customers are so now it is time to make your pitch.

If you're targeting several markets at once, it makes sense to segment your sales strategies and staff. Many firms divide their sales staff by corporate or private catering, or even by specific types of functions, such as weddings, receptions, dinners, or special entertainment-related events. Develop specialized staff; let them focus on a specific area, thus gaining greater expertise and familiarity with all the particulars of their assignment.

Once you have determined the type of business you are after, you have to do just that: go after it! Use lead referrals, advertising and—sometimes—aggressive cold calling. Work your leads like your livelihood depended on it.

The most successful salespeople are not the ones with the flashiest smiles, or most elegant presentations, but simply the ones who are the most persistent. Pay close attention to what conventions and groups are coming to town, as far in advance as you can gather the information.

One of the keys to developing leads is through networking your existing contacts. If the client is happy with your event, then you should try to get a few good words of recommendation as well. As mentioned before, ask if you may use their words of reference in your sales catalogs or brochures. Be sure to add all influential attendees of your functions to your database.

Once you have a client in place that you are trying to win over, be sure to protect yourself. Many new caterers are hungry for those first few sales, but they won't help turn your dream into profit unless the client can pay. Try to establish quickly and discreetly whether the client has sufficient funds to pay for your services. Aim to qualify them right away. If their budget still remains questionable, send them to your competition. Be suspicious when the promised deposits are not sent to you. If you already have a heavy commitment during the time of a proposed event, refuse, no matter how good a client is. Do not over-commit yourself and your staff.

Handling Inquiries

Most inquiries you get will be over the phone, so make sure you or your staff can answer the phone personally for as many hours as possible. Many times if someone does not get a quick response, they will just move on to the next caterer on their list. If you are part of a large business, consider hiring someone full-time to do this. If you are an individual owner, consider using your cell phone as your main number and carry it with you so you can answer those calls. Ideally, you'll be able to have someone answering the phone and responding to inquires six days a week from around 9 a.m. to 7 or 8 p.m.

The person answering the phone should be polite and knowledgeable. When someone calls in, the first step will be to check availability on the date the potential client needs services. It's harder to keep track of all these details if you are on the run and answering the phone yourself. If this is the case, make sure you always have an updated day planner so you can give the potential client an immediate response on availability. If you have someone in the office handling calls, you can computerize this information on a banquet inquiry form. Make sure the person answering phones fills this form out completely with all the information.

The potential client is likely to be calling several area caterers, so you should follow up in a few days and see if there are any other questions you can answer and try to set up a meeting. Showing initiative can take you a long way in the competitive catering business!

Meeting with the Client

Once you have someone interested in hiring you, one of the first things you will do is to meet with your client to find out about what type of event they want. This will be done before a contract is signed. When meeting with your client, it's important that you are professional and come to the meeting prepared. Be sure to bring, sample menus, any photos of past parties you have catered, samples of dishware, a contract, notepaper, pens, and references. If you are an on-premise caterer, be sure to show the client the facility when you meet, including the dining and bar areas and parking. Make sure to take thorough notes so you can refer to this information when drawing up the contract and planning the event.

Make a question list to take with you to make sure you've covered every aspect of every detail.

Here is a sample list:

- When does the reception start? When will the meal be served? What time will the event end?

- How many guests are you expecting?

- Is security needed?

- Do you need any signage?

- Should there be a checkroom available for guests' coats?

- What type of decorations does the client want? (Color of linens, flowers, balloons, etc.)

- Will someone be setting these up or will the caterer be responsible?

- When will the decorators need access to the room?

- What type of service does the client want?

- What type of china?

- Beverages?

- Will there be music? What times will the band be playing? Will there be dancing?

- Will the band be provided with dinner?

- Are there any audio-visual requirements?

- Is a photographer needed? Who will hire this person? When will photos be taken?

- What kind of room setup does the client want?

- Will there be a head table?

- Are there any programs or other printed material that need to be distributed to guests?

- Is there a formal seating chart?

- Are telephone or computer hookups necessary?

- Will there be a speaker?

- Any lighting requirements needed?

- Any special permits needed?

- How many cars will be expected? Will the client pay for parking or will the guests?

As you are listening to the client, try to pick what is most important. In general, people will have a vision of the type of event they want but it won't be grounded in reality. Part of your job is to figure out what is essential and what is not a priority in your client's mind. If the event is a wedding reception, the person may want to serve three different entrées—chicken, beef and fish. On the other hand, the budget for the event may only allow for two entrée choices. Try to communicate this information to your client in a positive way. Remember, everyone has budgetary limits. Rather than trying to force someone to spend more than they can afford and create potentially bad word-of-mouth advertising, try to adjust the client's expectations and still give them a memorable event.

SITE LIST

If you are an off-premise caterer, it is a good idea to hold one of your first meetings at the intended event location. This way you can see what kind of equipment and storage you have, and you can get an idea if you'll need to buy any new equipment to make the party work. Make sure to bring your notepad, tape measure and calculator on this trip. If the event is being planned far out in advance, it might also be a good idea to take your camera. That way you'll have a "memory jogger" when you get down to work on the details at a later date.

As you look at the facilities, ask your self these questions:

- How will the tables be set up? Is there a buffet?

- Is there room for a separate dessert and appetizer buffet?

- Where will drinks be set up?

- How many ovens are there and how much cold storage do you have?

- Will you need to bring auxiliary equipment?

- Are there pots, pans, etc., to use or will you need to bring them?

- Where will the dirty dishes be bused to and washed?

- Where does the trash need to go?

- Are there adequate restroom facilities?

- What is the parking situation? Will there be valet parking?

- Does the room require any special decoration?

You'll also need to know the timing of the day's event. If you are working on a wedding reception, for example, you should ask what time the ceremony is, when the guests will start arriving for the reception, and when appetizers and dinner should be served. Will there be toasts and bouquet tossing, and at what times? What time should the event wrap up?

If you are an off-premise caterer, it might be a good idea to make a site list to take to these meetings. One of the biggest challenges to an off-site caterer is how to deal with the variety of equipment and conditions you run into at various venues. It is especially easy to forget to check every detail in the beginning, so a site list would be a good way to make sure you cover everything and that you bring all the equipment you will need for the party— add any other questions you feel you should ask.

Following is an example of a site list.

SITE LIST	
Client	
Client contact information	
Event date	
Event time	
Type of event	
Indoor/Outdoor	
Venue address	
Outside parking	
Area for catering staff to unload and park	
Lighting	
Accessibility	
Dining area tables (provided or need to be brought in?)	
Size of dining area	
Buffet tables	
Bar	
Gift table	
Decorations	
Electrical outlets	
Heating/Air-conditioning	
Extensions	
Microphone/Podium	
Dance floor	
Stage	

SITE LIST	
Kitchen	
Stove	
Oven dimensions	
Grill	
Refrigerator and freezer space	
Dishwashing area	
Microwave	
Access to pots, pans, utensils	
Sinks	
Cleanup equipment (brooms, mops, etc.)	
Electrical outlets	
Counter space	
Pantry/Storage	

TYPES OF SERVICE

There are benefits and drawbacks to each type of service, and you'll want to keep these in mind while you're meeting with and negotiating with your client. The style of service will impact your event, the guests' interaction, and the quality of service you can give. The following table gives the advantages and disadvantages for various types of service.

TYPE OF SERVICE	ADVANTAGES	DISADVANTAGES
Plated	You control portion sizes and establish the pace of the meal. It's easier to create dramatic plate presentations and a romantic or elegant ambiance.	Requires a lot of planning.
Family Style	Food is easy to assemble and won't get cold quickly because it is being served from large serving dishes. Good for casual events, creates a sense of camaraderie.	No plate presentation. Passing dishes among guests can be awkward.
Casual Buffet (guests serve themselves)	Most food will be in place before event begins. You can offer a variety of dishes, guests can help themselves, and you don't have to seat everyone at once to begin serving.	Serving size not controlled, will need to replenish buffet, and have considerable leftovers. Hot items can be difficult to keep hot.
Formal Buffet (servers are used)	Servers allow people to move through buffet line quicker and determine portion size, fewer problems with running out of food. Can serve a whole carved meat to add elegance to event. Hot dishes are easier to keep hot because servers are paying strict attention to these.	There is the added expense of servers.

Your job as the caterer is to help your client navigate all the various options and possibilities to come up with an event that is outstanding yet still respects the client's budgetary limits.

Quotes and Contracts

Never give a quote over the phone. You want to meet with the potential client and make sure you understand exactly what they want before offering a quote or you may significantly underbid.

Make sure to write down every last detail of what the client wants. Record food selections, number of servers, length of event, number of guests expected, linens desired, extra services, and bar specifics. Once you leave the meeting with the client, analyze the information and crunch numbers before calling back with a quote.

Everything affects the price you come up with, so make sure you think through all the details. What is the occasion? Will the event require a light lunch or a large, multi-course buffet? What are the logistics involved with the location if the event is off-site? Will you need to supply additional cooking or cold storage equipment? Will you be cooking on-site? If the event is on-premise, what is the typical room charge associated with a room that will hold the desired number of guests?

Once the client decides on food preferences, prepare an outline for yourself that includes the following tasks:

- Food shopping
- Travel time to and from event
- Setup time
- Serving time

- Food prep
- Loading and unloading time
- Reheating and arranging food
- Cleanup time

This will help you determine your time, start to finish, because even though the event may be from 7 to 10 p.m., you'll be working long before and after the festivities! With this information and your pricing information, you will be able to develop a fair quote that will still ensure you make a profit.

WRITING A CONTRACT

Regardless of how well you know the person you are catering for or how nice he or she appears, you must have a written contract. Without a contract, you'll find yourself without a leg to stand on when attempting to collect from a non-paying customer. A contract is a binding agreement between two parties; the caterer is obligated to provide the food and service stated, and the other party, your client, is obligated to pay for this food and service.

When in the first stages of working with your client, it's important to take care of your needs and to protect your business. Many caterers start small, and their first clients are usually friends and family members. While it may seem uncomfortable to a friend or relative to sign a contract or give you a deposit, you should resist the temptation to skip these steps. Make sure all your agreements are committed in writing. In many states, only contracts in writing are enforceable. A written contract will encourage your client to ask for additional services to be provided during the initial phase of your negotiations. Think carefully about the tone of your contract. While you want to protect your business, you could alienate potential business with an aggressive tone. You can still convey the same information without being antagonistic. Templates and examples of contracts can be found at **www. catersource.com**.

Always ask for a deposit up front. Any time you do not receive a deposit, you are in danger of cancellation, even at the last minute. Deposit policies vary; some caterers ask for one-third when booking, another third one month prior to the event, and the remainder on the day of the event. Alternatively, a cater may receive 10 percent on booking, up to 50 percent a month prior to the event, and the balance on the day of the event. Your terms will be dictated by your cash flow needs.

Basic Contract Stipulations and Considerations

The following list of stipulations and considerations is intended as a guideline only. It is by no means exclusive; it is intended to draw your attention to a few basic requirements. When developing your contract template, bear in mind the following.

- **Personal details.** When composing a contract, first include your name, address, phone and fax numbers. Next, enter the client's name, address, phone and fax numbers.

- **Dates and times.** After indicating the date of the contract, state the day and date of the event to be catered, as well as the starting and ending times for the party. The exact amount of time allocated to each activity is especially important; if the caterer runs into overtime, an overtime charge should be applied against the client.

- **Make sure to nail down the minimum number of guests.** Establish, as closely as possible, the exact number of people to be in attendance. If this isn't possible, ascertain at least the minimum number of guests. Build in a clause that permits you to raise the price per person should you end up catering for less than the estimated minimum number of guests. You also should include a clause indicated that you need final numbers by a particular date. Most caterers ask for the client to give them a final guest count three days before the event. This allows the caterer an appropriate amount of time to shop and prepare the correct amount of food.

- **Determine a method for tracking the number of guests.** Some common methods for tracking guest numbers include tickets, plates issued, bundled/rolled silverware with a napkin issued, and by a turnstile. Today, many events are preceded by invitations that request an RSVP. The RSVP allows you to have a more accurate guest count and can greatly help the caterer on what to anticipate. If you have an event that is not by RSVP, you still need to know how much food to prepare.

Here is an easy formula to determine how many guests will actually show up at the event:

Number of guests invited x 0.66 x 1.15 = number of guests to anticipate. For example: 300 invited guests x 0.66 x 1.15 = 228 anticipated guests.

The 0.66 accounts for the number of no-shows, and the 1.15 accounts for the uninvited guests that will arrive.

- **Guard your reputation.** Regardless of how you arrive at your number, remember that if the caterer runs out of food, it's the caterer's reputation at stake. The guests won't know that the host underestimated the count, nor will they care. They'll just know that they're hungry, there's no food left, and it's the caterer's fault! Overcome this dilemma by covering your costs for producing extra food. Let the clients know that they're always welcome to take home any unused portions. Generally, caterers have a guarantee number as well as a real number for the guest count. This guarantee usually runs between 3 and 5 percent of the total. In other words, if the event is set for 200 people, the caterer will prepare food for 206 if their guarantee number is 3 percent.

- **Include a section in the contract that details the menu to be served.** Nothing should be left out, and nothing should be assumed. If you need to make major changes to the menu, and you probably will, draw up a new contract.

- **Event price.** An event price is established at the same time the client is shopping for a caterer. The contract must state that the price is an approximate estimate only. Include a clause that permits the caterer to adjust the price, based on unforeseen conditions. Large events are booked approximately six months in advance. Smaller events may happen on much shorter notice, but most caterers have guidelines for the latest date they can accept a job. For instance, a caterer may stipulate that he or she will book up to three days prior to a small event.

- **Payment policy.** According to the schedule agreed upon, include a clause stating unequivocally the method and time frame for the payments. In general, the larger and more expensive the event, the larger the deposit.

- **Staffing.** Include a section in the clause that states the number of staff to be provided, the hours they will work, as well as applicable charges for their services.

- **Define your policies regarding leftover food and alcohol.** This often may partially be determined by the event. If you are catering a 40-person dinner party at a client's house, you are likely to box and leave the leftovers. If, on the other hand, you are catering a wedding reception for 150 at a rented hall, you will probably take the leftovers back with you and divide amongst the staff; all the leftovers, that is, except a to-go plate for the bride and groom.

This is a nice gesture since the bride and groom rarely get to eat! You should also state your policy on serving alcoholic beverages to minors or those people who become intoxicated.

- **Cancellation/Refund policy.** Discuss in detail your policy regarding cancellations and refunds.

- **Caterer and client signatures.** Don't forget: without the necessary signatures, the contract is not legally binding.

Cancellations And Refunds

In the event of a cancellation, should you refund some, all, or none of the deposit? In general, there are no clear-cut answers to this, and you should determine it on a case-by-case basis. The timing of cancellations is crucial in determining your policy. If someone cancels months before the event, you probably can rebook the date. If, however, the client cancels a week ahead of time, you will probably not be able to rebook and you may lose deposits you made on rentals or money you have already spent on food purchases.

Many event locations, such as hotels, community halls and convention centers, often have a step refund policy. If a client cancels three months before the event, for example, the facility will refund the entire deposit. If the event is canceled a month before the event, the facility will refund 50 percent of the deposit and if the booking is canceled a week to a month in advance, 35 percent of the deposit will be refunded. If the event is canceled within the week of its occurrence, no refund is issued. This type of step policy helps to offset some of the costs the off-premise caterer may have already absorbed.

When deciding on the fairest course of action for your own cancellation/refund policy, consider the following issues:

If the client cancels at least a month before the scheduled event, you may want to:

- Refund the full deposit. In fact, you can very well use this policy as a selling point when a client is trying to decide between you and another caterer, for example.

- If the event is scheduled within a month of cancellation, discuss the matter with the client personally.

- If the cancellation happens at the last minute due to a tragedy involving one of the principals, for instance, it is best to wait a period of time before getting the client to discuss refunds.

When you're not sure how to handle the cancellation, postpone your decision; tell the client that you have to check your figures to see how much money and time has already been invested. This will give you time to calculate a reasonable amount to pay for costs you've already made. Refund the rest.

Client's Refusal to Pay

If you run into a situation where a client just won't pay, the first step is to send a personal letter requesting payment. It's very likely that your client simply forgot. Make sure to gently remind the client of the amount due and give the client a reasonable due date, such as ten days, to pay the balance.

If this doesn't work, try calling the client. The next step would be to have your lawyer draw up and send a standard collection letter. While it may seem silly, people really do sit up and take notice when they receive a letter from a lawyer. Remember, while this tactic might result in payment, it is likely to cost you a lawyer fee as well.

If nothing else works, you can try small claims court. This process is time consuming but not very expensive. In most states, claims are usually limited to between $1,200 and $2,000. Remember, however, that nothing guarantees the judge will rule in your favor. And even if he or she does, you are not guaranteed immediate payment.

Another route to try for delinquent payments is a collection agency, but these agencies take a fairly large cut, so you may want to try all other alternatives first.

The best and most expeditious way to get the money you need to cover your costs is to prepare a solid refund and cancellation policy that addresses all of the issues discussed above.

Sample Contract Agreement

The following sample may help you draw up your own catering contract agreement. Use it as a guideline only, and consider obtaining professional legal advice.

DAPHNE'S CATERING

In consideration of the services to be performed by [insert Caterer's name here] ("Caterer") for the benefit of [insert Client's name here] ("Client") at the event scheduled for [insert event's date here], 200_, ("Event") as set forth in the attached invoice, Client agrees to the following terms and conditions:

1. In arranging for private functions, the attendance must be specified and communicated to Caterer by 12:00 p.m. (noon), at least seven (7) days in advance. If the actual number in attendance is greater than the amount confirmed, Caterer cannot guarantee that adequate food will be available for all persons attending. If the actual number is more than 20 percent less than the number confirmed, Caterer reserves the right to increase the price per person.

2. In order to reserve the date of the Event, Client must deliver a copy of this Agreement to Caterer along with a Deposit ("Deposit") of 50 percent of the invoice amount. The balance is due and payable no later than the day on which the Event is scheduled to be held.

3. If Client fails to make any payments when due, this Agreement may be cancelled or rejected by Caterer, and Client agrees that Caterer shall not thereafter be obligated to provide any services hereunder. Client agrees that Caterer may retain 50 percent of the Deposit, as liquidated damages and not as a penalty, which represents a reasonable estimation of fair compensation to Caterer for damages incurred by Caterer resulting from such failure to pay or cancellation by Client.

4. Menu requirements are to be followed as discussed and agreed upon with Client. All food and beverage is subject to ___ percent sales tax and ___ percent service charge. No beverages of any kind will be permitted to be brought into the premise by Client or any of the guests or invitees from the outside without the special permission of Caterer, and Caterer reserves the right to make a charge for the service of such beverages.

5. Performance of this Agreement is contingent upon the ability of Caterer to complete the same and is subject to labor troubles, disputes or strikes; accidents; government requisitions; restrictions upon travel; transportation; food; beverages; or supplies; and other causes beyond Caterer's control that may prevent or interfere with performance. In no event shall Caterer be liable for the loss of profit, or for other similar or dissimilar collateral or consequential damages, whether on breach of contract, warranty, or otherwise.

6. Client agrees to indemnify and hold harmless Caterer for any damage, theft, or loss of Caterer's property (including without limitation, equipment, plates, utensils, and motor vehicles) occurring at the Event that is caused by persons attending the Event.

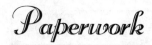

Now it's time to get down to the nitty gritty of event management. Once you have secured a contract, you'll have many details to attend to and there's a good amount of paperwork that can help you keep track of all these details.

EVENT ORDER SHEETS

Make sure to prepare an event order sheet and provide it to your service staff. This sheet will provide the staff with the information they need to make the function successful, and it will work as a list so they can double check their equipment and food.

An example of an order sheet follows. You can download a template of a worksheet from **www. restaurantbeast.com** and see another version of a similar worksheet on **www.wedoitallcatering.com**.

EVENT ORDER	
Customer:	Judith Jones
Contact:	Judith Jones
Phone:	555-555-5555
Event date:	12/14/06
Location:	J. Jones' house: 1516 Periwinkle Way
No. of guests:	60
Setup time:	5 p.m.
Event type:	Coworker Christmas dinner party
Schedule: 5 p.m. Caterer arrives 6 p.m. Guests arrive/serve appetizers/ open bar 6:30 p.m. Serve dinner 7:45 p.m. Serve dessert 9 p.m. Guests depart	**Rentals:** • Six 60" round linens • Six 10-foot rounds • Two 5-ft banquet tables for buffet

EVENT ORDER

Menu:

- Smoked salmon mousse on endive
- Fruit and cheese display with crackers
- New potatoes filled with sour cream and caviar
- Beef tenderloin glazed with reduced balsamic vinegar
- Wild mushroom cobbler
- Roasted green beans
- Bread and butter
- Individual chocolate soufflé cakes

Use and amend this sheet when you want to organize and plan for any special event.

CATERING AND EVENT CHECKLIST

Date of Event:		Time:	: am/pm to : am/pm	
Private or Open Event?		**Name of Party**		
DESCRIPTION OF EVENT				
Approx. Covers Last Event*:		**Sales Last Similar Event:**		$
Number of Guests:			* Approx. "Cover" formula: # of Seats x # of Hours	
MENU				

	PORTION PP	ORDER UNIT / PORTION #	ESTIMATED SERVINGS	AMOUNT TO ORDER / ADD TO PARS
Entrée				
1.				
2.				
3.				
Side Dishes				
Side 1				
Side 2				
Side 3				
Side 4				
Bread or Other				
1.				
Dessert				
1.				
2.				
3.				
Beverages				
1.				
2.				
3.				

CATERING AND EVENT CHECKLIST

CATERING AND EVENT CHECKLIST				
Other Ingredients/ Items to Order Increase				
1.				
2.				
3.				
4.				
5.				
6.				
7.				
8.				
9.				
10.				
11.				
12.				
13.				
14.				
15.				
16.				
17.				

CATERING AND EVENT CHECKLIST				
KITCHEN SETUP	**TIME TO DO**	**PERSON RESPONSIBLE**	**RETRIEVE ITEM FROM**	**PLACE ITEM WHERE?**
Product Prepping				
Prep Sheet Filled Out				
Prep Items Labeled				
Clean event area				
Equipment Setup				
Cooking Setup				
Tongs/#				
Spatulas/#				
Cold Side Dish Containers/ # plus backups				
Spoons for Cold Sides/ #				
Hot Dish Containers/ # plus backups				
Serving Spoons #				
Basting Brush				

Condiment Containers/ #				
Cold Holding Setup (40°)				
Aprons/#				
Food Handlers' Gloves				
Trash Cans Strategically Placed and Lined				
KITCHEN/ STAFFING PERSON	**POSITION**	**HOURS SCHEDULED**	**RATE**	**PRIVATE PARTY CHARGE?**

CATERING AND EVENT CHECKLIST

SERVICE SET-UP	TIME TO DO	PERSON RESPONSIBLE	RETRIEVE ITEM FROM	PLACE ITEM WHERE?
Table/Chairs Placement				
Tablecloths on Tables				
SERVICE SET-UP	**TIME TO DO**	**PERSON RESPONSIBLE**	**RETRIEVE ITEM FROM**	**PLACE ITEM WHERE?**
Condiments				
Beverages				
Cups				
Forks, Knives and Spoons				
Straws, Sugar, Cut Lemons				

GUEST BRINGING CAKE?				
Plates				
Cake Cutter				
Candles				

FULL BAR OR WINE?	Cash 'n Carry	Host Bar	Cork Fee?	Cost PP	$NA
Set Up Bar					
Register					

SERVICE STAFFING FOR EVENT/ PERSON	POSITION	HOURS SCHEDULED	RATE	CHARGE TO PARTY?
				NA
				NA
				NA
				NA
				NA
				NA
				NA
				NA
				NA
				NA
				NA
				NA
				NA
				NA
				NA
				NA
				NA
				NA
				NA
				NA

Make sure to record notes about the event; for example, if it is a public event, write down anything such as weather and product and staffing issues, and save in your event book for future reference.

BANQUET EVENT ORDERS

Most large caterers or those associated with a hotel or restaurant use Banquet Event Orders (BEO) to record the bar and buffet layouts, table settings, and other pertinent setup information. Many of these also include a room diagram. Smaller caterers would benefit from using these orders as well because small or large, a caterer lives and dies by the details.

In hotels, BEOs are prepared for each meal or beverage function and circulated to the affected departments a week or so before the event. They are usually sequentially ordered to help keep track of them.

A typical BEO contains the following information:

- BEO number
- Type of event
- Person who booked the event
- Beginning and ending time of event
- Menus
- Room setup
- Billing information
- Name of person preparing BEO

- Event date
- Client name and address
- Name of function room or event location
- Number of guests expected
- Style of service
- Prices charged
- Date BEO was prepared
- List of departments/persons receiving a copy of the BEO

- Special instructions (centerpieces, special accommodations, entertainment, etc.)

Following is a sample BEO:

THE MOVEABLE CHEF CATERERS BEO	
BEO #	16443
Date prepared:	6/2/05
Event date/ Event time:	8/9/05, 6 p.m. – 10 p.m.
Contact name and number:	Joe Smith, 555-555-5555
Event site:	Botanical Gardens
Group/type of event:	Parents' 50th anniversary
Count:	100
Moveable Chef contact:	Julie Krach
Billing:	50% deposit paid on 5/8/07; 50% by check on day of event

BANQUET SETUP

Set up area for cocktail area and appetizer display. Dinner will be buffet with 10 dining table rounds. Client will provide table linens, floral arrangements for buffet, and dining tables and decorations. Room will be decorated and ready for caterer by 4:30 p.m. on day of event.

THE MOVEABLE CHEF CATERERS
BEO

Appetizers

- Curried chicken salad in phyllo cups
- Cheese, fruit and cracker display with strawberries, grapes, brie, sharp cheddar, dill and Havarti, and assorted crackers
- Hummus and vegetables
- Smoked salmon and cream cheese rollups

DINNER

- Mixed green salad with champagne vinaigrette
- Smoked pork tenderloin with apple chutney
- Grilled chicken breast stuffed with leeks and mushrooms
- Roasted fingerling potatoes
- Haricot verts

DESSERT

- Client will provide anniversary cake. Servers to cut and serve with truffles and coffee.

SEATING

- There will be a head table with anniversary couple plus 8 other family members. Table to be round like other dining tables; place in front by stage.

ENTERTAINMENT

- Taped music for dinner (client will provide tape). A swing band will play after dinner.

Setting Up the Event

If you are doing on-site or off-site catering, you will need to be able to determine the number of people that can be seated in the room comfortably. Each setup also presents different challenges to the caterer servicing the function. There are common terms used in the catering industry for room setups as follows:

Banquet. This setup is used for weddings and most dinner and lunch events. It includes "rounds," which are round banquet tables that usually seat eight or ten people.

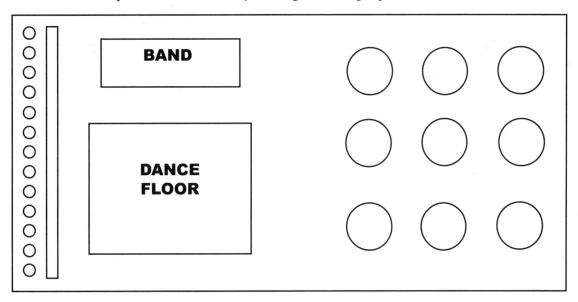

Classroom style. This setup is used for seminars and similar events. It is setup like a classroom with 6- or 8-foot long banquet tables facing the front of the room.

This setup is good for lectures and if you are going to use visual aids such as videos or PowerPoint. It is also good if you are going to be doing any testing of participants.

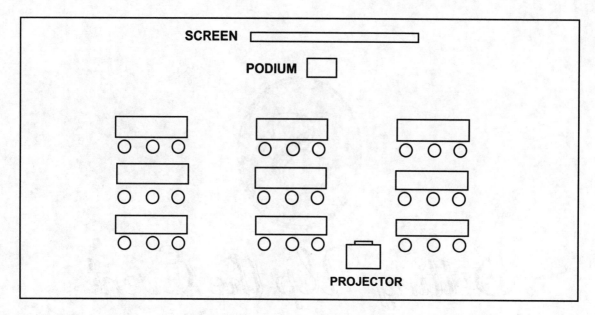

Boardroom style. This setup is often used for smaller meetings such as a board of directors' meeting. The room is usually setup with the participants around one large table. This setup works well for brainstorming activities and problem-solving exercises. It encourages informal conversation and active listening. If broken down into groups of small tables, this setup also works for group/team projects or discussions.

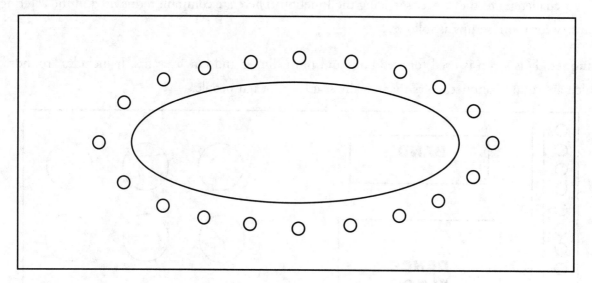

Theater style. This setup is the same as classroom style, but there are no tables, only chairs.

There are many variations on these basic setups, but there are some general conventions you will want to follow.

In a room that is set up specifically to be used for events, you want everything in your dining room setup to be symmetrical. Round tables should be evenly spaced and table legs should all be facing the same direction. Points of square tables should form a "V" shape over table legs. Also make sure your tables are of the same size.

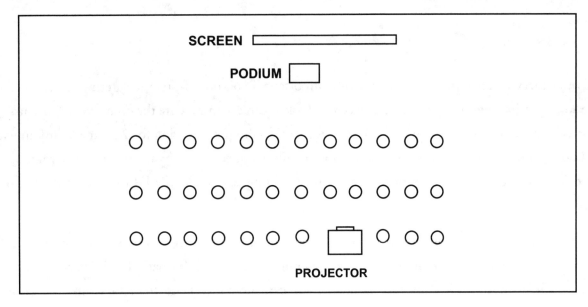

If you are catering a dinner in someone's home, this principle obviously will not hold true. When catering in a private home you will usually be using the client's furniture, and sometimes their dishes, so symmetry and likeness are less of an issue.

The typical dimensions for tables you can rent to use for catering functions in larger spaces are as follows:

- 60-inch round or 8-top—seats 6–10 guest

- 72-inch round or 10-top—seats 8–12 guests

- 66-inch round—seats 8–10 guests

- Banquet 6—30 inch by 6–foot rectangular table

- Banquet 8—30–inch by 8–foot rectangular table

- Schoolroom table—These rectangular tables are usually used for presentations or half of a buffet table. They are 18 or 24 inches wide and 6 to 8 feet long.

- Serpentine table—A crescent-shaped table usually used to make an oval-shaped buffet line. It is about one-fourth the size of a full round table.

- Half-moon table—A half–round table, usually used for the buffet line.

- Quarter-moon table—A quarter-round table, generally used as part of the buffet.

- Cocktail table—A small round table used for cocktail receptions. Sometimes chairs are used and sometimes just the tables. These are usually 18, 24, 30 or 36 inches in diameter.

- Oval—Usually measures 54 by 78 inches and is used for a dining table.

Tips for Room Setup

Always carry a calculator. This is especially important if you do off-premise catering. You'll need to do some math to figure out how each space you look at can accommodate the event you are discussing with clients. For example, if you are talking with a bride about a reception for 200 in a ballroom with 4,000 square feet, you have to determine how many banquet rounds you can fit in the room. You also need to account for space for the buffet, the wedding cake table, the DJ or band, a dance floor, and a bar.

If you only do on-site catering, once you know the size of your facility and how many people will fit in the various setups, all you have to do is keep a binder with this information in it. Keep this binder handy when meeting with potential clients so you can show the client different setups and options for the use of your facility's space.

Software. To help with room setups there are specialized software packages available. Most of the larger hotels use software that can determine room capacities. You can find event-planning software at **www.certain.com**. Their program Event Planner Plus costs $500. Along with creating room layouts, this software will track attendance, create a budget, track travel and lodging arrangements, compare vendor quotes, and create task lists. Another Web site, **www.catermate.com**, also offers software that can be used for room layouts, client tracking, event sheets, and more.

Accessories. Often the food is only part of an event. You will need to find out if this is the case. Does the event include a presentation or seminar? You will want to talk to the client about additional needs such as a podium, a riser for speakers, easels, projectors, lighting, head tables, and background music.

The main factors to keep in mind for room setup, whether you are catering on-site or off-site, are amount of floor space, room appearance, location and utilities.

FLOOR SPACE

The amount of floor space in a room is one of its most critical features to your clients. If you are an on-premise caterer, make sure you know the exact dimensions of the rooms you are using. If you are an off-premise caterer, get this information from the facility or guest, or bring a tape measure to get measurements yourself.

The space in a room affects every part of the event. Foremost, because of fire codes, the size of the room will determine how many guests the room can accommodate. The fire code maximum is a good guide to use when determining the available space for stand-up events like cocktails parities or sit-down events that require theater seating. Keep in mind that a buffet reception or sit-down dinner will require more space for tables and other equipment, so these events will accommodate fewer people.

TABLE ALLOWANCES

If you are hosting a sit-down dinner event, you should allocate 10 square feet per guest if using rectangular banquet tables for seating. If you are using rounds, you need to allow for 12.5 feet. And don't forget about aisle space. You, your guests, and your servers will need this for maneuverability. Aisles between tables and around food and beverage tables should be at least 48 inches wide. Cross aisles should be 6 feet. Also, tables should be at least 48 inches away from a wall. Don't forget about handicap seating, if you are expecting a disabled person at the event. Someone in a wheelchair will require more seating and aisle space.

Events such as weddings or retirement parties will often have a head table for the guest of honor. Head tables typically need 25 to 100 percent more space than regular dining tables.

DANCE FLOOR AND ENTERTAINMENT

If the event has a dance floor, you'll need approximately 3 square feet of dance floor per guest. If you are a smaller caterer, you can rent a floor that comes in 3 by 3-foot sections (you'll need one section for every three guests). For a band you will need about 10 square feet per band member. Drum sets, however, usually require 20 square feet. You may also want a riser for the band. Most of these are 4 by 4 feet or 4 by 8 feet.

You may need additional space depending on the type of entertainment and program the event has. You may need room for a podium and speaker, an audiovisual setup or strolling musicians.

CATERER'S SPACE

Along with guest space and entertainment space, you'll need to have a good idea of how much space you need for your own setup. If the event will have a cocktail reception and a meal, you will need space for both functions. For a reception area, you'll need about 6 to 10 square feet per guest.

BUFFET

If the event has a buffet, you'll need space for all the buffet tables. An 8-foot banquet table will need about 24 square feet for the table and 60 square feet for aisle room (100 if you need access from both sides of the table). To determine how many banquet tables you'll need, you need to know the menu, number of guests, length of time for dining service, type of service equipment required, style of service, and any flower arrangements that will go on the buffet. In general, you need about 2 feet of table to accommodate each dish. Style of service is very important in estimating the amount of space needed. French and Russian service each require twice as much space as others.

BEVERAGE STATIONS

For a nonalcoholic beverage station, such as a hot beverage station, you'll need a similar amount of space as you do for a buffet setup. Bars will require more space for ice, backup stock, coolers for beer and wine, and bartenders. The smallest amount of space that should be used for a bar is 42 square feet, but it's more likely you will need 150 square feet if you want the bar to function comfortably.

UTILITY SPACE

You should also plan space for tray jacks and side stands so guests have a place to discard empty plates and glasses. You may or may not want to include garbage cans in this space. These areas will need approximately 3 square feet of space.

Room Appearance

All clients are interested in the event room's appearance. Unlike restaurateurs, caterers serve people food only for special occasions. Therefore, the room must be special as well. These factors should be considered:

- Lighting
- Temperature
- Color

- Smell
- Sound
- Visibility

- Walls
- Layout

If you are an on-site caterer, you will be limited to whatever rooms your business has to offer. Usually there is some variety in size and décor of these rooms since most large operations want to attract a variety of business. If you are an off-site caterer, it is likely that the venue will be selected before you enter the process, so you will need to deal with whatever the client's choice is.

And while you may not have input on the room selection itself, you can have an effect on the setup. For example, if the event has a speaker and you need to setup a microphone and podium, be sure not to locate the podium next to an entrance. The comings of goings of guests will interrupt the speaker and the audience's focus on the speaker. If a video is being shown, try to setup the screen so the entrances to the room are on the sides of the screen. This way a latecomer won't have to walk in front of the projection.

The "perfect" room is highly subjective, so most of this will depend on what your client's taste is and what type of ambiance they are trying to create for the event. If it's a wedding, they are likely to want a room that can have the lights dimmed after dinner and that has warm, rich tones and a large space for dancing. If the event is a "Sweet 16" party, the client may want something brighter and they may not need as much floor space.

Guests tend to like to eat in a fairly well-lit room. Vibrant colors such as red, hot pink, and yellow stimulate the appetite. Darker colors such as dark green or blue tend to dull it. Table placement at receptions and buffets also affects food consumption. For example, an appetizer table that is placed against a wall only allows guest access from three sides. Therefore, if you are trying to cut down on the amount of appetizers or desserts you need to supply, you may want to consider positioning the appetizer or dessert table against a wall.

LOCATION

The farther an event room is from the preparation kitchen, the more difficult it becomes to offer unlimited option for foods. In a hotel or restaurant situation, this is less of an issue. Even so, if the event room is located at the other end of the building, it may be difficult to serve something like soufflés, which would likely deflate before they even hit the table.

For off-premise catering this is obviously more of an issue because food is often traveling across town rather than across the building. We'll discuss the logistics of off-premise catering in the next section.

DRINK AND BAR STATIONS

Bar setups are usually simpler than food setups, but you still need to keep a number of factors in mind. If you are just serving beer and wine, you will still need a place to store full and empty bottles, glasses, and devices for keeping beer and white wines cold. If the event requires a full bar, you will need to store additional glasses, bottles, mixers and garnishes.

Bar areas need to keep the following in mind:

- **Sufficient working space.** Make sure you have enough room for at least one bartender and one bar back.

- **Sufficient storage space.** Make sure you have enough space for all the stock, empties, paper products, garnishes, mixers and ice.

- **Prevent liquor access to minors.** Be sure to keep a bartender staffing the bar at all times. If a client does not want to hire a bartender and would rather just have guests help themselves, you might want to include a waiver of responsibility in your contract so that you are not responsible if a minor obtains alcohol.

- **Allow for proper accounting of drinks served.** How you account for alcohol served will depend on how you arranged this with your client in the initial contract. If it is a cash bar, you will want a register or ticket system in place. If the host is paying for all the beverages, make sure your bartenders are placing the empties in a particular area so you can go back and count them at the end of the event to determine how much the client should be charged.

Coffee service is probably the simplest and most profitable drink service you can provide. A coffee service area should include:

- Cups and saucers
- Regular coffee

- Decaf coffee
- An assortment of tea bags
- Lemons
- Spoons
- Hot water for tea
- Sugar and sweetener
- Cream
- Cocktail napkins

If you are hosting a morning event, make sure to have the coffee station setup bright and early. This is the first place people will seek out, and you'll definitely have a grumpy crowd on your hands if that first cup isn't ready when they are.

Keep in mind that your guests can drink 5 gallons of coffee in 15 minutes at a morning function, so keep the pots brewing.

Also, be sure to place coffee condiments such as cream and sugar off to the side. Adding these ingredients takes longer than filling a cup of coffee; placing them in front of coffee urns will just hold up the line.

Buffet Setup

Buffets are popular because they let the host offer their guests an array of foods to choose from and they are often less expensive than sit-down meals.

When setting up the buffet line, one trick to help food cost is to place lower-cost food items at the beginning of the line so guests fill their plates with these and will have less room for the more costly items. Also, try using a 9-inch dinner plate rather than 10-inch. Likewise, having a chef serve the more costly items, such as the prime rib, will cut down on the amount of food people will put on their plate since they are "being watched."

When deciding where to setup the buffet tables in a room, avoid doorways so you can prevent traffic jams.

CONFIGURATION

When setting up the table, you may want to consider setting up a double buffet line, depending on the number of guests. You can usually estimate 100 guests per buffet line. If the event is time-sensitive, however, such as a corporate lunch, you may want to bring this number down. For breakfast events, guests tend to arrive in twos or threes rather than a large group, so you can probably get by with one buffet line for every 100 guests. If you set up a buffet line for 50 guests, you can serve your guests in about 15 minutes. For an hors d'oeuvres/cocktail buffet event, you can estimate one hors d'oeuvres table for every 50 guests. You also may want to consider setting up a wider buffet line. If you have a lot of items, a long buffet table can be broken up with curved tables. You can also add height and drama to your buffet by placing cardboard boxes under the tablecloths. These little pedestals create wonderful areas to place beautiful dishes.

If you include an "action station"—a station that a chef will man throughout the event, serving guests directly—you will need to allot enough space for this. Usually these are placed at the end of a buffet or in an area by itself.

DISHES

When looking at the types of dishes to use on your buffet, do not try to include all servings in one dish. It is more attractive if you do smaller dishes because you can replace a half-eaten dish with a fresh one, making guests' dining experience much more pleasurable. In addition, guests will usually take smaller portions from smaller dishes, afraid that may be all there is. This will help ensure you don't run out of food and everyone gets at least one serving. Each dish should hold 25 to 30 servings, and your runners can replace the dishes throughout the event as necessary.

The dishes you use will depend on the event. You might rent a plain white set from the china rental company, or your client might want you to use his grandmother's china set for the event.

ACCESSORIES

Buffets are more than just the food in dishes on the table. Your buffet tables will also require linens and decorations. Depending on the event, you might need flowers or even an ice sculpture. If you have blanket spots on the table, fill them with flowers, napkins, dishes of fruit, or similar items. If the event has a theme, you will probably want the buffet decorations to echo this theme. For example, many brides have specific colors for their wedding. If you are catering a wedding reception, you will want to use these colors in linens and any floral arrangements.

You can make interesting centerpieces for your buffet and dining table with ribbons, baskets, candles, plants, or fresh or dried flowers.

You should also get skirting for buffet tables. If you work in a large hotel or restaurant, you will have access to this through the housekeeping department. If you are a smaller caterer, this is something you can get from the rental company that supplies your tables, china, silverware and glasses. Skirting usually comes with clips or Velcro for attaching the skirts to tables. Plastic clips are either standard or angled. Standard will fit a table with a 3/4-inch thick tabletop. Angled clips are used for tabletops 1/2-inch thick. You should attached clips every 2 feet to avoid sagging. Most skirting is 29 inches long, accommodating a 30-inch-high table.

If you are skirting an 8-foot buffet table, you will need 22 running feet (two 8-foot sides and two 3-foot sides equals about 22 running feet).

UTILITIES

The types of utilities available can be an issue for larger events or events with speakers, bands, or audio-visual presentations. Concerns about utilities available may include:

- Type of electricity
- Maximum lighting
- LCD, TV, radio, and DVD
- Maximum wattage
- Number of lighting controls in the room
- Paging system
- Number and types of electrical outlets, phone jacks, ISD outlets, built-in speakers

Dining Table Decor

Dining tabletops will need to be decorated beautifully for any event. The tabletops should echo the theme and formality or informality of the event itself. If there is a buffet, the dining tables will also complement the buffet décor. Each cover should have a place setting that includes a plate, silverware, napkin and glassware, depending on the event. If you have a buffet, however, you will not have plates set at the table; these will be picked up at the buffet.

NAPKINS

The napkin is a very import part of the place setting, and caterers should consider the napkin fold as well as the color.

Fold. You may want to create a fancy fold and place the napkin in the center of the plate, or you might want to do an accordion fold and fan the napkin out of the wine glass. If the event is casual, you may want to roll the silverware in a brightly colored napkin with an equally bright ribbon. Flat folds are usually good for outdoor events because of the wind.

Color. White is the most common color used, but you can play with color schemes, using light or dark colors as appropriate. You can also mix and match. For example, for a large group you may want to do half the table in black tablecloths with white napkins and the other half in the reverse color scheme. Don't limit yourself to only solid colors; sometimes a floral pattern or geometric pattern may be the right choice for an event. Remember to discuss these choices with your client. When renting or gathering your linen for an event, be sure you have linen and skirting for all buffet and service tables, linen for all dining tables, and dining napkins and beverage napkins. Depending on the event, these may be cloth or paper.

TABLETOPS

Make sure to pad the tabletops (and buffet tables) before covering them with tablecloths. This will help minimize the noise created by dishware. You can purchase padding fairly cheaply or talk to your rental company to see if it is something they can supply.

Like the buffet table, the choice of dining china is up to you and your client for each event. Work closely with your client to choose appropriate dishes for the event. If it is a graduation picnic, you won't want fine china, but if the event is a golden anniversary party, you might want to consider using some family china or something special from your rental company.

Table Presentation

When setting tables, be sure to adhere to the following etiquette.

The cover. This is the space—about 24 inches by 15 inches—within which one place is set with china, silver, linen and glass. An imaginary line may be drawn defining this area to assist in laying the cover.

Linen. A silence pad, if used, should be placed evenly on the table so that the edges do not hang down below the tablecloth. The tablecloth is laid over the silence pad or undercover or directly over the table with the center fold up and equidistant from the edges of the table. All four corners should fall an even distance from the floor. The cloth should be free from wrinkles, holes and stains.

When doily service is used, the doilies should be laid in the center of the cover, about 1 inch from the edge of the table. Silverware is placed on the doily.

FIGURE 1. "Table Cover Setup" using 16" x 12" doily and showing space allowance for a 24" cover arrangement.

1. Napkin

2. Fork

3. Bread and butter plate

4. Service plate

5. Water glass

6. Dinner knife

7. Teaspoon

8. Cup and saucer

The folded napkin is placed at the left of the fork, with open corners at the lower right and about 1 inch from the front edge of the table. For formal dinners when a service plate is used, the napkin may be folded and placed on the service plate.

Silver placement. Knives and forks should be laid about 9 inches apart, so that a dinner plate may be easily placed between them. The balance of the silverware is then placed to the right of the knife and to the left of the fork in the order in which it is to be used (placing the first used at the outside and proceeding toward the plate). The handles of all silver should be perpendicular to the table edge and about an inch from the edge. Forks are placed at the left side of the cover, tines pointed up. Knives are placed at the right side of the cover with the cutting edge turned toward the plate.

FIGURE 2. Cover arrangement for main breakfast course.

1. Plate of toast

2. Fork

3. Breakfast plate

8. Bread and butter plate

9. Water glass

10. Creamer

---

4. Knife	11. Coffeepot on underliner
5. Teaspoon	12. Sugar bowl
6. Saucer	13. Sugar spoon
7. Cup	14. Salt and pepper shakers

Spoons are laid, bowls up, at the right of the knives. The butter spreader is placed across the top edge or on the right side of the bread and butter plate, with the handle either perpendicular or parallel to the edge of the table, the cutting edge turned toward the butter plate. The butter spreader is properly used only when butter is served and a bread and butter plate is provided. Sometimes when a sharp steel-bladed knife is used for the meat course, a small, straight knife for butter is laid at the right of the meat knife.

Oyster and cocktail forks are placed at the extreme right of the cover beyond the teaspoons or laid across the right side of the service plate underlying the cocktail glass or the oyster service.

Silver for dessert service—the iced teaspoon and the parfait or sundae spoon—are placed just before the respective course at the right side of the cover. The dessert fork is laid at the right side of the cover if it is placed just before the dessert is served.

Breakfast or luncheon forks, salad forks and dessert forks are placed next to the plate in order of use; the spoons are arranged to the right of the forks, in order of use, beginning in each instance with the first course (on the outside) and working toward the center of the cover. When knives are not used in the cover, both the forks and spoons are placed to the right of the cover.

FIGURE 3. Cover arrangement when a dinner salad is served as separate course.

1. Plate of wafers   4. Bread and butter plate

2. Salad fork   5. Butter spreader

3. Salad plate   6. Water glass

China and glassware placement. The bread and butter plate is placed at the left of the cover, directly above the tines of the meat fork. The water glass is placed at the right of the cover, immediately above the point of the dinner knife.

Wine, liquor and beer glasses, if applicable, are placed to the right of the water glass. When a butter chip is used, it is placed to the left and on a line with the water glass, toward the center or left side of the cover.

Sugar bowls and salt and pepper shakers are generally placed in the center of small tables. When wall tables for two are set, the sugar bowl and shakers usually are placed on the side nearest the wall or the side nearest the room rather than in the center of the table. When an open-topped sugar bowl is used, a clean sugar spoon is laid to the right of the bowl.

When a large table is being setup and several sets of sugars and creamers are needed, the cream pitchers and sugar bowls may be placed at equal distances down the center of the table. Guests can more conveniently handle them if the handles are turned toward the cover. When several sets of salt and pepper shakers are used on a large table, they may be placed between the covers on a line parallel with the bases of the water glasses.

FIGURE 4. Cover arrangement for appetizer course of a formal dinner.

1. Napkin with hand roll in center   7. Dinner knife

2. Salad fork   8. Teaspoon

3. Dinner fork

4. Service plate

5. Underliner

6. Cocktail glass

9. Soup spoon

10. Cocktail fork

11. Water goblet

12. Salt and pepper shakers

FIGURE 5. Cover arrangement for dessert course for luncheon or dinner.

1. Dessert plate

2. Dessert fork

3. Teaspoon

4. Coffee cup and saucer

5. Water glass

6. Individual creamer

7. Ashtray

8. Sugar bowl

In addition to these conventions, the following rules should be observed.

- Napkins should be folded carefully with folds straight and edges even.

- Individual creamers should be washed and thoroughly cooled before being filled with cream. A container with a slender spout is used for filling if a cream dispenser is not available. Care should be taken not to fill creamers too full.

- Ashtrays should be collected and cleaned frequently, especially during the serving period; a clean one should be provided each time newly arrived guests are seated at the table.

- Serving trays should be kept clean and dry, to protect both the waitperson's uniform and the serving-table surface. The top of the tray should be wiped clean before it is loaded, to prevent the bottoms of the dishes from being soiled.

- Ice cubes or cracked ice should be clean and free of foreign matter; ice cubes should be handled with tongs and cracked ice with a special scoop or serving spoon. Ice should be transported in containers dedicated for ice only. Ice should be considered a food item.

- Butter pats need to be chilled and a pan of ice made ready before serving.

- Chairs should have crumbs dusted off after each guest has left. Backs, rounds and legs of chairs should be carefully dusted every day.

- Silver or stainless should be cleaned according to the special directions of the restaurant. When a cream polish is used, it should be rubbed with a soft cloth or a small brush over the surface and well into the embossed pattern of the silverware. Then the silver should be thoroughly washed, rinsed, and polished with a dry cloth to remove all traces of the silver cream.

HEAD TABLE ARRANGEMENT

If you are catering a wedding reception and have a head table, place the bride and groom at the center with the bride to the groom's left. The best man will go on the bride's left, followed by a bridesmaid, groomsman, etc. The maid of honor will be on the groom's right, followed by groomsman, bridesmaid, etc. Make sure you have enough room at the head table to accommodate the entire wedding party.

For centerpieces, mimic themes you have on the buffet tables, if there are any. Make sure these are aesthetically pleasing and appropriate for the event. There's nothing more annoying than sitting at a table at an event with a centerpiece that is eyelevel, making you unable to see the person you are talking to across the table, so be sure to consider height when you are deciding on centerpieces.

Flower arrangements are always popular centerpieces; but candles, breadbaskets, ice sculptures and knickknacks can be considered as well. If you are using fresh flowers, be sure to pick them up the day of the event so the flowers are still fresh and beautiful. Many caterers use a round mirror as a base for a centerpiece display. This reflects the flowers or flickering candles, creating a lovely atmosphere. If you use a mirror base, be sure it is smudge-free with no fingerprints!

General Rules for Table Service

Since there are several methods of table service, each food service unit must follow the method appropriate to its particular conditions, and each member of your serving staff must learn to follow the serving directions exactly so that service will be uniform throughout the unit. The following rules are approved by social custom:

- Place and remove all food from the left side of the guest.

- Place and remove all beverages, including water, from the right of the guest.

- Use the left hand to place and remove dishes when working at the left side of the guest, and the right hand when working at the right side of the guest. This provides free arm action for the server and avoids the danger of bumping against the guest's arm.

- Place each dish on the table, the four fingers of your left hand under the lower edge, and your thumb on the upper edge, of the plate.

- Never reach in front of the guest, nor across one person in order to serve another.

- Present serving dishes from the left side, in a position so that the guest can serve himself. Place serving silver on the right side of the dish, with the handles turned toward the guest so that he may reach and handle them easily.

- Do not place soiled, chipped or cracked glassware and china or bent or tarnished silverware before a guest.

- Hold silverware by the handles when it is laid in place. Be sure it is clean and spotless.

- Handle tumblers by their bases and goblets by their stems.

- Do not lift water glasses from the table to fill or refill; when they cannot be reached conveniently, draw them to a more convenient position.

- Set fruit juice and cocktail glasses, cereal dishes, soup bowls and dessert dishes on small plates before placing them in the center of the cover, between the knife and the fork.

- When it accompanies the main course, place the salad plate at the left of the forks, about 2 inches from the edge of the table. When the salad is served as a separate course, place it directly in front of the guest.

- Place individual serving trays or bread and rolls above and to the left of the forks. Place a tray or basket of bread for the use of several guests toward the center of the table.

- Place the cup and saucer at the right of the spoons, about 2 inches from the edge of the table. Turn the handle of the cup to the right, either parallel to the edge of the table or at a slight angle toward the guest.

- Set tea and coffeepots on small plates and place above and slightly to the right of the beverage cup. Set iced beverage glasses on coasters or small plates to protect tabletops and linen.

- Place individual creamers, syrup pitchers, and small lemon plates above and a little to the right of the cup and saucer.

- Place a milk glass at the right of and below the water glass.

- Serve butter, cheese and lemon wedges with a fork. Serve relishes, pickles and olives with a fork or spoon, not with the fingers.

More and more, food service operations are using booth or banquet-type seating. It is extremely difficult to carry out proper table service in these situations. The general rules for booth service are as follows:

- Serve everything with the hand farthest from the guest; use your right hand to serve a guest at your left and your left hand to serve your guest to your right.

- Remove soiled plates with the hand nearest your guest while substituting the next course with the hand farthest from your guest.

Breakfast Service

Good breakfast service is important because guests are not always at their best in the morning. Foods served for breakfast are most palatable when they are freshly prepared and when they are served at the correct temperature. Often you will want to serve breakfast in courses unless your client especially requests that the whole meal be served at once. Cooked foods and hot beverages should be brought to the guests directly from the serving station and under no circumstances allowed to remain on the serving stand to cool while the customer finishes a preceding course.

Order of service for breakfast:

1. When fresh fruit or fruit juice is ordered, it is desirable to serve it first, and then to remove the soiled dishes before placing the toast and coffee.

2. When customers order a combination of cooked fruit, toast and coffee, they may ask to have the whole order served at once. Place the fruit dish, set on an underliner, in the center of the cover, the plate of toast at the left of the forks, and the coffee at the right of the teaspoons.

3. When the breakfast order includes cereal and a hot dish, the service procedure may be as follows:

   a. Place the fruit course in the center of the cover.

   b. Remove the fruit service.

   c. Place the cereal bowl, set on an underliner, in the center of the cover. Cut individual boxes of cereal partway through the side near the top   so the guest may open them easily.

   d. Remove the cereal service.

e. Place the breakfast plate of eggs, meat or other hot food in the center of the cover. Place the plate of toast at the left of the forks. Place the coffee service at the right of the spoons.

f. Remove the breakfast plate and the bread plate.

g. Place the finger bowl, filled one-third full of warm water. At times the finger bowl is placed after the fruit course when fruits that may soil the fingers have been served.

Luncheon Service

Catering luncheons may have time restraints due to guests having to return to work. If this is the case, make sure your service is efficient but not rushed.

Order of service for luncheons:

1. Fill the water glasses three-fourths full of iced water.

2. Place chilled butter on a cold bread and butter plate.

3. Place the appetizer in the center of the cover.

4. Remove the appetizer when the guest has finished.

5. Place the soup service in center of cover.

6. Remove the soup service.

7. Place entrée plate in center of cover.

8. Place individual vegetable dishes (if used) above the cover.

9. If salad is served with the main course, place the salad at the left of the forks, about 2 inches from the edge of the table.

10. Place tray or basket of bread and rolls at the left of the salad plate.

11. Place hot beverages above and a little to the right of the cup and saucer, with individual creamer above the cup.

12. Place an iced beverage or milk at the right and a little below the water glass.

13. Remove the main-course dishes.

14. Remove any extra silver not used for the main course.

15. Crumb the table, if necessary.

16. Place dessert silver to the right of the cover, with fork nearest the dessert plate, if fork and teaspoon are used. When several teaspoons are placed, the dessert fork may be laid on the left side, to "balance the cover."

17. Place the dessert service in the center of the cover.

18. Serve hot coffee, if requested.

19. Remove dessert dishes and silver.

20. Place the fingerbowl on the underliner (when one is used) in the center of the cover.

Dinner Service

Catered dinners are often the most leisurely of all the meals. Although the guests should be allowed plenty of time to complete each course, long waits between courses should be avoided. Your serving staff should watchfully observe the guests during the meal in order to serve the next course promptly and to comply with any requests made by the guests for special service.

Order of service for dinner:

1. From the left, place the appetizer or hors d'oeuvres service in the center of the cover. A tray of canapés and hors d'oeuvres is often offered to the guest. In this case, an empty plate should first be placed before the guest and the tray of hors d'oeuvres then offered.

2. Remove the first-course dishes.

3. Place the soup service in the center of the cover.

4. Remove the soup service.

5. When the entrée is served on a platter, place it directly above the cover. Lay the serving silver at the right of the platter. Place the warm dinner plate in the center of the cover.

6. When plate, or "Russian," service is used, place the dinner plate in the center of the cover.

7. Place salad at the left of the forks when it is served with the main course.

8. Place beverages to the right of teaspoons.

9. Offer rolls or place them to the left of the salad plate.

10. Remove the main-course dishes when the guest has finished.

11. When salad is served as a separate course following the main course, place the salad fork at the left and the salad plate in the center of the cover.

12. Remove the salad service.

13. Crumb the table if necessary.

14. Place silver for the dessert course.

15. Place the dessert service in the center of the cover.

16. Serve hot coffee or place the demitasse.

Special attentions to observe when serving:

1. Serve hot food hot, on heated dishes.

2. Serve cold food chilled, on cold dishes.

3. Inquire how food is to be cooked:

    a. Eggs: fried or boiled, how many minutes.

    b. Steak: rare, medium or well-done.

    c. Toast: buttered or dry.

4. Refill water glasses whenever necessary during the meal.

5. Serve extra butter when needed.

6. Refill coffee on request and according to management policies. Bring more cream if necessary.

7. Serve granulated sugar with fresh fruit and unsweetened iced drinks.

8. Place silver necessary for a course just prior to serving.

    a. Soup spoons on extreme right of teaspoons.

    b. Cocktail fork to right of soup spoon.

9. Offer crackers, melba toast and other accompaniments or relishes with appetizer and soup courses, according to policies of management.

10. Provide iced teaspoons for ice drinks and place parfait spoons when a parfait is served. Place soda spoons and straws with malted milks, milkshakes and ice cream sodas.

Clearing the Table

The following are standard procedures for clearing tables:

1. After any course, dishes should be removed from the left side, except the beverage service, which should be removed from the right.

2. Platters and other serving dishes should be removed first when clearing the table, or they may be removed as soon as empty.

3. The main-course plate should be removed first, the salad plate next, followed by the bread and butter plate.

4. The empty milk or beverage glass is removed from the right side after the main course.

5. The table should be crumbed by using a small plate and a clean, folded napkin. This is especially important when hard rolls or crusty breads are served.

6. Hot tea and coffee service should be left on the table until the completion of the dessert course.

7. The water glass should remain on the table and be kept refilled as long as the guest is seated.

8. Replace soiled ashtrays with clean ones as often as necessary throughout the meal.

When a guest is seated at a table and it is necessary to change a soiled tablecloth, turn the soiled cloth halfway back, lay the clean cloth half open in front of the guest, and transfer the tableware to the clean cloth. The soiled cloth may then be drawn from the table and the clean one pulled smoothly into place. If this exchange of linen is accomplished skillfully, the guest need not be disturbed unduly during the procedure. Soiled linen should be properly disposed of immediately after it is removed from the table

Event Timing and Staffing

Service timing is a critical function during events. You will already have discussed this with your client before the event. It is important that during the event this timing flows without a catch and no bottlenecks interrupt the flow of service.

About 15 minutes before meal service, you should start calling the guests. You can do this by having the host make an announcement, servers can circulate through the room to let the guests know the meal is beginning, or you can dim the lights or ring chimes. In general, a salad course will take 20 to 30 minutes and an entrée will take 30 to 50 minutes from the time the platters are served to the time they are removed. Desserts are usually finished in 20 to 30 minutes. A typical banquet service will generally wrap up in 1.25 hours for lunch and 2 hours for a dinner event.

STAFFING THE EVENT

Once you have all the details for an event, you'll want to start thinking about staffing. If you operate a large organization, you may have several events on one day and you might need to do some juggling. Even if you are a smaller operation, you may need to juggle schedules. If you hire freelance servers, for instance, these individuals will have catering events that they work for other establishments as well, so be sure to arrange serving and cooking staff early so you don't get left in the lurch with no one to serve the guests.

Depending on the type of event, you will need to schedule the following types of positions:

- Food captain
- Food server
- Cocktail server

- Food runner
- Bus person
- Bartender or sommelier

Service personnel are responsible for a wide variety of tasks, including the following:

- Napkin folding
- Table setting
- Bar setup
- Serving food and beverages
- Opening wine bottles
- Hot and cold beverage service
- Busing tables
- Tableside preparation
- Handling last-minute requests
- Dealing with intoxicated guests
- Directing guests to other areas of facility, such as restrooms and places to put gifts

- Table setup
- Buffet setup
- Presetting food on dining tables
- Taking orders from guest for drinks or food
- Pouring wine
- Crumbing tables
- Carrying trays of food
- Handling complaints
- Taking coats

The number of servers you will need for a particular event depends on a number of factors:

- Length of party
- Number of guests
- Style of service

- Menu
- Timing of event
- Room setup

If you are serving a large luncheon for corporate executives, for example, you will need a large waitstaff. A wedding reception is also likely to require a large staff. For other parties you and one server may be enough. If you are catering a buffet brunch for a bar mitzvah, for example, you could replenish and serve the buffet, bring an assistant to work in the kitchen, and have one server clean up and get drinks for guests.

Consider this example: You are catering a wedding reception for 100 people with a large selection of hot and cold hors d'oeuvres, a buffet dinner with roasted salmon and cucumber sauce, seared beef tenderloin with horseradish sauce, green salad, bread, wild rice pilaf, roasted vegetables, and wedding cake. The hot hors d'oeuvres will be passed and the salads will be preset on the tables. There will be two bars: one for alcoholic drinks and one for soda, iced tea and water. Champagne and cake as well as after-dinner coffee will be served while the guests are seated.

For this type of function you will need a kitchen manager and cook for a few days before the party as well as a pastry chef if you are making the wedding cake (most caterers hire this function out to bakeries that specialize in wedding cakes). On the day of the event you will need two bartenders and three servers who will also bus and break down the tables.

Regardless of the situation and event, do not to skimp on service staff. Catered events are generally special occasions, and people want quality service for their event. By skimping, you run the risk of substandard service and an unhappy client.

The minimum number of service staff you need can vary from 1 server for every 8 guests to 1 server for every 40 guests, depending on the style of service. The minimum you should use for a sit-down dinner with American-style service is 1 server for every 20 guests. You can have one server take two rounds of ten people. If you are using bus people, you can schedule one bus person for every two servers.

If the event uses a more elaborate service style, such as Russian, you will need 1 server for every 16 guests. If it is a buffet event, you can have 1 server for every 40 guests. However, you need servers to replenish the buffet table so you may want to schedule a food runner for every 100 to 125 guests.

If the event is large, you will also want to position yourself as, or hire, a captain to oversee the activity in the dining areas. The rule of thumb is to schedule 1 captain for every 250 guests.

UNIFORMS

The more formal your catering business, the more dressed up your staff should be. Having uniformed staff catering an event is more businesslike and professional. In fact, it gives the staff a sense of belonging. Make employees feel that they're members of an identifiable team. Clearly, the smartest and classiest type of outfit for catering staff is a white tuxedo shirt, black pants and a bow tie (usually black). At the very least you should have aprons printed with your company's name and logo. Here are some general suggestions about choosing the right style of uniform for your catering operation.

Management. As the owner or manager, you have the choice of wearing the same uniform as your staff. Preferably wear something that indicates you're the boss. Consider a red cummerbund and a different-colored bow tie.

Kitchen staff. Chefs, cooks and kitchen personnel should be in white shirts, coats and aprons. Hats or caps are a must.

Waiters/Waitresses. The traditional uniform for waiters and waitresses is black pants or skirt with a white shirt and a black bow tie.

Part-timers. Part-timers are generally required to maintain their own uniforms. Either have your staff buy the necessary garments or buy a supply yourself. Give a set to each new staff member, but be wary of deducting the cost from their paychecks.

Spare garments. Have a few extra tuxedo shirts and pants available for emergencies. Staff will appreciate your thoughtfulness.

Sample Catering Dress Code:

- Black skirt/pants and white tux shirt
- Hair pulled back
- Black socks for men
- Conservative makeup for women
- Dark, clean, shiny shoes
- No earrings for men
- Short and clean nails

General appearance and hygiene. Insist that employees their uniforms at the start of their shift. Make it a routine that they wash their hands thoroughly before handling or serving food and that they keep their hands away from their faces and hair at all times. You are perfectly within your rights to ask staff to use an unscented deodorant and an antiseptic mouthwash in addition to brushing their teeth frequently.

Your staff are the ones who leave a lasting impression on the guests. Regardless of how well your customer service has been with your client, if the client's guests are not happy, your client will not be happy either. First impressions are lasting, and you must remember that you are marketing your services at every event you cater. One great comment from a guest can lead to many referrals, but one even slightly poor comment could blacklist you from many more events and possibilities.

Calculating Food Amounts

This is one of the most difficult calculations a caterer has to make. While there are some general principles to follow, your knowledge of human nature will guide you through this process as well.

In general, the rule of thumb is 1 to 1.5 pounds of food per person, but this rule can vary significantly depending on the type of event you are catering.

If you are catering a wedding reception, people will expect a good amount of food. If, however, you are catering a corporate lunch, you might expect to prepare less for the same number of people. People tend to eat lighter for lunch, and in a corporate setting, less emphasis is be placed on the actual food being served.

Hors d'oeuvres are probably the most difficult aspect of an event to determine a food amount for. The amount depends on a number of factors including the type of hors d'oeuvres you serve, the time of day, how long of a time lapse there is between cocktail hour and dinner, and if there even is a dinner to follow at all.

If you are serving a meal as well as hors d'oeuvres, try to keep appetizer/cocktail hour to just that–an hour. You should have at least four different types of appetizers with six to eight pieces per person, so for a party of 50, have about 350 to 400 hors d'oeuvres total. If you are not serving a meal, you will obviously want more. Increase the ratio to 12 to 15 pieces per person for these parties.

If you are serving hors d'oeuvres that do not come per piece, such as dips and cheese platters, calculate about one ounce as one piece. Usually for 100 people with a variety of hors d'oeuvres, you'll want 2 ounces of cheese person (12.5 pounds). You can either do this as a variety of cheeses on a cheese bard with grapes and strawberries and crackers, or you might want to do a baked Brie in phyllo crust and goat cheese or blue cheese in phyllo cups with sun-dried tomatoes and toasted nuts.

The following chart will help you determine amounts for other courses you may be serving at parties. It is based on a buffet menu, so remember that at most events that include a buffet, people will tend to take a little of each item served. If you are planning a sit-down event, use the following as loose guide to portions.

FOOD		INDIVIDUAL PORTION SIZE	FOR 50 BUFFET GUESTS
Soup	As first course	8-10 oz	2½ gallons
	As entrée	1½ – 2 cups	4 gallons
Green salads	Romaine	¼ head	8 heads
	Red leaf	⅓ head	12 heads

FOOD		INDIVIDUAL PORTION SIZE	FOR 50 BUFFET GUESTS
	Tomatoes, cucumber, radish, etc	3–4 slices	6 cups
	Salad dressing	1–2 tablespoons	1½ quarts
Poultry entrée	Boneless	½ pound	14–16 pounds
Beef, lamb or pork entrée	Boneless beef roast	½ pound	14–16 pounds
	Bone-in roast	14–16 ounces	30 pounds
	Steaks	16–24 ounces	30 pounds
	Ribs	1 pound	28–32 pounds
	Lamb	4 chops	84–98 chops
	Ground meat	½ pound	14–16 pounds
Seafood/ Shellfish	Soft shell crab	2	50
	Fillet	6–8 ounces	16 pounds
	Shrimp	5–7 (large)	14 pounds (large)
	Lobster	5–6 ounces medallion meat or 1 lobster	12½ pounds medallion meat
	Scallop	4–6 ounces	10 pounds
	Oysters/Mussels/Clams	6–10 as entrée 4–6 as appetizer	200–325 as entrée 160–240 as appetizer
Vegetables	Asparagus, broccoli, cauliflower, green beans, carrots	3–4 ounces	8 pounds
	Potatoes	1 (5–6 ounces)	12 pounds
	Eggplant	⅓	12 (medium)
	Corn, peas, lima beans	3–4 ounces	7 pounds
	Zucchini, yellow squash	4–5 ounces	8 pounds
Grains	White rice (dry)	3–4 tablespoons	2½ quarts

FOOD		INDIVIDUAL PORTION SIZE	FOR 50 BUFFET GUESTS
	Brown or wild rice (dry)	2–3 tablespoons	2 quarts
	Beans (dried)	¼ cup	2 quarts
	Couscous	⅓ cup	2½ quarts
	Polenta	⅓ cup	2½ quarts
Pasta	Dry	2–3 ounces	6 pounds
	Fresh	4 ounces	8 pounds
	Stuffed pasta (tortellini, ravioli, etc.)	4–5 ounces	10 pounds
Pasta Sauce	Cream	½ cup	5 quarts
	Tomato based	½ to ⅔ cup	1½ gallons
Casseroles	Quiche	One, 4-inch slice	Four 10-inch tarts
	lasagna	1–1½ cups	Three 13" x 9" pans (32–48 cups)
Breads	Dinner rolls, muffins, croissants, etc.	1½	7 dozen
Dessert	Ice cream	6 ounces	2 gallons
	Sheet cake	One 2"x2" piece	1/2 sheet cake
	Cheesecake	One 2" slice	Four 9-inch cakes
	Pie	One 3-inch slice	Four 9-inch pies
	Bar cookies	1–2	5½ to 6 dozen
	Cookies	2–3	6–8 dozen
	Mousse	¾ cup	Four 8"x5" bowls
	Bread pudding, tiramisu	1 cup	Four 9"x5" bowls

You never want to be caught with not enough food—whenever you are uncertain, always side with more food rather than less. If you run out of food, the negative reaction will always outweigh the extra cost you would have incurred had you bought more food.

Beverage Functions

Beverage functions are usually part of a food event. Most include both alcoholic and nonalcoholic beverages. At the least, these would be accompanied by appetizers. Most clients see the beverage function as a way for guests to mingle and socialize at the event before the meal.

For formal/traditional beverage functions, you may want to stick to the tried and tested. For this type of function, most clients prefer a standard drinks menu: red and white wine, a domestic light and regular beer, some soft drink brands, drink mixtures, and at least one brand of each Scotch, gin, vodka, bourbon, rum, tequila and Canadian whiskey.

Cater to today's preferences for reduced alcohol or alcohol-free beverages as well. Current trends indicate a decline in the sale of alcoholic beverages, particularly hard liquor, with a corresponding increase in the sales of light, import and microbrew beers, as well as specialty drinks.

Tastes vary depending on location and audience. Be aware that there are geographic differences in the consumption of spirits. For instance, the number of drinks consumed on average per person at a black-tie gala with reception and dinner, in Las Vegas is 5.5, in Chicago it's 5.0, and in San Francisco it's only 2.5 drinks per person.

Beverage Menu Planning

In order to plan effectively for a beverage event, the caterer needs to discuss priorities with the client beforehand. For instance, is the main purpose purely social where guests can recharge their batteries, or is it designed to offer an opportunity for networking? Whether beverage service is scheduled to take place before or after a meal will also affect the types of drinks to be served at the function. Clarify all these issues with your client. This way you'll be able to suggest the beverage menu that exactly meets their requirements.

Off-premise caterers, in particular, must be knowledgeable about the brands and qualities of various beverages. Clients are guaranteed to ask for your advice. Expertise in this area may mean the difference between being selected or rejected by the client.

When planning a beverage event, make sure you take into account the demographics of the group. For example, women will usually drink less than men, and typically women will prefer wine or clear liquor, where men will prefer darker liquor and beer.

To calculate required beverage quantities, use the following formula:

Total Ounces = # of Guests x Average # of Drinks per Person x Ounces per Drink

To work out the total quantity, divide the total ounces by the bottle size.

For soda and juices, take the total number of bottles of spirits and multiply by 3.

For ice, use two to three pounds per person.

HARD LIQUOR AND WINE

At a reception, the average person will consume three hard liquor drinks or three glasses of wine. If you have a 100-person party, plan on 50 percent of the people drinking wine, so you will need 30 750-ml bottles of wine. Current trends also suggest that 30 to 40 percent of the people drinking wine will drink red wine. For the same party, plan on ordering the following in hard liquor.

# OF BOTTLES	TYPE
1	Gin
1	Canadian whiskey
3	Vodka
2	Scotch
1	Rum
2	Bourbon
1	Brandy/Cognac

BEER

A barrel of beer contains 31 gallons, or the equivalent of 13.8 cases of 12-ounce bottles (24 bottles to a case and 2.25 gallons per case). Typically, the kegs of draft beer that are used at most on-premise establishments are actually half-barrels. Assuming a one-inch head, there are approximately 200 12-ounce servings per keg or about 150 16-ounce servings, varying slightly with the type of glass used.

NONALCOHOLIC

You should also plan to have sparkling water, fruit juices, tonic, club soda, sugar-free beverages, iced tea, nonalcoholic beer and wine, and sodas. When establishing the drink menu, be sure to check with your client on whether or not there are certain brands of liquor or certain types of beer or wine they prefer. Some clients will be very specific; others will want you to make those decisions.

Pricing

Most clients are more concerned about the price per drink, price per bottle, and labor charges than about the specific brand names to be served at the catered event. The most common pricing procedures are a cash bar, an open bar, a combination cash and open bar, and a limited–consumption bar.

At a cash bar guests get drinks themselves and pay for them at the bar. Some hosts will subsidize the price per drink and then have their portion added to the catering bill.

An open bar means that guests do not pay for their drinks. For this type of bar, the host picks up the tab and the total is added to the catering charge.

A combination bar allows guests to have a certain number of drinks that the host pays for, and the guest is responsible for paying for all subsequent beverages. The combination bar is becoming increasingly popular, as it is a good way to limit liability for the host while still being gracious and providing some alcoholic beverages at no expense to the guests.

A limited-consumption bar is priced by drink. The host decides how much he or she can afford and when the cash register meets that amount, the bar closes. Of course, the bar can reopen as a cash bar if so desired.

There are various ways for the caterer to charge for drinks:

- Per drink
- Per hour
- Per person
- Flat rate
- Per bottle

PER DRINK

Cash bars that are subsidized by the host generally use the per-drink method. If this method is used, the bartender keeps a tally and the portion the client is picking up is presented as part of the bill. Alternatively, the guests will simply be charged the per-drink charge throughout the event.

Prices are generally set according to a cost percentage. Hard liquor is typically based on 12 to 18 percent and wines and beers are priced to yield a cost percentage of 25 percent.

Here's an example of drink prices to consider for an event:

Well drinks	$4.50
Premium brands	$5.00
Wine by the glass	$4.00
Domestic beer	$3.00
Imported beer	$3.50
Soft drinks	$1.50
Bottled waters	$1.50

PER BOTTLE

For open bars the most common charging method is by the bottle. To use this method, you'll need to take a starting inventory of your beverages before the event and compare this to the end inventory. This method generally is a little less expensive for the client.

PER PERSON

Generally, you will calculate an average consumption level that takes into consideration the amount and type of drink consumed and then charge the host a per-person fee.

PER HOUR

The per-hour method is similar to the per-person method, but you'll usually include a sliding scale for this method. For example, the host might pay $1,000 for the first hour of the event, then $500 each for the last two hours. Make sure you keep the number of guests in mind when using this method.

FLAT RATE

A flat-rate charge is based on the assumption that guests will have two drinks each during the first hour of the event and one drink for each hour following. Be careful with this method: sometimes you win and sometimes you lose.

Regulating Beverage Service

No matter how you charge for drinks, it is a good idea to regulate the amount of alcohol per drink and maintain an accurate inventory. Drinks need to be mixed properly so customers do not complain about drinks that are too strong or too weak. In addition, over-pouring and spillage can seriously reduce your profits.

ALCOHOL INVENTORY CONTROL

If you decide to maintain a beverage or liquor inventory, you should take steps to ensure accuracy. This way you will avoid running out at events and can also circumvent other problems such as employee theft. Check out the following options:

- **AccuBar** is an excellent example of a computerized inventory system. Customers report a 50 to 80 percent time savings when using the AccuBar system. It's easy to learn: most users are up and running within 30 minutes. The patented technology eliminates the need to estimate levels; simply tap the fluid level on the bottle outline. Once you tap the bottle outline, data entry is complete. There is no further human intervention. Since no data entry or third party is involved, reports are generated immediately. It also provides a running perpetual inventory. Transfers between locations and returns of defective items are also covered. AccuBar also helps gauge which items aren't selling, allowing you to consider stocking something else that might bring a better return. AccuBar also recommends what needs to be ordered from each supplier based on current perpetual, par and reorder points.

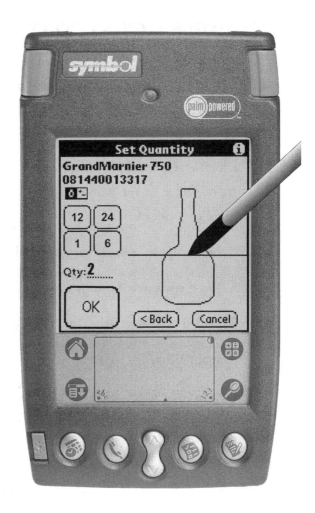

The order is totally customizable. When a shipment arrives, simply scan the items, and any discrepancy from what was ordered is caught immediately. AccuBar can also track food, glassware, china, and other essentials.

- **The Accardis Liquor Inventory System** is another option to save time and money and eliminate over-pouring and theft. Since 1987, Accardis Systems has been controlling liquor inventory costs. Accardis was the originator of scanning and weighing bottles to control inventory. The alcohol inventory system has proven to be fast and accurate. It will lower your costs while increasing your profits. Most clients recover the cost of the liquor inventory system in only a few months. The Cyclops Falcon scans and weighs liquor bottles electronically and then downloads the data to our PACER 4.0 for Windows software. Pacer prints out all the management reports on a station-by-station basis. The liquor inventory system also tracks all purchases and requisitions and can be used for liquor, beer, wine, supplies, hats, T-shirts, etc. Cyclops Falcon gives the user complete control of beverages at a fraction of the cost of most other systems. For more information, contact Accardis Systems, Inc., 20061 Doolittle Street, Montgomery Village, MD 20886. Call 1-800-852-1992 or visit **www.accardis.com**.

ALCOHOL SERVING CONTROL

Once your inventory is managed, you should also address alcohol service. From beer to mixed drinks, there are a number of products available to reduce waste and spillage. Here are some options:

- **Liquor-control systems (LCS).** The use of technologically advanced portion-control systems is becoming increasingly commonplace in today's drinks industry. LCSs are particularly effective at controlling liquor costs. They can also virtually eliminate employee theft. LCSs are marketed on the basis of a typical return on investment within 12 months. The following suppliers offer LCSs:

  Berg Company • **www.berg-controls.com** • 608-221-4281

  AzBar • **www.azbaramerica.com** • 214-361-2422

  Bristol BM • **www.bristolnf.com/liquor.htm** • 709-722-6669

  Easybar Beverage Management Systems • **www.easybar.com** • 503-624-6744

- **Easybar Beverage Management Systems** has multiple solutions for beverage portion control. The Easybar CLCSII is a fully computerized beverage-dispensing system that controls beverage pour sizes, improves bartender speed, and ensures perfectly portioned drinks and cocktails. This system also prevents product loss by eliminating over-pouring, spillage, breakage and theft. It accounts for all beverages dispensed through the system 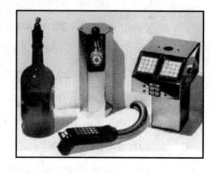 and boosts receipts by lowering costs and increasing accountability. Also available is the Easypour Controlled Spout System. This offers control for drinks that are dispensed directly from a bottle. The controlled pour spouts allow only preset portions to be dispensed and will not allow drinks to be dispensed without being recorded. Easybar's Cocktail Station creates cocktails at the touch of a button. The cocktail tower can dispense up to 48 liquors plus any combination of 10 juices or sodas. It mixes cocktails of up to five ingredients, and ingredients dispense simultaneously to cut pour time. All ingredients dispense in accurate portions every time.

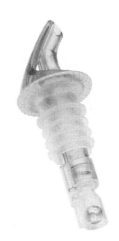

- **Precision Pours** (**www.precisionpours.com**) manufacturers measured liquor pours, gravity-feed portion control systems, and bar accessories. By eliminating over-pour and spillage with the Precision Pour™ 3 Ball Liquor Pour, users save money on every bottle served. If your bartender over-pours just 1/8 ounce per drink, your loss could be up to four drinks per bottle. The Precision Pour™ 3 Ball Liquor Pour allows bartenders to pour liquor with one hand while mixing with the other, speeding up drink production. Also, since there is no need to use a messy shot glass, additional time is saved on cleanup.

- **Look into ready-made bar mixers.** These can save a tremendous amount of time and preparation. Zing Zang manufacturers a complete lines of bar mixers. Visit **www.zingzang.com** for details or to view their product line.

WINE CONTROLS

- **Winekeeper** produces a line of dispensing and preserving systems for wine. Their use makes enjoying fine wine an extended and pleasurable experience. Winekeeper units consist of handcrafted, custom-quality cabinetry and employ proven nitrogen gas preservation technology. Single bottle units to larger commercial units are available. Custom applications, designs and finishes are available. For more information contact Winekeeper at 625 E. Haley Street, Santa Barbara, CA 93103, phone 805-963-3451, or visit **www.winekeeper.com**.

- **OZ Winebars** are another option for serving wine by the glass. The traditional way for wine refrigeration is opening a bottle and placing it in a refrigerator. It is not only slow and inefficient, it ends up speeding up the deterioration of the wine through oxidation, reducing your wine sales  profitability. With unrefrigerated wine, this process is even faster. OZ Winebars is a wine refrigerator designed specifically to store and dispense both red and white wine. OZ Winebars has an advanced commercial system for managing, refrigerating, preserving and serving opened wines. OZ Winebars extend the serving life of your wines and provide your staff a clean, efficient vehicle for your wine service program in an exciting, authoritative ambience for your customers. For more information, contact OZEM Corp, 832 Harvard Drive, Holland, MI 49423, phone 866-617-3345, or visit **www.ozwinebars.com**.

OTHER SERVING INNOVATIONS

- **Motoman's RoboBar™.** This is a complete, self-contained robotic bar that serves mixed drinks, draft beer, wine, sodas and juices, highlighting potential applications in the growing service sector. RoboBar features a UPJ dual-arm robot with a compact NXC100 controller housed in the base of the robot. The two manipulator arms on this unique robot each have five axes of motion, and the base also rotates to provide an eleventh axis of motion. The end-of-arm tooling consists of simple parallel grippers. A safety enclosure is included. Programming is easy, and the user interface is intuitive and graphics-based. The system is designed to use a magnetic card scanner to authorize drink service. After a valid card swipe, the customer uses a touch screen to choose a beverage. The Motoman UPJ dual-arm robot selects a cup, and then fills it with the appropriate beverage(s) and ice, if desired. The robot then passes the drink to the customer via an automatic turntable located at the side of the cell. "Robots are fascinating to watch, and the entertainment factor alone makes RoboBar a customer magnet" says Ron Potter, Motoman's Senior Director of Emerging Robot Markets. "But RoboBar not only out-draws the competition, it also out-pours and out-performs, while improving profits and pleasing customers—giving establishments a big advantage in the 'bar wars,'" he continues. "RoboBar doesn't take tips, so customers can spend more money on drinks. RoboBar is never late for work and doesn't get tired. Interaction with customers is always friendly. Plus, it doesn't drink on the job or dip into the till—and smoke doesn't bother the robot," he explains. For more information on Motoman products and services, visit the corporate Web site at **www .motoman.com**, call 937-847-6200, or write to Motoman Inc. at 805 Liberty Lane, West Carrollton, OH 45449.

Service

You also need to consider labor charges for your bartending and cocktail serving staff. If the event is large and the client is spending a good deal of money on food already, you may want to consider waiving these charges. You'll still make your profit and you'll win some points with the client, which might lead to future business.

You'll need one bartender for every 85 to 100 guests. If everyone arrives at the event at once, however, or time is an issue, you might want to hire one for every 50 to 75 guests. Generally, the labor charge for bartenders is $125 for the first hour, $75 for the second, and $50 per hour thereafter. If you hire cocktail servers, the charge is similar.

Some clients offer to provide their own bartender. Be wary of this because more often than not, their choice is Uncle Louis who has decided to be a designated driver and is not adequately trained or capable of performing to your high standards. Guests will assume that the bartenders are part of your staff so their behavior must be kept to the same high standards as other staff.

GENERAL CONVENTIONS

In order to be taken seriously in the catering business you have to know the business and its terminology, and liquor has it own set of rules.

All liquor can be divided into two basic categories: well items and call items. Some restaurants and caterers establish a three-tier system: well, call and premium liquor.

Well items are house liquors. They are called well items because they are in a well speed rack in front of the bartender. Well liquors are used when a customer orders a particular drink without specifying a brand; for example, a Scotch and soda or a bourbon and water. For each major type of liquor, such as bourbon, gin, vodka, Scotch, tequila, rum, brandy and rye, you will need to select a well or house brand. The well liquor you select must be a popular and recognized brand that is moderately priced.

Call items are the more expensive, higher-quality types of liquor. Customers order these by the particular brand name; for example, a Cutty Sark Scotch and soda or a Jack Daniel's bourbon and water. Call items are sometimes called back bar items because they are usually stored on the shelves behind the bar.

Premium liquor is top-of-the-line liquor that few customers order, and it typically has an additional surcharge.

Whiskey

All whiskeys are distilled from fermented grains. Commonly used grains are barley, rye, corn and wheat. All whiskeys are aged in oak barrels. From this aging process they obtain their characteristic color, flavor and aroma. Most whiskey consumed in this country is produced in the United States, Canada, Scotland or Ireland.

Whiskey can be divided into two basic types: straight whiskey and blended whiskey.

STRAIGHT WHISKEY

Straight whiskey is a whiskey that has never been mixed with other types of whiskey or with any neutral grain spirits. Straight whiskey itself has four major types, discussed below.

Bourbon whiskey is named for the Bourbon county in Kentucky where the whiskey was originally produced. Bourbon must be distilled from grain mash containing at least 51 percent corn. (Suggested: 1 well bourbon and 3 to 6 call items.)

Rye whiskey has the similar amber color of bourbon, but the flavor and aroma are different. Rye whiskey must be distilled from a fermented mash of grain containing at least 51 percent rye. (Suggested: 1 well rye and 1 to 2 call items.)

Corn whiskey must be distilled from fermented mash of grain containing at least 80 percent corn. (Suggested: 1 call item only.)

Bottled-in-bond whiskey is usually a rye or bourbon whiskey that is produced under the supervision of the United States government. The government ensures that the whiskey is aged at least four years, is bottled at 100 proof, is produced in one distilling by a single distiller, and is bottled and stored under government supervision. Since the government bonds these steps, the whiskey is referred to as "bottled in bond." The government does not guarantee the quality of the whiskey, it only ensures that these steps have been completed under its supervision. (Suggested: 1 to 2 call items.)

BLENDED WHISKEY

Blended whiskey is a blend of straight whiskeys and neutral grain spirits. It must contain at least 20 percent, by volume, of a straight whiskey and be bottled at no less than 80 proof.

Canadian whiskey is a blend produced under the supervision of the Canadian government. This whiskey is usually lighter bodied than most American whiskeys. (Suggested: 1 well and 3 to 6 call items.)

Scotch whiskey is produced only in Scotland. All Scotch blends contain malt and grain whiskeys. The unique smoky flavor of Scotch is derived from drying malted barley over open peat fires. In recent years the popularity of single malt Scotch and other whiskies has grown phenomenally.

MALT WHISKEY

Many bars have a vast selection of hard-to-find single malts, and they are very expensive and profitable.

Single-malt whiskey is the product from a single distillery and has not been blended with any other whiskeys. Only water is added before it is bottled, and in the case of "cask strength" bottlings, not even that. There are bottlings with an alcohol percentage of over 60 available. (Suggested: 1 well Scotch and 4 to 8 call items.)

Irish whiskey is produced only in Ireland. This whiskey is usually heavier and fuller bodied than most Scotch blends. The malted barley used in the distilling process is dried over coal-fired kilns. This drying process has little or no effect on the whiskey's taste. (Suggested: 2 to 3 call items.)

Other Liquor

Vodka was originally produced in Russia from distilled potatoes. Now produced in various countries, vodka is commonly made from a variety of grains, the most common of which are wheat and corn. It is bottled at no less than 80 and no higher than 110 proof. During the distillation process, it is highly refined and filtered, usually through activated charcoal.

Vodka is not aged. It is colorless, odorless and virtually tasteless. Because of these traits, it is a very versatile liquor that can be mixed with almost anything. In addition, it can be served straight, chilled to taste. (Suggested: 1 well brand at 80 proof and one at 110 proof, and 2 to 3 call items; 1 to 2 should be imported.)

Gin is distilled from a variety of grains and is bottled at 80 proof. Every gin manufactured has its own distinctive flavor and aroma. The aroma is derived from a recipe of juniper berries and other assorted plants. Gin is usually colorless and is most often used in making the popular martini cocktail. Vacuum-distilled gin is distilled in a glass-lined vacuum at a lower than normal distilling temperature. This process tends to eliminate the bitterness found in some gins. (Suggested: 1 well and 3 to 4 call items; 1 to 2 should be imported.)

Rum is distilled from cane syrup, which is the fermented juice of sugar cane and molasses. It is bottled at no less than 80 proof. Most rums are a blend of many different types of aged rums. Dark rums often have caramel syrup added for color. Rums can be classified into two major types: light and heavy bodied.

Light-bodied rums are dry and light in color due to a lack of molasses. Among the light-bodied rums are two varieties: gold label and white label. The gold is often of slightly better quality and is darker and sweeter; the white is paler and slightly stronger in flavor. (Suggested: 1 well 80 proof and 1 to 2 call items.)

Heavy-bodied rums have been distilled by a different and slower process. Because of the slowness of this process, the rum contains more molasses, which makes the rum darker, sweeter and richer. (Suggested: 1 well 80 proof, 2 to 3 call items and 1 to 2 high-proof items.)

Brandy is traditionally distilled from a mash of fermented grapes but may be produced from other fruits. There are many different types available.

Cognac is perhaps the finest of distilled brandies. It is produced only in the Cognac region of France. Usually it is a blend of many different types of distilled cognac of the region. Cognac may be aged for as long as fifty years or more.

Armagnac brandy is similar to cognac but slightly drier in taste. It is produced only in the Armagnac region of France.

Applejack brandy is distilled from the cider of crushed apples. Calvados (an apple brandy) is produced only in Normandy, France. In the United States, Applejack is often bottled in bond.

Fruit-flavored brandies have a distilled brandy base with a flavor ingredient added. These are commonly used in blended cocktails. A good selection of the more popular types will be needed.

Tequila is usually produced in Mexico or the American southwest. It is distilled from the fermented mash of the aqua or century plants, which are cacti. Tequila is usually clear, although some types may have a gold tint. The smell and taste are distinctive. Tequila is used primarily in making margarita cocktails. Also in recent years there has been a wide increase in the variety of "premium" tequilas.

Tequila can also be chilled and served straight as a "shooter" with a beer chaser. (Suggested: 1 well and 2 to 3 imported call items.)

Cordials and liqueurs are created by the mixing or pre-distilling of neutral grain spirits with fruits, flowers or plants to which sweeteners have been added. Cordials and liqueurs are all colorful and very sweet in taste, which is why they are usually served as after-dinner drinks. There are a wide variety of cordials and liqueurs available.

A good selection of cordials and liqueurs would include 15 to 25 of these. There are approximately 10 to 12 different types that you must stock because of their popularity or because they are used in making certain cocktails. (All cordials and liqueurs should be call items.)

Vermouth is not classified as liqueur or liquor at all. It is actually a wine flavored with roots, berries or various types of plants. Vermouth is used almost exclusively in making martinis and Manhattans. There are two basic types: dry and sweet.

Dry vermouth is usually produced in America or France. This variety has a clear to light goldish color. It is used primarily in martini cocktails. One good well item is all that is required.

Sweet vermouth is a darker reddish wine with a richer, sweeter flavor. It is most often produced in Italy. Sweet vermouth is primarily used in making Manhattan cocktails. One good well item is all you need.

Beer

Whether packaged in bottles or kegs, beer should be treated as a food product. Always keep in mind that it is a perishable commodity with a limited life span. To ensure the freshness and full flavor of bottled beer, it's essential to adhere to a few simple procedures. The two biggest enemies of beer are exposure to light and temperature extremes, and the best way to combat them is to store beer in a dark, relatively cool place.

There are five basic categories for the hundreds of brands of beer are produced:

- Lagers, the most popular type produced today.

- Ales, which contain more hops and are stronger in flavor.

- Porter, stout and bock beers, which are all heavier, darker, richer and sweeter than the first two.

Beer is available in bottles, cans or on a draught keg system. Of the hundreds of brands available, fewer than a dozen are primarily demanded by customers. However, it should be noted that the popularity of "microbrewed" beers has come on very strong. Beer is a perishable item, so you'll want to buy the other, less popular brands you'll carry in bottles or cans to preserve their freshness. Most draft systems can handle three separate kegs; if your business warrants it, use all of them.

Imported beers have gained increasing popularity in recent years. Although they are 50 to 100 percent more expensive than domestic beers, customers still demand the more popular ones. There are three to four of these imported beers that you should always stock.

Light beer is produced with fewer calories than other beer and has developed a great demand within the past five years. One or two light beers should be included on your list.

Bar Terminology

Proof: The measurement of alcohol in an alcoholic beverage. Each degree of proof represents a half percent of alcohol. For example, a bottle of liquor distilled at 90 proof is 45 percent alcohol.

Grain Neutral Spirits: Colorless, tasteless, usually odorless ethyl alcohol distilled from grain at a minimum of 190 proof. Grain neutral spirits are used in blending whiskies and in making other types of liquor/liqueur.

Shot or Jigger: A unit of liquor ranging from 3/4 ounce to 2 ounces. Most restaurants/caterers pour 1-1/4 to 1-1/2-ounce shots for cocktails and add slightly less to blended drinks.

Straight Up: Refers to a cocktail that is served with no ice—usually a martini, Manhattan or margarita. A special chilled, long-stem straight-up glass should be used. Liqueurs and cordials that are served straight up may be poured into pony glasses.

On the Rocks: Refers to a cocktail, usually a straight liquor, such as a Scotch, or a cordial, served over ice. Although most cocktails are served over ice anyway, certain cocktails and liquors are just as commonly served without ice. In such cases the bartender or cocktail waitress must ask the customer which way he or she prefers.

Twist, Wedge and Slice: The fruit that garnishes the cocktail glass. A twist is a lemon peel. A wedge or slice is usually a piece of lime or orange.

Press: A fruit press used to squeeze the juice of a fruit garnish into the cocktail.

Bitters: Commercially produced liquid made from roots, berries or a variety of herbs. It is, indeed, bitter, and a dash or two is used in some cocktails.

Virgin: A drink that contains no alcoholic beverage, such as a virgin piña colada or a virgin Bloody Mary.

Back: Refers to either water or coffee and indicates that along with the cocktail ordered, the customer would also like a separate glass of water or cup of coffee.

Rimmed: Either salt, sugar or celery salt around the rim of a cocktail glass. Usually Bloody Marys, margaritas and salty dogs are served this way. The bartender prepares a rimmed glass by wetting the rim of the glass with a wedge of fruit; then twirls the glass in a bowl of the salt or sugar desired.

Shaken: A cocktail that is shaken in the mixing glass before being strained.

Stirred: A cocktail that is stirred (not shaken) in the mixing glass with a spoon before being strained.

Wine

With the popularity of wine drinkers soaring, many caterers must know their wines and wine terminology. There are more nuances to wine service than the service of other alcoholic beverages. Many people enjoy drinking wine with food, so the service of wine involves a greater knowledge of the wine itself than with other alcoholic drinks. If someone orders a Scotch and soda for dinner, they don't worry whether it goes with the lamb special. When a guest orders wine, however, they usually try to pair it with the food they are ordering.

Most caterers use 750-milliliter wine bottles. They may also offer splits of wine or champagne, which are generally half the size of a regular bottle. Most caterers also stock larger bottles of house wines to use for individual glass service.

WINE TERMINOLOGY

It is important that your servers know the basics of wine, the most common grape varieties, and how people discuss wine. Your servers should be able to discuss color and smell ("nose") and taste ("palate"). You may also want them to be able to distinguish more subtle color differences. Is the wine yellow like a Chardonnay or is it clearer like a Pinot Grigio?

Some of the terms people use to describe smell and taste include dry, sweet, earthy and smoky. They may also say that a wine's taste is reminiscent of another flavor, such as raspberries or pepper. Most importantly, your servers should know which wines in your establishment are sweet and which are dry. This will be the main category upon which guests will base their wine decisions. For helpful advice about wine language, visit **www.demystifying-wine.com**

Franklin Miami Publishing's guide "*How to Read Wine Labels*" summarizes all you need to know about interpreting the information on wine labels. Go to **www.franklinmiamipublishing.com**.

Wine and Food

Your servers should know how to suggest what wine will complement what entrée. You can help them out by including this information on your menu if there is room, but servers still need to know how to make suggestions for your customers.

REDS

- Light-bodied (Gamay, Sangiovese, Pinot Noir)—Red meats, roasted poultry, oily fish such as salmon.

- Medium-bodied (Merlot, Syrah, Zinfandel, Malbec)—Veal, pork, venison, game birds.

- Full-bodied (Cabernet Sauvignon)—All red meats, duck, lamb.

- Semi-sweet—Dessert; never before dinner, as the sweetness will spoil the customer's appetite.

WHITES

- Dry light-bodied (Pinot Grigio, Pinot Blanc, some Rieslings)—Shellfish, some seafood.

- Semi-sweet—Seafood.

- Medium-bodied (Sauvignon Blanc, Gewürztraminer, some Chardonnays)—Roasted poultry, oily fish such as salmon, steak.

- Full-bodied (Chardonnay)—White meats, seafood.

ROSÉ

- Dry light-bodied—Can be served in place of either dry white or red wines.

- Sparkling wine/champagne.

- Dry—May be served in place of dry white wines; complements most foods.

- Semi-sweet—May be served in place of semi-sweet whites; does not go with as much as a dry sparkling wine.

FORTIFIED AND DESSERT WINES

- Sherry—soup course.

- Sweeter wines go well with fruit and dessert.

- Some, such as Port or Sauterne, can go with a savory appetizer such as Stilton cheese.

WINE RESOURCES

There are many books and magazines on wine. Some of the more respectable ones include:

- *Exploring Wine: The Culinary Institute of America's Complete Guide to Wines of the World*

- Robert Parker's *Buying Guide*

- Oz Clarke's *Encyclopedia of Wine*

- *Wine Atlas* by Hugh Johnson

- *New Sotheby's Wine Encyclopedia* by Tom Steven

- *Hachette Wine Guide 2002*—Recognized as "The French Wine Bible"

- *The Definitive Guide to French Wine*—This Hachette guide contains over 9,000 wines described by 900 experts.

For online resources try the following:

- Wine Spectator: **www.winespectator.com**

- Wine and Spirits: **www.wineandspiritsmagazine.com**

- Wine Enthusiast: **www.wineenthusiast.com**

- Tasting Wine: **www.tasting-wine.com/html/etiquette.html**

- The American Institute of Wine and Food: **www.aiwf.org**

- Wines.com: **www.wines.com**

One of the best ways to train your serving staff about wines is to let them taste it. Hold regular wine tastings for your servers. Make wine-tasting cards, and have them fill out the cards about the specifics of the wines they are tasting. Many times your wine vendors can be called upon to help with such training. You should also hold sessions that include tasting menu items so that the servers can understand why a Cabernet Sauvignon is a good choice with a steak, but a better selection with fish maybe a Sauvignon Blanc. You can train servers how to pour wine from the bottle by using empty bottles with colored water.

TASTING TIPS

When tasting wine, you use many senses:

- **Sight:** You can tell several things from the color of a wine, including its age. White wines grow darker with age and red wines grow lighter.

- **Smell:** Smell is an important part of wine tasting. In order to smell all the nuances in a wine, you want to swirl the wine in your glass to "open it up." Swirling allows air to combine with the wine. To swirl, hold the glass by its stem and rotate in a small circle. After swirling the wine, smell it and try to describe the aroma

- **Taste:** When tasting wine, you should take a small amount into your mouth and hold it at the bottom of your mouth. Draw in air through a small hole in your lips and let the air cross the wine in your mouth, allowing it to bubble.

The following list provides you with some descriptive terms for wine:

Aggressive: The wine that has slightly high tannins or acid.

Astringent: The wine that has very high tannins or acid.

Beefy: A full-bodied wine.

Big-Full-Heavy: A full-bodied wine that is high in alcohol and has good balance.

Body: The texture or taste of the wine in the mouth.

Bouquet: Used to describe the smell of wine as it matures in the bottle.

Bright: A young wine with fresh and fruity aromas and flavors.

Chewy: A very rich and intense full-bodied wine.

Corky or Corked: A spoiled wine.

Crisp: A noticeably acidic wine, but the acid does not overpower the wine.

Delicate: A quality wine that is light and well balanced.

Dense: A full-flavored wine or wine with a deep color.

Dried Out: A wine that has lost its fruitiness.

Dry: Refers to the lack of sweetness in the wine.

Earthy: A wine that tastes of soil.

Flabby: A wine lacking acidity.

Flat: Having low acidity, or refers to a sparkling wine that has lost its bubbles.

Finesse: A high quality well balanced wine.

Finish: The flavor a wine leaves in the mouth after the wine is swallowed.

Forward: An early maturing wine.

Fragrant: A wine with a floral aroma or bouquet.

Fresh: A simple, well-balanced, fruity wine.

Jammy: A wine with a concentrated fruit flavor.

Legs: The drops of wine that run down the inside of the glass after swirling.

Light: Refers to the wine's body and alcohol content.

Mature: A wine that is ready to drink.

Meaty: A full-bodied wine with rich flavors.

Metallic: A wine with a tin-like flavor.

Moldy: A wine with a mold-like aroma or flavor.

Nose: The aroma or bouquet of a wine.

Nutty: A wine with a flavor or aroma of nuts.

Off: A wine that is flawed or spoiled.

Overdeveloped: A wine that has past its prime.

Oxidized: A wine that has been exposed to air. This exposure has changed the quality of the wine from good to bad.

Peppery: A wine with a spicy, black pepper flavor.

Robust: A wine with a powerful flavor.

Round: A wine with a well-balanced, mellow, and full-bodied flavor.

Semi-Sweet: Refers to the underlying sweetness of a wine.

Sharp: A wine with too much acid.

Simple: A wine with few characteristics that follow the initial impression.

Smoky: A wine that has a smoky aroma.

Soft: A wine that is mellow and well balanced.

Sour: A wine with a lot of acidity.

Tart: A wine that is high in acid and leaves a sharp, sour note in the mouth.

Tired: A wine that has been over aged.

WINE LABELS

In the United States, wine labels have the following information:

- Name of wine
- Name of importer
- Country of origin
- Sulfite advisory

- Name of producer/name and address of bottler
- Name of shipper
- Alcohol content (as a percentage of volume)
- Government warning

Labels may also include:

- Quality of wine
- Vintage
- Type of wine

- Growing region
- Descriptive information

Wine labeling regulations are determined by the regulatory body in each country, so wines from areas other than the Untied States may contain different information on their labels.

SERVING PROCEDURES

Wine is a delicate substance. It must be cared for and served properly in order for it to taste the way it should. Each delivery must be properly received and stored away from light, heat sources and vibrations. Wine must be stored on its side or at enough of an angle to keep the cork moist. Should the bottle be stored upright, the cork will soon dry out and allow air to seep into the bottle and spoil the taste of the wine.

The most important consideration in serving wine is to make certain it is at the proper temperature. Much of the wine's flavor, bouquet and body will be lost if it is served too cold or too warm. Most people know that red wines should be served at room temperature, but this is a confusing statement. "Room temperature" in Europe is 10 to 15 degrees cooler than in North America. For clarification, the list below gives the commonly accepted serving temperatures for each wine. However, these are not steadfast rules, as taste is an individual experience, and individuals have different preferences. Always serve wine in the manner the customer wishes.

- White and Rosé   46°–50°F

- Red Wines   62°–68°F

- Champagne and Sparkling Wine   42°–48°F
  (Serve in an ice bucket with water.)

Always ask the customer when he or she would like the wine to be served or with which course. Red wines should be opened as soon as possible and placed on the table so that they may "breathe." This allows air to enter the bottle, which is supposed to release the wine's flavor and bouquet. Many experts will argue that this step is unnecessary because of the minimal amount of air actually exposed to the wine at the neck of the bottle. Whether or not it is effective, it should always be done for appearance's sake. White wines and champagnes may need to be chilled prior to serving, so take the wine order as soon as possible.

Steps for proper wine service:

- Always place a napkin behind the bottle.

- Display the bottle to the person who ordered it (usually the host). Give him plenty of time to examine the label; he will want to make sure it is the wine and vintage desired.

- The wine opener used should be the waitperson's folding pocketknife with the open spiral corkscrew and smooth edges.

- With the knife blade, remove the capsule and foil.

- Clean the neck and bottle with the napkin.

- Hold the bottle firmly, and slowly insert the corkscrew into the center of the cork. Stop about two-thirds of the way through the cork. Don't go all the way, as this may result in putting a few pieces of the cork into the wine.

- With the bottle on the table, steadily pull straight up. Do not jerk out the cork.

- After opening, check the cork for dryness, and place it end up on the table so that the host may examine it.

- When the host is satisfied, pour about an ounce into his glass. He must approve of the wine before the other people in the party are served.

- The customer has the prerogative to reject a bottle of wine at any stage of the service. However, once the bottle is opened, his reasoning for rejection must be due to there being something wrong with the wine itself, not because he doesn't like it. If a bottle is rejected, it should be removed from the table and brought to the kitchen where the manager may examine it and act accordingly. Some distributors may issue a credit for damaged bottles, however there is usually no obligation to do so, particularly with older, more expensive bottles.

- It is customary to pour all the women's glasses first and the host's last. When you are finished pouring a glass, give the bottle a slight twist; this will prevent any dripping. Always pour wine with the label facing you.

Opening sparkling wine and champagne:

- Always use a napkin behind the bottle to stop drips, and although it rarely happens, it is possible that the bottle may split from the internal pressure.

- Remove the foil and wire muzzle.

- Remove the cork by turning the bottle, not the cork. Always point the bottle away from people. The cork should be removed slowly and carefully; it should never explode open with a gush of champagne.

- Special champagne glasses may be used, however it is perfectly acceptable to serve champagne in tulip-shaped wineglasses.

- A stuck cork may be removed by placing the neck of the bottle under a stream of hot water for a few seconds. The heat will build up pressure on the inside of the bottle making it easier to extract the cork.

Cocktails

Of the hundreds of varieties of cocktails, about 25 of the more common ones are ordered 90 percent of the time. In order to obtain consistency among them, a recipe and procedure manual should be developed. This manual should contain cocktail ingredients and amounts, which cocktail glass should be used, garnishes, pertinent serving instructions, and preparation procedures.

There are several excellent bartender guides available that list all the various cocktails and how to prepare them. One of these books should be kept at the bar. Occasionally a customer will order a drink that you will not know, nor will it be listed in the book. Usually this is because the customer is pronouncing it wrong or it is some variation of another cocktail. Politely inform the customer that you are not familiar with the cocktail; many times he or she can tell you how to prepare it.

Below are some of the most commonly ordered cocktails:

- Screwdriver
- Manhattan
- Mai-Tai
- Piña Colada
- Old Fashioned
- Tequila Sunrise
- Gimlet
- Margarita
- Martini
- Cosmopolitan

- Black and White Russians
- Gibson
- Bloody Mary
- Stingers
- Coffee drinks
- Juice or punch drinks
- Collins drinks
- Fizzes
- Daiquiris
- Sours

MIXERS

You will need to have bar mixers, juices and garnishes. Here is a list of the most common.

Juices

- Orange juice
- Cranberry juice
- Pineapple juice

- Tomato juice
- Lime juice
- Lemon juice

Fresh Fruit

- Oranges
- Limes
- Bananas
- Strawberries

- Lemon peels
- Lemons
- Pineapple

Soda

- Coke or Pepsi
- Soda water
- Sprite or 7-Up
- Ginger Ale

- Tonic water
- Diet Coke or Diet Pepsi
- Sparkling or mineral water
- Purified water

Mixers—Misc.

- Sweet-and-sour

- Orgeat syrup bar mix

- Coconut cream
- Grenadine
- Gitters

- Worcestershire sauce concentrate
- Tabasco sauce
- Sugar-saturated water

Garnishes

- Cherries
- Stuffed olives
- Cocktail onions

- Kosher salt
- Celery salt
- Super-fine bar sugar

MIXING TECHNIQUES

Stirring. Add the ingredients to the glass with ice and stir with a spoon. Cocktails that are stirred: Manhattan and Rob Roy.

Shaking. Put ice into a cocktail shaker. Pour other drink ingredients over ice. Cover and shake for about ten seconds or until frost forms on outside of shaker. Remove the lid and strain the ingredients (this method allows you to serve a cold drink with no ice). Shaken drink examples: Tom Collins, Margaritas, and Daiquiris.

Blending. Combine all the ingredients and ice in a blender. Drink examples: frozen Daiquiris or Margaritas and Piña Coladas.

Garnishes

Garnishes are part of the entertainment of drinking. There is nothing worse than a customer seeing less-than-fresh garnishes laying in a tray from the previous night that are about to go into her drink. They look bad and cost operators money in waste. Calculate how much is needed and cut just enough.

Heads turn when customers glimpse a pair of sunglasses or plastic animals hanging off a cocktail. Try using dry ice; a triple garnish of orange, lime and lemon slices; a cluster of grapes for the glass of wine; a choice of olives, such as almond- or garlic-stuffed olives; a lemon twist wrapped around a coffee bean; a skewer of oversized cherries; or a pickled okra sprout. Garnishes add finesse and style and can become your trademark. Be creative: review some food-garnishing books and let your inventive chef have a crack at some ideas.

WHIPPED CREAM

All coffee drinks and many blended drinks use whipped cream as a topping or garnish. Real whipped cream is simple and inexpensive to prepare. The alternative to real whipped cream is the widely used aerosol can of non-dairy whipped cream. Real whipped cream is superior to the canned variety. The taste, texture and quality of the ingredients are incomparable.

Though there are many recipes, real whipped cream is made primarily with sugar, vanilla and heavy or whipping cream. Real whipped cream is often used in the kitchen for topping desserts and other items and can also be made by whipping the ingredients in the blender at the bar.

FRESHLY SQUEEZED JUICES

A most impressive demonstration of quality is the use of freshly squeezed juices. Throughout the evening the bartender can extract fresh juice for cocktails that use the juice of oranges, grapefruits, lemons and limes. The additional cost of using fresh juices is passed on to the customer through higher drink prices.

Added Touches

Sometimes the only element that separates successful caterers from those that fail is the small professional touches of excellence. This extra effort implies that a tremendous amount of care and attention has been made to provide the highest level of quality possible. Some simple inexpensive suggestions for bar service enhancements are offered below.

HEATED SNIFTERS

Snifter glasses should always be warmed prior to pouring brandy and certain cordials. Brandy heated in a warm glass has a stronger aroma and flavor that is preferred by most people.

To heat the brandy snifter, pour near-boiling water into the bottom third of the glass. Let it sit for two to three minutes. Before using, wipe the entire glass dry with a clean bar towel. Coffee drink glasses and mugs should also be preheated as described to maintain the coffee's temperature. You may also preheat glasses by filling them with tap water and microwaving them for 15 to 30 seconds.

FROSTED BEER MUGS

Beer mugs and glasses should be frosted prior to use. Aside from adding aesthetic value to the beer, chilled glasses help maintain it at the proper drinking temperature.

Stock a supply of the mugs in a cooler set at 31° - 33°F. When the mugs are removed from the cooler, condensation will occur, leaving the frosted glass with a thin layer of ice. Mugs must be dry when placed in the cooler. Should they contain droplets from a recent washing, this excess water will freeze onto the mug. When defrosted by the warmth of the beer, this ice will melt, diluting the beer, and depriving the customer of its delicate flavor.

CHILLED COCKTAIL STRAIGHT-UP GLASSES

Chilled cocktail straight-up glasses must be kept ice cold, as the cocktails themselves contain no ice. These glasses are used almost exclusively for straight-up martinis, Manhattans, gibsons and margaritas. If there is no cooler space available to keep a supply chilled, bury them stem up in crushed ice. Glasses must be shaken dry before using.

FLAMING LIQUOR

Certain cocktails require that they be set aflame prior to serving. Extreme care must be used by employees and customers when handling these cocktails. Preheat the glass and warm the entire cocktail before attempting to ignite it. Remove a teaspoon of the cocktail and set it aflame. Pour the flaming liquid carefully back into the cocktail.

Fire regulations in your area may prohibit any open flames, such as those from candles, flaming food and flaming liquor. Contact the local fire department to learn of its restrictions.

FRESH FRUIT DAIQUIRIS

Fresh fruit daiquiris are incomparable in quality to daiquiris that are made from fruit-flavored liqueurs. Aside from being a misrepresentation, substituting fruit-flavored liqueurs for real fruit is unnecessary. Fresh fruit is available in most places year-round. The small additional cost is outweighed by the resulting quality of the cocktail.

FLOATING CORDIALS—POUSSE CAFE

The most attractive cordials served use a variety of liqueurs, which are floating in layers, one on top of the other in the same glass. Although it appears complicated—if not impossible—to create, the floating cordial is rather simple.

Liqueurs and cordials have different densities, thus enabling liqueurs with lower densities to float atop those with higher densities. The trick is to pour the liqueur carefully on top of the preceding one. This is best accomplished by pouring each liqueur over an inverted spoon. The rounded bottom of the spoon will diffuse the liquid over the one below and no mixing will occur. Be certain that all ingredients given in the recipe are poured in the exact order listed.

CREATING THE PEACOCK EFFECT WITH NAPKINS

Undoubtedly you have seen in fancy bars the stacks of cocktail napkins displayed like the feathers of a peacock, all jutting out in a different circular direction. Although this appears to be a painstakingly difficult and time-consuming task, it is easily and quickly created. The bartender can prepare an entire night's napkins in less than five minutes.

Place a two-inch-high stack of cocktail napkins on the bar. Place a small highball glass on its side in the middle of the stack. Press down on the glass and rotate it two to three inches to the left. Move the glass around to each side until the napkins are all feathered out evenly. This is an extremely simple procedure, which results in elegant-looking napkins.

Legal Implications of Alcoholic Beverage Catering

The beverage caterer needs to be fully aware of state and local municipality liquor laws, as well as the legal implications of providing bartenders to serve alcoholic beverages. To sell alcoholic beverages, you must have a license. For off-premise caterers, there are three possible scenarios:

1. You may be permitted to serve but not sell alcoholic beverages. In this case, you have to provide payment to the retail liquor vendor, with the client's check payable to that liquor vendor, for the amount of purchase.

2. You may obtain a temporary license to sell liquor at a specific event, at a specific date and time.

3. In some states (for example, California), you can obtain a license to sell and serve alcohol on a regular basis.

An on-premise caterer must have the right type of license to serve liquor. A full tavern license is usually needed to serve spirits, wines and beers. In some parts of the country, a hotel or conference center may not be able to serve liquor if it does not possess a private club license.

ILLEGAL LIQUOR SALES

No matter where you are located in the country and what type of catering you do, certain types of liquor sales are always illegal.

Serving alcoholic beverages to minors is a serious offense. You cannot sell alcoholic beverages to anyone under 21 years old in the United States. There are exceptions in some states when a minor is in the presence of his or her parents or major-age spouse.

Serving alcohol to intoxicated individuals. While there is a legal criterion for considering a person to be intoxicated (a blood alcohol concentration of .08 to .10, depending on the state), there is no sure-fire way of telling whether or not a person is intoxicated. Play safe—don't serve alcohol to anyone who appears to be intoxicated.

Blood alcohol concentration (BAC) is an indicator of how much alcohol is in the bloodstream. Alcohol is absorbed directly into the bloodstream from the stomach and intestines. Know the stages of intoxication.

STAGES OF INTOXICATION	
Level 1:	**Level 2:**
• Guest gets louder. • Guest may become overly friendly.	• Guest may have difficulty walking. • Speech may be slurred. • Guest may become argumentative. • Guest may have reduced muscle coordination, may have trouble picking up change, etc.

To help prevent intoxication:

- Always check IDs.
- Offer guests food when drinking.
- Serve each guest only one drink at a time.
- Try to keep track of how much a guest consumes.

If you serve an intoxicated guest or a minor and he or she causes an accident, the facility, server and host may be liable for damages to the injured person. In some states, under dram shop legislation, you'll be held at least partially responsible. You cannot defend yourself if it is proved that the facility's employees served a minor or a legally intoxicated guest.

Social-host laws. Some states have social-host laws; other states have neither dram shop nor social-host laws. But whichever way you look at it, you don't want to get involved in a legal battle that could ruin your business.

Beverage functions that do not offer food. Check with the Alcohol Beverage Commission. Establish whether you're allowed to cater for an alcoholic beverage-only function. The Alcohol Beverage Commission will also be able to advise you of the rules regarding clients who want to bring in their own liquor. You may, for instance, be prohibited from offering free liquor or reduced-price liquor.

Alcoholic portion regulations. To avoid overcompensation of alcohol, some local municipalities restrict the amount of alcohol you can put into each drink. You may not be allowed to serve doubles, boilermakers and pitchers of beers, or drinks that contain multiple liquors like Mudslides, Long Island Iced Teas and Scorpions.

You will likely serve alcohol at a majority of your catering events. If served wisely and conscientiously, it can add immeasurably to the client's satisfaction, and it is also a boon to bottom-line profits.

Staffing and Personnel

One of the biggest challenges you face as a caterer is labor issues. These concerns include hiring chefs, kitchen personnel, service staff (both full- and part-time) and sales staff. A recent report published by the National Restaurant Association, **www.restaurant.org**, mirrored the concerns of the operators on this point. Staffing for catering is an ongoing activity because your requirements fluctuate widely.

There are a lot of people out there willing to work for you on a per-hour basis; it is by no means an easy job to cultivate potential employees. Be aware that many staff members will be variable-cost employees who tend to work for other caterers as well. They may well leave you on short notice for full-time permanent employment elsewhere. It is a fact that the labor shortage frustrates your efforts to build and retain adequate staff. Below are some practical suggestions about resolve the staffing issue.

Recruitment

Most catering businesses rely mainly or entirely on on-call staff, although larger companies employ a few permanent, full-time staff such as a chef, kitchen manager, receptionist, and sales and marketing personnel. Develop a list of reliable people to call on for work. Many people in the catering industry are willing to work long hours, so offer these people employment before soliciting new and untried employees.

The key to staffing is to strike a proper balance between regular staff handling the day-to-day operations and part-timers on-call. Error on the low side when determining the size of the regular day-to-day staff; after all, it's easier to bring in additional staff during busier times than to cut staff when it's slow and ask them to come back later.

The first position you need to consider is chef. If you are a small operation and you are the chef, consider hiring a sous chef or kitchen helper to assist with the prep work. If you don't already have someone in mind, check with area culinary schools. You can always find a student ready to make a little extra cash.

You may also want to consider hiring a part-time baker or finding a good outside baking source. Baking takes a lot of time, and it is one function that many caterers outsource.

Waitstaff are probably the most important positions you will need to consider as a caterer. Not only is it the waitstaff interacting with the client and guests, but the waitstaff does most of the setup and cleanup work as well as serving food and drinks. While most events use servers as bus people, if the event is large, you may want to consider hiring bus people too.

Other positions you might find in larger catering operations include:

- Drivers
- Office staff
- Production assistant (order food, shop, pack, and stock)
- Cleaning staff
- Party coordinator/account manager

Don't forget to consider the cost of payroll when you are figuring out which positions to hire and whether a position should be full-time, part-time or on-call. Normally the payroll costs, as a percentage of sales, should be between 20 to 30 percent. Don't forget to take into account the cost of benefits paid in addition to the hourly wages. Don't overtax your business with too many full-time employees. Most businesses find that payroll and benefits are their highest overhead costs.

Bear in mind that the labor cost is your only area of flexibility. Initially, you will need to work as long as 12 to 14 hours a day in order to establish a positive cash flow, but it is likely you will continue to work these hours as your business grows and succeeds.

HIRE FOR FIT

The key to hiring good, competent employees is to put aside personal prejudices and select one applicant over another only because you feel he or she will have a better chance of being successful at the job. What a potential employee is qualified and capable of doing is often quite different than what he or she will actually do.

You're goal in hiring employees is to find the best possible fit for the job. As a service organization, you will be looking for employees with strong customer-service attitudes. By hiring the right person for the job, you save money and time on searching for, hiring and training replacements. You'll also save costs associated with additional FICA and unemployment insurance payments, overtime pay to cover unfilled positions, and fees for advertisements and employment agencies. You also have fewer turnover and morale problems to worry about.

Like most things in management, hiring the right employees requires planning. The first considerations to take into this planning are federal regulations concerning hiring employees. Make sure you know the rules before you start. A great resource for federal laws is the U.S. Department of Labor's Employment Law Handbook. To access this information, see **www.dol.gov /asp/programs/handbook/main2.htm**. The U.S. Department of Labor's Elaws at **www.dol.gov/ elaws** also provides business owners with interactive tools that provide information about federal employment laws.

Other useful guides on human resources and making hiring decisions can be found at Uniform Guidelines on Selection Procedures at **www.uniformguidelines.com/uniformguidelines.html#3** and The Council on Education in Management's Web site at **www.counciloned.com**.

RECRUIT FOR TEAMWORK

When hiring, you want to find people who are going to pitch in and help. Basically, you want people who can function well as part of a team. When recruiting, avoid superstars, and seek both technical skills and evidence of being good with people. You may want to ask about teams they have been on (sports or other). Also ask how they may have handled conflict with fellow workers in the past.

In general, there are four personality types that function well in a team environment. The best teams have a balance of all four, and members understand the different types and roles. Keep your eyes open for these types of individuals:

1. **The contributor.** Technically adept, task-oriented, born trainer. Excellent leader in kitchen or detail-oriented bus staff.

2. **The collaborator.** Goal-oriented, quick to help out. Excellent in front-of-the-house staff.

3. **The communicator.** Process-oriented, great floor manager, server, greeter, good trainer, attentive listening skills for problem solving.

4. **The challenger.** Candor and openness helps team explore better ways of doing things, highly principled, willing to disagree, blow whistle.

The best scenario is to get a good mix of these types working for you. Make sure your recruitment strategy takes into account the differences among people and doesn't place an unwarranted, and undesirable, emphasis on hiring people who are just like you or just like other key members of your company.

RECRUITING SOURCES

So where do you find good employees? Running an advertisement in the local paper is always the first thing that comes to mind, but this may not be your best resource for employees. Consider the following alternatives as well:

Promoting from within. Promoting from within is an excellent source. Hosts and bus people are often anxious to be promoted to serving staff because of the increase in income and prestige. Serving staff may want to move into sales or clerical positions. Kitchen staff may also want to explore new responsibilities. Not only does this method motivate your current workers, it saves you money on training because these people already know a great deal about the establishment and position.

Employee referrals. Ask your employees if they have friends or relatives who are looking for work. Often an employee won't recommend a friend unless they are sure this friend is not going to embarrass them by doing a poor job, so you are likely to get good employees this way. Offer an incentive to employees for helping you recruit. You could offer an employee a $25 bonus for each referral; if the person works out and stays on for a year, give both the employee and new hire a cash bonus at the end of that year.

Open house. Hold an open house to find new employees. This strategy is particularly effective if you're looking to fill several positions at once. These take more work than a regular interview, but it may be worth it. Get your managers or other employees to help. Make sure to advertise the open house.

Off-site recruiting. Restaurant trade shows are excellent places to recruit! Consider using other events for recruitment purposes such as wine tastings, food festivals, and career fairs.

Industry organizations and Web sites. Many industry Web sites have pages for posting jobs and résumés. Check out a few of the following sites:

- American Culinary Federation: **www.acfchefs.org**

- National Restaurant Association: **www.restaurant.org**

- Nation's Restaurant News: **www.nrn.com**

- Restaurantbeast.com: **www.restaurantbeast.com**

- Monster.com: **www.monster.com**

Area colleges. Many college students are looking for a source of income and a schedule that can work around their classes. Many of these colleges also offer culinary arts or restaurant management programs.

Catering professionals. When recruiting for sales and management personnel, the best sources are professional associations. Many catering professionals belong to the National Association of Catering Executives (NACE), **www.nace.net**.

Yipeee, Inc. For caterers who prefer to have someone else maintain a qualified labor pool, Yipeee, Inc, **www.yipeeeinc.com**, in New York City, runs a database of more than 500 freelance service professionals—from waiters and waitresses to maitre d's and bartenders. "We're a full-resource company that provides event management, event staffing and consulting in the catering and restaurant industry," says Karen DiPeri, Yipeee Executive Vice President. "We screen, qualify and select seasoned service professionals. Having well-trained professionals can really make a difference at a catered event."

Culinary schools. Check out local and national culinary schools. They usually have a spot on their Web pages for people to post résumés. Some examples include:

- Culinary Institute of America: **www.ciachef.edu**

- Sullivan's University, Louisville, Kentucky: **www.sullivan.edu/programs/program2.htm**

- New England Culinary Institute: **www.neculinary.com**

- The National Restaurant Association's Web site has a listing of culinary/hospitality schools across the country. For more information log onto **www.restaurant.org/careers/schools.cfm**

THE RECRUITMENT AD

If you do run an ad, be sure to carefully study other hospitality employment ads in the paper. How are they written? What types of information are important? You should also spend some time thinking about what type of information you want to emphasize about your organization and the position.

- Do you offer better benefits than most of your competitors?

- Do you emphasize a fun work environment?

- Do you need someone who already has some food service skills or do you prefer to train someone from the ground up so they don't come in with any preconceptions or bad habits?

Make a list of all the information you feel is important to include in your ad, then start writing. Refer back to those ads you examined before for language hints. Remember, most papers charge by the word so you will want to get your ad across as concisely as possible. Also remember that a classified ad is a marketing tool. You are trying to attract good potential applicants so use exciting language to make potential applicants want to work for you.

Just as there are alternative recruiting methods in general, there are alternatives for classified ads. Of course, the local paper is always one option, but think about area college papers, local magazines, hospitality Web sites, and community bulletin boards.

Hiring

Once you know what type of staff you need and you've decided on a method to recruit them, it is time to begin the hiring process. It may be daunting, with many twists and obstacles, but a little knowledge and a lot of preparedness will overcome them.

Employee Screening

Screening job applicants will enable you to reject those candidates who are obviously unsuitable before they are referred for a lengthy interview. This saves both the business and the applicants time and money. The preliminary screening can be done by an assistant manager or someone knowledgeable about the operation's employment needs and practices.

Potential job candidates may then be referred to the manager for intensive interviews. All applicants should leave feeling they have been treated fairly and had an equal opportunity to present their case for getting the job. As previously stated, this is an important part of public relations. Who knows; the applicant who just left may be your next customer.

A good and informal way to screen candidates is to have job candidates fill out an application form. The application form gives you information about the person's skills and experience. The following tips will help you streamline your application process.

Application file. You should keep applications on file for a year. It is a good source to use to look for potential employees the next time you have an opening. Rather than advertising, look at your application file first. Was there anyone who stood out that you didn't have an opening for before?

References. Make sure your application form has a spot for the candidate to list references, and then use this information. Many future problems can be avoided if you call two or three references. Ask the reference what job the candidate performed, what time period he worked there, if the candidate got along with supervisors and coworkers, and if the reference would ever consider hiring the person again.

You may also want to check criminal records, driving records, workers' compensation records, federal and state court records, credit ratings, education, and previous employment information.

APPLICANT TESTING

You may want to consider including job skills tests in your application process. Perhaps you could give the candidate a short math test or ask him or her to demonstrate how they would wait on a customer.

Don't use employment tests to screen people with Disabilities, unless you can show that the tests are job-related and consistent with business necessity. For information concerning the American with Disabilities Act (ADA) visit the ADA Web site at **www.usdoj.gov/crt/ada/adahom1.htm**.

Base your preliminary screening on the following criteria:

- **Experience.** Is the applicant qualified to do the job? Examine past job experience. Check all references.

- **Appearance.** Is the applicant neatly dressed? Remember, she will be dealing with the public; the way the applicant is dressed now is probably better than the way she will come to work.

- **Personality.** Does the applicant have a personality that will complement the other employees' and impress customers? Is he outgoing but not overbearing?

- **Legality.** Does the applicant meet the legal requirements?

- **Availability.** Can the applicant work the hours needed? Commute easily?

- **Health and physical ability.** Is the applicant capable of doing the physical work required? All employees hired should be subject to approval only after a complete physical examination by a mutually approved doctor.

- **Application.** Make certain the application is signed and dated.

All applicants at this point should be divided into one of the three following categories:

1. **Refer for hiring.** Send applicant to the manager for an interview and, if feasible, to the department head where the job is open.

2. **Reject.** Describe the reasons for rejection and place the application on file for future reference.

3. **Prospective file.** Any applicant who is not qualified for this position but may be considered for other areas of the business should be placed in a prospective applicant file.

Interviewing

The application will give you some information about a potential employee, but the job interview will give you more. When interviewing, don't use a script; have a conversation. Focus on what animates the candidate. Ask open-ended questions and look for thoughtful responses. Have other employees participate in the interview process so that you can compare impressions. Look for new hires who will be open to cross-training and new opportunities. Ask how they feel about taking on new responsibilities and what other positions they would like to learn. Here are some guidelines that will help you through the interviewing process.

Be systematic. Before you go into an interview, prepare a list of questions. Also, be sure to read the application before you sit down for the interview. Have the job description, expected work hours, pay information, and general policies in front of you. Discuss these details with the candidate. Inform the applicant of the time frame within which he or she will be notified about the position. Ask if the applicant has any questions before you finish the interview.

Interview with no disruptions. Conduct interviews in a quiet place, such as a back table during a slow period. Most catering owners like to hold interviews and accept applications in the mid to late afternoon between lunch and dinner rushes. Be sure to eliminate distractions. Ask your staff not to interrupt you and leave your cell phone and pager on your desk.

Develop a rapport. Job interviews are stressful. Take a few moments at the beginning of an interviews to chat and put the applicant at ease. This will let the person relax and the interview will be more successful.

First impressions. The interview is where you get your first impression of your potential employee. Notice what they are wearing. Remember, this is the first impression your customers will get as well. You can also get a feeling for their punctuality. Did they arrive on time? Better yet, did they arrive five minutes early? Do they seem organized? Do they have all the information they need to fill out the application?

Look for a passion for service. Often this is more important than a lot of past experience. People with nontraditional backgrounds are often more flexible. Remember that people skills are more important than technical skills; you can easily teach the technical skills. Does the candidate look you in the eye? Does he or she smile? Do they seem warm and friendly or aloof? What does their body language tell you? Someone who sits back with his or her arms folded sends a negative signal. Someone sitting forward, however, signals interest and eagerness. Look for employees with outgoing personalities who will be good with clients and guests.

Note appearance. Be sure to pay as much attention to the interviewee's appearance as to what he or she says. Notice if the applicant appears clean, well-groomed, and appropriately dressed for the interview. Does the person have good posture? Is he or she chewing gum? Does the person smile frequently?

Treat all applicants considerately and show a genuine interest in them, even if they have little or no chance of obtaining the job. Every applicant should be treated as a potential customer, because they are.

Be on time. Make certain that you are on time and ready to receive the applicant. Arriving late or changing appointment dates at the last minute will give the applicant the impression that you are unorganized and that the business is run in the same manner.

Know the job being offered. You cannot possibly match someone's abilities with a job you do not know or understand completely.

Ensure privacy. All interviews must be conducted in privacy, preferably in the interviewer's office. Interruptions must be kept to a minimum.

Set applicant at ease. Have comfortable chairs and beverages available. Speak in a conversational, interested tone.

Answer questions. Applicants will be full of questions about the job, its duties, the salary, etc. Newspaper advertisements tell only a little about the job and your company, so allow plenty of time for this important discussion.

Listen. Whenever possible, let the applicants speak. You can learn a great deal about them by the way they talk about themselves, past jobs, former supervisors, and school experiences. Watch for contradictions, excuses, and, especially, the applicant being on the defensive or speaking in a negative manner. Avoiding subjects is an obvious indication that there was some sort of problem there in the past; be persistent about getting the whole story, but don't be overbearing. Come back to it later if necessary.

Be neutral. Never reveal that you may disapprove of something an applicant has done or said; always appear open-minded. On the other hand, don't condone or approve of anything that is obviously in error.

Catch 'em off guard. Always ask a few questions they don't expect and aren't prepared for: What do they do to relax? What are their hobbies? What is the last book they read? Try to understand their attitudes, personalities, and energy levels.

Discuss previous employment. Perhaps one of the most useful things you can ask when interviewing prospective employees is, "What were your favorite parts of your previous job?" Look to see if the things they liked to do with previous employers fit with the things you'll be asking them to do for you. This is critical; it is important to cross-train employees to do as many jobs as possible, and it helps to know which of those jobs will be a good fit.

Often in interviewing prospective food service employees you'll get two types of applicants: those who say they prefer the "people part" of the job (talking to people, serving customers, running the cash register) and those who like the "food part" of the job (chef, salad prep, line cook). Most applicants will be fairly honest about what they like to do.

Ask scenario-based questions: What would you do if a customer complained "The soup just doesn't taste right," or "What would you do if your seemingly happy patron did not leave any tip at all?" This reveals whether the person knows what to do or has good judgment.

You can't rely on scenario questions to reveal what the applicant will actually do when faced with the situation in real life. Take your question one step further and ask about a specific time when he or she encountered a situation in the past, and then probe for details about the candidate actually did. Some ideas include: "Tell me about a time when a customer complained about the quality of the food you served. What was the problem? How did you react? What was your role in the resolution? What did you learn from the experience?" These questions are based on the truism that the best predictor of future behavior is past behavior.

Interview Legally

There are two basic types of interview problems: 1) interviewer deficiencies that can be improved with training, and 2) discriminatory actions or impacts that may result in compliance actions or lawsuits. There is no way to guarantee that you will never be sued. However, employers can do several things that will minimize the risk.

Employers should:

- Design questions carefully.

- Ask only pre-planned questions.

- Ask the same questions of every applicant.

- Document responses carefully.

- It is very important that the interview be documented in two ways: 1) notes taken during the interview, and 2) notes that recap what happened and support a recommendation or rejection after the interview is over. Create forms and instructions for people other than yourself who are involved in the hiring process.

- Be aware of any bias and work to rectify it.

- Treat every applicant with respect and dignity.

- Consider rejected applicants' challenges.

- Pay particular attention to your rejection methods. Although most applicants are rejected, ensure that the methods are professional, respectful and kind.

- Provide an internal method for rejected applicants' to challenge the rejection.

- Audit your process.

Do not wait for a third party to review your records and advise you that your selection process is flawed or discriminatory. Review your process annually for compliance with the affirmative action plan and know what your selection rates are. In the event that there appears to be an adverse impact, fully investigate the matter. Advise management of risks and enlist managers in finding solutions.

UNLAWFUL PRE-EMPLOYMENT QUESTIONS

Note: This section is not intended to serve on behalf of, or as a substitute for, legal counsel, or even as an interpretation of the various federal and state laws regarding equal and fair employment practices. The purpose of this section is to act as a guide to the type of questions that may or may not be legally asked of a potential employee.

A thorough discussion of this subject with both the state and federal labor offices and with your lawyer would be in order. Standard employment applications may be purchased at your office supply store. Before you use these forms, let your lawyer examine one to make certain that it doesn't contain or insinuate any questions that might be considered illegal.

The Federal Civil Rights Act of 1964 and other state and federal laws ensure that a job applicant will be treated fairly and on an equal basis, regardless of race, color, religious creed, age, sex or national origin. In order to support these regulations, you cannot ask certain questions of applicants in regard to the aforementioned categories.

There is a fine line between what may and may not be asked of applicants. Use basic common sense in regard to the type of questions you ask. Any illegal question would have no bearing on the outcome of the interview anyway, so avoid questions that are related to or might evoke an answer that infringes upon the applicant's civil rights.

Age/date of birth. This is an area of great concern for establishments with liquor, wine or beer licenses. Age is a sensitive pre-employment question because the Age Discrimination in Employment Act (**www.eeoc.gov/policy/adea.html**) protects employees 40 years old and above. It is permissible to ask an applicant to state his or her age if it is fewer than 18 years or if you are hiring for a bartending position. You may only ask for a date of birth for internal reasons; for example, computations with respect to a pension or profit-sharing plan, this information can be obtained after the person is hired.

Drugs, smoking. It is permissible to ask an applicant if he or she uses drugs or smokes. The application also affords an employer the opportunity to obtain the applicant's agreement to be bound by the employer's drug and smoking policies. It also affords an employer an opportunity to obtain the applicant's agreement to submit to drug testing.

Other problem areas:

- Questions concerning whether an applicant has friends or relatives working for the employer may be improper if the employer gives a preference to such applicants.

- Questions concerning credit rating or credit references have been ruled discriminatory against minorities and women.

- Questions concerning whether an applicant owns a home have been held to be discriminatory against minority members, since a greater number of minority members do not own their own homes.

- While questions about military experience or training are permissible, questions concerning the type of discharge received by an applicant have been held to be improper, because a high proportion of other-than-honorable discharges are given to minorities.

The Americans with Disabilities Act prohibits general inquiries about disabilities, health problems, and medical conditions.

Here is a list of prohibited questions, some of which are obvious but used to illustrate the point:

- How tall are you?

- What color are your eyes?

- Do you work out at the gym regularly?

- Do you or anyone you know have the HIV?

- Did you get any workers' comp from your last employer?

- How old are you?

- Have you been in prison?

- Are you really a man?

- Do you rent or own your home?

- Have you ever declared bankruptcy?

- What part of the world are your parents from?

- Are you a minority?

- Is English your first language?

- I can't tell if you're Japanese or Chinese. Which is it?

- So which church do you go to?

- Who will take care of the kids if you get this job?

- Is this your second marriage, then?

- Are you gay?

- Are you in a committed relationship right now?

- How does your boyfriend feel about you working here?

QUESTIONS YOU CAN AND SHOULD ASK

Start out by reviewing the applicant's work history and ask if anything would interfere with the person getting to work on time. Ask specifics about experience: Has the candidate ever served wine? How many tables have they waited on at one time? Have they made salads before?

Here are some specific questions you may want to ask:

- What are your strengths?

- What are your weaknesses?

- How would your current (or last) boss describe you?

- What were your boss's responsibilities?

- What's your opinion of them?

- How would your coworkers or subordinates describe you professionally?

- Why do you want to leave your present employer?

- Why should we hire you over the other finalists?

- What qualities or talents would you bring to the job?

- Tell me about your accomplishments.

- What is your most important contribution to your last (or current) employer?

- How do you perform under deadline pressure? Give me an example.

- How do you react to criticism?

- Describe a conflict or disagreement at work in which you were involved. How was it resolved?

- What are two of the biggest problems you've encountered at your job and how did you overcome them?

- Think of a major crisis you've faced at work and explain how you handled it.

- Give me an example of a risk that you took at your job (past or present) and how it turned out.

- What's your managerial style like?

- Have you ever hired employees; and, if so, have they lived up to your expectations?

- What type of performance problems have you encountered in people who report to you, and how did you motivate them to improve?

- Describe a typical day at your present (or last) job.

- What do you see yourself doing five years from now?

Include open-ended and behavioral questions as well.

- If you were serving a guest that appeared to have had too much to drink, what would you do?

- If a guest is served the wrong order or an improperly prepared order, how would you handle the situation?

- If a customer is on a restricted diet, what types of menu items would you suggest?

For more information about legal and appropriate interview strategies, visit

- **www.doi.gov/hrm/pmanager/st13c3.html**

- **www.doi.gov/hrm/pmanager/st13c.html**

- **www.restaurant.org**

OTHER INTERVIEW TIPS

Make sure to take notes during the interview. This will make it easier to compare potential candidates when you make your hiring decision.

A panel interview. In food service establishments, interviews are typically conducted by managers. You may want to think about including others in the interview process. If you're hiring a new server, for instance, you may want the serving captain to interview with you. This person may think to ask important questions you wouldn't. Do not include too many people, however, or you're likely to make the candidate a bundle of nerves.

Rehiring. Consider rehiring talented former employees. By rehiring someone you will save time and money on retraining. Do not, however, just throw the person back on the front lines. Give the rehire the same information as new hires and give them the appropriate amount of training.

Interview red flags. Watch out for individuals that show too much interest in hours, benefits, wages and titles during the interview process. This interest can signal a person that isn't too interested in work. Also, look for long lapses of time in the work history section of the application. Ask the person what they did during this time. They may simply have taken time out to raise children or it could signal a trouble spot.

WHAT TO LOOK FOR IN POTENTIAL EMPLOYEES

Many owners/managers fall into the "warm body" trap when hiring. Unfortunately, this practice is widespread and can cause many more problems than it solves. Turnover in the restaurant industry tends to be high, and you will find yourself short on staff. Given the hectic, demanding nature of the hospitality world, this is stressful for everyone and this is what tempts you to hire the first person that walks through the door. Ultimately, this only leads to higher training and hiring costs because this person often does not work out in the long run.

When hiring, make sure to take the time to carefully select your candidates. Here are some attributes to look for in this process:

Stability. You don't want employees to leave in two months. Look at past employment records. Stability also refers to the applicant's emotional makeup.

Leadership qualities. Employees must be those who are achievers and doers, not individuals who have to be led around by the hand. Look at past employment positions and growth rate.

Motivation. Why is the applicant applying to your operation? Why the food service industry in general? Is the decision career-related or temporary? Does the applicant appear to receive his motivation from within or by domineering others, such as a spouse or parent?

Independence. Is the applicant on his own? Does he appear to be financially secure? At what age did he leave home? And for what reasons?

Maturity. Is the individual mentally mature enough to work in a stressful environment? Will she be able to relate and communicate with other employees and customers who may be much older.

Determination. Does the applicant seem to always finish what he starts? Does he seem to look for, or retreat from, challenges? Examine time at school and at their last job.

Work habits. Is the applicant aware of the physical work involved in catering employment? Has the applicant done similar work? Does the applicant appear neat and organized? Look over the application; is it filled out per the instructions? neatly? in ink? Examine past jobs for number and rate of promotions and raises.

THE FINAL SELECTION AND DECISION

Reaching a decision and selecting who to offer the position to is often difficult. You may have many applicants who are qualified and would probably become excellent employees, but which one do you choose?

Always base your choice on the total picture the applicants have painted of themselves through the interviews, résumés and applications. Gather advice from those who interviewed or had contact with the individuals. Not only will this help you reach the correct decision, but will also make the rest of your staff feel a part of the management decision-making team. Whomever you select, he or she must be someone you feel good about having around, someone you hopefully will enjoy working with, and whom you feel will have a very good chance of being successful at the job.

When you offer him or her the job, make certain the applicant fully understands the following items before he or she accepts your offer.

Salary. Starting pay, salary range, expected growth rate, the day payroll is issued, company benefits, vacations, insurance, etc.

Job description. List of job duties, hours, expectations, etc.

First day particulars. Time, date and to whom he should report to on the first day of work.

Rejecting Applicants

Rejecting applicants is always an unpleasant and difficult task. The majority of the applications will be rejected almost immediately. Some applicants will ask the reason for rejection. Always be honest, but use tact in explaining the reasoning behind the decision. Avoid confrontation, explaining only what is necessary to settle the applicant's questions. Usually it will be sufficient to say, "We accepted an applicant who was more experienced," or "who is better qualified."

As mentioned before, some applications may be transferred into a "prospective file" for later reference. Inform the applicant of this action, but don't give the impression that he or she has a good chance of being hired, nor state a specific date when you will be looking for new employees.

Create a Personnel File

Once the applicant is hired, a personnel file should be set up immediately. It should contain the following information:

- Application.

- Form W-4 and Social Security number.

- Name, address and phone number.

- Emergency phone number.

- Employment date.

- Job title and pay rate.

- Past performance evaluations.

- Signed form indicating receipt and acceptance of Employee Handbook/Personnel Policy Manual.

- INS Form I-9. You are required by law to have employees provide proof of citizenship an fill out an I-9 form. For more information on I-9 forms, log onto the U.S. Immigration and Naturalization Service Web site at **www.ins.usdoj.gov**. For information about work place discrimination, visit the Federal Consumer Information Center at **www.pueblo.gsa.gov/ call/workplace.htm**.

Employee Handbook and Orientation

One of the first training materials your new employees will see is an employee handbook. Federal law mandates that all employers, regardless of size, have written policy guidelines. Employee handbooks/ policy manuals are used to familiarize new employees with company policies and procedures and serve as guides to management personnel.

POLICY MANUAL

Formally writing down your policies could keep you out of court; prevent problems and misunderstandings; save time spent answering common questions; and help you look more professional to your employees. Explaining and documenting company policy to your employees has been proven to increase productivity, compliance and retention. Here are some of the most common inclusions:

TOPICS TO BE COVERED IN EMPLOYEE HANDBOOK		
Standards of Conduct	Employee Conduct	Bonus Plan
Absenteeism and Punctuality	Work Performance	Performance Reviews
Neatness of Work Area	Availability for Work	Benefits Program
Personal Telephone Calls	Personal Mail	Benefits Eligibility
Mandatory Meetings	Communications	Insurance
Employee Relations	Problem Resolution	Insurance Continuation
Use of Company Vehicles	Disciplinary Guidelines	Personal Appearance
Confidentiality of Company Information	Safety	Conflicts of Interest

TOPICS TO BE COVERED IN EMPLOYEE HANDBOOK		
Violence and Weapons Policy	Workplace Monitoring	Holidays
Severe Weather	Suggestions	Vacation
Orientation	Equal Employment Opportunity	Bereavement Leave
Harassment	Criminal Convictions	Social Security
Personnel Files	Employment References	Pre-Tax Deductions
Employment of Relatives	Outside Employment	Military Leave
Rehiring Former Employees	Searches	Medical Leave of Absence
Substance Abuse	Solicitations & Contributions	Family Leave of Absence
Company Property	Office Equipment	Employee Discounts
Tools and Equipment	Employment Classification	Workers' Compensation
Hours of Work	Break Policy	Jury Duty
Recording Time	Overtime	Unemployment Compensation
Salary and Wage Increases	Payroll	Educational Assistance
Travel Expenses	Reimbursable Expenses	Job Abandonment
Voluntary Resignation	Performance-Based Release	Acts of Misconduct
Termination Procedures	Other Forms of Separation	Affidavit of Receipt

Lack of communication along with inadequate policies and guidelines have been cited as major factors in workplace legal disputes. Failure to inform or notify employees of standard policies has resulted in the loss of millions of dollars in legal judgments. Simply not being aware that their actions violated company policy has been an effective defense for many terminated employees. For this reason it is important to have the employee sign a document stating he or she has received, reviewed, understands, and intends to comply with all policies in the manual.

If you have ever written a policy document before, you know how time consuming it can be. Even if you were a lawyer, it would likely take you 40 hours to research and write a comprehensive employee manual. To pay someone to draw one up for you can cost thousands of dollars. Atlantic Publishing has put together a standard employee handbook guide for the food-service industry. The template contains all of the most important company handbook sections, and it's written in Microsoft Word so that customizing and printing your manual will be as easy as possible. The program currently sells for around $70 and is available at **www.atlantic-pub.com**, and 1-800-814-1132.

When writing your employee manual, keep these simple writing tips in mind:

- Write for your audience. Make sure the tone, style, and language reflect the audience you are writing for.

- Organize your material before you begin writing.

- Make sure to revise and edit. It's also a good idea to have someone else read your handbook. A second pair of eyes often catches mistakes you might have missed.

- Use simple, direct language, and avoid wordiness.

- Use the active voice—instead of saying, "The server was taking the drink order" say, "The server took the drink order." Active voice keeps your manual much more immediate and it emphasizes your subject (the employee or trainee) rather than the object.

- Use gender-neutral language.

ORIENTATION

Time spent orienting, training and motivating new staff is time well spent. Happy, well-informed employees are more likely to stay put and save you the hassle of going through the whole recruitment process. But where do you start? Consider the following:

Provide new staff with an overview. For example, sum up your philosophy and the purpose of your business. Provide new employees with the handbook. Get the general manager to welcome them, personally. Give new employees a tour of the property. Introduce them to their supervisors and colleagues.

Explain the rules. Explain and demonstrate the main rules and regulations regarding the job—on day one, not when the first problem arises.

Give new employees a space to call their own. Allocate parking and locker room spaces. Assign name-tags.

Training. Once initial orientation has been completed, start the training process. This is usually conducted in groups or consists of on-the-job training.

The responsibility for training varies depending on the size of your organization. Large operations may have an HR department that will coordinate much of the orientation process. If you are a one-man show, you get to do it all. Someone who knows catering and has served in the position better performs specific, job-related training.

Training may be informal but be sure to include some formal training in areas of high importance or that demand high levels of regulation. High-class service, for instance, demands continual training. A good resource for training guidelines is the The Food & Beverage Committee of the Hotel Sales & Marketing Association International. It has developed training guidelines that caterers can use to help new staff become familiar with all relevant operating activities.

Orientation Training

A complete orientation of the trainee to his or her new job and new company is an integral part of the training process. The entire orientation may not even take thirty minutes, but it is so often overlooked and new employees are left to fend for themselves. Give the new employee a good introduction before he or she starts the actual training. Described below are some basic orientation practices.

- Introduce the new employee to yourself and the company.

- Introduce the new employee to all of the other employees.

- Introduce the new employee to his or her trainer and supervisor.

- Explain the company's employee and personnel policies. Present the Employee Handbook/ Personnel Policy Manual.

- Outline the objectives and goals of the training program:

  a. Describe the training and where and how it will take place.

  b. Describe the information that will be learned.

  c. Describe the skills and attitudes that will be developed.

Set up a schedule for the employee. It should include:

- The date, day and time to report to work during training.

- Who will be doing the training and who the supervisor is.

- What should be learned and accomplished each day.

- The date when the training should be completed.

At this point, the trainee may be presented to the trainer. Ideally, the employee's regular supervisor does all of the training. The trainer must be a model employee who is thoroughly knowledgeable about and experienced in the job. He or she must be able to communicate clearly and have a great deal of patience and understanding.

The trainee must be taught the how, why, when and where of the job. This is best accomplished by following the trainer's example and methods. After confidence is built, the employee may attempt to repeat the procedure under the watchful eye of the trainer.

The trainer must gauge how fast the trainee is learning and absorbing the material against the established time schedule.

Compare the trainee's production to that of an experienced worker. Written and practical tests can be given to evaluate how much material is being absorbed and utilized. Add new material when the old material has been assimilated. Relate the old material to the new as you continue to train the employee.

Once the employee has completed the training, the trainer should prepare a final written report and evaluation for the personnel file. This report should describe the strengths and weaknesses of the trainee, his or her knowledge of the job, quality of work, attitude, and a general appraisal of the employee. Solicit feedback about the training program from the employee. Use the information to revise and improve the training program.

It sounds like a great deal of work, and if you are just opening a business it is tempting to brush over this training and attend to what might be considered more pressing business matters. However, nothing could be more pressing than making sure you have the resources in place to serve your clients and their guests with impeccable standards.

Orientation Package

Orientation is more than just job-related training; it is a process for new employees to get a sense of belonging and feel like they know how things are done in your company. Here is a list of things you may want to include in the orientation packet, if they are not already included in the employee handbook:

- Scheduling procedures
- Uniform requirements
- Employee benefits
- Employee meal policy
- Tip-reporting procedure (or if tips are automatically included in catering cost)
- Policy on employee eating or drinking leftovers
- Pay periods and clocking-in and out procedures
- Job description
- Safety and emergency plans
- Copy of the menu and wine list
- Copy of an employee call list

A sample orientation checklist follows. As you go through orientation with an employee, check things off that you have covered. When orientation is complete, put the completed form in the employee's personnel file.

ORIENTATION CHECKLIST

Employee Name:_____ Hire Date:_____

Introduction

____ Welcome the employee

____ Give employee the history of company (how business began, target audience, event specializations, theme, organization chart, etc.)

____ Mission (talk about attitude towards guests, food quality, mutual respect of coworkers, how to handle problems, etc.)

Tour

____ Tour of facilities

____ Introduction to coworkers

Policies

____ **Appearance/dress code**

    ____ Uniform

    ____ Hygiene

    ____ Name tags and aprons

    ____ Jewelry and hair

____ **Conduct and Attitude**

    ____ Attendance/punctuality

    ____ Finding subs

    ____ Behavior in front of guests

    ____ Attitude towards guests and coworkers

____ **Time Card**

____ **Job performance**

    ____ Job description and expectations

    ____ Work schedule

    ____ Probationary period

    ____ Training period

    ____ Training program

    ____ Performance reviews

____ **Pay**

    ____ Time period and when checks are issued

    ____ Wage

    ____ When employee will receive first paycheck

    ____ Policy on wage increases and promotions

EMPLOYEE CHECKLIST

___**Hiring Paperwork**

___W-2

___Insurance forms

___I-9

___Tip declaration

___Alcohol serving policy

___**Safety**

___Kitchen/knives

___Fires

___Preventing accidents

___Reporting accidents

___Emergency procedures

___**Sanitation**

___Washing hands

___Cleaning

___Safe food temperatures

___**Discipline**

___Drug/alcohol use

___Verbal and written warnings

___Progressive discipline policy

___Giving away food

___Fighting

___**Personal Visits/Calls**

___**Breaks**

___**Smoking**

___**Emergency Information**

___**Parking**

___**Sexual Harassment**

___**Employee Theft**

___**Requesting Time Off**

___**Benefits**

___Insurance (medical, dental, life, etc.)

___Sick time

___Vacation

___Workers' compensation

___Promotions

___Awards programs

___Meal policy

___401(k)

Signature of Employee:_____ Date:_____

Signature of Manager:_____ Date:_____

ORIENTATION RESOURCES

A good online resource for information on how to develop an orientation program is "Deliver the Promise" at **www.deliverthepromise.com**. This site also offers information on strategies to retain employees, as well as mentoring and coaching. They also offer an online employee orientation. Also visit HP Invent at **www.hp.com** for information on their employee orientation service.

Training and Motivating

As important as it is to get qualified, trainable employees hired; to make any training program work, the owner or manager must get involved.

YOU AS THE LEADER

As the owner, you are the leader of your team of employees. Here are some tips that will help you to become a successful leader.

Leadership qualities. What makes a good leader? Think back to bosses you had during your early years in food service. Who stands out and why? You probably remember the managers that respected employees, showed concern for their staff, and were not afraid to pitch in wherever needed. These are all qualities that make a good leader.

Participate. Whenever you see that your employees need help, pitch in. Whether that means answering the phone or pouring a glass of water, you show your employees that you care about the success of the operation and that you acknowledge and value the work done by each member of the team.

Know yourself. Know your own strengths and weaknesses; capitalize on the former and minimize the latter. If you have poor math skills, hire an accountant to compensate for this weakness. If your people skills are strong, make sure you spend a lot of time on the floor with your employees and customers.

Be part of the team. Pitch in when someone is missing. Your employees will appreciate your effort and respect you for lending a hand rather than managing from on high.

Accept differences. Always remember that your employees are individuals. Accept the different styles of your employees, but always expect good performance. Be alert to the training and development needs of each individual employee. Meet those needs.

Be fair and consistent with policies and procedures. Treat all your employees equally. Don't show favoritism. If you dock one employee's pay for an unexcused absence, don't look the other way when the next employee is a no show with no excuse.

Reinforce positive behavior. The saying "you catch more flies with honey" is true. You are more likely to get the behavior you want out of your employees if you reward them for acceptable behavior. While you always have to discipline for inappropriate behavior, let them know they did a good job and that you appreciate it.

Share your vision. Help your employees relate to the bigger picture. Employees can easily get bogged down by detail and focus on one dish or one table, to the detriment of the rest of their duties. It can be difficult for them to step back and see how their behavior might affect the business and profits as a whole.

Encourage communication. Make an effort to encourage your staff to communicate with each other and yourself. Let them know that you want to know what they need and what they appreciate. By understanding their needs, you'll make working together much easier.

Encourage new ideas. Be careful not to assemble a team of "yes men." Creative solutions to problems come from diverse points of view, so don't surround yourself with other management team members who think just like you do. Encourage those who disagree to speak up as well. You may, for example, want to consider rotating meeting leaders to make sure your own point of view isn't the only one heard.

Support creativity. Be creative when looking for solutions. In meetings, when you are looking for solutions, state your target/problem simply and clearly. Often solutions are to be found within a range of possibilities with no single answer being right. Begin by brainstorming, and appoint one or two recorders to keep track of all ideas. Halfway through, change recorders and freshen the mix of the group. Encourage people use their imaginations, and consider the suggestions logically and inventively.

Manage conflict. Conflict resolution is a tricky part of being a leader. Remember, conflict is not always a negative thing and can often be useful. Encourage people to speak up about what bothers them. Engage in active listening when dealing with a conflict. Also be sure to set norms for politeness, good behavior, and honesty.

Teamwork

While you may be the leader in your catering company, you can't do everything, so you need to rely on the people you so diligently hired to help you out. This means you must establish and support a team environment. Teamwork can increase your productivity, improve decision making, maximize the use of your human resources, and make better use of your inventory. With effective teamwork you can improve the bottom line, but teams often need a little bit of help to become effective, so teamwork training is often in order. Before you go out and start building your team, you need to know what a team is and how it functions.

WHAT IS A TEAM?

A team is a manageable number of people with similar or coordinated functions working together for the common goal of providing seamless service. Usually 2 to 25 people (ideally 10 to 15 people) make a manageable number of people. You can think of teams as front-of-the-house teams and back-of-the-house teams. If you have a large staff, one particular position could be a team or your teams could be organized by shift.

The members of a team must have common goals, similar or complementary functions, and equal responsibility for team performance. Everyone should have the same definitions of team and teamwork for the teams to work.

To delegate responsibility, you must choose team leaders. These people do not necessarily have to be the best performers, but they should be people who can motivate and train others and carry a full load. They will be the naturals, the ones to whom others naturally look. Make sure you have more than one leader for each team, so that changing schedules can be accommodated and no shift will be without a team leader.

Goals established by you alone will never be fully accepted by the group. You need to encourage your employees to share in the tasks of goal setting and determining the criteria used to assess whether or not goals have been achieved. By allowing employees to participate in decision making, you allow employees to take ownership of their jobs and of the operation. When this occurs, employees are much more willing to go the extra mile and ensure performance standards are being maintained. If they have a stake in the decision making, they have a stake in the outcome.

TEAM BUILDING

Any type of food service business requires teamwork. Servers must have the cooperation of the kitchen staff and the kitchen staff must have the cooperation of the dining room staff. All employees must be able to work harmoniously with all other fellow employees if they are to achieve good results.

The easiest way to build a team is to demand courteous behavior. This is not an easy task in a busy catering operation, but it is absolutely necessary. Just as employees are required to be respectful and polite with clients and guest, so they must be with their fellow employees. Using "please" and "thank you" often and respecting the manner and working habits of others go a long way toward creating a harmonious team environment.

Be sure to engage in team-building behavior yourself. A team falls apart easily if you as the leader fail to reinforce the fact that they are a team working for a common goal. Let members get to know each other in a casual setting. Perhaps have a staff party, and take instant photos of teams and put them on bulletin boards in the back of the facility. You could also create a scrapbook that includes personal details, pets, family, and personal goals. Update it regularly.

If one member of a team doesn't perform, the whole team suffers and team trust is compromised. Be sure to reward good behavior, but also set conditions for poor behavior, and make sure everyone knows the standards. It is not useful simply to say, "Don't make mistakes," or "Don't have accidents." Find out why an employee is having problems, and work together to find the cause and a solution.

Also remember that not all teams are the same. Kitchen team members are more specialized and less likely to switch functions. Front team members have primary but not fixed responsibilities and are more likely to interchange functions, covering for each other to ensure smooth service. Make sure all team members understand the differences and what their own responsibilities are.

A slowdown in one function can upset the entire flow of service to all customers. The team leader can define and assign secondary task responsibilities during the daily meeting. Sometimes a buddy system works well to adjust front-of-the-house staff to shift away from the "not-my-job" syndrome and do whatever it takes to deliver great service every time.

Teamwork Training

There are online sources available to help train your management and staff in teamwork. For training materials and information on teamwork training, try **www.conferencecontent.com/content_ teambuilding.htm**.

BUILDING TRUST AND TEAM SPIRIT

Every person in the organization is important and has a critical role. Ensure that employees know their role in your organization and how their job fits into the organization's overall goals. If you ask the dishwasher what he does and he replies, "I wash dishes," you need to get to work on team spirit. If he replies "I make sure that the business can function properly, by providing a constant supply of clean dishes," then you have already succeeded.

As an owner/manager you can foster team spirit by:

- Paying your employees at least as much as your competitors and allowing for adequate employee benefits.

- Organizing a secure working environment.

- Providing rewards for those employees who do things right, especially from day one.

- Disciplining those who keep doing things wrong and those who like to stir trouble.

- Practicing firm and fair leadership.

- Encouraging employees to solve day-to-day customer service problems, themselves and by supporting their decisions.

- Creating opportunities for the best staff members to move up in the company.

- Projecting a lively image by conducting upbeat staff meetings, while including staff in the planning and organization of the operation.

- Remaining flexible with your employees. Most catering employees work several jobs because most caterers do not hire large full-time staffs. Your workers are going to be juggling multiple events as well as families and other responsibilities. Work with them on scheduling; if you try to be flexible with them, they will reward your efforts by being flexible and loyal.

Employee Motivation

People are motivated to work hard for employers who care about them. By creating a caring work environment, your employees will take the extra effort to make your establishment a better place. Here are some practical and common-sense approaches to providing a motivating work environment.

Take and use employee suggestions. Make sure your employees know that you value their opinions by utilizing their suggestions.

Act. A sure way to develop a poor attitude in staff is to retain someone who is not performing up to standards. Work to train the employee. If the individual is still not making the grade, take action and fire the employee. Not only is it necessary from a customer service standpoint, but it also shows your staff that you are serious about keeping a strong team environment.

Inform. Include your employees in your decision-making processes and explain what the clients' expectations are. Give them credit for knowing how to do their jobs well.

Provide benefits. In an effort to professionalize the service, some caterers with regular employees pay regular wages every two weeks and include health and dental insurance, 401(k) plans (with 25 percent matching contributions), paid vacations, and merit-based raises. Having these additional benefits will motivate your employees to do a good job. This also promotes longevity. Although it may not be as attractive for the student who wants to work short shifts or flexible schedules, the more mature employees will be very interested.

Praise. One of the greatest motivators is praise. Praise motivates employees to produce results and it reinforces positive behavior.

UNCONVENTIONAL MOTIVATORS

Benefits, raises, and a caring environment are tried and tested ways to motive employees. Try some creative, inexpensive ways as well.

Films. Use films such as "Apocalypse Now" to show how passions lead to outstanding results. You can have a night out with the staff. If you don't have an event on a particular Monday, hold a screening. Bring popcorn and other snacks, and have a discussion about the themes from the movie that you want to discuss afterwards.

Trips to farms. Take your serving staff to an organic farm or local winery to help with food and wine education.

Inspire. Don't just manage your employees; inspire them! Inspiration will help lead them to the next level of productivity and it will guarantee exceptional service to your guests.

Pitch in. Show your staff that no job is too small by doing some of the smallest jobs yourself. Help bus tables on a busy night, or put on an apron and rub elbows with the dishwasher when he or she falls hopelessly behind.

Pat on the back. Inspiration can come from an action as simple as a pat on the back. Make sure you tell your employees when they do a good job and communicate that you are proud they are a part of your team. The time for this type of feedback is in the moment. Don't wait a week to say good job, do it right now!

Show respect. It's simple. People are more likely to work hard for someone who respects them. Give them some responsibility. For instance, instead of making them come to you when someone sends an entrée back, give them some guidelines to work with, then let them handle the situation.

Employee poker. A more general contest involves a deck of cards and the best poker hand. At the beginning of the week (or event), tell your employees that each time you spot an example of good service, you will give that employee a card. At the end of the week (event), the employee with the best poker hand wins a prize.

COMPENSATION

It's a well-known fact that when caterers gather to discuss their trade, one of the most controversial topics is whether to pay catering staff as independent contractors or as employees. If you consider the fact that you need not pay the employer's share of Social Security and Medicare taxes, unemployment taxes and workers' compensation insurance for your independent contractors, the amount of savings could amount up to 20 percent of total payroll expenses. When considering the prickly subject of compensation, you need to be clear about the following issues.

Federal laws. Federal laws establish the minimum wage, currently at $5.15 per hour. You may pay people as little as $2.12 per hour, if the wages and their tips equal the minimum wage. Be aware of the child labor laws that affect caterers who employ young people to bus/wash dishes and set tables. To find out more about federal labor and wage regulations, you can visit the U.S. Department of Labor Web site at **www.dol.gov**.

Employee benefits. What are your obligations? Required employee benefits are usually paid as payroll taxes. In addition to federal taxes, some states also require employers to contribute to their unemployment benefit programs and the state-operated workers' compensation programs. As a general rule, the minimum cost of required employee benefits equals approximately 15 to 18 percent of your total payroll expense.

Discretionary benefits. For example, health, dental, optical and life insurance may be offered to employees at a reduced rate. Consider providing stock option plans, 401(k) plans, free meals, paid vacation time and sick days, insurance coverage for dependents, formal training, etc.

Unions. Bear in mind that unionized properties tend to adopt generous overtime pay policies, as well as very favorable holiday pay schemes. You may be required, for instance, to pay double time instead of time and a half for all overtime worked.

Contractor versus employee. If the IRS reclassified your independent contractors as employees, you would need to pay the employee benefits for as long as they went unpaid. There also may be penalties assessed by the IRS. If you contract for a party and arrange for the client to pay the staff direct, then you'll need to scrutinize the contract between yourself and the client, carefully. You'll also have to establish who exactly is responsible for supervising the workers—you or the client? State laws vary, so be aware of the issue. Log onto the IRS's Web site for information pertaining to federal taxes at **www. irs.gov**.

Compensation packages. Typical compensation packages in the food service industry include salaries, wages, commissions, bonuses, tips, etc. Management positions usually receive predetermined salaries. Bonuses and commissions, however, may also be part of their compensation package.

Sales and marketing staff may be on monthly, weekly or hourly pay, totally on commission, or a combination. In catering, commissions usually fall in the range of 2 to 10 percent, but they can vary from area to area.

When calculating commission, don't forget to exclude delivery and rental charges, service charges, etc. It usually boils down to paying a commission on gross food and beverage charges. Remember, commissions reinforce productivity. Apart from your reps, also consider offering your administrative sales people who produce results a level of commission on top of their salaries. Don't hesitate to reward these employees.

Generosity. Most food preparation staffers are poorly paid, with wages slightly above minimum wage. Give your staff all that you can afford. You'll have a better chance of getting them on short notice for that last-minute event.

Pay for transport time. Pay for the hours spent traveling one-way when you are transporting your staff to an off-premise catering event. It's a formula that works for both the employer and the employee.

Overtime. Overtime should be pre-planned and approved by the management. It should not be confused, however, with the hours of catered events that extend beyond the planned stop time. In this situation, you'll need to pay your staff for the extra hours worked.

Leftovers. When figuring the number of servings you will need for an event, plan to have enough to feed your workers. Catering and restaurant staff don't get many breaks in the real world, and your staff will love you for thinking of their food needs.

Maintaining Performance Standards and Conducting Performance Reviews

As an employer, you need to monitor employee performance to ensure performance levels stay within your high standards. People tend to forget and slack off after a period of time, so it's very important for you to closely supervise your employees and correct these slippages when they occur.

Your job is not over when training is complete. You still need to give your employees feedback on how they are doing, letting them know if they are maintaining the performance standards your expect. One way to do this is to develop ways to monitor employee performance and communicate how they are doing. There are two general ways to monitor employee performance: informal and formal.

INFORMAL PERFORMANCE MONITORING

This type of monitoring is done on a day-to-day basis and includes actions such as observing employees at work, tasting food, and checking in with customers. Of course this is only part of the informal monitoring process; you must communicate to them when they are performing well and when they need to improve.

When communicating with employees about performance issues, you will most likely be praising or criticizing. Many managers focus too heavily on criticizing employees for poor performance, thinking this is the best or only way to change behavior. Praise for work done well can be a strong reinforcement for the behavior you want to see. Employees need to know what they have done right as much as what they have done wrong. Praise motivates employees to do a good job by building confidence and pride. Constant criticism will only make an employee resentful rather than a good performer.

When criticizing an employee's performance, be sure to be respectful—give them the benefit of the doubt and always listen. Make sure you get all the facts before making a judgment. Criticism, when done constructively, is beneficial in improving employee performance and building their skill level. Here are a few tips on making constructive criticism.

Criticize the action not the person. It is the action that is wrong, not the person doing the task. Do not criticize an employee's character or intelligence.

Don't focus on the trivial.

Be clear. Make sure you are clear when explaining what the employee is doing incorrectly and explain the correct way to accomplish the task.

Don't get angry. Anger will only provoke fear and cause a loss of motivation in your employees.

FORMAL PERFORMANCE MONITORING

Formal performance monitoring goes beyond the daily observing of employee behavior. Formal performance monitoring focuses on particular aspects of job performance, and you will need to develop specific ways to monitor these aspects. You will need to set standards, measure performance, and provide employees feedback on their performance.

Setting standards. Make sure your standards are specific and clearly defined. They should also be achievable so employees do not become frustrated.

Measuring performance. Measurements should be fair and communicated to all employees.

Feedback. Setting standards and measuring performance is useless unless you communicate the standards and tell the employee how he or she is doing. People cannot change inappropriate or unwanted behavior if no one tells them to. Employees not meeting the standards need to be told and corrective action must be taken. Employees who are meeting or exceeding the standards need to be praised and recognized for their efforts. Feedback should be given regularly.

The following are some ways to measure performance:

- **Comment cards.** Comment cards are a good source of information for measuring performance. Since they are anonymous, people are usually quite candid in their remarks.

- **Talk with guests.** Always make it a practice to walk around the event and check in with the guests on how their meal and service was. Most people appreciate the attention and concern, and many will be very honest in their comments.

- **Talk with your client.** Make sure to get feedback about the service level of your staff. You may not always see what goes on—perhaps your receptionist is gruff on the phone or your servers were too friendly with certain guests.

ANNUAL PERFORMANCE REVIEWS

Performance reviews are another important way to give your staff feedback on how they are doing. These should never take the place of regular feedback; they should be used in conjunction with them. Remember that nothing you say in a review should come as a surprise to your employee. Always give your staff regular feedback, both positive and negative. Performance reviews focus on how the employee is doing overall rather than focusing on specific tasks or job areas.

Typically, the manager or supervisor completes an evaluation form and then shares and discusses it with the employee during a meeting. The purpose of the performance review is to maintain good performance and improve poor performance. They serve a purpose in your training program because they provide you with information on types of training the employee needs or wants.

Remember, you are evaluating an employee's performance in relation to the standards you have set up. Refer to the job lists you established when developing your performance review forms.

Intent of reviews. The results of performance reviews are two-fold. First, you must use a review in order to judge how well the employee is doing his or her job and whether or not the employee is eligible for a wage increase. Additionally, and perhaps more importantly, reviews are used to set goals for employees.

Setting goals. When setting goals for improving performance, be sure to make them concrete.

Types of review. In general, there are two kinds of performance reviews. One uses input just from the employee's supervisor; the other type uses input from other staff members as well. Many companies, recently, have switched to a performance-review system that involves other staff members. This type of review, called "360-degree feedback," involves the supervisor collecting information from staff members who work with the employee. The supervisor then takes the staff input information and his assessment of the employee and uses this information during the evaluation interview. At no time are names used, so the other employees can feel comfortable giving honest feedback. The site **www.360-degreefeedback.com** has specific information pertaining to the 360-degree feedback process. Additional sites with human resources information include the International Association for Human Resources Information at **www.ihrim.org**, **www.business.com/directory/human_resources/index.asp**. and The Society for Human Resource Management at **www.shrm.org**. You also can download performance appraisal forms and related material for $39.95 at **www.performance-appraisal-form.com**.

Self-review. Before you conduct the review, ask the employee to review themself and to bring this review to the session. This will help you to understand how they see themself.

Be specific. Don't just tell your employee they need to improve, explain how they need to improve. Give them specific behaviors you would like to see improved and tell them how to go about making positive changes.

Be fair. It's difficult to review someone, but be as fair and consistent as you possibly can.

Let the employee speak. Performance reviews should be a dialogue, not a lecture. Be sure to let your employee talk about what he or she thinks they do well and where they might need improvement.

Discuss what the employee does well. Don't just focus on the negative. Be sure to give praise where praise is due.

Maintain a review schedule. Give your employees annual reviews. You may want to schedule all reviews during a month that is always slow. You could also schedule reviews for employees' anniversary dates. For new employees, schedule a review in the first couple of months to give them immediate feedback on their new job.

Review questions. Some of the behavior you will want to address in reviews includes the person's relationship with others, their problem-solving skills, accountability, enthusiasm, and team spirit. Structure your questions accordingly. Focus questions on the following areas:

- Does the employee fulfill his or her job duties?
- Does the employee use sound judgment in keeping a safe work environment?
- Does the employee assist others with work?
- Is the employee responsible and punctual?

Use a rating system for the questions. Be sure to include an area for comments on the form as well; if someone is not performing their duties, you will want specific information on the problem areas.

Review location. A performance review should always be conducted on neutral ground. Don't conduct them in your office; the person you are reviewing is likely to feel threatened. The review should not feel like a disciplinary interview; it should be a dialogue between you and an employee with the goal of making the employee more productive. You may want to conduct the review off premises or you could go to another room. It's also very important that reviews be conducted in private, so make sure you will not be interrupted.

HANDLING DIFFICULT EMPLOYEES

Unfortunately, everyone is not going to be a model employee, and you will have to deal with difficult employee situations. As a manager you have to address the issue and try to find a way to solve it. Difficult employees come in all shapes and sizes. Here are just a few of them:

The new employee. A difficult employee in the sense that he or she does not yet know what is expected, and he or she needs training in order to reach the desired performance level.

Inconsistent employee. He or she often performs well, but just as often the employee performs poorly. You know this particular person is capable of doing the job because he or she has shown you that on various occasions. Oftentimes these employees require much more feedback than other employees to get them on track.

Unbalanced employee. Often very good at one job task, but only so-so at others. You may have a cook that is an excellent sous chef, but this same employee leaves the kitchen a wreck after the shift.

Mediocre employees. Does just good enough. They show up on time and do their jobs, but they do not really produce high-quality work.

Less-than-mediocre employee. Nearly falls short of doing their job. Often wastes time and is rarely productive.

The bad employee. Does little work, has a high absenteeism rate, and does very few tasks correctly.

Here are some of the warning signs that you may have a difficult employee:

- Poor work quality
- Complains a great deal
- Does not follow direction
- Blames others for mistakes

- Absenteeism is high
- Shows little initiative and does not cooperate
- Is defensive when approached about problems
- Does not interact well with coworkers

Once you have identified poor employees, you have to do something about them. Most organizations suggest using a progressive disciplinary policy when discipline is necessary.

Take corrective action. Explain the problem to the employee. Identify the performance problem and talk about the reasons the problem is occurring. Make sure the employee understands the job performance expectations, and talk about ways to correct the undesired behavior. Remember, the emphasis is on improvement, not punishment.

Only after coaching and counseling has been tried several times should a manager move on to disciplinary action. Once disciplinary action does start, it should take place in several phases.

Oral warning. The first step in a progressive disciplinary policy is usually an oral warning. The employee will be warned by the manager in a private conversation that includes what is expected of the employee; a chance for the employee to explain his behavior; suggestions for correcting the actions, and further disciplinary action will occur if the actions continue. Even though this step is called "oral," you should be sure to make a written record of the warning and include it in the employee's personnel file.

Written warning. If the employee repeats the offense, you will record it as a written warning and include it in the employee's personnel file. The manager reviews the warning with the employee and the employee signs it, indicating he or she has received the warning and understands.

Suspension or termination. Some discipline policies allow for a suspension step between written warnings and termination and others don't. You will need to decide which type of policy best fits your operation. If you do include a suspension step, the seriousness of the offense should determine the length of time of the suspension (all suspensions are without pay).

Terminating an employee is a serious step to take. An employee can be terminated due to the frequency or serious nature of misconduct. Very serious offenses, however, may be grounds for immediate termination without following the above progressive disciplinary steps. If you terminate an employee, you will want to be sure to include this paperwork in the employee's personnel file as well.

When you create a progressive discipline policy, keep the following in mind:

- Be sure your policy is appropriate for your business and your employees.

- Make sure you specifically list what behaviors will be subject to the policy and which behaviors will result in immediate dismissal. For example, if an employee is chronically late, you may wish to use your progressive disciplinary policy. If an employee has been stealing, state that this type of behavior will result in immediate termination.

- Make sure you advise all employees of the policy. You can let new employees know in their orientation. If you need to communicate the information to current employees, include it on the agenda of a company meeting and make sure all employees receive a written copy of the policy.

- Make sure to determine how you want to document the policy (that is, how you want to maintain a record of oral warnings, written warnings, and termination paperwork), and decide how long to keep the information on file.

Developing a Training Program

To develop a training program you must first develop a training policy. This policy outlines your commitment to the goals of training your staff in a cost- effective manner. Decide when and how often training will be conducted, who will conduct the training, what training records should be maintained, and how costs will be monitored.

Once the policy is in place, you must decide on what your actual training needs are. Some signals that indicate training might be an appropriate solution for a problem include:

- Dissatisfied clients
- Employees confused about their jobs

- Low morale
- Low productivity
- Sanitation issues
- Employee theft
- Substandard products or services
- Low sales
- High waste
- High employee turnover
- Low number of repeat business or referrals
- High level of employee fighting

While many of these may be apparent in the average day, there are a number of ways to help determine training needs.

Surveys. Conduct surveys among your staff to see what type of training they want or feel they need.

Observations. One of the most effective ways to determine training needs is by being on the floor and seeing what goes on day to day.

Guest/Client comments. Guests' comments, whether written or verbal, are excellent sources for determining training needs.

Employee meetings. Involving employees in setting standards for performance can go a long way in ensuring they follow the established standards. An informal meeting with employees to discuss what they see as the reason for low performance will help get the employees to buy into the solution for the problem. And if the employees buy in, there is a much higher chance for success.

ESTABLISHING TRAINING OBJECTIVES

Once you have determined you training needs, you can turn your attention to training objectives.

Make sure you determine performance-based objectives. Most managers can identify the problem and state a general solution, but fewer are able to translate the solution into performance-based, measurable goals employees will be able understand and achieve. For example, the problem may be that employees are unbuttoning their uniform blouses and shortening their uniform skirts so they look like street clothes. A general training objective to solve this problem might be, "Teach employees how to wear the uniform." While this statement does address the problem overall, it does not give employees a way to actually achieve the goal. A better training objective would be, "Teach employees how to wear the uniform to remain stylish but not provocative." This statement gives your employees an actual tasks to focus on, and you can develop a training plan to address this problem with specific actions.

JOB DESCRIPTIONS AND JOB LISTS

While some of the training you will do is general and does not involve specific job responsibilities, most of the training you engage in will. Therefore, before you can actually begin designing your training plan, you must have written job description and job lists for each position in your operation.

There are many books on writing job descriptions, such as *Writing Job Descriptions* by Alan Fowler and *A Guide to Writing Job Descriptions Under the Americans with Disabilities Act* by Robert L. Duston. Atlantic Publishing also offers food service job description software (**www.atlantic-publishing.com**). In addition, the National Restaurant Association has developed *Model Position Descriptions for the Restaurant Industry*. This book has over 40 job descriptions and can be ordered by calling them at 1-800-482-9122.

When writing job descriptions, you need to include:

- Job title.

- Title of supervisor.

- Job summary—a general description of the position and its responsibilities.

- Essential functions or primary responsibilities—this section outlines the various tasks involved with the job. Always be sure one of these is "all other duties as assigned" so you have the flexibility to change responsibilities over time as the operation's needs change. This also provides employees an opportunity to grow within their positions.

- Qualifications and special skills.

JOB LISTS

Before you can teach someone a job, you must be able to break that job down into discrete steps. A job list is a list of all the duties a person in a particular position must perform. These lists can help managers in hiring, training, and evaluating employees.

To develop these lists, you should break all jobs down into broad categories (customer service, opening duties, kitchen duties, etc.) and then group tasks associated with the job under these categories. Think about every single thing you can that is associated with a particular job function when developing these lists. Remember, for someone who has never preformed the job before, no task is too small to mention. You might consider having an employee or employees help you with these lists or you might want to trail an employee while creating the lists yourself.

You'll need to make a determination of how detailed you want these lists to be. This may depend on the experience level of the staff you typically hire. Also keep in mind that these lists are not constant. Jobs will change over the course to time—make sure your job lists change as well!

For training purposes you can make checklists by putting a blank before each task so you can check it off as the employee masters that particular skill. These duties should be listed as specifically as possible so there is no confusion about the actual duties you want employees to perform.

Some sample job checklists follow.

BUS PERSON JOB LIST

Name:_____ Reports to:_____

Hire Date:_____

Employee must be able to:

(When employee has mastered each task, please place a check mark beside the task)

General

____Hospitable to guests

____Neat appearance

____Punctual and has a good attendance record

____Was trained in and follows correct procedures for finding subs

____Company policies including scheduling, pay, break times, and sexual harassment policy

____Personal hygiene

____Safe food handling

____Heimlich Maneuver

____Safe workplace procedures

Setup Duties

____Inventory and stock bar

____Preparing drink garnishes

____Properly preparing dish water and sanitizer for dirty glasses

Service Duties

____Prepare bar specialty drinks, such as Rusty Nails, Martinis, Manhattans, and Gin and Tonics

____Be able to operate a cash register and make change

____Be astute as to the amount of alcohol a patron has consumed

____Be able to wash drink glasses and restock beverages

____Be able to select the appropriate drink glass for the appropriate beverage

Closing Duties

____Inventory and stock bar

____Put away drinkware and garnishes

COOK JOB LIST

Name:_____ Reports to:_____

Hire Date:_____

Employee must be able to:

(When employee has mastered each task, please place a check mark beside the task)

General

____Hospitable to guests

____Neat appearance

____Punctual and has a good attendance record

____Was trained in and follows correct procedures for finding subs

____Company policies including scheduling, pay, break times, and sexual harassment policy

____Personal hygiene

____Safe food handling

____Heimlich Maneuver

____Safe workplace procedures

Prep Work

____Use scales and measuring

____Fill out prep sheets

____Practice HACCP principles devices for preparing foods

____Rotate food properly

Opening Duties

____Reheat soups and other leftovers properly

____Turn on ovens, fryers, grills, and steam tables correctly

____Properly stock steam table and cold storage

Service Duties

____Must be able to safely use ovens, fryers, grills, steam tables and refrigeration units

____Must be able to slice, dice, and mince

____Must be able to use food scales properly and follow instructions for standardized recipes

____Timely preparation of hot foods

____Keep foods out of the temperature danger zone

JOB BREAKDOWNS

The next step is to prepare job breakdowns. These are more detailed than job lists, showing what needs to be performed, the materials needed, and steps in performing the job. These breakdowns are great tools to use for individual training, such as when you have a new employee.

If you currently do not have job lists and job breakdowns, be sure to involve your employees in developing these. It is essential to get people actually doing the job to provide feedback on these tools.

Job breakdowns are useful for training in many ways. They can be used to plan training and as outlines for teaching. The job breakdowns give trainers a logical progression for their training sessions. Job breakdowns are also important in setting standards for evaluation.

The following is one example of a job breakdown.

Bartender Job List—Serving Beverages

WHAT TO DO	HOW TO DO IT
Greet customers	Greet customers warmly as soon as they are seated and introduce yourself by name. Set a beverage napkin in front of customers and ask if they would like to see a wine list or cocktail list.
Take drink orders	Take woman's orders first, if possible. Write the order on a guest check using standard abbreviations. Make sure to find out preferences such as garnishes and on the rocks or straight. Suggest the most popular cocktails, call brands, or wines if the customer is unsure of these. You may also offer the customer a taste of a wine if you have a bottle of that particular wine open.
Set up the drinks	Make sure you use the proper glassware for each drink order. Put ice in drinks that require ice. Garnish drinks properly, and make sure garnish is fresh and attractive. If a drink should be served at a particular temperature, make sure you do so. Always use the stem to carry glasses—do not touch the glass rims.

DESIGNING THE PLAN

Before beginning any training program, you need to decide what your particular training needs are. What is necessary for your employees to learn and what skills must your employees have to meet your performance standards? A training plan lists what will be done by whom, when, and how so that the training objectives can be met.

Before beginning your program, decided what your training goals are. Put these goals in writing so everyone knows what the expected outcome of training is. When writing these objectives or goals, be sure to list the behaviors you want employees to learn or engage in and identify how a particular task will be evaluated.

Here are some examples of written goals, whether or not they are effective, and why.

WRITTEN GOAL	EFFECTIVE OR INEFFECTIVE	WHY
After the training,. the employee will be able to engage in good employee practices.	Ineffective	Too general to be meaningful.
The employee will be able to prepare menu items according to standard recipes.	Effective	Specific information on what you want the employee to do.
The employee will be able to name four important factors in providing excellent customer service.	Effective	Specific and measurable.
The employee will learn how important excellent customer service is.	Ineffective	Not specific; doesn't give employee any means for providing excellent customer service.

Remember, good training goals need to be specific and they need to be measurable. If your goals have these two characteristics, employees will have a solid understanding of what is expected of them and you will have a solid criteria for measuring and evaluating their performance.

Your training program will be made up of many training plans. Once you have determined your training goals, develop these plans to help you determine who needs what type of training in your organization. You might want to use the following checklist to determine the answers to these questions.

Here is an example to show how this checklist can be used effectively. Assume you're training objective is to ensure that all employees are familiar with proper hand-washing technique. Fill in the following checklist:

Checklist

- **What should be learned?** Proper hand-washing technique.

- **Who should learn it?** All employees.

- **How much needs to be learned?** The entire correct hand-washing procedure, length of time, area to wash, when to wash, and why it is important.

- **When and where should training occur?** Before each shift, in the kitchen (training should take about 30 minutes).

- **What training method should be used?** Lecture (why hand-washing is important) and demonstration.

- **How will I evaluate if the training was successful?** Ask each trainee to demonstrate method after class and through management observation following the class.

Follow Up

As with the simple hand-washing example above, it is very important to follow up on training and ensure employees are following the training they received and acting in the manner you desire. You may need to involve yourself with coaching or simple retraining sessions with employees to remind them of the training objectives and the appropriate behavior.

Coaching

Once training is completed, your job isn't done. Managers need to continually show employees that they care about helping them do a good job. Managers must communicate with employees and let them know they are available for counseling, talking, and questions.

Coaching is an important but often-overlooked component of any training program. Coaching allows you to interact with employees after training to refocus their attention on procedures and reinforce that they are doing a good job. Coaching focuses on accomplishments, job duties, and observations. It is designed to correct and improve an employee's ability to do a job.

There are two principles of coaching to which managers need to pay attention:

1. **Involvement.** Employees have to be personally involved in their goal setting and in achieving results.

2. **Understanding.** The manager and employee must be certain they both have the same understanding of the problem or situation. This is done by actively listening to the employee and ensuring that you are hearing what the employee is really saying.

In general, there are two forms of coaching: formal and informal.

FORMAL COACHING

Formal coaching is usually conducted by interviews or pre-interview evaluations with the employee. In these situations you can control the direction of the conversation by asking questions or you can let the employee guide the interview. The objective of these interviews is to inform the employee about his or her job performance, help the employee understand his or her strengths and weaknesses, give the employee a chance to make a development plan, or give the employee a chance to make decisions related to his or her job performance.

When conducting interviews, keep the following interviewing techniques in mind:

- Make sure to keep your questions understandable. If an employee does not understand the question, he or she can not act upon the information.

- Try to stay on topic during the interview, asking questions that relate to the situation/issue being discussed.

- Make the employee feel comfortable. There may be a need to engage in some small talk in order to achieve this.

- Keep questions specific. General questions may confuse the employee as to how to answer.

- Ask open-ended questions (questions that require more than a "yes" or "no" answer). This will help employees think through a situation.

INFORMAL COACHING

Informal coaching is just a function of supervision. It occurs when you walk around the establishment and observe and interact with employees. As you are doing this, be sure to keep these coaching goals in mind:

Reinforcement. When an employee is performing according to or above expectations, be sure to stop and recognize this. Praise the employee and make sure he or she knows that you recognize their good work.

Restatement of expectations. Also be sure to repeat your expectations for a job as you are conducting day-to-day business. Often employees forget information they learned in training sessions or get busy and sloppy about their work. By reminding employees what you expect of them, it will help reinforce the appropriate actions.

Employee training and motivation are two very complex and important aspects of managing a successful business. Take the time to learn how to perform these tasks effectively, and continually monitor your own performance to improve. Your management skills will improve and your profitability and job satisfaction will likely follow suit.

Tipped Employees

One of the biggest payroll challenges facing the owners and managers of retail beverage and food operations is getting employees to report and pay taxes on their tips, as required by the IRS. Complying with the intricacies of the tip reporting and allocation rules can be difficult and confusing. Tip tax laws are constantly changing. You must use extreme caution in this area; get assistance from your accountant or attorney.

Once you have consulted with your accountant or attorney, you will need to make sure your front-of-the-house employees are trained in this area. You might want to ask your accountant or attorney to make this presentation with you.

IRS TIP AGREEMENTS

The IRS is continuing its emphasis on a multi-year strategy to increase tax compliance by tipped employees. Originally developed for the food and beverage industry, this program has now been extended to the gaming (casino) and hairstyling industries.

There are two arrangements under this program that, depending on their business, employers in specific industries can agree to enter into: The Tip Rate Determination Agreement (TRDA) is available to the gaming and the food and beverage industries, and the Tip Reporting Alternative Commitment (TRAC) is available to the food and beverage and the hairstyling industries.

First introduced in 1993, the TRDA set the stage for a new way of doing business at the IRS. This arrangement emphasizes future compliance by tipped employees in the food and beverage industry by utilizing the tip rates individually calculated for each retail beverage and food outlet. In addition, as long as the participants comply with the terms of the agreement and accurately report their tip income, the IRS agrees not to initiate any examinations during the period the TRDA is in effect.

TRAC emphasizes educating both employers and employees to ensure compliance with the tax laws relating to tip income reporting. Employees are provided tip reports detailing the correlation that exists between an employee's charged tip rate and the cash tip rate. In general, the IRS district director will not initiate any examinations on either the employer or employees while the agreement is in effect if participants comply with the provisions of the agreement.

The overall response to TRDA and TRAC has been very positive among employers who seek to foster compliance from their employees in a manner that is relatively simple and that makes good business sense. In addition, there are benefits for both the employer and the employees.

Participation in one of these programs is voluntary, but you may only enter into one of the agreements at a time. The 1998 tax legislation specifies that IRS agents can't threaten to audit you in order to convince you to sign a TRDA or TRAC agreement.

The big benefit for you as an employer is that you will not be subject to unplanned tax liabilities. Those who sign a TRAC or a TRDA agreement receive a commitment from the IRS that the agency will not examine the owner's books to search for under-withheld or underpaid payroll taxes on tip income. There are benefits to employees also, including increases in their Social Security, unemployment compensation, retirement plan and workers' compensation benefits.

Under TRDA, the IRS works with you to arrive at a tip rate for your employees. At least 75 percent of your tipped workers must agree in writing to report tips at the agreed-upon rate. If they fail to do so, you are required to turn them in to the IRS. If you do not comply, the agreement is terminated and your business becomes subject to IRS auditing.

TRAC is less strict but requires more work on your part. There is no established tip rate, but you are required to work with employees to make sure they understand their tip-reporting obligations. You must set up a process to receive employees' cash tip reports, and they must be informed of the tips you are recording from credit card receipts.

TIP CREDITS FOR EMPLOYERS ARE POSSIBLE

As an employer you may also be eligible for credit for taxes paid on certain employee tips (IRS Form 8846). You will not, however, get credit for your part of Social Security and Medicare taxes on those tips that are used to meet the federal minimum wage rate applicable to the employee under the Fair Labor Standards Act. This is also subject to state laws. You must also increase the amount of your taxable income by the amount of the tip credit.

The credit is effective for your part of Social Security and Medicare taxes paid after 1993, regardless of whether your employees reported the tips to you or when your employees performed the services.

Effective for services performed after 1996, the credit applies to the taxes on tips your employees receive from customers in connection with providing, delivering or serving food or beverages, regardless of whether the customers consume the food or beverages on your business premises.

ADDITIONAL INFORMATION ON TIP REPORTING

The following IRS forms and publications relating to tip income reporting can be downloaded directly from the Web site **www.irs.gov**. Under the heading Forms and Publications by Number, you will find:

- Pub 505—Tax Withholding and Estimated Tax

- Pub 531—Reporting Tip Income

- Form 941—Employer's Quarterly Federal Tax Return

- Form 4137—Social Security and Medicare Tax on Unreported Tip Income

- Form 8027—Employer's Annual Information Return of Tip Income and Allocated Tips

EMPLOYEE TIP REPORTING "FREQUENTLY ASKED QUESTIONS"

Employee tips are taxable income. As income, these tips are subject to federal income tax and Social Security and Medicare taxes, and may be subject to state income tax as well.

Q: What tips do employees have to report?

A: If you received $20 or more in tips in any one month, you should report all your tips to your employer so that federal income tax, Social Security and Medicare taxes—maybe state income tax too—can be withheld.

Q: Do employees have to report all their tips on their tax return?
A: Yes. All tips are income and should be reported on your tax return.

Q: Is it true that only 8 percent of employees' total sales must be reported as tips?

A: No. You must report to your employer all (100 percent) of your tips except for the tips totaling less than $20 in any month. The 8 percent rule applies to employers.

Q: Do employees need to report tips from other employees?

A: Yes. Employees who are indirectly tipped by other employees are required to report "tip-outs." This could apply to bus persons, for instance.

Q: Do employees have to report tip-outs that they pay to indirectly tipped employees?

A: If you are a directly tipped employee, you should report to your employer only the amount of tips you retain. Maintain records of tip-outs with your other tip income (cash tips, charged tips, split tips, tip pool).

Q: What records do employees need to keep?
A: You must keep a running daily log of all your tip income.

Q: What can happen if employees don't keep a record of tips?

A: Underreporting could result in your owing substantial taxes, penalties, and interest to the IRS and possibly other agencies.

Q: If employees report all their tips to their employer, do they still have to keep records?

A: Yes. You should keep a daily log of your tips so that, in case of an examination, you can substantiate the actual amount of tips received.

Q: *Why should employees report their tips to their employer?*

A: When you report your tip income to your employer, the employer is required to withhold federal income tax, Social Security and Medicare taxes, and, maybe, state income tax. Tip reporting may increase your Social Security credits, resulting in greater Social Security benefits when you retire. Tip reporting may also increase other benefits to which you may become entitled, such as unemployment benefits or retirement benefits. Additionally, a greater income may improve financing approval for mortgages, car loans, and other loans.

Q: *If an employee forgot to report their tip income to their employer, but remembered to record it on their federal income tax return. Will that present a problem?*

A: If you do not report your tip income to your employer, but you do report the tip income on your federal income tax return, you may owe a 50 percent Social Security and Medicare tax penalty and be subject to a negligence penalty and, possibly, an estimated tax penalty.

Q: *If employees report all their tips, but their taxes on the tips are greater than their pay from their employer, how do they pay the remaining taxes?*

A: You can either pay the tax when you file your federal income tax return or you can reach into your tip money and give some to your employer to be applied to those owed taxes.

Q: *What can happen if employees don't report their tips to the IRS?*

A: If the IRS determines through an examination that you underreported your tips, you could be subject to additional federal income tax, Social Security and Medicare taxes and, possibly, state income tax. You will also be awarded a penalty of 50 percent of the additional Social Security and Medicare taxes and a negligence penalty of 20 percent of the additional income tax, plus any interest that may apply.

Q: *What is an employee's responsibility under the Tip Rate Determination Agreement (TRDA)?*

A: You are required to file your federal tax returns. You must sign a Tipped Employee Participation Agreement proclaiming that you are participating in the program. To stay a participating employee, you must report tips at or above the tip rate determined by the agreement.

Q: *What is an employee's responsibility under the Tip Reporting Alternative Commitment (TRAC)?*

A: Directly tipped employee: Your employer will furnish you a written statement (at least monthly) reflecting your charged tips:

You are to verify or correct this statement.

You are to indicate the amount of cash tips received.

When reporting your cash tips, keep in mind that there is a correlation between charged tips and cash tips.

You may be asked to provide the name and amount of any tip-outs you've given to indirectly tipped employees.

A: Indirectly tipped employee: You are required to report all your tips to your employer.

TIP RECORDS

It is in your company's best interest to insist that all employees accurately report their income from tips. The IRS will hold you responsible. Establishments that do not comply are subject to IRS audit and possible tax liabilities, penalties, and interest payments. As a precaution, if you have any employees who customarily receive tips from customers, patrons, or other third parties, we recommend you keep the following additional information about tipped employees:

- Indicate on the pay records—by a symbol, letter or other notation placed next to their name—each tipped employee.

- Weekly or monthly amount of tips reported by each employee.

- The amount by which the wages of each tipped employee have been increased by tips.

- The hours worked each workday in any occupation in which the employee does not receive tips, and the total daily or weekly earnings for those times.

- The hours worked each workday in any occupation in which the employee receives tips, and the total daily or weekly straight-time earnings for those times.

LARGE FOOD OR BEVERAGE ESTABLISHMENTS

You may meet the definition of a "large food or beverage establishment" if you employ more than ten employees. If you do, the law requires that you file Form 8027, Employer's Annual Information Return of Tip Income and Allocated Tips, with the IRS.

If you meet the definition, the law requires that you report certain tip information to the IRS on an annual basis. You should use Form 8027 to report information such as total charged tips, charged receipts, total reported tips by employees and gross receipts from food and beverage operations. Also, employers must allocate tips to certain directly tipped employees and include the allocation on their employees' W-2 forms when the total of reported tips is less than 8 percent.

You can get a copy of Form 8027 and its instructions by calling 1-800-829-3676. You can also get copies of most forms by dialing 703-368-9694 from your fax machine.

TIPS-REPORTING POLICIES

Be sure to advise all new hires about your tip-reporting procedures. Have this procedure in written format and review it annually. Consider the following issues:

Who has to report tips? Employees who receive $20 or more in tips, per month, are required to report their tips to you in writing. When you receive the tip report from your employee, you should use it to figure the amount of Social Security, Medicare and income taxes to withhold for the pay period on both wages and reported tips. For more information on employer tip-reporting responsibilities, visit the IRS's Web site at **www.irs.gov** and look at Publication 15, Circular E, "Employer's Tax Guide." For more information on employee responsibilities, look at Publication 531, Reporting Tip Income.

Supreme Court ruling. In June 2002, the Supreme Court ruled that the IRS can estimate a restaurant's aggregate tip income and bill the business owner for its share of Social Security and Medicare taxes on unreported tips. This ruling puts a greater burden on restaurateurs and other food service businesses to make sure employees declare all tip income, because it is likely they will be overcharged by the IRS if they incorrectly estimate the tips earned. Because this ruling is so recent, it is unclear exactly how it will affect tip-reporting procedures for catering owners. Currently, the laws are not affected by the court's recent ruling and employees are still legally responsible for reporting all tips to their employers once a month. In turn, employers are still responsible for reporting these amounts to the IRS and paying the FICA tax on the amount.

How to train your servers about tip reporting. Include this information in your orientation packets for new hires. You also may want to purchase a tip-reporting kit from **www.restaurantworkshop. com**. These kits include educational materials that you can distribute to your servers. Also consider inviting an accountant to do a training session with your servers.

Restaurant industry action. The National Restaurant Association is lobbying Congress to ask that they clearly state that the IRS cannot use the aggregate assessment method to pressure employers to police tipped employees as to their tipped income. Obviously, this matter is not completely settled; to keep current with information related to IRS rules on tip reporting, log on to the IRS's Web site at **www.irs.gov** and the National Restaurant Association's Web site at **www.restaurant.org**.

Resources. The Tip Reporting Education Kit from the National Restaurant Association includes posters, payroll-stuffers, manager checklists, and employee brochures to help you convey the tip-reporting laws to your employees. The National Restaurant Association also offers "Legal Problem Solver for Restaurant Operators," which can be purchased on their Web site at **www.restaurant.org**

Pricing and Menus

Whether you are an individual caterer working out of your home or a director of the catering services of a large hotel, you will be responsible for developing both standardized and customized menus. If you own your own business, you will be solely responsible for menu development. If you work for a large catering operation, banquet sales associates in conjunction with chefs are usually responsible for this task.

You'll want to consider how much customization you want to do. Large hotels generally work from a limited number of set menus. If you are in business for yourself, you have more freedom to decide if you want to offer your clients a set number of menus with preset items or customized menus. You might want to do both.

Menu Setting

If you want to offer set menus, you need to think about what types of items you want to include and what categories of items.

Menus can be broken into:

- Menu groups
- Menu categories
- Menu items

1. Decide what menu groups you will offer. Groups include appetizers, entrées, soups, desserts, etc.

2. Decide what categories to offer within these groups. For entrée choices you could offer beef, poultry, seafood, pork, vegetarian, lamb, and veal. Then you must decide how many

dishes you will offer in each category. You may have four beef dishes, three seafood entrées, two poultry, and one vegetarian, for example.

3. Decide on the dish itself. There are numerous recipe sources you can call on. Buy cookbooks and experiment with recipes you find there. Get online and look for recipes; thousands of sites. And don't forget to use the creativity of your kitchen staff.

When creating menus, make sure to keep the demographics of your clients in mind. Think about the average age, sex, ethnic background, socioeconomic background, and dietary restrictions of guests. If you are catering an event for a group of senior citizens, for example, you will want to avoid heavy, spicy and exotic foods. One of the first questions the client will have is the per-person price. When you meet with him or her, be sure to bring some menu examples. If these examples are exactly what the client is looking for, you can give a solid per-person price. If you need to create a new menu, these examples will at least give the client a ballpark figure. You can get back to him or her in a couple of days after you have worked up the menu and costs.

Menus can be classified in a number of ways. They may be classified by the type of meal they serve: breakfast menus, lunch menus, and dinner menus. They can also be classified by how items are priced:

- **A la carte** menus price everything separately, including salads and side orders.

- **Semi a la carte** menus usually include a side (such as a vegetable and potato) and a salad with the main entrée, but they price soups, desserts and appetizers separately.

- **Prix fixe** menus offer a complete meal at a set price. This may include an appetizer, entrée and dessert, or it can be a five-course meal. Fixed pricing includes all menu items and gives a price per person.

Below are some menu examples you can use. You should keep copies of examples for a variety of types of events, such as a buffet dinner, a plated dinner, and an appetizer-only menu.

Filet Mignon
Wild Rice Pilaf
Mixed green salad with balsamic vinaigrette
Roasted haricot vert
Assorted mini desserts
$37.00 per person

With mixed pricing, the customer gets a set price with the option of changing different courses for an additional charge per person.

Appetizers
Please add $3.50 per guest
Cheese and fruit board
Endive with curried shrimp mousse
Lobster spring rolls with basil oil
Raspberry and brie phyllo cups

Desserts
Please add $4.75 per guest
Flourless chocolate cake with raspberry coulis
Pumpkin crème brûlée
Gingered pear tart
Passion fruit sorbet with coconut tuiles

Individual course pricing offers each menu item as a separate item with a separate per-person price:

Entrées (choose 1)

Cedar planked Copper River salmon	19.95
Filet mignon with gorgonzola butter sauce	16.95
Seared duck breast with fig compote	22.95

Salads (choose 1)

Arugula and mixed green salad with orange vinaigrette	2.50
Wilted spinach with warm bacon vinaigrette	2.25
Pear and Maytag blue cheese with port vinaigrette	3.25

Vegetables (choose 1)

Roasted summer squash	1.50
Grilled green beans with sun-dried tomato sauce	2.00
Roasted asparagus with lemon and Parmigiano-Reggiano	3.50

Starch (choose 1)

Polenta triangles	3.00
Whipped sweet potatoes	3.25
Roasted new potatoes with rosemary	3.00

Dessert (choose 1)

Espresso crème brûlée	7.00
Raspberry mocha torte	8.75
Key lime cake with homemade coconut ice cream	8.25

The basic types of menus used in catering service include

- Breakfast, lunch, and dinner menus
- Reception menus
- A la carte menus
- Hors d'oeuvre menus
- Special function menus
- Beverage menus

The types of items you include in each menu will be based on:

- Style of service
- Kitchen's skill level
- Customer needs
- Food production capabilities (equipment available, etc.)
- Price range needed to make a profit
- Type of cuisine
- Knowledge of food trends

Menu Planning

Planning the menu is a lot more than merely selecting menu items that are enjoyed and demanded by your clientele. Menu planning includes arranging equipment, personnel, and food products into an efficient unit that will be affordable and in demand by the public.

As you create your menu, think about what you want to say. What do you want to communicate to your customer? Make decisions about the categories to use, what to call different dishes, and how many dishes to have. Think about the size of your kitchen and skills of your staff. If your kitchen is small, you may want to limit the number of items you place on the menu. If you have a schooled and highly skilled kitchen staff, you may be able to prepare a greater number and greater variety of dishes.

All menu items selected must fit into the physical workings of the kitchen. Thus, the menu should be finalized prior to designing, selecting equipment for, and laying out the kitchen. This is necessary for maximum efficiency of time, labor and equipment. The design and layout of the kitchen and work areas must meet the needs of the menu. If it doesn't, the entire operation will become slow, disorganized and inefficient. Inefficiency can only result in a drop in employee morale and in the business's profit margin. So, when sitting down with your client to plan the menu of a particular event, you have to keep your kitchen space in mind. Make sure you don't let clients talk you into something that would be impossible for you to produce well. Make suggestions for comparable replacements.

Just as the kitchen must meet the demands of the menu, the personnel employed to prepare the menu items must be selected to fit into the design of the kitchen. Careful consideration must be given to the number and type of employees needed. Is the menu simple enough for inexperienced workers to prepare, or are the skills of a professional, more experienced chef needed? Will the food be prepared ahead of time or at the event? When will these employees be needed and for how long? Will there be enough room in the kitchen for everyone to work at the same time? Who will supervise them?

Service will also affect your menu planning. Select the style of service that fits your party. Whether you decide on a buffet, a picnic, or a formal sit-down meal, select recipes that are suited to that style. While a curried lobster bisque would be perfect for an evening wedding reception, it probably would not work for the neighbor's annual summer picnic. Additionally, remember that some foods do not hold well and should not be used for a buffet.

Here are some additional points to keep in mind when creating your menus:

- The menu item must be of superior quality.

- The raw materials used in preparing the item must be readily available year-round at a relatively stable price.

- The menu item must be affordable and demanded by your clientele.

- The menu item must be acceptable to the preparation and cooking staff you use.

- The raw materials used in preparing the menu item must be easily portioned by weight.

- All menu items must have consistent cooking results.

- All menu items must have a long shelf life. Food items prepared ahead of time and not utilized may not be sold for as long as 36 hours.

- The storage facilities must accommodate the raw materials used in preparing the menu items.

- Menu items should be creative.

RECIPE GUIDELINES

The first rule of thumb for choosing recipes for your event is to never plan to include a recipe in a party menu that you haven't prepared at least once before. Use the following proportions as guidelines for how many new recipes to include on a menu:

- Up to 20 percent can be challenging/new recipes.

- Sixty to seventy percent all-done-ahead-of-time recipes.

- Twenty to forty percent are purchased and you only need to serve.

Prep time. As you create menus, you also need to evaluate each dish for the amount of preparation time required and the cost of the ingredients. Try to strike a balance between expense and time involved. You should create a recipe file and include this time on your recipe cards. This will help you in determining ingredients needed and labor costs. A great resource for keeping a record of your recipes and menus and for costing is ChefTec software.

Time constraints. Plan recipes and quantities appropriate to the time frame of the event. You may be able to serve only nibbles at a cocktail reception, for example, while if you have invited guests for a three-hour party, the host should serve enough cocktail fare and hors d'oeuvres to provide a filling meal.

If you are short on time during an event, consider having salads preset on the tables. Also think about the size of the items you serve and the number. Larger vegetables, such as whole asparagus spears, are harder to dish out than chunks of vegetables. In addition, serving more than three vegetables on a buffet will slow service as people decide which one to take or take additional time serving a little of all the offerings.

Balanced food groups. Aim to include a range of elements from the four basic food groups: meat, fish, or other protein; fruits and vegetables; breads and vegetables; and milk and dairy products. Balance is about creating a meal of complementary flavors, colors, textures, and harmony. For example, if you are serving a buffet dinner, you will probably have two to three entrée choices. Don't make all the choices beef; offer a beef dish as well as a seafood and vegetarian option. Keep color in mind when creating your buffet table; make sure the table isn't monochromatic.

Seasons. Many restaurants and caterers are focusing on seasonal foods these days, and it will bring a certain quality to your menus. Using seasonal items can often be cheaper as well. With catering operations, guests are often booking parties months in advance, however, so it's important to mentally skip ahead and think about what will be available at the time of the party rather than at the time of the booking. You should develop new menus seasonally. Have alternative plans should a product become unavailable or priced out of your budget. In fact, it's standard in the food service industry for quality food service establishments to change their menus every quarter. The rule of thumb is to track your mix. Replace less popular items with new ideas every three months.

Add variety. Make sure you avoid repetition in your recipes and menus. Generally, your client won't be impressed if you duplicate cooking methods or style of preparation within the same menu. Don't choose, for example, chocolate mousse for dessert, if the appetizer is salmon mousse. Also, do not repeat ingredients on the menu. If you are a hotel caterer and a guest is using your services over a period of time for a conference, this is especially important.

Track item popularity. You should also develop and use a tracking sheet to keep tabs on the popularity index of your menu items. For example, if your menu consists of items Chicken Marsala, Roast Halibut, Vegetarian Lasagna, Porterhouse Steak, and Veal Picatta, and at the end of three months you've sold 1,082 Marsalas, 28 Halibut, 486 Lasagnas, 602 Porterhouse Steaks and 497 Veal Picattas, then remove Halibut from your menu for the next quarter, if not permanently. Offer another type of fish entrée in its place.

Menu trends. So, where do you get ideas for the menus you present to clients? A good way is by keeping up to date with eating and dining trends. You can translate these trends to reflect your clients' desires and budget. Understand that most clients are budget-conscious—a strong demand for value is the present-day concern. However, being in fashion gives people a sense of identity. For instance, the trend towards spicier food nationwide, sparked by the Cajun craze, is now commonplace on catering menus. Don't be afraid to experiment with new menus.

There are several current trends in catering you may want to be aware of when designing menus for events:

- **Themed events.** These may be tied into an occasion that is being celebrated or some more generic theme, like a tropical buffet.

- **Stations.** For a stationed event, you setup several serving areas and offer different cuisines at each. Often ethnic cuisines are used for these: one station may be Italian, the second is Chinese, and a third is a dessert station.

- **Hands-on parties.** These events let people participate in the food preparation. These are run similar to a hands-on cooking class. Today's sophisticated guests like to participate and show off their culinary skills. Consider setting up an action (or assembly) station. Introduce hands-on customer involvement for some aspects of the food preparation. How about a "tartar station," where guests are invited to select their salmon, beef or other raw meats? Let them put the meat through the appropriately labeled grinder themselves and position their plates to catch it.

There are many ways to keep up with food trends:

Join trade organizations and subscribing to trade magazines. Three of the main trade organizations to look into are:

- National Association of Catering Executives
  2500 Wilshire Blvd., Suite 603, Los Angeles, CA 90057; 213-487-6223

- National Institute for Off-Premise Catering
  1341 N Sedgwick, Chicago, IL 60610; 800-633-7736

- National Restaurant Association
  www.restaurant.org, 311 1st St NW, Washington, D.C. 20001; 800-424-5156

Restaurant Industry Forecast. This report is available from the National Restaurant Association. The document provides information concerning forecasted restaurant industry sales and forecasted trends. Currently industry leaders see the following trends: ethnic menus, including Mexican, Southwestern,

Asian, Indian, Caribbean, and Cajun; the take-out market; lean and healthy menu choices; and items made with fresh ingredients and homemade products.

Eat out often. See what other restaurants and caterers are doing. What works for them and what doesn't? You can learn from your competitors' successes and mistakes!

Subscribe to magazines such as *Gourmet* and *Bon Appetite*. These magazines are designed for the general public and will help you define current food and dining trends.

Don't forget industry magazines. Magazines such as The American Culinary Federation's *The National Culinary Review* and *Special Events Magazine* are excellent sources for current food and dining trends. *The National Culinary Review* is available to members. You can find membership information on the Web at **www.acfchefs.org**. *Special Events Magazine* can be found at **www.specialevents.com**.

Watch television. These days cable television is loaded with food shows with everything from Martha Stewart to the Iron Chef. Keeping tuned in will help you keep current.

Travel. What a fun way to stay current with food trends! If you are able to, travel and eat out. This will expose you to trends from other areas of the country and around the world. It will also help to inspire you and spark your own creativity when working in your kitchen.

Themes

One of the biggest trends in catering today is themes. In fact, often enough it's the food itself that determines the theme of the event. For instance, if a client wants to have Tuscan food or a South American menu, the décor and the rest of the party theme will flow from that. Because customers get tired of the same thing, themes allow you to make each event unique. Some of the most popular events could be those with a heartland cuisine or Native American foods theme. Consider turning even such basic presentations as afternoon breaks for corporate meetings into "themed" events. Or offer a "healthy break" with granola bars and fresh fruit or a "chocoholic break."

Try to create something original and out of the ordinary for these events. Use all five senses. Some ideas for themes parties are listed below.

- Old Mexico—taco bar, interactive fajita bar, piñatas

- State Fair/Fourth of July/Circus—create variations on the hot dog, hamburger grill out

- Oktoberfest—German beer, bratwurst, cream pugs, strudel, German music and polka dancing

- Western theme—use a chuck wagon dining approach, frontier days, rodeo, or hoe down

- Location themes—Paris, Rome, Hong Kong, New York

- Eras—1800s, 1920s, 1960s, etc.

- Sports themes

- Historical themes

If themed events will be a major part of your business, you might want to invest in some permanent props you can use. You can find props anywhere, including party stores. Check out local ethnic shops, Goodwill and flea markets as well. Be creative!

WEDDINGS

Weddings may be seen as the ultimate in theme catering. Some caterers only cater weddings while others avoid them like the plague. While wedding catering can be extremely lucrative (the average couple spends $22,000), it is also probably the most stressful type of event to cater because the wedding party is so stressed about making the day perfect.

When you meet with the prospective wedding client for the first time, you need to make them understand that you can make the event as special and perfect as they desire:

- Make sure to take lots of notes.

- Share their enthusiasm; get as excited about their day as they are.

- Build trust and confidence in your abilities.

Portion Control

Determining the various quantities and portion sizes for the menu items will help you calculate the cost of the menu. It will also help you determine the food quantities needed for purchasing, preparation and production purposes.

The general rule for developing a portion size is to use the largest portion feasible but charge accordingly. It is far better to serve too much food than too little. The crucial element, which must be constantly reinforced, is that every menu item—entrées, side dishes and some desserts—must be a specific weight and size. Portion control is the basis for the business's entire cost-control program. Its importance cannot be overstated.

Portion controlling all food items is an effective way to control food costs, but it also serves another important function: It maintains consistency in the final product. Once the precise recipe is developed, the completed menu item should look and taste exactly the same regardless of who prepared it.

Portions may have a variance of up to, but not exceeding, half an ounce. Thus, if the set portion size for a steak is 12 1/2 ounces, the steak may range from 12 to 13 ounces. Any amount over 13 ounces must be trimmed. A light steak should be utilized for something else. Although a 1/2-ounce variance may seem like a small amount, in actually it will add up very quickly.

Since portion controlling is such a vital kitchen function, purchase the best scales available. A good digital ounce scale will cost upwards of $200. However, this investment will be recouped many times over from the food cost savings it will provide. Purchase at least two ounce-graduated scales for the kitchen and always keep a third available in reserve. One floor-type pound scale with at least a 150-pound capacity will be needed. This scale will be used to verify deliveries and raw yields. All scales should have a temperature-compensating device.

Maintain these scales per the manufacturers' instructions; clean them periodically and oil when necessary, and they will provide years of service. To ensure the accuracy of the scales, test them periodically with an item of known weight. Most good scales come with a calibration kit.

For practical reasons some food items, such as dressings, sauces and butter, are portioned by weight. However, they should still be portion controlled by using proper-sized spoons and ladles. Soups and condiments must be placed in proper-sized serving containers.

At each work area of the kitchen, place a chart listing the portion sizes and other portion-control practices. All employees must use the measuring cups and spoons and the recipe manual when following recipes. Remember that the basis for the food-cost program you are developing is based upon the knowledge that every item has a precise portion size.

Determining portion size for quantity production can be tricky. Let's say you are catering a lunch party for a high school graduation. You expect 200 guests, which will include the graduates and their relatives. Your menu is grilled chicken breast served with mango salsa, pasta salad, fruit, mini focaccia sandwiches with pesto and olive tapenade, and mini dessert bars. You figure each person will eat 3 ounces of chicken. As you are shutting down the buffet line you realize you have only gone through about half the chicken! What happened? It could have been a number of things. First, at least a third of your guests were teenage girls. Teenage girls do not eat fashion-model portions, so your overage may be do to this. On the other hand, the event was held on a hot and humid afternoon, so people may have been eating lighter in general. The moral of the story is that many factors are going to affect portion size; some of these you can control, others you can't.

Some general guidelines to follow for individual portion sizes follow.

GENERAL GUIDELINES FOR INDIVIDUAL PORTION SIZES	
Appetizers	6 to 8 individual pieces
Meat entrée	6- to 8-ounce portion for dinner 3 to 5 ounce portion for lunch
Potato	1
Rice	⅔ to ¾ cup
Pasta	1 to 1½ cups
Mini desserts	2 to 3

Menu Planning and the Client

When planning specific menus for clients, remember that your job is to give the customer the kind of food and service they want, when and where they want it, at the price that they specify, while still producing a profit for your company. So, the more you know about your clients, the more likely you are to meet their goals and, of course, your goals.

When you meet with your client to discuss the menu, project competence and confidence. Use your menu as a powerful tool to project an image of a company striving to create something special, fresh and custom-designed for your client. Describe your dishes in a thoughtful manner. Avoid clichés.

Make sure you include budget in the conversation at the earliest opportunity. You'll save time this way and eliminate fruitless discussions about a menu for an event that wasn't feasible in the first place. Find out what the client's budget is, then start asking questions.

- What type of service does the client want?

- How much food do they want? Is it a full meal or just a light snack?

- What kind of food?

- Is the event formal?

- How much and what kind of beverages?

- Do they want appetizers passed?

- Should alcoholic beverages be served during dinner?

- What type of decorations does the client want?

As you ask these questions, see where the client's priorities lie. If she is an obvious gourmand, you'll want to spend more of the budget on food. Make suggestions for where to save money in some areas so more can be spent on food. You're also likely to find that the client is willing to spend a little more than what they initially tell you, so don't be afraid to up sell during your meeting.

Be sure to steer clients away from ideas that simply won't work. On those occasions when a client suggests an idea fraught with challenges, approach the situation carefully. Begin by complimenting them on their idea. After a moment, slowly bring your objections to light, as though they are coming to you after you considered their proposal in greater depth. "That's a good idea," you might say. "I'm wondering, though, if we served such a large salad, would that make your guests less likely to enjoy the rest of the dinner that we're planning." (Secretly, you know that you would have to rent large salad plates for the dish the client has in mind). "Have you seen the picture of our chef's Waldorf salad? This would make a great impression as a first course." As always, the secret to keeping everyone happy is compromise.

Check with the client about any guests with special diets. Most chefs or caterers should and do accommodate special requirements for health, lifestyle or religious reasons. The general rule is that if it's in the building and you want it, you'll get it. The price is then adjusted accordingly and the magnitude of that adjustment depends on the magnitude of the request.

When planning larger events, make sure you have a vegetarian option available because the odds are you will have a vegetarian in the room. By being attuned to your customers' needs, you will impress all their guests and probably find yourself getting more business from these people in the future. You should also try to have fruit to offer for dessert for anyone who may have dietary restrictions, such as cardiac patients or diabetics.

Types of Service

The type of service you use for an event will play a large role in the menu ideas you offer your client, so this is one of the first questions you should ask. The menus for a sit-down dinner for 40 and a reception for 300 are going to be very different. A menu that may work very well for a plated meal may not work at all for a buffet service event. If your customer is trying to save money, a buffet will be cheaper because of the food setup and you will not need to hire as many servers to staff a buffet as you would a plated dinner. On the other hand, if the occasion is very formal, a plated dinner is more appropriate. Ask your customer questions to determine the tone of the event; this will help you determine the appropriate service.

- How formal is the occasion?

- How many people will be in attendance?

- Do you have any thoughts on items you would like served?
- Do you want people to mingle or to have a specific place to sit?

The following are service styles the client might want for the event.

French. Classical French service uses a six-person dining staff. Because of the high cost, this is inappropriate for catering, but aspects of this service are often included in catering operations. For example, a Caesar salad or flambé dessert might be prepared tableside at a sit-down dinner. (You should consider adding an extra per-person charge for this service.)

Russian. This service is well suited for parties with tables of 6 to 12 guests at each table. Food is served from large platters. Servers portion and serve the food at each table directly to the guest. Today this service is seen in what many people call "family-style" dining.

American. American service is what is most commonly used for catered events. All food is prepared and served on plates from the kitchen. The main course, vegetable and starch all come on one plate and a plate cover is used to keep items warm as the staff is plating all the covers to take out simultaneously. Once in the dining room, the wait-staff can serve a large party very quickly.

Buffet. All items are plated and served from a main table. The guests come to the table and portion and serve themselves. Sometimes servers assist guests, but not always. While this type of service requires fewer dining room staff, it does take longer in setup time and it takes more time for the overall service with guests moving through the line rather than having servers bring the food to their tables.

Menu Design

While menu choices at a restaurant are made by the individual diner, catering menus are normally decided by several people. Catering menus are often reviewed in customers' own homes or offices prior to meeting with any food service personnel. The customer is also likely to be reviewing menus from several different operations at the same time. Because of this, the appearance of the catering menu takes on even greater significance as a marketing and communication tool.

The design format of catering menus is often determined by the sales presentation cover because the menu is part of a sales packet. The most common size is an overall dimension of 9 inches by 12 inches, because this will easily fit into a business envelope. The most common format is a two panel with pockets.

As a communications tool, the menu's prime function should be to maximize sales and profits. There are many ways to catch the customer's attention. One of these involves item placement on the menu. Generally, the catering industry uses a single-page format that is included as part of a sales package. There are other formats available, however.

DESIGN FORMATS

Single Page

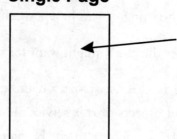

The top half of a single-page menu should contain the items to which you want to draw attention.

Two Panel

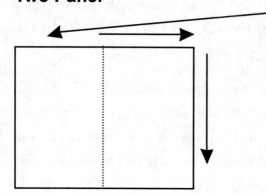

On a two-panel menu, customers first focus on the left-hand side of the open menu just as if they were reading a book. They then continue across the top of the page all the way to the right, and down the right- hand side.

Three Panel

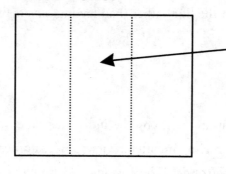

The three-panel menu gives you a total of six areas to use for menu copy. With these menus, the eye focuses in the center.

Multi Page

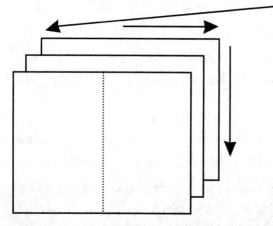

It is more difficult to find the focal point on a multi-page menu. Each page spread becomes a "mini menu" with its own focal point.

Your menu reflects your identity, so take time to plan the design and layout of the menu as well as the items that will be included on it. It can include graphics, such as the establishment's logo, and text.

Menu Psychology

A well-designed menu influences what people choose to buy. Everything from the type to the color to the item placement affects what your client may choose. As with any advertising, you can direct your customer's attention to particular areas and items and influence their purchasing decisions.

In our culture, people's eye movement goes from left to right and starts at the top of the page. Different menu formats will require different item placement because of the way the human eye moves across the page. This eye movement can also be influenced by any kind of box or graphic image that will make the reader move his or her eye away from the normal pattern. By placing items you want to sell in areas such as these, you are more likely to see them sell.

Your menu is your vehicle for telling your clients what your business is. If you cater corporate lunches, let your menus say this! Design them to reflect these values. If speed is one part of your identity, think about how you can reflect this in your menu. What colors and graphic elements denote speed? Perhaps some of the menu items could have graphic elements that look like the trails the Road Runner left in old cartoons. Red is often a color used for sports cars, so you may want to use red and other bright colors for your menu.

LAYOUT

How the text looks is also important. Be sure to have enough "white space" on the menu. A menu that is cluttered is very hard to read and annoying to clients. Work closely with your printer and designer on typeface styles and sizes. You want a typeface that echoes the theme or style of operation or the event you are catering. Above all, make sure the type is readable.

Your printer has access to catalogs and can explain some of the nuances of choosing typefaces, but here are some basics:

Typefaces appropriate for menus:

- Serif (Prime Rib)
- Sans serif (**Prime Rib**)
- Script (*Prime Rib*)

Serif fonts have tiny accents at the ends of character strokes, such as Times New Roman. Sans serif fonts do not have accent strokes, such as Arial. It looks more modern. Script fonts should only be used occasionally, as these font styles are difficult to read, especially in paragraphs, or "body" text.

Here are some other suggestions for designing your menu's physical appearance:

- Using uppercase letters for food categories or to draw attention to a special or original item. Use lowercase letters for item descriptions.

- Use bold or italic type to break up large blocks of text.

- Don't use more than three type styles on your menu.

- Type size, which is measured in points, should be no smaller than 12 point which is the size you are reading here.

This is 8 point type

This is 9 point type

This is 10 point type

This is 14 point type

This is 20 point type

This is 24 point type

This is 36 point type

This is 48 point type

Kerning, the spacing between letters, can be adjusted to make your text more readable.

Leading, the spacing between lines of text, should be at least 3 points between lines for maximum readability.

GRAPHIC ELEMENTS

If you decide to incorporate graphic elements into your menu, you can easily add simple geometric designs in a word processing program. If you want pictures, however, there are several options.

If you have a photograph, work with your printer to incorporate this.

You can download clipart from online sources, such as **www.clipart.com.** If you want an original illustration, check around area colleges. You can probably find a student artist at a reasonable price.

MENU PRODUCTION

Other elements you will need to consider when you go to print your menu are paper type and weight, color, and ink.

The quality of paper you use will be partially determined by how permanent your menu is. If it changes often, you may want to choose a lower-quality, lower-priced paper stock. If your menu isn't likely to change often, you may want to go with higher-quality paper for increased durability. In general, a heavier paper stock, usually called "cover stock," works well for menus. Regular letter paper is 20 pound, which cannot stand up to constant handling as well as a heavier stock.

Finally, you need to decide the color of your menu paper. Be sure the colors you pick for your menu are echoed in your identity as a whole. Many office supply stores offer laser printer papers you can use for your menu and menu cover. You can also order papers online at **www.ideaart.com**.

Menu design software is another option. The software is generally very easy to use, with built-in templates, artwork, etc. Your finalized menu can be printed on a laser printer. Color, clipart, photos, artwork, and graphics may be added. One such software program is Menu Pro™.

MENU DESIGN DOS AND DON'TS

- Leave some "eye breathing room." A menu with too much text will overwhelm your customer and underwhelm their dining experience.

- Make sure the type size is large enough to read, especially if you cater to an older demographic. Don't go below 12 point type. Make sure that the type style is readable as well.

- Put some thought into how much or how little descriptive text you want on your menu. Don't waste space describing common items.

- Work on your menu layout yourself, don't leave it to the printer. The printer can balance the menu and make it aesthetically pleasing, but you know what items you want to emphasize. If you feel unsure about how to approach this, many cities have menu consultants you can hire to work with.

- Be sure to proofread and have some one else proofread your menu before sending it to the printer. There is nothing more unprofessional than a menu with typos!

To Start

Cedar-Planked Salmon Salad

Salmon grilled on a cedar plank, served with an herbed couscous lentil salad

$4.95

Blue Cheese Baklava

Layers of phyllo, Maytag blue cheese and honeyed almonds

$3.75

Salads

Wilted Spinach with Warm Honey Vinaigrette

$2.25

Pear and Maytag Blue Cheese with Port Vinaigrette

$3.25

Entre'es

Seared Tuna with Black Pepper Crust

Served with braised bok choy and wasabi mashed potatoes

$22.95

Filet Mignon with Gorgonzola Butter Sauce

6-oz portion grilled to your taste and served with fresh-
roasted asparagus and sweet potato latkes

$18.95

Orcchiette with Garlic Cream Sauce

Served with haricot vert and Italian bread

$13.95

Maple-Glazed Pork Chops

Two 6-oz pork chops glazed with a maple soy sauce and served with
whipped sweet potatoes and roasted apple rings

$16.95

Desserts

Chocolate Espresso Crème Brûlée

$7.00

Raspberry Mocha Torte

$8.75

Menu Text

Menu text can influence what your customers choice to purchase. Menu copy should clearly communicate what the customer will receive so there are no surprises. Be sure that your menu items are spelled correctly. Nothing can turn a client off faster if you miss this type of detail. You can get some help in this area with a computer program called Menuspell©. The program was created by Arno Schmidt, C.E.C., Former Executive Chef of The Waldorf-Astoria Hotel, and lists 25,000 menu items.

Let the copy reflect your identity and the client's event in tone and formality, and be sure not to make any false claims. Diners are becoming more and more sophisticated, and if you claim the mashed potatoes are homemade, make sure they really are. Making false claims will only lead clients feeling taken advantage of, and ultimately you will lose customers and future potential profits.

Here are some ways to improve or write your menu copy:

- Use short phrases in your descriptions.

- Use descriptive, food-related words; for example, say "roasted" rather than "cooked."

- Don't overuse adjectives.

- Over-descriptive words and phrases can confuse the customer.

If you were a client, which description would be likely to influence you to decide to order this item?

- Veal Parmigiana – Tender veal lightly breaded and fried to perfection, then smothered with thick marinara sauce and topped with layers of melted provolone cheese, served with a mound of linguini.

- Veal Parmigiana – Lightly breaded and fried veal topped with marinara sauce and provolone cheese. Served with a side of linguini.

While both descriptions convey the same information, the first one actually has the opposite of the desired effect. The first one almost makes you feel too full from just reading the description; the second description is more likely to make you crave the item.

There are three general categories of menu copy:

1. Name of the item

2. Descriptive copy

3. General copy

NAME OF ITEM

The name of the item is obviously what the item is called: hamburger, filet mignon, or roasted chicken. Names can also be less obvious: Lisa's Favorite Salad, Mountain Burger, or Theater Steak. These types of items will need more of the next category, descriptive copy.

DESCRIPTIVE COPY

Descriptive copy includes ingredients, method of preparation, and any side dishes that accompany the entrée. All of these do not need to be included with each item description. If something is grilled, you really don't need to say any more about it. Common ingredients do not need a description, but if you are serving foie gras, you may need to include a few descriptive phrases!

The most important and trickiest of these categories is the description. Some caterers have long, detailed descriptions while others are very brief. How do you determine what is right for your business? What kind of food do you serve? Are ingredients common to most households or do you offer a variety of exotic foods?

Foreign words can be used in a description, but be careful. If it is not self-explanatory, explain the phrase. If your customers feel intimidated to ask for a definition, you might lose sales on that item.

The following is information usually included in descriptive copy:

- Preparation method (grilled, sautéed, fired)
- Main ingredients
- How it is served/accompaniments
- Grades and freshness claims
- Geographic origin (Copper River salmon, Dover sole, etc.)

GENERAL COPY

General copy is general information about the establishment, such as ownership and contact information. Many catering menus do not include this as a part of a menu, but as part of the total selling brochure, they might offer a potential client.

Price Placement

When you place the prices on the menu, you want the client to read the description of the menu item before reading the price. Rather than using dot leaders and placing prices in a row along the right-hand side of the page (Example 1), try placing the prices right after the last word of the item's description (Example 2); this will help shift the focus away from the prices.

<table>
<tr><td colspan="2" align="center">**EXAMPLE 1**</td></tr>
<tr><td colspan="2">

Shrimp Lo Mein

Shrimp, vegetables, scallions, egg noodles, and soy sauce 7.95

Cashew Chicken

Crispy chicken, ginger brown sauce, roasted cashews, and vegetables 6.95

Pepper Steak

Onion, ginger peppercorn beef, and vegetables 8.95

</td></tr>
</table>

<table>
<tr><td align="center">**EXAMPLE 2**</td></tr>
<tr><td align="center">

Shrimp Lo Mein

Shrimp, vegetables, scallions,

egg noodles, and soy sauce 7.95

Cashew Chicken

Crispy chicken, ginger brown sauce, roasted

cashews, and vegetables 6.95

Pepper Steak

Onion, ginger peppercorn beef, and vegetables 8.95

</td></tr>
</table>

ARRANGEMENT OF TEXT

Just as important as price placement is how the menu text is arranged. Menus are arranged logically in the order the courses are served: appetizers, soups and salads come before entrées, and desserts are the final menu item. While eye flow is important, the client must still easily be able to locate the food course he or she wants.

Restaurant consultants agree that item placement is extremely important and it affects product sales. Customers are most likely to remember the first and last things they read or hear the most. (Think of the last time you were at a party and were introduced to several people at one time. Whose names could you recall?) By placing the items you want to sell (the items that yield the highest profits) first or last, you increase the chance of selling them. Additionally, you can draw attention away from other menu items by placing them in the middle of the list.

Look at the following example menu quickly, then look away. Which items do you recall?

ENTRÉES

Baked Trout with White Wine Herb Sauce $18.95

New York Strip with Roasted Potatoes $19.95

Double-Cut Maple Glazed Pork Chops with

Whipped Sweet Potatoes $16.95

Beef Tenderloin Kabob over Wild Rice Pilaf $20.75

Roast Chicken with Cornbread Sage Stuffing $15.75

Eggplant Napoleon with Goat Cheese $14.75

Hopefully you recalled the trout, the strip steak, the chicken, and the eggplant. If this was your catering menu, you might place those four items on the menu in those spots because you want them to sell well. You want to sell the trout and steak because they will increase your profits. The chicken and the vegetarian option will have low food costs, so selling those will also help your profit margin.

Sample Menus

It is always beneficial to study other caterers' menus, especially your local competition, to compare design and pricing. To follow are some sample menus from actual catering companies with a short summary about each.

- **Heaven's Bakery** catering menu is a full-color, half-fold (5.5" x 8.5") menu. It is created in-house utilizing Microsoft Word so it can be easily changed, printed and customized.

Ripe seasonal fresh fruit arranged with assorted cheese serve with crackers

Assorted platter (serves 20)................ $ 60.00

Baked fresh daily

One Dozen ....$ 25.00

Two Dozen ....$ 45.00

Build your own breakfast tray. Choose from fresh oven baked Muffins, Butter Croissants, Turnovers, Bars and Cookies

Breakfast Tray (serves 12)................... $ 25.00

Sodas, Tea and Lemonade...................... $ 1.59

Bottled Water or fruit Juice .... $ 1.85

Coffee (cream, sugar and cups included)..... $ 1.59

Large Chocolate Covered Strawberries *(Seasonal)*

12 .... $ 24.00   24 .... $ 45.00

Ordering Time Frame:

- Your needs can often be met with very short notice, however the following lead times are preferred

Delivery:

- Free delivery within Greenbelt area.
- Nominal delivery charges will apply to other areas.
- A small order fee of $10.00 will be added to order less than $40.00, which will be waived if you arrange to have your order picked up at our Bakery.

Please email us at customercare@heavensbakeryinc.com for additional information or call us at 301-220-0691.

since 1984

Heaven's Bakery
Cookies & Cakes

Catering Menu

Heaven's Bakery at Forestville Mall
3261 Donnell Drive
Forestville, MD 20747
P. 301-568-3144

Heaven's Bakery at Beltway Plaza Mall
6092 Greenbelt Road
Greenbelt, MD 20770
P. 301-220-0691

Catering
Phone: 301-220-0691
Email: info@heavensbakeryinc.com

Please visit our website at
www.heavensbakeryinc.com

An unbelievable moist cake: (Select from)
Carrot , German Chocolate, Plain Yellow, Chocolate Yellow, Chocolate Chocolate, Coconut, Rum and Fruit Cake

Small (serves 10)...................... $ 30.00

Large (serves 20)....................$ 55.00

The ultimate chocolate dessert!

Small (serves 12)...................... $ 24.00

Large (serves 24)....................$ 45.00

Beautifully crafted to your specifications for your office, wedding or any other occasions. Each cake is custom made fresh everyday. Please place order 36 hours in advance.

Flavors & Fillings

Flavors: Yellow cake, and/ or Chocolate Cake

Fillings: Strawberry, Raspberry, Lemon, Pineapple and Custard

Sizes & Pricing

1/4 Sheet (serves about 15) .... $20.00 to $40.00
1/2 Sheet (serves about 30) .... $40.00 to $65.00
Full Sheet (serves about 60) .... $65.00 to $95.00

Round and Stacks Cakes are also available. Please email us at info@heavensbakeryinc.com for additional information or call us at 301-220-0691.

A assortment of our famous fresh baked cookies:
Chocolate Chip, Snickerdoodles, Chocolate Chip w/ Walnuts, Peanut Butter, Oatmeal Raisin, Macadamia Chocolate, M&M Cookies and much more! *(Select one or any combination to meet your needs...)*

Small (serves 8)...................... $ 25.00

Large (serves 16)....................$ 45.00

Our famous melt in your mouth cheesecakes:
Plain, Strawberry, and Cherry,
Cheesecakes are available

Small (serves 8)..................... .$ 25.00

Large (serves 16)....................$ 45.00

A fresh selection of seasonal fruits such as pineapple, melon and berries in a colorful arrangement for any exotic occasion

Small   (serves 10)................ $ 30.00

Medium (serves 15)................$ 40.00

Large   (serves 25)................$ 60.00

A selection of gourmet cheese with crackers

Small   (serves 10)................$ 40.00

Medium (serves 15)................$ 50.00

Large   (serves 20)................$ 60.00

• **Maya's Mexican Restaurant** is a restaurant that has expanded to a catering service, all with a continued commitment to bring customers the best Mexican food experience. Their professionally designed menu is a full-color tri-fold featuring exquisite food photography. The colors emphasize the Mexican theme with bold purples and oranges.

- **University Catering's** menu is also created in-house in Microsoft Word. It is a very extensive 28-page menu with a complete offerings. It is full size, 8.5" x 11", and in color.

- **Food Evolution** features a full-size, 8.5" x 11" black and white menu. It focuses on weddings and is an elegantly simple 6-page menu.

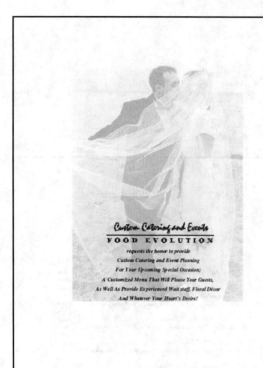

Custom Catering and Events

FOOD EVOLUTION

requests the honor to provide
Custom Catering and Event Planning
For Your Upcoming Special Occasion;

A Customized Menu That Will Please Your Guests,
As Well As Provide Experienced Wait staff, Floral Décor
And Whatever Your Heart's Desire!

Custom Catering and Events

FOOD EVOLUTION

Hors d'oeuvres

Tuxedoed Servers will Serve Your Hors d'oeuvre Selections on Silver Trays
Garnished with Fresh Herb Bundles Tied with Raffia...

Polenta Cornucopia
with Chevre Mousse Garnished with Roasted Red
and Yellow Peppers
1.75 per piece

Oriental Spoon with Duck or Vegetarian Dumpling
Drizzled with Plum Sauce
1.75 per piece

Chilled Cucumber, Strawberry, Tomato
and Fennel Gazpacho and Pineapple Soup
Served on Tequila Shot Glasses
2.00 per piece

Crisp Tortilla Tuille with Grilled Shrimp
Topped Chunky Guacamole and Cilantro Garnish
2.00 per piece

Mini Mignon Steak
Set on Buttered Brioche Round
with Herbed Horseradish Sauce
2.00 per piece

Smoked Salmon Layered with Nori and Sushi Rice
Topped with Pickle Ginger and Wasabi Cream Sauce
2.00 per piece

Crab Rangoon
Served with Mango Dipping Sauce
1.75 per piece

Mint Crusted Baby Lamb Chop
With Pistachio Fums
3.50 per piece

Mini Beggars Purse
Filled with Curried Chicken Salad and Tied with Leek Thread
2.00 per piece

Skewered Chicken
With Coconut Peanut Sauce to the Side
1.75 per piece

Mini Potato Pancake
Dolloped with Apple Chutney
1.75 per piece

Pear and Brie Quesadillas
With Fresh Fruit Salsa
1.75 per piece

Wasabi Lime Crab Salad
In Cucumber Flower
2.00 per piece

Additional Hors d'oeuvres Available

Custom Catering and Events

FOOD EVOLUTION

Estimate

Food Evolution
Would like to assist you with formulating a budget.
We have created an estimate of all costs.
The estimate reflects the lower end of the per person cost range.

Please keep in mind,
your menu choice, equipment rental, venues and other variables
may increase in your final cost.

We would love to offer you a taste!
After you decide on you preliminary menu and wedding ideas,
it would be our pleasure to schedule a tasting of your choices.

Estimated Per Person Charges With Plated Chicken Entree

Passed Hors d'oeuvres	$ 5.50
Seated Dinner Menu	$ 26.25
Mixers and Ice Only	$ 3.50
Service Staff	$ 20.00
Tabletop Rental Equipment	$ 12.00
Linen	$ 4.00
Delivery	$ 1.00
Subtotal	$ 72.25
8.5% Sales Tax	$ 6.14
Total	$ 78.89

A 50% Deposit Is Due Upon Signing Contract.

Payment In Full Is Due Five Days Prior to Your Event.

Truth and Accuracy in Menus

Careful consideration must be taken when writing the final menu to ensure its complete accuracy. Be aware of the unintentional inaccuracies you may have in the menu and the governmental regulations regarding this.

Due to the actions of a few unscrupulous restaurant operators in recent years, a crackdown on the entire food service industry has been declared by certain regulatory agencies. All states have one or more laws which basically say that any organization selling a product must not misrepresent the product in any manner with intent to deceive. Many states have specific "truth in menu" legislation.

Every statement made, whether it be orally by the waiter/waitress or written in the menu description, must be completely accurate. For example, "fresh bay scallops" must never be frozen; they must be bay, not sea or ocean, scallops. "Real maple syrup" must be 100 percent real maple syrup. "Imported baby spring lamb" must be imported, baby, spring lamb. Words and descriptions to watch are fresh, real, imported, baby, 100 percent, BBQ or barbecue, pure, natural, homemade, etc. The description printed on the menu must be exactly the product you are serving.

You may be wondering how you can possibly write an enticing menu that will not read like a grocery list yet still remain within the boundaries of the law. The trick is to be creative in writing the descriptions. State precisely what the product is, but modify the sentences to make the product sound enticing. Creative printing and the use of artwork will boost the appeal of the menu.

NUTRITIONAL CLAIMS ON MENUS

If you decide to include menu items that are marketed as healthy (for example, heart healthy, low fat, reduced fat, cholesterol-free, etc.), make sure you have the nutritional information for these items readily accessible.

Since 1997 restaurants and caterers have been included in the FDA's nutritional labeling laws. Any establishment that uses health or nutrient content claims on its menu must comply with these regulations. If you use a symbol to designate these dishes as healthy, such as a heart rather than text, you must comply with regulations.

Basically, the regulations state that if you make health claims on your menu, you must be able to demonstrate there is a reasonable basis for making such claims. There is some flexibility in how you must establish the claim, but you must be able to show customers and officials that the claim is consistent with the claims established under the Nutrition Labeling and Education Act.

Make sure you are familiar with the FDA's definition of terms. While you may think a menu item with 20 grams of fat is low fat, the FDA may not define it this way. To find out more about FDA regulations, you can go to their Web site at **www.fda.gov**.

NUTRITIONAL PRIMER

Since healthy eating is a current food trend in the industry, it wouldn't hurt to go over a few nutritional basics so you can determine if you should include such items on your menu.

There are six basic categories of nutrients: proteins, fats, carbohydrates, minerals, vitamins, and water. In general, for menu planning, the main categories you need to focus on are carbohydrates and fats. Carbohydrates are starches, sugars, and fiber. These make up the bulk of a healthy diet and are an important energy source for the body. Examples of carbohydrates are sugar, potatoes, bread, rice, pasta, and fruit. Vegetables also contain carbohydrates, but in much lesser amounts.

Fats are a concentrated energy source and provide approximately twice the amount of calories as proteins or carbohydrates. There are saturated fats and unsaturated fats; the difference relates to the chemical structure. Saturated fats are more solid than unsaturated and include shortening and butter. Unsaturated fats are considered healthier and include olive oil and canola oil.

Many people in the United States suffer from heart disease or other chronic illnesses such as diabetes. These people are likely to be guests at any event you cater, so you should familiarize yourself with the various diets they have to follow and include menu items that they can eat. If you ask your client about any special diets in your initial planning meetings, you will also go a long way in showing the client that you are a detail-oriented, savvy caterer.

If you include nutritional information on your menus, make sure the information is correct and clear. You may want to consider hiring a dietitian to check your menu items. There are also software programs available that will do nutrition calculations. ChefTec software does nutritional calculations. Nutribase is another nutritional software you can find at **www.nutribase.com**.

Ways to Provide Your Customers with Healthy Menu Alternatives

If you do not currently offer healthy menu alternatives and would like to do so, there are several ways to do this. There are many sites that provide healthy recipes, such as the American Institute of Cancer Prevention at **www.aicr.org**, the American Heart Association at **www.deliciousdecisions.org**, and the American Diabetes Association at **www.diabetes.org**.

There are also many good healthy cookbooks in print nowadays. The following is a list of a few:

- *Vegetarian Cooking for Everyone* by Deborah Madison

- *The Joslin Diabetes Gourmet Cookbook* by Bonnie Sanders Polin, Ph.D. and Frances Towner Giedt

- *The French Culinary Institute's Salute to Healthy Cooking* by Alain Sailhac, Jacques Pepin, Andre Soltner, and Jacques Torresn (faculty at the French Culinary Institute)

- *Healthy Latin Cooking* by Steve Raichlen

- *Good Food Gourmet* by Jane Brody

- *Heart Healthy Cooking for All Seasons* by Marvin Moser, M.D., Larry Forgione, Jimmy Schmidt, and Alice Waters

- *Moosewood Restaurant Low-Fat Favorites* by the Moosewood Collective

- *Canyon Ranch Cooking* by Jeanne Jones

If you do not want to spend the time developing new recipes to include healthy alternatives, you can probably change some of your existing recipes. Try incorporating the following suggestions into your current menu program.

- A vegetarian entrée.

- One entrée without a butter or cream sauce.

- A greater selection of salads.

- Whole grain breads as part of a bread basket.

- Low-fat mayonnaise as a sandwich condiment.

- Sorbet as a dessert option.

- A simple fruit dessert such as baked pears that is low in sugar and fat.

- Smaller portion sizes on some of your entrées.

- Reduced-fat/reduced-calorie salad dressings.

- Substitute chicken broth for milk in mashed potatoes.

- Replace the cream or whole milk in a recipe with skim milk.

- Replace butter on vegetables with lemon and herb.

- Replace sour cream with yogurt.

- Make your own stock or pick a canned stock that is low in sodium.

- Try serving oven-baked fries rather than French fries.

- Use local fresh produce, meats, and other products.

- Use olive or canola oil instead of butter or shortening.

FOOD ALLERGIES

A food allergy can be very serious and even life threatening. Symptoms can include hives, nausea, vomiting, shortness of breath, and anaphylaxis, a severe respiratory reaction.

Some of the most common allergies are to nuts, eggs, shellfish, peanuts, and wheat. When designing your menu make sure ingredient information is available and you talk with your client about any guests who might have these allergies.

To find out more about food allergies, contact the International Food Information Council at 202-296-6540 or visit their Web site at **www.ific.org**.

CASE STUDY: WORD FROM THE EXPERTS

HEAVENS BAKERY

LOCATION: Washington, D.C.

SERVICES: Heavens Bakery is a family owned business that has been in business since 1984. They focus on knowing their customers. They strive to accommodate everyone's tastes and preferences and treat their customers like family.

Catering is highly customized business, so we have to do a lot of research in how we can specifically meet all of our clients' needs. The best way to sell a dish is to sell it as a package deal to our regular clients to try. In most cases, they love it enough to order it the next time.

We market our products online because it gives us visibility and also an additional place where people can look at our menu. We like to think all of our clients are special, and we accommodate to each individual's special needs. We feel that so many businesses focus on their own food and employee issues that they miss out on what is truly important: focusing on the customers.

Our signature item is a cookie called Snickerdoodle. It is our best seller for both of our locations, selling about 1,500 lbs plus a week. Since our Forestville location is close to military base, lots of military familes move yet still drive hours to buy our Snickerdoodle. Most people who also travel a lot say they been to lots of cookie stores but they never had Snickerdoodle like ours. Honestly, the key is that we use the best-quality butter and other ingredients, and even with higher and rising cost of raw products, we never compromise quality over profit by using any lesser-quality raw materials.

Food Presentation and Production

Time is a critical element when you're a caterer and timing even more so. Many foods can be prepared several days—even weeks or months—in advance and wrapped and stored in either your refrigerator or freezer.

To ensure that you have all the details covered, you should have a production plan for each event. This plan will list the amounts of finished foods and beverages needed, when they must be ready, and when they should be made. The plan will also include setup timing and procedures. If you work in a large facility, the banquet manager and chef will need copies of these with their banquet event orders so they have time and the necessary items for the party. Often in large operations chefs will need to requisition supplies, and that might take a couple of days. If you are a sole proprietor, you will need a few days to shop and make calls for all the items necessary.

When determining how much food to get, you will need to make sure you have enough to cover the guarantee plus a certain percentage over. If there are to be 100 guests, plan on an additional 10 percent. If the guarantee is for 100 to 1,000, plan for an additional 5 percent, and if the guarantee is over 1,000, prepare for an additional 3 percent.

Sit-down dinners are easier to plan since amounts will be pre-portioned for guests. If the main course is a 6-ounce cooked piece of beef, for example, and the expected yield from the raw beef is 75 percent, you will need to get 55 pounds of beef for a party of 100; this will serve 110 people.

While a buffet is more difficult to estimate, there are some general rules of thumb. In general, guests will eat approximately seven pieces of hors d'oeuvres in the first hour of a reception. In addition, blue-collar workers will generally eat and drink more than white-collar workers. Furthermore, people tend to eat and drink less in a very crowded room because it's more difficult to maneuver to the appetizer tables and bar.

Advance Preparation

Food prep for catering events generally begins a day or so before the day of the event. There are several items that can be prepared early that will hold up well until the day of the party. For example, the following can be prepared the day before:

- Cheese trays (covered and refrigerated, minus the crackers)

- Cut and bagged fruit and vegetables (except strawberries)

- Pastries (bake)

- Fruit and vegetable trays (arranged)

- Dips

- Pastries (stuffed)

- Meats that require sauces (in most cases)

- Strawberries (wash and slice)

- Vegetables

- Cheese blocks

- Breads and crackers

The larger the function, the more advanced prep you'll want to do. But be sure you aren't sacrificing quality by preparing items early that need to wait to the day of the event. While you will want to make the salsa the night before so the flavors meld, don't prepare the egg casserole because it will be rubbery and dry by the time it is served. You could, however, break all the eggs you will need and mix them with the cream and refrigerate the mixture to save some time the day of the party.

You can also plan ahead for other non-food items to make the day of the event less stressful. A full-service caterer may spend the week before an event preparing food, décorating the event space, underlining plates with doilies, polishing silver and mirrors, and folding napkins—anything that can be handled ahead of time. Attend to little details. Clean and polish utensils such as tongs, spoons and ladles.

Here are some guidelines for production concerns with specific types of food.

Vegetables. On the day of an event, store broccoli, carrots, celery, cauliflower and radishes in an ice bath to keep them fresh and crisp. A vegetable tray for a typical event might contain chopped broccoli, celery, carrots, cauliflower, cucumbers, yellow squash, zucchini and radishes. If you're serving 100 guests, you'll need about 10 pounds of vegetables (net weight).

Fruit. For the fruit trays, peel, core, remove seeds and chop/slice honeydew, cantaloupe, strawberries, blueberries, raspberries, bananas, oranges and apples. A fruit tray for 100 guests will require around 20 pounds of fruit (net weight). Some fruits, such as apples and bananas, have to be kept in lemon juice to prevent them from turning brown. Don't wash strawberries until the last minute—they get soggy quickly.

Sandwiches. Many events offer small sandwiches for guests. Slice any meats such as roast beef, ham, turkey or salami on the day of an event to prevent them from drying out. This also applies to the accompanying vegetables and garnishes such as lettuce, tomato and red onion. Sliced cheese should be laid out and presented attractively. If you're serving 100 guests, you'll need approximately 20 pounds of meat for sandwiches on cocktail breads. For regular-sized sandwiches, you'll need about 30 pounds of meat per 100 guests.

Breads. Place a moist paper towel on top of the breads/rolls until just prior to service to keep them soft and moist. Most breads become hard and unpalatable if left out even for a few minutes. Use miniature seeded rolls for an added touch. They seem to stay softer longer as opposed to the typical cocktail breads that dry out quickly. Also offer cocktail rye, wheat and pumpernickel.

Seafood. Seafood items need careful attention. No shortcuts here. Fresh fish, including salmon and trout, must have clear, glassy eyes (not cloudy) and must be slime-free. Avoid seafood or fish that smells of ammonia—a clear indication that it's unfit for consumption.

Punch. When using a punch fountain, don't use a punch recipe that has sherbet or any kind of fruit pulp—the particles will clog up the fountain. Serve this type of punch recipe from a glass or crystal punch bowl instead.

Food Presentation

Today's clients expect more than quality food at a catered event; they want their socks knocked off by the food presentation as well. "People do eat first with their eyes," says Frank Puleo, owner of Framboise Catering in New York City, vice president of Culinary Expressions International and NCA president. When it comes to presentation, take a tip from Puelo, who often caters at exotic venues.

For example, Puleo catered one recent event at the Air France terminal in the Newark, New Jersey, airport. "The husband was taking his wife to Paris for her 40th birthday and wanted a surprise party with a few of their friends and family as a send-off," says Puleo. To dazzle guests, Puleo employed an in-house artist to customize each catered event from passing platters to plate presentations. For a recent event at the Rock and Roll Hall of Fame Museum, the artist arranged the food around 45s and small guitars on the serving and passing trays. "We use a lot of different vegetables to try to get a mix of color, texture and height on a plate and garnish with fresh herbs," says Puleo.

Food that is presented well is perceived to have more value by the customer, and your prices for well-plated food can be on the higher side of the price continuum.

PLATE PRESENTATION

Three elements comprise plate presentation:

- Dish type and size
- Portion size
- Garnish

You must provide the appropriate plate sizes for menu items, or kitchen staff may be prone to over-portioning for plated events. If a salad that should be plated on a salad dish is put on a dinner plate, the pantry person is likely to add more salad so the item is not swallowed up by the dish. You should include plate size information on your standardized recipe.

Garnish

Garnish is often overlooked in recipes and in presentation. For minimal cost, garnish can add to the appearance of your plates. Garnish can be anything from simple chopped parsley to sauces drizzled across the plate in a décorative manner. It's the slice of lemon on top of your salmon or the cheese croûtons in the soup.

Along with the actual garnish ingredients, think about how you want the food to be arranged on the plate. Factors to consider when arranging a plate include the following:

Layout. Usually a plate consists of a meat, a starch, and a vegetable. Think about where you want the customer to focus. Most times you want the customer to focus on the most expensive item on the plate (this will enhance the perceived value of the meal). The main element of the plate is usually the meat, so you want your customer to focus on that.

Balance. You must also take the balance of the plate into consideration. By balance we are referring to the weight of the items on the plate. Line is also important because a strong line has strong eye-appeal. A strong line helps to draw the customer's eye to the plate.

Dimension/height. Dimension or height also adds to a plate's appeal. Use molds to mound potatoes or rice and lean meat up against these mounds to create height and a three-dimensional plate. Do not overdo the height factor, however. You do not want to overwhelm the taste of the food by the presentation. Do not over-stack, or over-portion, a plate.

As an example, rather than just putting the sliced roast pork beside the mashed potatoes and green beans, tie the pieces together. Place the mound of potatoes in the center of the plate and fan the slices of pork around it, leaning against the mound. Tie the green beans into a bundle with a steamed chive and angle them on the other side of the potatoes. Think of the plate as a canvas and see what you can create.

Color. Color is also important in plate presentation. Learn and use the color wheel when designing your plates and platters. Red, yellow and blue are primary colors. Orange, green and purple are secondary colors. On the color wheel, the secondary colors are opposite the primary colors, and these opposite colors will appear more intense when beside each other on a plate. For example, red tomatoes served with green kale, purple grapes with yellow cheddar cheese. You can achieve a more subtle plate affect by using colors adjacent to each other on the color wheel. For example, use cantaloupe and watermelon for a fruit cup or asparagus topped with hollandaise sauce. Try to get maximum eye-appeal.

Texture. Also keep texture in mind. Food is more appealing when served with contrasting consistencies. For instance, serve a golden baked puff pastry cup with a seafood mousse. The pastry will heighten the smoothness of the mousse.

Finally, keep in mind that the guest is eventually going to eat the masterpiece you have just created; don't make it difficult to reach around garnishes or to cut into food.

Guidelines for Tray and Platter Selection and Design

Choose service platters according to the occasion, but keep the color of food in mind when deciding on which serving dishes to use as well. In general, vivid dishes stand out against white backgrounds, while at the same time showing off your food to its best advantage.

Presentation on platters is very similar to plate presentation. The goal on a buffet or a dinner plate is to create eye-appeal, and the design principles remain the same.

Be sure to introduce a focal point—an area on the platter to which the eye is automatically drawn. For instance, the platter setup might consist of straight and curved lines, with a centerpiece of salad garnish cascading from the focal point. Perhaps, try to create a straight-line effect, with lines radiating from the centerpiece. Also be sure that the food is properly molded, cooked, sliced, faced or sequenced.

Display unattractive dishes in exciting or special tableware. Dishes such as creamed chicken and chili will immediately appear more enticing. As with plate presentation, height is another important factor of presentation. Create an illusion of height by positioning a large piece of un-sliced roast or galantine in the center of the platter; a rack of ribs is always an impressive option. Or, build a stack of sliced meats with whole pieces of fruit interspersed between the layers. Consider using an acorn squash filled with a sauce or salad. Remember, do not over-stack or over-portion.

Chef Mike Bentz of Crackerjack Catering is an expert at creating tempting and appetizing platters. Pictured on the previous page are some examples of his fruit, shrimp, vegetable and cheese platters.

The Extra Step

In the catering world you are almost always working at events that are special occasions, so people want a special meal that looks terrific rather than just eye-appealing. Here are some suggestions for wowing guests with your presentation.

"People eat with their eyes first, not their mouths." Make food attractive so you can turn even the simplest foods into something wonderfully appealing! Presentation must be visually appealing. To be a successful caterer, food must be good, but so should the food presentation. It takes creativity, common sense and pride to achieve the perfect results. If you have a crudities display, for example, try cutting the vegetables into interesting designs: make radish roses and carrot flowers. Make sure you garnish plates and platters and do not overload the plates with food.

- **"T" or serpentine arrangement**. Use this proven-successful setup for wedding receptions. A "T" arrangement allows guests to serve themselves from both sides of the table, thus preventing long lines and allowing more time for socializing. Display the food in a "lust" setting.

- **Personalize the layout for each event.** For example, décorate the tables with flowers of every color, or shining silk and lamé fabric. Alternatively, use glass block and mirrors. You also can create height on the buffet table by putting boxes or cake stands under the tablecloths and putting some platters on top of these stands. Think about the personality of the client as well. Does the bride have a fondness for a particular flower? Incorporate these into the centerpieces.

- **The elegant dessert.** For guaranteed "wow," serve a stunning dessert such as "The Three Berries" dessert. It consists of a dish of fresh berries arranged on leaves, then a simple sauce of crème fraiche, or raspberries served separately. There is nothing complex about this dessert—it's the presentation that makes it special. Keep it simple, but go for impact. If you are not comfortable with your baking skills (as many caterers are not), find an excellent bakery to make your desserts. To find a dessert supplier, check with area restaurants. Most restaurants do not have in-house pastry chefs anymore, so if you find one that has wonderful desserts, ask the owner or manager who supplies them.

- **"Less is more."** Create an exquisite carrot "chrysanthemum." Simply place a tiny sorrel and scallop soufflé on a nest of beet purée. It's sure to impress your guests and is far more effective than a platter decorated with a mass of fluted vegetables and piped decorations. The key to achieving impact is to arrange foods with a sense of scale and proportion.

- **Create an illusion of "effortlessness."** One of the best secrets of effective food presentation is to make it look as if it's been effortlessly prepared. Achieve this by placing your food in interesting patterns. Choose an exquisite garnish or decorate the platter with a single ingredient. This strategy for food arrangement never fails.

- **Tailor your arrangements to reflect a client's individual requirements.** Pay special attention to the different dishes being presented, as well as their size. Put dynamic patterns into use. Nothing can be more boring than seeing all dishes on a table arranged in the same manner!

- **Diagrams.** Create diagrams in order to organize your thoughts for food presentation. This will help you in placing, sizing and shaping your foods. It is time well-spent.

TRIED AND TRUE "WOW" FACTORS

The following suggestions offer tried and tested ways of really making a splash! Consider incorporating some of them into your repertoire.

- Create a Napoleon appetizer. Layer crisp phyllo pastry or deep-fried wonton layers with savory fillings.

- Try a fresh look for the classic Mexican seven-layer dip. Instead of serving this in the traditional-style dish, try serving individual portions in martini glasses.

- A fish cooked whole. Leave the head on. Deep fry, roast or steam the fish.

- Butterfly (spatchcock) a chicken or other fowl. Grill it flat.

- Using a mandolin, slice Yukon Gold potatoes, fry them, and use these for salad croutons.

- Use a wild rice waffle as the base for a savory appetizer.

- Sweet tamales of walnut and cinnamon. Serve with crema fresca.

- Add a twist to serving caviar—combine with a vodka tasting session.

- An entrée with impact. Serve a ten-inch porcini mushroom with minimal garnish.

- Cut salmon into strips and interlace the strips to create a basket weave square for steaming.

- Grill jumbo Thai prawns in the shell; serve on a giant banana leaf.

- Serve blackberry and blueberry sorbets in hot-pink tulip glasses.

- Poach peaches (with the stem on) in red wine with cardamom-vanilla sauce.

- Serve heart-shaped ravioli on a brilliant red sauce for a Valentine appetizer.

- Add edible flowers and flower petals to salads and desserts for that extra special touch.

- Instead of sifting confectioners' sugar, cocoa, cinnamon or ground nuts through commercial paper doilies, let your imagination soar by making your own templates. Trace designs on manila file folders, then cut out using a razor-sharp box cutter or mat knife.

- To make red or yellow pepper curls, fillet the peppers and slice in very thin strips. Put the strips in ice water for several hours and they will curl.

- Fry sage leaves to top poultry or pork dishes.

- For a festive touch, dust mint sprigs lightly with confectioners' sugar before using to garnish a dessert plate or platter.

- To "paint" the sauce on a dessert plate, pool a little of the sauce in the bottom of a plate. Then, with a second sauce of contrasting color in a squirt bottle with a fine tip, make a series of concentric circles in the first sauce. Finally, at regular intervals, draw a knife tip or poultry pin across the sauce rings, creating a wavy effect.

- To "paint" hearts in sauce, squirt the second sauce into a ring of dots, spacing them about an inch apart. Stick a knife tip or poultry pin in the center of a dot, pull it to the right or left, up or down, forming a heart. For two-toned hearts, place a smaller dot of contrasting color inside each large dot.

- To save time, pipe rosettes or dollops of whipped cream onto foil-covered baking sheets and freeze. Transfer to self-sealing plastic bags, label and date, and store in the freezer. Then all you need to dress up a dessert is top each portion with a rosette or dollop of frozen whipped cream. They will thaw in ten minutes or less.

Presentation-Enhancing Products

While your own creativity and skill is vital to food presentation, there are a number of products that can enhance your designs. Check out the following:

- **Floralytes, Submersible Floralytes and LED Candles.** Enhance any atmosphere with battery-operated lighting. Perfect for affairs with low lighting to create an elegant touch. For more information, visit **www. chillinproducts.com**.

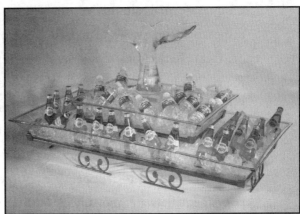

- **Gourmet Display, www.gourmetdisplay.com**, offers a wide variety of presentation products including beverage housings, pastry cases. cubes and staircases, ice carving pedestals, juice dispensers, ornamental iron, tiers, epic edge trays, riser rim mirror trays, serving stone trays, and acrylic and mirror trays. Two examples are pictured below.

- **America - America Corporation** produces a line of elegant birch wood commercial servings trays that are totally dishwasher safe. They are exceptionally lightweight and handsome. They also dry faster than plastic trays and can support heavy loads. A variety of colored trays are also available or you can have them customized with your company's logo. For more information, **www.america-amer-icabirchtrays.com**.

DISPOSABLE PRODUCTS

You may also want to investigate disposable items. These can be very useful for serving as well as transport.

WNA Comet, **www.wna.biz**, manufacturers a variety of disposable products that are versatile and attractive. These timesaving products can help achieve a high-class look. Following is a summary of some of their product lines:

- **Reflections™** cutlery has a look that takes disposable cutlery to a new level of sophistication. Reflections™ has the same shine and silver-sparkle as stainless steel cutlery, giving consumers a unique, formal alternative to white or black disposable cutlery. Available in a spoon, knife or fork, Reflections™ single-use silverware is the only solution addressing both the need for a formal presentation and the high costs associated with renting or owning permanent flatware. Caterers estimate that loss and accidental disposal result in the need to replace 15 to 30 percent of permanent flatware annually. A 600-unit case of Reflections™ has the same average cost of 11 permanent flatware settings. In addition, for the cost of renting just one stainless flatware setting, Reflections™ provides at least 5 settings.

- **Masterpiece™ dinnerware** combines the expensive appearance of painted china with the convenience of a premium, heavyweight disposable. Offered in two standard designs and a holiday print, Masterpiece™ is a distinct upscale line that enhances food presentation and distinguishes with impeccable style and grace. The Premiere stock pattern is simple sophistication printed gold on ivory, while the Bordeaux stock design is a more contemporary burgundy imprint on white. With Masterpiece™ dinnerware,

breakage, cleanup costs, washing and transportation expenses are all eliminated. The Masterpiece™ dinnerware is perfect for caterers who specialize in event or corporate catering and food service management companies that specialize in stadium and arena skybox catering, restaurants, country clubs, and hotels and resorts with pool patios.

- **Classicware's®** timeless elegance captures the look of fine china, adding a touch of class to any occasion. A heavyweight yet disposable design in clear, black or white makes this attractive dinnerware a durable alternative to china, paper and foam products. Offering four plate sizes, 10-ounce bowl, serving bowl, trays, utensils, and a wide variety of drinkware, Classicware® completes any occasion. The graceful curve of the Classic Crystal™ drinkware complements the scalloped edge of Classicware® dinnerware to deliver a stunning presentation equivalent to fine crystal and china. Fluted tumblers and stemware create the impression and sparkle of fine-cut crystal. Conveniently, Classicware® single-service drinkware eliminates glassware breakage worries.

- **Classicware® beverage products.** One-Piece Wine Glass and One-Piece Champagne Flute capture the timeless elegance of fine-cut crystal and combine it with the convenience of single-service. With single-service plasticware you eliminate glass breakage worries and reduce labor costs for cleanup, washing and return transportation. Plus, the one-piece construction saves over $4 (per 100 count case) in costly assembly labor versus two-piece disposables. The Classicware® One-Piece Wineglass and One-Piece Champagne Flute, with their sophisticated designs, can be used in place of crystal when a disposable product is more practical. The Classic Crystal™ 50-Ounce Pitcher is perfect for any cold beverage, from water to carbonated drinks, sangria to beer, and iced fruit drinks to margaritas. The sleek clean lines of the pitcher silhouette are accented by a crystal-cut design that offers the elegance of glass or crystal combined with the convenience of single-service.

- **CaterLine®.** From rigid platters and bowls to compartment trays to serving utensils, CaterLine® products offer versatile beauty in strong, durable designs. This servingware is designed for strength and will not bend or buckle under even the heaviest loads. Sophisticated shapes of round, rectangle, oval, triangle and square are offered in assorted sizes and colors allowing caterers to differentiate themselves by mixing shaped trays and bowls for a truly unique display. To fully complete any presentation, CaterLine® brings you strong, disposable serving utensils that reduce

the costs to clean and replace lost permanentware and allows "drop and go" convenience. Offering a utensil for any occasion, CaterLine® truly delivers the whole catering presentation.

- **CaterLine® Pack n' Serve.** Ease the transition from preparation to presentation with CaterLine® Pack n' Serve bowls, which combine the convenience and value of a disposable bowl to transport food with an upscale look that allows you to utilize the same product for display. The subtle fluting on the bowls and lids enhances the food presentation and package appearance. These bowls are available in clear and black with clear dome lids. Bowls are offered in sizes from 24 to 320 ounces. The bowls offer superior sidewall strength and leak-resistant lids that seal in freshness. In addition to the ample-size tabs on both the lid and bowl to facilitate openings and closings, Pack n' Serve bowls stack for

stability during transport. Each size bowl nests into the lid of not only that size, but also the next size up.

Sabert Corporation, **www.sabert.com**, also offers a wide variety of disposable products. Sabert's elegant product styling makes food look great. All platters, bowls and utensils are available in an extensive selection of styles and sizes. All products are food service tested for superior performance and designed with food service operators' needs in mind. Sabert's product solutions incorporate superior resistance to cracking and crushing since they are manufactured from the same tough materials used in beverage packaging.

Sabert knows that people eat with their eyes first and its product solutions are designed to be easy on the eyes. From the crystal clarity of the lids to the array of sophisticated colors, customers will be impressed. Like clarity and color, design is important when you are trying to turn a good first impression into a lasting one.

Sabert Nova Plus Platter

Following is a summary of Sabert's product line:

- **The Queen Ann Collections.** A traditional design with a touch of royal formality.

- **The Europa Gold Collections.** Designed to convey a sense of European charm and panache.

- **The Mulberry Hill Collections.** A chic and contemporary motif with unpretentious sophistication.

- **The Seashell Collections.** Designed to evoke an air of fresh refinement, the distinctive curved contour is perfect for the tasteful serving of condiments.

- **The Nova Plus Collection.** An exotic jet-black color is emphasized by an embossed, swirl pattern that dresses up any special event.

- **Round and Oval Platters.** Classic simplicity just right for any occasion.

Genpak is another manufacturer and supplier of food service packaging. Their Quality to Go® Line features snack, sandwich and dinner foam hinged containers, foam bases with clear lids, foam and plastic serving bowls with lids, clear hinged containers, paper cones and soufflé cups, foam serving trays, and several lines of foam, laminated foam and plastic dinnerware. Visit **www.genpak.com** to view and order samples or call 518-798-9511 for more information.

Genpak products

For the environmentally conscious, Biocorp, Inc., **www.biocorpaavc.com**, offers biodegradable and compostable bags, liners and food service ware. Their extensive line of cost-effective, quality products makes organic recycling feasible. Biocorp has developed an exciting line of food service ware including plates, cups, bowls, lunch boxes and cutlery.

CASE STUDY: WORD FROM THE EXPERTS

THE RESULTS GROUP

LOCATION: Nashville, Tennessee

SERVICES: Michael Attias operates a restaurant in Nashville, Tennessee, and helps restaurant owners add or expand a catering profit center through his company, The Results Group. You can download his FREE Report: Tapping Into Your Hidden Catering Profit$ at www.ezRestaurantMarketing.com.

ADVANCED MARKETING FOR CATERERS By Michael Attias

A customer list is a caterer's most valuable asset. Not only does it show a potential buyer where your business comes from, but it is a license to print money by targeting your existing customers when a sales boost is needed. If you don't have a customer list, you need to start building a customer database today.

I'll give you an example of the value of a customer database. A couple of years ago we added onsite catfish fries to our option of caterings. I sent out a simple one-page letter letting our customers know about the new service. One of the people on the list was a factory that was shutting down and we should've taken them out of our database. They received the letter, called us up and booked a safety luncheon worth over $5,000 from a letter that cost about fifty cents to mail. At the event, the talk of a Fourth of July event came up, and we booked a $4,000 event. So, this one letter to somebody who shouldn't have even been in my database was responsible for over $9,000 of business.

Pre-season bookings, new menu offerings, and existing services should all be sold via direct mail and contact to your customer database. It will yield your highest marketing ROI.

Cost Controls

resently throughout the entire food service industry, operating expenses are up and income is down. After taxes and expenses, restaurants that make money, according to the National Restaurant Association, have bottom lines at 0.5 to 3.0 percent of sales. This tiny percentage is the difference between being profitable and going under, and it drives home the importance of controlling your costs.

Most small business owners find that setting prices and controlling costs are two of the most difficult tasks they undertake. While this affects everyone in the food service industry, these issues are even more difficult for the caterer. And the smaller caterer suffers the most. If you are part of a larger operation or a catering operation in a hotel or restaurant, food cost is not as big of an issue. If you are a sole proprietor, however, and you have food left over from a party on Tuesday, you won't be able to save it for the soup at lunch on Wednesday as a restaurant might do. This being said, it is important for an operation, small or large, to control costs and price food in order to make a profit.

According to government statistics, a restaurant investor has a 1 in 20 chance of getting his or her money back in five years. Furthermore, the consensus of many successful restaurateurs is that 80 percent of the success of a food service business is determined before it opens. This means you must prepare, and part of that preparation is integrating an ongoing cost-control program into your business.

This can be doubly important if you are fortunate enough to start out doing great business. This is because high profits can hide many inefficiencies that will surely expose themselves during times of low sales. Too many people become cost-control converts only after suffering losses; this is shortsighted. The primary purpose of cost controls is to maximize profits, not minimize losses. Controlling costs works because it focuses on getting the most value from the least cost in every aspect of your operation. By keeping costs under control, you can charge less than the competition or make more money from charging the same price.

What Is Cost Control?

A lot can be done to control costs, and it begins with planning. Cost control is about numbers. It is about collecting, organizing, interpreting, and comparing the numbers that impact your bottom line. They are what tell you the real story of what's going on in your operation.

Cost control is not accounting or bookkeeping: these are the information-gathering tools of cost control. Cost control can be defined by explaining its purposes:

- To provide management with information needed for making day-to-day operations decisions.

- To monitor department and individual efficiency.

- To inform management of expenses being incurred and incomes received, and whether they fall within standards and budgets.

- To prevent fraud and theft.

- To provide the basis for the business's goals (not for discovering where it has been).

- To emphasize prevention, not correction.

- To maximize profits, not minimize losses.

Cost control is an ongoing process that must be part of the basic moment-to-moment breathing of your business. A continuous appraisal of this process is equally as integral to the functioning of your operation. There are five key elements to an effective cost-control strategy:

1. Planning in advance.

2. Procedures and devices that aid the control process.

3. Implementation of your program

4. Employee compliance.

5. Management's ongoing enforcement and reassessment.

Furthermore, your program should be assessed with the following questions:

- Do your cost controls provide relevant information?

- Is the information timely?

- Is it easily assembled, organized and interpreted?

- Are the benefits and savings greater than the cost of the controls?

This last point is especially important. When the expense of the controls exceeds the savings, that's waste, not control. Spending $30,000 on a computer system that will save you $5,000 in waste is ineffective.

Standards are key to any cost-control program. Predetermined points of comparison must be set, against which you will measure your actual results. The difference between planned resources and resources that are actually used is the variance. Management can then monitor for negative or positive variances between standards and actual performance and will know where specifically to make corrections. These five steps illustrate the uses of standards:

1. Performance standards should be established for all individuals and departments.

2. Individuals must see it as the responsibility of each to prevent waste and inefficiency.

3. Adherence—or lack of adherence—to standards must be monitored.

4. Actual performance must be compared against established standards.

5. When deviations from standards are discovered, appropriate action must be taken.

Your job is to make sure standards are adhered to. Be sure your staff is using measuring scoops, ladles and sized bowls, glasses and cups, weighing portions individually, portioning by count, and pre-portioning. These are all useful tools to make sure standards are met and your cost-control program implemented effectively.

Critical Areas of Cost Control

The following seven areas are central to any food operation and are therefore crucial elements of cost-control records.

Purchasing. Your inventory system is the critical component of purchasing. Before placing an order with a supplier, you need to know what you have on hand and how much will be used. Allow for a cushion of inventory so you won't run out between deliveries. Once purchasing has been standardized, the manager simply orders from your suppliers. Records show supplier, prices, unit of purchase, product specifications, etc. This information needs to be kept on paper.

Receiving. This is how you verify that everything you ordered has arrived. Check for correct brands, grades, varieties, quantities, correct prices, etc. Incorrect receivables need to be noted and either returned or credited to your account. Products purchased by weight or count need to be checked.

Storage. All food is stored until it's used. Doing so in an orderly fashion ensures easy inventory. Doing so properly, with regard to temperature, ventilation and freedom from contamination, ensures food products remain in optimum condition until being used. Expensive items need to be guarded from theft.

Issuing. Procedures for removing inventory from storage are part of the cost- control process. Head chefs and bartenders have authority to take or issue stock from storage to the appropriate place. This is a much more important aspect of cost control than it seems, because in order to know your food and beverage costs, you need to know your beginning inventory, how much was sold, and your ending inventory. Without this data you can't determine accurate sales figures.

Rough preparation. How your staff minimizes waste during the preliminary processing of inventory is critical.

Preparation for service. Roughly prepared ingredients are finished off prior to plating. The quality and care with which this is done determines the amount of waste generated in preparation of standard recipes.

Portioning/Transfer. Food can be lost through over-portioning. Final preparation should be monitored regularly to ensure quality and quantity standards are being adhered to. This is such a crucial element to cost control that many managers are assigned to monitor order times, portions, presentation, and food quality with an eagle eye.

Types of Losses

There are three general types of losses that can affect you cost controls:

1. Operational   2. Direct   3. Potential

OPERATIONAL LOSSES

Operational losses are unavoidable and just a part of doing business. Still, the amount of operational loss can be controlled if you put cost-control measures into place.

Here are examples of operational loss:

- China and glassware breakage
- Food over-production
- Poor food purchasing and receiving
- Theft
- Improper scheduling of labor
- Lack of telephone controls

- Flatware and linen loss
- Beverage over-pouring
- Utility waste
- Lack of preventative maintenance
- Lack of inventory rotation and storage policies

OPERATIONAL LOSS CONTROL

China and Glassware Breakage

By following a few simple rules and techniques, both you and your staff can greatly reduce losses from breakage and keep your glassware, tableware, and equipment supplies from turning over unnecessarily.

- Always have your employees use hot pads when serving meals, thereby reducing breakage incidents when a plate is "too warm." You'll save money in food and tableware inventory, as well as insurance costs.

- Ensure that all employees using dishwashing machines give your glassware and tableware ample time to cool before they handle them. When glassware or ceramics are heated, they have a far lower breakage point and are much more likely to develop small cracks or break.

- Make it clear to your kitchen staff that ceramic bowls are not to be used for things like whisking of eggs or stirring of contents. Such actions radically damage your tableware and dramatically lessen their usable lifespan. Provide plastic ware or metalware for these sorts of activities.

- Have employees dry all silverware before putting it away for an extended period. This simple activity will not only check that every piece of cutlery is actually clean, but will also cut down on rust over a long period.

- Ensure any glassware properly fits your glass racks, especially in the dishwasher. If they don't have a snug fit, glasses will do a lot of bouncing around during the wash cycle and while being transported; this will bring their failure date closer.

- Are your dishes and bowls easy to handle? Quite often what looks great on a table can be hard for an employee to manipulate, causing breakage. Similarly, if your plates aren't easily stackable and thick enough to take the wear and tear of daily life, you could be wasting money. When choosing dinnerware for your business, take more than just looks into account.

- Never allow your bar staff to use glasses as ice scoops. A tiny chip of glass falling into your ice bin can cause a great deal of injury, and bar glassware certainly isn't designed to shovel rocks of ice. Along the same lines, any time a glass breaks in or near an ice bin, the entire ice bin needs to be emptied and the contents disposed of before it can be used in the preparation of another drink.

- Staff should never touch the upper half of a glass in the act of serving a drink. It's unhygienic, it looks terrible to the customer, and the glass will be much more susceptible to breakage if it's being regularly handled in this manner.

- Stemmed glasses are far more susceptible to breakage than most other types of glasses, and usually more expensive. All staff should take extra care in the handling of these items, perhaps even to the point of washing them only by hand.

- All glasses and plates need to be inspected, if only briefly, before they're used to fill an order. A lipstick smudge, chip, crack, or remnants of a previous meal or drink are not only off-putting to a customer, but also hazardous to the customer's health.

- Limit the number of dishes stacked on the warming table, by the dishwasher, and in storage areas. Placing large amounts of dishes on top of each other causes great stress at the bottom of the stack, and will see your tableware break far sooner than it should. Avoid piling them any more than a dozen high.

- Avoiding unnecessary handling and transportation of dishes and glassware is a good way to keep it from breaking. If the journey your dishware takes from the dishwasher to the warmer to the counter to the table is a long one, think about ways to eliminate steps from the process. Is the warmer next to the washer? Do your staff stack loaded dish racks when they're just out of the washer, adding another step to the process? Use your space to your advantage, and not only will you save on breakage, you'll also find your labor is more productive.

Flatware and Linen Loss

- Keep an inventory of your cutlery, crockery, serving equipment, glassware, napkins, tablecloths, silverware and prep equipment. All of this equipment costs you money. If these items are accidentally thrown out or if every staff member took a few glasses, a tablecloth, a few plates, and some silverware home with them over the course of a month, that is a huge dollar loss.

- If you use paper napkins, consider purchasing recycled paper-based products as a cost-effective, environmentally sound alternative. You'll also be showing your clientele that your establishment is environmentally conscious.

- If you use a linen service to have napkins and tablecloths cleaned, it might be worth investigating whether it would be more cost effective to set up your own small laundry area on the premises. Having your kitchen staff also responsible for laundry duties, and paying to have a washer and dryer installed, may seem expensive, but if you never have to pay for a linen service again, that initial expense may be quickly recovered.

- If your own on-premise laundry area is out of the question, consider using a linen rental service. Each week you rent a certain number of linens, and at the end of the week, the service replaces them, hauls away the old ones, and cleans them. This saves you labor, worry and, hopefully, price.

- Your employees' uniforms can cost you a great deal of money initially, but if you make your uniform choices something that your employees will likely wear outside the business, basic black shirts, pants and skirts, for example, you'd be more than justified in asking the employees to cover half the purchase cost. Make it easy on them: let them pay a little out of their wages each week. If you're not asking them to wear something garish, they shouldn't have too many complaints.

- An apron doesn't just keep your staff from staining their clothes, it also provides a uniform look to your employees, and makes them far more noticeable as staff. If you're providing uniforms for your people, supplying an apron to preserve your employees' clothing could save you a bundle in wear and tear.

Food Over-production

- Ensure all employees adhere to portion standards. If the portions your staff is serving are just 10 percent more than you're budgeting for, you're giving away a whole lot of money every month. This holds true from the size of a slice of meat to the amount of salad and dressing served with each meal.

- Compel your chefs to follow your established recipes. Recipes have two purposes: 1) to ensure consistency, and 2) to control costs. Following these practices will keep food costs from getting out of control, and having a consistent quality for all your meals will enhance the way your business is perceived.

- Ensure your chefs are not overcooking meals. This results in lower portion yields as well as delays in serving, which will combine to increase your bottom-line expenses.

- Discourage "free handing it." Also be sure your staff is using scales, measuring cups, measuring spoons, and appropriate ladles. Often cooks will free-hand it after awhile, and this will lead to over-portioning.

- Does your staff use trim items from meal preparations in other meals? For example, meat trimmings can be used for soups to great effect, celery leafs can be used as garnishes, and pastry off-cuts can be re-rolled and used, rather than wasted.

- Maintain a fixed menu for your business, one that allows you to keep a smaller inventory and a fairly simple price list for employees to remember. When you do offer specials, fashion them around whatever ingredients you bought at a great price that week, or items in your inventory that you would like to move. If you do use a seasonal menu, try to use local growers for lower produce prices, and design seasonal menus that allow you to use ingredients in several dishes so you can order in bulk.

- Ensure your kitchen staff weighs all meat portions and ingredients before cooking them to meet recipe specifications on every meal. Often when you purchase from suppliers, you're paying by the pound, so if your portions are too large, you're losing money on every meal. Trim where necessary, and maintain consistency wherever possible.

- Let your employees be aware that they are to portion out all condiments, sauces and breads according to the number of guests at a table. If they put more bread on the table than is needed, your patrons will inevitably eat more and order less. Similarly, if the bread is thrown away and not used, it is wasted money.

- How much meat is your chef trimming away? Is he or she cutting off more meat than fat? Excessive trimming will dry your meat when cooking, leading to poor-quality results

- Be certain your kitchen staff uses the correct-sized dish for each menu item. If they are serving a salad on a dinner plate, they will probably serve too much since the prescribed portion will look small on the dinner plate.

- Having standardized recipes and measuring equipment available to your staff won't help you reduce costs unless your staff knows how to use them and what your expectations are. Train all new employees and spend time retraining existing staff at regular intervals. Make sure cooks know exactly what ingredients go on the Vegetable Lover's Pizza and servers know how much bread goes into the bread baskets.

Beverage Over-pouring

Controls for determining dispensing costs, recording sales, and accounting for consumed beverages can be done three different ways:

1. **Automated systems that dispense and count.** These range from mechanical dispensers attached to each bottle to magnetic pourers that can only be activated by the register. These systems are exact, reduce spillage, and cannot give free drinks. Basically, liquor can't be dispensed without being put into the system.

2. **Ounce or drink controls.** This requires establishing standard glassware and recipes, recording each drink sold, determining costs of each drink, comparing actual use levels to potential consumption levels, and comparing actual drink cost percentage to potential cost percentage.

3. **Par stock or bottle control.** This is a matter of keeping the maximum amount of each type of liquor behind the bar, then turning in all empty bottles for full ones. No full bottles are given without an empty one coming in. A standard sales value per bottle is determined based on the drinks it makes. A sales value is determined from consumption and compared to actual sales for variances. If less was sold than consumed, investigate.

Poor Food Purchasing and Receiving

An efficient purchasing program incorporates standard purchase specifications based on standardized recipes resulting in standardized yields that, with portion control, allow for accurate costs based on portions actually served.

Ordering effectively is impossible unless you know your inventory. Before an order is placed, counts of stock should be made. Many software programs are able to determine order quantities directly from sales reports, but without this kind of system, you must inventory what you have on hand before ordering. The taking of inventory must be streamlined, because it must be done as frequently as you order.

Whether your inventory system is by hand or computer, it has many purposes. It should provide records of what you need, product specifications, suppliers, prices, unit of purchase, and product use levels. The inventory system should increase the accuracy of inventory, make it easy to detect variance levels in inventory, and facilitate efficient ordering.

The following suggestions will help you to have a more efficient purchasing and receiving program no matter how much business you do.

- Talk with your delivery person and order-taker. Try to speak with the same people every time you deal with them and build a relationship of trust. Ask what items they have in stock that are an exceptionally good deal this month or are of greater quality than normal. Ask them if they can discount an item if you buy a larger quantity or if you settle your invoice early. A good relationship with a vendor can be a great cost savings in many ways.

- Do you use fixed orders? Often a fixed order will see you granted a small discount because it allows the vendor to accurately plan their own purchases, but if you're buying more than you need over the long run, this deal might cost you more than it saves you. Review all standing orders at least every quarter, reducing or increasing where necessary, and keep your inventory at a productive level.

- Use your suppliers' Web sites. Many of the larger food suppliers, such as SYSCO, have Web sites on which you can place and track orders. Like SYSCO, they may also have links to current market reports and information on new products. You can visit SYSCO's Web site at **www.sysco.com.**

- Do you monitor markets regularly for lower prices? Perform monthly price checks for food, beverages and supplies, and if you spot someone selling cheaper than your supplier, ask them to match the price. A supplier trying to get, or keep, your business may offer discounts, bonuses and incentives that can save you a bundle.

- Don't over-purchase. A long-term saving may be offset by additional storage costs, spoilage, and by having your finances tied up in stock that won't give a return on your investment for some time.

- Change your menus to accommodate large price shifts. When the price of beef soars, consider raising your main menu prices to accommodate, or change your menu items to use pork, chicken or another meat with an acceptable price level. Keeping your profit margin stable is a very important aspect of your business.

- When considering the purchase of a new food or beverage product, ask if you can test a sample before you make your decision. Not only is free stock always a nice thing to have, but testing a new item properly is essential if you don't want to deal with unforeseen problems later.

- The person who handles your inventory counts of food and beverages should also be responsible for creating lists of what needs to be ordered. Keeping the main responsibility of deciding purchasing quantities with the person closest to the inventory assures you won't go overboard with your buying habits.

- Never pay for any shipping invoice not signed for by an employee from your establishment. If nobody working for you is prepared to put their signature on paper to say that a delivery arrived and that it was in the order it was supposed to be in, then you shouldn't pay the bill until you can investigate it further.

- Let employees know that they're responsible for whatever they signed for. If a box is supposed to contain 20 steaks and only contains 19, that should be pointed out and noted when the delivery first comes in. If the discrepancy isn't pointed out to the delivery driver, either you're going to lose money or your employee needs to cover the difference. If you'd rather not use such a harsh tactic, you still need to be sure the employee knows his or her responsibility. You may want to issue a warning the first time this happens and then let the employee know if it happens again what type of disciplinary action you will take.

- The longer your inventory sits without being put away, the faster it will spoil. Don't let deliveries sit, waiting to be properly handled; ensure they're delivered at a time when your staff have the flexibility to put them away. And never let deliveries be dropped off early in the morning or when nobody is on duty. Goods sitting on your back doorstep will be invariably stolen, spoiled, and a lure for rodents and bugs.

- Demand that returned or refused items are marked and initialed by the delivery person, on the packing slip, and then put back on the truck, before the driver leaves your establishment. It's far harder to send goods back and be credited for them when they've been sitting in your cool room for two days.

- Always check expiration dates, and anything with an expired date should be refused or sent back.

- Check your kitchen scales for accuracy. Your scales need to be checked on a weekly basis to ensure complete accuracy, and that you are not billed for product you haven't received.

- Is your scale adequate to check the weight of incoming orders? You should be able to quickly check if you are receiving 50 pounds of hamburger or only 45 pounds, and if you don't have scales, consider purchasing them. To purchase kitchen scales online, visit the following:
  - Scale World: **www.scaleworld.com**
  - Scale Man: **www.scaleman.com**
  - Itin Scales: **www.itinscale.com**

Lack of Inventory Rotation and Storage Policies

The storage habits of your operation can end up costing you big money if they're not as productive as they could be. It doesn't take much effort to embrace proper storage methods, and the upside is less spoilage, easier access, and the maximum use of your available space.

Make sure you have purchasing and storage specifications in place for your staff to follow. These specifications should include specific product information for placing orders, correct storage temperatures, and a rotation policy for stock.

Use the first in, first out (FIFO) for all your inventory products so items do not sit on shelves and spoil. Minimize food loss in storage: keep frozen food at 0 degrees; food in dry storage areas should be stored at temperatures around 50 degrees; keep food in dry storage on shelves at least 6 inches from the floor and the wall; make sure the staff is storing raw meat on shelves below raw produce; and be sure that fresh fish is being kept on ice in the refrigerator to maintain the proper temperature of 30 to 34 degrees.

- The improper stacking of storage containers can result in spills, breakage, and accidents. Ensure that if you use storage containers, they stack properly and are easily handled.

- Stacking items on top of one another in your cool room might seem to be the most productive way to utilize your limited space, but such a system makes cleaning and access to certain items very difficult. A good shelving system that is flexible enough to allow you to easily change shelf heights will make good use of space, but also makes every item in your fridge easier to get to and make cleaning a breeze.

- When you receive deliveries like flour, sugar and salt in large five-gallon buckets, reuse them for storing dry materials. Buckets like these are usually airtight and designed for maximum protection of the contents, so rather than tossing them, clean them, re-label them, and utilize them.

- Don't automatically use fresh fruit and vegetables if canned alternatives can be used without dramatically cutting back on meal quality. Canned tomatoes, artichoke hearts, chili peppers, pineapples, pears, etc., can all be used in many meals without a loss in flavor, and the trade off is a big drop in price and spoilage rates. For example, in a tomato-based pizza sauce, most people would be hard-pressed to tell the difference between a canned product, a pre-prepared product from a jar, or fresh tomatoes.

- Rotate stock when receiving deliveries. There's no better time to perform a stock rotation than when you're first putting away fresh items. Failure to do so can make it harder to differentiate what's new and what's old down the road.

- Discard food past the expiration date. Don't let food lay around that has passed its expiration date. Potentially hazardous food that has been prepared in-house can be stored for a maximum of seven days at 41°F or lower.

Utility Waste

Your yearly power bill will run well into the thousands. Even the smallest cost-saving procedure can save you hundreds of dollars a year if you stick with it.

- Save on your electricity bills by ensuring that your dishwashers are running the garbage disposal only as needed. Leaving it running continually is expensive.

- Do you really need your dishes to be power-dried at the end of the dishwasher cycle, at all times through the day? Leave the dishes to air dry, thereby saving energy and reducing your operating expenses.

- Use lower-watt light bulbs, and be sure to look for "longer lasting" light bulbs that don't require as much energy. Halogen lights are a good alternative. They are more expense to purchase, but they last longer than fluorescent lights. Additionally, the use of mirrors throughout your establishment will maximize your lighting effects, as well as give your room the illusion of increased space.

- Use timers for all of your lights in case employees forget to shut them off at the end of the day. The use of timers will ultimately create savings in your electrical costs, and can also be used as a break-in deterrent to give the impression someone is in the building late at night.

- Dishwasher water temperature should be set at the lowest point allowed by local health department guidelines to conserve the energy needed to heat your water. Save even more electricity by actually turning the dishwasher "off" when not in use. Leaving an appliance switched on for hours at a time costs your business money.

- Many air-conditioning systems are designed to be working at a low rate, even when the temperature is perfect, just to keep air flow moving. If you have windows and doors that can be opened during a nice breezy day, have the A/C turned off altogether and save this big power-user for times when you really need it.

- Often employees will carelessly leave a light on in walk-in coolers when they walk out, costing you big money over the long term in wasted electricity. Consider using a timer or motion detector on these lights so that a few minutes after an employee leaves the lights, they automatically turn off. Also be sure that employees shut walk-in and reach-in doors completely. This can be a huge energy drain.

- The coils on the back of your refrigerators and coolers work far less effectively when they're clogged with dust, ice and grease. Ensure that at least every two months, a staff member turns off the refrigerators for ten minutes and cleans the coils thoroughly.

- Most utility companies have departments devoted to helping you reduce power costs. Call your local electricity supplier and ask them to send someone out to help you keep costs, and waste, to a minimum. Typically this service is offered at no charge.

- Look into switching service providers. In many areas, gas and electric companies have become deregulated. If your business is in one of these areas, you should do some research to see if your current carrier is giving you the best rates you can get.

- Replace furnace filters on a regular basis. Clogged filters can cause a furnace to overheat and shut down.

- Have a contractor look at your property to calculate your building's heat loss. All buildings lose heat through windows, doors, the roof, etc. Have someone look at your building to pinpoint areas you may need to look at. Perhaps your windows need weather-stripping, or you may need to add additional insulation in spots.

- Ensure that your stoves aren't turned on until they're likely to be needed. Often the first thing staff members do when they enter your kitchen for a shift is turn on the stoves, but is it worth heating your stove for an hour before anyone actually orders a meal?

- Kitchen fuel expenses should ideally be kept under 0.5 percent of your food sales. If your own expenses are higher than that rate, perhaps you could benefit from purchasing new cooking equipment with better gas economy. Talk to your gas supplier about ways to keep your bills down.

- Have the thermostats on your ovens checked at least bi-monthly. If your thermostats are off-kilter, you could be using more or less gas than you need to, with potentially disastrous results concerning the quality of your meals and your expenses.

- Ensure that your stoves, hot plates, microwaves and ovens are located far away from coolers and air-conditioning vents. If your hot plate is being "cooled" by an air conditioner, you'll be spending more than you need to on gas just to keep it at a level temperature.

- Make sure your chef and kitchen staff use lids when appropriate. Not only do foods heat faster with lids, but they also get far better use out of the heat generated. If chefs are braising or stewing, the lid should be on.

- Have your staff on the lookout for steam leaks when you have your pots and pans covered. Steam will escape naturally if a lid isn't fastened, but if it's coming from one spot only and a little too easily, then your lid might be out of shape and allowing energy to be wasted.

- Use the proper-sized pots and pans for individual burners. Placing a ten-gallon pan on the smallest burner on your stove will consume far too much energy in cooking, while placing a tiny pan on a huge burner will see most of the energy being used completely wasted.

- Have your kitchen staff keep foil burner trays under the burners, saving time in cleaning and keeping your energy focused on the food.

- Use thermometers in refrigerated units and ovens. Place thermometers in these and monitor them on a regular basis to make sure all of your units are functioning properly and food is being stored at the correct temperatures.

Theft

In most operations the majority of theft occurs at the bar. Hourly workers tend to steal stuff, not cash, because that's what they can get their hands on. Keeping food away from the back door and notifying your employees when you are aware of theft and are investigating can have a deterring effect.

- If practical, try to rotate your employees so that they are not working with the same people constantly, minimizing the opportunities to scheme and steal from the business.

- Conduct regular surprise inspections throughout the facility. If anything is out of place or suspicious, investigate further and take preventative action. Using daily inspections is much more likely to spot an employee being dishonest or a system that isn't working well than waiting for a catastrophe.

- Have your employees place any mistakes on a shelf for management review and notation as to why and how the mistake occurred. Using and sticking to this method will make certain that employees and managers take spoilage and waste seriously, as well as deter theft.

- Implement a robbery plan for your employees. If the unthinkable should occur, you want to ensure that both your employees and clients are as safe as possible, and that your cash is hard to get to. Talk to a security expert and your local law enforcement officials to determine the best plan of action in the event of a robbery.

- Always be sure to lock your bar inventory when the bar is not open for service. This will actively deter employees and wandering customers from engaging in petty theft, and allow you to identify exactly when any losses occur. Additionally, make sure you have locks on all of your storage areas, and establish rules as to who has access to the keys. Your local locksmith can not only help you with locks, but also with more sophisticated measures, such as closed circuit cameras and card swipe systems.

- Keep a lock on your storage area and ensure that only a select number of responsible managers and employees have control of those keys. This way, if something goes missing, you can narrow down the possibilities of who was responsible.

- Limiting access to your office areas will prevent theft of valuables and valuable information.

- When designing or refitting a kitchen, locate your freezers and walk-in coolers as far from the back door as possible. Making it harder to sneak out high-cost items can only benefit your fight to avoid loss through theft.

Lack of Preventative Maintenance

Most businesses fail to realize that preventative maintenance can be a far more cost-effective manner of keeping appliances running at peak efficiency.

- Check your ice machine regularly. Is it working properly? Is there water buildup? Is the machine making more ice than you need, and is that ice the right shape to suit your needs? Try to have your water lines run through or past your refrigeration system so that the ice machine doesn't have to work so hard to cool the water it uses to freezing temperature. Also have a professional repair person confirm that the machine is set to peak efficiency for your business.

- Keep a list of all appliances, model numbers, name brands, warranties and expiration dates, and service phone numbers so that when something does break down, you have all the information possible to assist with arranging the service call. Labor costs will be reduced if you have enough information at hand for your repair person, than to have him come out to see it himself, go back for a part, and come out again to fix it.

- Create a checklist outlining maintenance schedules, taking note of equipment capacities and which items are most likely to break down under stress. A well-maintained kitchen unit will last longer and keep replacement expenses low.

- Buy a small toolbox and fill it with the basic maintenance supplies. Small and basic repairs can often be performed by management or a knowledgeable service employee, saving a service call and a great deal of money. Replacing a knob on the stove from one you have in stock is much more cost effective than calling for repairs.

- Consider keeping a repairperson on retainer. Paying a flat $100 to $250 monthly fee to a person with skills in the electrical, carpentry, landscaping and plumbing areas is a cost-effective alternative to hiring specialized contractors in each profession.

- At least once a year, have a heating and air-conditioning contractor come in and review your equipment to ensure that everything is working properly. While this expense may seem easily erasable, a regular service will not only keep downtime to a minimum and ensure peak hardware productivity, but it will also save you money by catching small problems before they become major ones. This thinking translates to all your major equipment.

- Replace burners, handles and timers as needed. Check these to prevent food burns, spoilage due to improper cooking times and methods and to prevent any workers from getting injured on the job.

- Check overlooked solutions to malfunctioning equipment before you start calling for service repairs. Make sure that the appliance is plugged in and double check all breakers or fuses. Many appliance also have a reset button on them to get them restarted.

Improper Scheduling of Labor

The overall objective in scheduling is to place the most efficient employee at the job and shift where he or she will achieve maximum productivity at minimum expense. The greatest tool management has in controlling labor costs is scheduling. Scheduling is most often poorly done when it becomes more of problem than a solution. In many cases the employee's schedule is scribbled on a piece of paper or, worse, verbally communicated with little thought as to what is actually needed.

- Set up clear responsibility guidelines for all managers and employees to ensure everyone knows exactly what's expected of them. If your staff is neglecting certain tasks, create extra levels of middle management so that everyone is responsible for their own job and ensuring others do their jobs too. Develop daily plans for specific tasks, and make a checklist to ensure those tasks are handled on time.

- When your own schedule becomes crowded and difficult to control, don't be afraid to delegate tasks. Some people feel like they're losing control when they have others help them with their work, but the real loss of control comes when you can't get your tasks completed on time.

- Set performance standards for your employees and post them for all to see. This way, if a job goes unperformed, there can be no excuses as everyone knows who does what.

Lack of Telephone Controls

Most business operators don't even look at their utility bills, but those that do can often find ways to reduce their monthly outlays on phone calls with a little smart thinking and forward planning. If you have an employee constantly using your line to make long-distance phone calls, you are not only paying them to waste time talking on the phone, but they're also stealing long distance from your business.

- How long do your employees spend on the phone? Do they use it while on a break, at lunch, before work, after work, or during time that they should be spending on customers? Make it a blanket rule that employees should not have access to phones unless they are engaging in specifically outlined business activities such as taking orders and reservation calls.

- Make a pay phone available for your employees' needs in calling home or calling for rides. This will not only save you money, but it can actually make you money as most pay phone operators work on a profit-share basis with the establishment they're in.

- If employees must use your office phone, consider keeping a log of all employee phone use and where the call was made so that any toll charges can be paid by the employee, not your business.

- Consider unlimited calling for your fax line. If your fax seems to be always in use, this may save you additional fees and taxes. Call your communications carrier for more information.

- You may want to consider having a cell phone or cordless telephone handy so you can address business calls while you're moving about your establishment. If you do not have a cordless telephone, you will constantly be called back into the office to answer the phone, which will not only cost you time in your daily activities but also money.

- When calling a vendor, don't use their direct number if it will be a long-distance call. Instead, use their 800 number, and let them foot the bill for your continuing business.

- Compare long-distance rates and carriers available in your area at least once every three months. Are you getting the best deal? Consider changing your telephone carrier if you can get a better deal, and always ask for a rate better than advertised. You'll be surprised how often you can get what you ask for. To compare long-distance phone rates between multiple suppliers, try using Lower My Bills (**www.lowermybills.com**) or the Telecommunication Research and Action Center (**www.trac.org**).

DIRECT LOSSES

Direct losses are revenue losses and they come from a number of different areas, but there are three main sources for caterers: 1) un-collectable bills, 2) disputed charges, and 3) complaints.

- **Uncollectible bills happen in all businesses, unfortunately.** Even when you conduct a careful credit check of a potential client, these may occur. Do your best to research upfront, but if you have uncollectible bills at the end of the year, you may want to talk with your accountant or tax advisor to see if this money can be written off as a business expense.

- **Disputed charges are usually the result of careless bookings.** This could be a dispute about the final guest count, additional items that were ordered last minute, or items the guest assumed were provided at no cost. The best way to avoid these types of losses is to document everything. Make sure the contract you provide the client to sign includes as much information as possible on pricing and services so you don't have to worry about these losses down the road.

- **Complaints, like uncollected bills, are inevitable.** The adage "You can't please all the people all of the time" is definitely true. While some complaints may be valid and others may not, you need to follow up on all of them. Take complaints seriously, and try to resolve them because they will affect your future business.

POTENTIAL LOSSES

Potential losses do not directly stem from the operation; they are caused by issues such as poor management, lack of insurance, and lack of safety procedures. Examples of this type of loss include:

- Food poisoning
- Employee accidents
- Fire losses
- Food objects found in food
- Guest accidents
- Intoxicated guest liability

The best strategy for protecting yourself against this type of loss is to have adequate insurance coverage and a sanitation and safety plan in place. We'll talk more about these plans in Chapter 14.

Kitchen Controls

Kitchen management is very important to the overall profitability of a catering company. This is where waste is managed and procedures are put in place and enforced to ensure maximum efficiency. The key to this process is the Kitchen Director.

THE KITCHEN DIRECTOR

The Kitchen Director is the head cook, and in a small catering company, it is usually the owner. The primary objective of the Kitchen Director is to establish the maximum operating efficiency and food quality of the kitchen. The Kitchen Director oversees prep cooks and ensures that all food products are ordered and accounted for.

Areas Of Responsibility

- All personnel in the kitchen.
- Controlling waste and food cost.
- Training of kitchen personnel.
- Enforcing health and safety regulations.
- Scheduling his or her own time.
- Holding kitchen staff meetings.
- Communicating possible problem areas to the manager.
- Food quality.
- Ordering, receiving, storing, and issuing food products.
- Morale of the kitchen staff.
- Scheduling all kitchen personnel.
- Maintaining a clean and safe kitchen.
- Filling out forms for kitchen controls.

Kitchen Procedures

The Kitchen Director is responsible for establishing the kitchen procedures and controls that will ensure efficient kitchen operation. There are five key procedures that can make or break the kitchen and ultimately the catering business altogether:

1. Purchasing
2. Inventory and control
3. Receiving and storing
4. Rotation procedures
5. Issuing

PURCHASING

The goal of purchasing is to supply your business with the best goods at the lowest possible cost. There are many ways to achieve this, but most of all the buyer must develop favorable working relations with all suppliers and vendors. A large amount of time must be spent meeting with prospective sales representatives and companies.

Purchasing is a complex area that must be managed by someone who is completely familiar with all of the needs of the business. It is best to limit the purchasing responsibilities to one or two people. The reasons for this are greater buying power and better overall control. Price is not the top priority; it is only one of the considerations in deciding how and where to place an order.

You need to have reliable suppliers that you can count on to deliver items and who will go out of their way to accommodate your requests. This flexibility is built over time and does not necessarily come from the cheapest provider.

INVENTORY CONTROL

The first step in computing what item and how much of it to order is to determine the inventory level, or the amount needed on hand at all times. To determine the amount you need to order, you must first know the amount you have in inventory. Walk through the storage areas and mark off on an inventory sheet the amount of product you have on hand. Determine how much you need to have based on your upcoming commitments. The difference between the two is the amount you have to order.

Add on about 25 percent to cover unexpected usage, a late delivery, or a backorder at the vendor. Experience and food demand will reveal the amount an average order should contain. By purchasing too little, you may run out of supplies; ordering too much will result in tying up money and putting a drain on cash flow.

It is tempting to buy large amounts of items to save money by volume purchasing, but you must always consider the cash-flow costs. It is best to set up and adhere to a buying schedule based on what you know you need and what you have on hand.

A Want Sheet is made available for employees to write in any items they may need to do their jobs more efficiently. This is a very effective form of communication; employees should be encouraged to use it. You should consult this sheet every day. A request might be as simple as a commercial-grade carrot peeler. If the one that was being used just broke, this small investment could save you from an increase in labor and food costs.

RECEIVING AND STORING

Most deliveries will arrive during business hours so you must be available to sign for them and ensure that each item is delivered to the required specifications. Receiving and storing each product is a critical responsibility. Costly mistakes can come about from a staff member who is not properly trained in the correct procedures. Slight inaccuracies or improper storing of perishable items could cost you hundreds, even thousands, of dollars.

Watch for a common area of internal theft. Collusion could develop between the delivery person and the employee receiving the products. Items checked as being received and accounted for may not have been delivered at all as the driver simply keeps the items.

All products delivered to your business must:

- Be checked against the actual order sheet.

- Be the exact specification ordered (weight, size, quantity).

- Be checked against the invoice.

- Be accompanied by an invoice containing current price, totals, date, company name, and receiver's signature.

- Have their individual weights verified on the pound scale.

- Be dated, rotated, and put in the proper storage area immediately.

- Credit slips must be issued or prices subtracted from the invoice when an error occurs; the delivery person must sign over the correction.

Keep an invoice box (a small mailbox) in the kitchen to store all invoices and packing slips received during the day. Mount the box on the wall, away from work areas. Prior to leaving for the day, the receiver must bring the invoices to the manager's office and place them in a designated spot. Extreme care must be taken to ensure that all invoices are handled correctly. A missing invoice will throw off the bookkeeping and financial records and statements.

ROTATION PROCEDURES

All food items need to be rotated to ensure that the oldest items in inventory are used first. The first in, first out (FIFO) method of rotation is used to ensure that all food products are properly rotated in storage.

The FIFO method uses these principles:

1. New items go to the back and on the bottom.

2. Older items move to the front and to the left.

3. In any part of the operation, the first item used should always be the oldest.

4. Date and mark everything. (For resources, visit **www.dissolveaway.com** or call 1-800-847-0101.)

TEMPERATURE RANGES FOR PERISHABLE ITEMS	
All frozen items	-10°–0°F
Fresh meat and poultry	31°–35°F
Produce	33°–38°F
Fresh seafood	33°–38°F

TEMPERATURE RANGES FOR PERISHABLE ITEMS	
Dairy products	33°–38°F
Beer	40°–60°F
Wine (Chablis, rosé)	45°–55°F
Wine (most reds)	55°–65°F

ISSUING

All raw materials from which portionable entrées are prepared, such as meat, seafood and poultry, must be issued on a daily basis. Whenever one of these bulk items is removed from a freezer or walk-in, it must be signed out

When a part of a case or box is removed, the weight of the portion removed must be recorded. A preparation form will show that the items signed out were actually used for company purposes, and you can compute a daily yield on each item prepared. At any one of these steps, pilferage can occur, so the sign-out procedure acts as a deterrent. Products such as dry goods or cleaning supplies may be issued in a similar manner.

Kitchen Cleanliness

Kitchen cleanliness must always be of constant concern to both you and your employees. A maintenance company should not clean in the kitchen; most have not been trained in the cleaning procedures that must be used in the kitchen to maintain food safety requirements.

A maintenance company should only be used for cleaning and washing the kitchen floor. All the rest of the kitchen cleaning and maintenance should be the responsibility of the staff.

All employees must be made aware that their daily cleanups are as critical as any of their other responsibilities—perhaps more so. The most effective cleanup policy to institute is to make each employee responsible for his or her own area. Every workstation must have its own cleaning check-off sheet for the end of each shift. Seal them in plastic so that a grease pencil can be used to check off each completed item. Every employee must have his or her cleanup checked by a manager.

You must inspect employee cleanup carefully and thoroughly. Once a precedent is set for each cleanup, it must be maintained. At the end of a long shift some employees may need encouragement to get the desired results.

Example cleaning checklist:

Place a check mark on all completed items.

____ 1. Turn off all equipment and pilot lights.

____ 2. Take all pots, pans and utensils to the dishwasher.

____ 3. Wrap, date and rotate all leftover food.

____ 4. Clean out the refrigerator units.

____ 5. Clean all shelves.

____ 6. Wipe down all walls.

____ 7. Spot clean the exhaust hoods.

____ 8. Clean and polish all stainless steel in your area.

____ 9. Clean out all sinks.

____ 10. Take out all trash. Break down boxes to conserve space in dumpster.

____ 11. Sweep the floor in your area.

____ 12. Replace all clean pots, pans and utensils.

____ 13. Check to see if your coworkers need assistance.

____ 14. Check out with the manager.

Perpetual Inventory

The perpetual inventory is a check on the daily usage of items from the freezers and walk-ins. This form is used in conjunction with the Sign-Out Sheet, and when completed, will ensure that no bulk products have been stolen from the freezer or walk-ins. List all the food items that you have on hand. At the beginning of the period, write on a grid/chart the amount you have of each item–this is your start figure. At the end of each day, count all the items on hand and enter this figure on the end column. Compare this end figure against the product that was signed out during the day. Check the invoices every day for the items delivered that are in your perpetual inventory. Ensure that all items signed off as being delivered are actually in the storage areas. Should there be a discrepancy, check with the employee that signed the invoice.

The number of items you start with plus the number you received in deliveries minus the amount signed out by the preparation cooks must equal the number on hand. If there is a discrepancy, you may have a thief.

Should you suspect theft in the kitchen or elsewhere, record the names of all employees who worked that particular day. If theft continue to occurs, a pattern will develop among the employees who were working on all the days in question. Compute the perpetual inventory or other controls you are having a problem with at different times of the day, before and after each shift. This will pinpoint the area and shift in which the theft is occurring. Sometimes placing a notice to all employees that you are aware of a theft problem in your company will resolve the problem. Make it clear that any employee caught stealing will be terminated.

Sequence of events:

____ 1. Determine the purchase

____ 2. Purchase the amount needed.

____ 3. When product is delivered, follow the receiving and storing procedures.

____ 4. Enter the amount on the Perpetual Inventory Form.

____ 5. Preparation cooks compute the opening counts.

____ 6. Sign out the product as needed.

____ 7. Verify amounts by comparing the inventory totals with amounts prepared and amounts ordered.

A tightly controlled kitchen is more efficient, and even though the control system seems cumbersome at first, it becomes second nature in no time. No one can afford to lose product, and following the types of procedures outlined will help curb or at least identify sources of loss.

Controlling Food Cost

One of your biggest costs is food. In order to control food costs effectively, there are four things you need to do:

1. Forecast how much and what you are going to sell.

2. Purchase and prepare according to these forecasts.

3. Portion effectively.

4. Control waste and theft.

In order to do these things effectively, you must have standards to which you rigorously adhere. Here are two main standards that will help you sustain quality, consistency and low cost.

1. **Standardized recipes.** Since the recipe is the basis for determining the cost of a menu item, standardized recipes will ensure consistent quality and cost. Standardized recipes include ingredients, preparation methods, yield, equipment used, and plate presentation.

2. **Standardized purchase specifications.** These are detailed descriptions of the ingredients used in your standardized recipes. Quality and price of all ingredients are known and agreed upon before purchases are made, making the recipe's cost consistent from unit to unit, week to week.

STANDARDIZED RECIPES

Use of a standardized recipe ensures quality and consistency of menu items and it helps with cost control and pricing. And while you may be a one-person show in the early days of your business, starting a recipe file from day one can save time later when you do have different people cooking and consistency becomes more of an issue.

Some of the advantages to using standardized recipes are:

- Ensures product consistency.

- Helps make the kitchen run efficiently.

- Helps with employee training.

- Improves cost control by controlling portion size.

- Helps create inventory and purchasing lists.

- Lists item cost, which makes it easy to access and use this information for pricing.

When developing your recipe file:

- Test all recipes in your kitchen. Your kitchen's oven may cook muffins quicker than the oven used to create the recipe. If you don't test and find this out, your cooks will constantly burn the muffins because they are using the wrong cooking time.

- Have ingredients listed in the order they are used.

- Check for correct ingredient amounts.

- Make sure the sequence of work is clear.

- Make sure you have all the necessary equipment to prepare the recipe. If your staff is using various pans to cook something because you don't have the correct size, the item will not turn out the same each time and you are forfeiting consistency.

- Give dry ingredients' measure by weight and liquid ingredients' by volume, and be sure you have a scale to measure the weighed amounts.

- Make sure that you or a designated person record any changes to the recipe over time.

- Use it! Make sure you enforce the use of standardized recipes with your kitchen staff.

You may want to use index cards and an index cardholder, or you may want to use a three-ring binder with recipe sheets inserted into transparent envelopes that can be easily wiped clean. Be sure to organize your file in a meaningful way. Group all the appetizers together, all the entrées together, all the soups, all the salads, and all the desserts.

The information you should include on your recipe form should follow this system:

- **Name of item.**

- **Recipe number/identification** within file system.

- **Yield.** Total quantity the recipe will prepare.

- **Portion size.** This may be listed by weight or number of pieces. You may want to include what size of utensil to use for serving. For example, use the 6-ounce ladle for a cup of soup.

- **Garnish.** Be specific and make sure every plate goes out looking the same. This includes plate setup. You may want to draw a diagram or include a photograph to show your staff how the chicken should lean against the polenta squares, and the asparagus should sit at an angle on the other side of the chicken.

- **Ingredients.** List ingredients in order. Make sure to list quantities of ingredients used, and keep the abbreviation used for quantities standard. If you use "oz" for ounce in one recipe, make sure you use it in all your recipes. Give the physical state of ingredients—are the nuts whole or chopped? Is the flour sifted?

- **Preparation instructions.** Be sure to include any preheating instructions. Use the correct terms for instructions. Do you want the eggs mixed into the batter or folded into it? Should the employee stir or mix with an electric mixer? Be sure to include any precautions or special instructions—if someone is preparing caramel, caution them that the sugar water is extremely hot and that they should take the mixture off the heat before adding the cream. This also should include pan sizes and preparation, cooking temperature, cooking time, how to test for doneness, and instructions for portioning.

- **Finishing.** Describe any finish the product needs, such as brushing with oil or melted chocolate drizzled on top. Also include how to cool and at what temperature the product should be held. Can it sit at room temperature or does it need to be refrigerated?

- **Cost.** Not all caterers include cost on the recipes. If you do, the recipe can be a resource in everyday ordering as well as menu design. Include every ingredient and every garnish for accuracy. You will need to look at product invoices to get unit prices, then determine the ingredient cost from this. Total the cost of each ingredient for your total recipe cost. This can then be divided by the number of portions and you will have a portion cost as well.

Below is an example of a standardized recipe.

Recipe No. 126 Portion Size: 1.5 cups	Name: Blue Ridge Jambalaya Yield: 40 portions	Cost per Portion: $0.90
Ingredients	**Weight/Measure**	**Cost**
Chicken, boneless breast cut in 1-inch pieces	4 lbs	$8.00
Andouille sausage, sliced	2 lbs	$5.58
Celery, chopped	16 cups	$3.16
Red peppers, chopped	8 each	$6.00
Onions, chopped	4 each	$0.40
Garlic cloves, minced	8 each	$0.17
Short grain brown rice, dry	6 cups	$4.74
Beer	32 oz	$3.50
Chicken stock	60 oz	$1.72
Canned diced tomato	60 oz	$2.12
Tabasco sauce	4 tsp	$0.03
Parsley (garnish)		$0.04
Cornbread (side)		$0.58
		$36.04

Directions

Trim chicken and cut into 1-inch pieces. Heat vegetable oil in a large sauté pan. Add chicken and cook through. Add sausage and heat through. In a large stockpot, sauté onion, garlic, celery, and red pepper in oil. Add rice and coat rice with oil. Turn heat down to low, add beer and broth a little at a time, allowing the rice to absorb the liquid before adding more. When rice has simmered about 15-20 minutes, add tomato, chicken and sausage. Continue cooking until done and rice is tender (about 1 hour). Add Tabasco, salt and pepper. Portion out the jambalaya into smaller containers to cool. Can refrigerate or use immediately for service.

Service

Serve in a dinner bowl with a piece of cornbread on the side. Top with parsley.

YIELD COSTS

Once you have standardized recipes in place, you can determine the per-plate cost of every dish. In order to do this you need to know what the basic ingredients cost and the edible yield of those ingredients for each dish. There are a number of necessary terms for this process.

- **As-purchased (AP) weight.** The weight of the product as delivered, including bones, trim, etc.

- **Edible portion (EP) weight.** The amount of weight or volume that is available to be portioned after carving or cooking.

- **Waste.** The amount of usable product that is lost due to processing, cooking, or portioning, as well as usable by-products that have no salable value.

- **Usable trim.** Processing by-products that can be sold as other menu items. These recover a portion or all of their cost.

- **Yield.** The net weight or volume of food after processing but before portioning.

- **Standard yield.** The yield generated by standardized recipes and portioning procedures—how much usable product there is after processing and cooking.

- **Standard portion.** The size of the portion according to the standardized recipe, also the basis for determining the cost of the plated portion.

- **Convenience foods.** Items where at least a portion of the preparation labor is done before delivery. These can include pre-cut chicken, ready-made dough, etc.

These factors allow you to calculate plate costs. The food cost of convenience foods is higher than if you made them from scratch, but once you factor in labor, necessary equipment, inventories of ingredients, more complicated purchasing and storage, etc., you may find that these foods offer considerable savings.

To cost convenience foods, simply count, weigh or measure the portion size and determine how many portions are there. Then divide the number of servable portions into the AP price. Even with their pre-preparation, a small allowance for normal waste must be factored in, often as little as 2 percent per yield.

Costing items from scratch is a little more complex. Most menu items require processing that causes shrinkage of some kind. As a result, if the weight or volume of the cooked product is less than the AP weight, the EP cost will be higher than the AP price. It's a simple addition of the labor involved and the amount of saleable product being reduced. Through this process, your buyer uses yields to determine quantities to purchase, and you discover optimum quantities to order that result in the highest yield and the least waste.

FOOD-COST PERCENTAGE

This basic ratio is often misinterpreted because it can be calculated so many ways. Basically, it is food cost divided by food sales. However, whether your food cost is determined by food sold or consumed is a crucial difference. Also, for your food-cost percentage to be accurate, a month-end inventory must be taken. Without this figure your food-cost statement is inaccurate and therefore basically useless. This is because your inventory will vary month to month—even in the most stable environment—because months end on different days of the week.

Distinguishing between food sold and consumed is important because all food consumed is not sold.

- Food consumed includes all food used, sold, wasted, stolen or given away to customers and employees.

- Food sold is determined by subtracting all food bought at full price from the total food consumed.

Maximum allowable food cost (MFC) is the most that food can cost and still return your profit goal. If at the end of the month your food-cost percentage is over your maximum allowable percentage, you won't meet your profit expectations. To better understand this, follow this calculation:

- Write your dollar amounts of labor costs and overhead expenses, excluding food costs. Refer to past accounting periods and yearly averages to get realistic cost estimates.

- Add your monthly profit goal as either a dollar amount or a percentage of sales.

- Convert dollar values of expenses to percentages by dividing by food sales for the periods used for expenses. Generally, don't use your highest or lowest sales figures for calculating your operating expenses.

- Subtract the total of the percentages from 100 percent. The remainder is your maximum allowable food-cost percentage (MFC).

Actual food-cost percentage (AFC) is the percentage you're actually operating at. It's calculated by dividing food cost by food sales. If you are deducting employee meals from your income statement, then you are calculating cost of food sold. If there is no deduction for employee meals—which is true for most operations—then the food cost you're reading is food consumed. This is always a higher cost than food sold, and if inventory is not being taken, the food cost on your income statement is just an estimate based on purchases and isn't accurate.

Potential food-cost percentage (PFC) is also called your theoretical food cost. This is the lowest your food cost can be because it assumes that all food consumed is sold, and that there is no waste whatsoever. It is found by multiplying the number sold of each menu item by the ideal recipe cost.

Standard food cost (SFC) is how you adjust for the unrealistically low PFC. This percentage includes unavoidable waste, employee meals, etc. This food cost percentage is compared to the AFC, and is the standard that you should meet each period.

Prime food cost includes the cost of direct labor along with the actual food cost. This is labor incurred because the item is made from scratch—baking pies and bread, trimming steaks, etc. When the food cost is determined for these items, the cost of the labor needed to prepare them is added. So prime cost is food cost plus necessary direct labor. This costing method is applied to every menu item needing extensive direct labor before it is served to the customer. Indirect labor cannot be attributed to any particular menu item, and is therefore overhead. Prime cost is the total cost of food and beverage sold, payroll, and employee benefits costs.

Beverage cost ratio is calculated when alcoholic beverages are sold. It is determined by dividing costs by sales—calculated the same way as food consumed. A single beverage ratio can't be standardized because the percentage will vary depending on the mix of hard alcohol, wine and beer. Spirits run a lower cost percentage than wine and beer, and, as such, it is recommended that alcoholic beverages be split into their three categories.

Beverage sales do not include coffee, tea, milk or juice, which are usually considered food. Wherever you include soft drinks, know that it will reduce the overall food cost since the ratio of cost to selling price is so low.

Inventory turnover is calculated by dividing cost of food consumed by your average inventory. This is your beginning inventory plus your ending inventory divided by two.

Ratio of food to beverage sales is simply the ratio of the respective percentages to your total sales.

Contribution margin is your gross profit. It is what remains after all expenses have been subtracted from 100 percent.

Closing point is when the cost of being open for a given time period is more expensive than revenue earned. This means that if it cost you $2,000 to open today, and you only made $1,800, your closing point expense will be $200.

PRICING FOR PROFIT

The prosperity of any catering business is often directly attributable to its menu. The objective of this section is to present guidelines for planning a successful and profitable menu. As a general approach to pricing a catering event, you should consider the following guidelines:

- Determine how much your competitors charge for the same service.

- Determine your costs for producing the food items.

- Use the total cost of all your raw materials for a particular recipe to calculate your overhead and labor cost.

- Add up a year's total cost, like rent, insurance, business taxes, utilities, depreciation, etc. (not including food and related expenses). From this total you derive your daily overhead expense.

- Calculate your labor costs in the same way.

Obviously menu pricing is a major component of menu management. When you put a price on menu items, your overall goal is to realize a profit. Pricing is based on a markup of cost, which is figured by determining food cost, sales history, and profit margin. But a complete pricing strategy does not end there. Pricing decisions are influenced by indirect factors as well:

- Human psychology
- Market conditions
- Location/ Atmosphere

- Service style
- Competition
- Customer's willingness to pay

Customer psychology is an indirect pricing factor that must be kept in mind. Psychologically, prices that end in odd amounts like 9 or 5, are perceived as lower than a price that end in zero. So, $12.95 is lower than $13.00 in the customer's mind. When the difference involves three digits or four digits, the difference in perception is increased: $9.95 is perceived as less than $10.00.

Market conditions affect every industry. When the economy is bad, caterers are likely to see less profit because people may be eating out and traveling less. Prices are demand or market driven. The market will ultimately be a large determinant of your prices. In the end, what it costs you to produce a particular menu item will not matter if the price is so high that no one will buy it. Your prices need to not only reflect the cost of the item but what the competition is charging and what the customer is willing to spend on an item.

Location and atmosphere are also important in determining menu prices. If you buy red snapper in Seattle, the price you expect to pay as a customer is greater than what you would expect to pay for the same in Athens, Georgia, because red snapper is more readily available in Georgia.

Client's willingness to pay is perhaps the most important factor. All the other factors make no difference if your client thinks your prices are too high for what they are receiving. Remember, your clients aren't concerned with your costs. They are concerned with getting their money's worth.

Pricing

Once you understand where your costs are coming from and you have a general idea about your pricing strategy, you need to put solid numbers on each of your menu items.

There are many ways to price a catered event simply because there are so many factors to be taken into account. First, you'll need to calculate all the direct costs of the event—the food and labor costs—as well as the indirect ones, such as licenses, office supplies, marketing and advertising. These calculations need to be made before approaching the client with a written contract to accept the cost for your food and services.

In general, the basic formula for price setting is as follows:

Labor + Food/Supplies + Overhead + Profit Margin = Price

Most caterers break the formula down this way:

1/3 Labor + 1/3 Food/Supplies + 1/3 Profit = Selling Price

LABOR COSTS

Your kitchen staff members are usually treated as regular employees; servers are often hired as independent contracts. The labor for both these categories need to go into your price calculations.

Let's look at a detailed example:

You host a party for 200 people. It takes your cook 10 hours to prepare at an hourly rate of $10, so you need to add $100 to the total.

Likewise, if it took four servers four hours each to serve the meal, you need to add their fee. (Generally, servers are paid by four-hour periods. Currently the going rate is between $75 and $95 for four hours.)

4 servers at $75 (4 hours each) = $300

Total labor cost = $100 (cook) + $300 (servers) = $400

Divide the total labor cost by the number of guests, and you have the additional charge for labor that needs to be reflected in your per-person price.

$400 ÷ 200 = $2

FOOD COSTS

In general, caterers (and restaurateurs) seek a food cost that is approximately 30 percent of their revenue. To determine the food cost of a particular menu item, you will need to cost out the recipe. Usually food cost is expressed as a percentage of the menu price or of overall sales. Food cost of a specific menu item is figured by dividing the cost of the ingredients for the item by the menu price. This figure is usually expressed as a percentage.

$3.80 (ingredient food cost) ÷ $12.50 (selling price) = 0.30 (30% food cost)

Example:

Let's say one of your menu items is a pan-seared duck breast with an orange-loganberry sauce. First, you must look at your invoices and determine the cost of ingredients for a single serving. This cost needs to include the duck, the sauce ingredients, and any side dishes and garnishes. Your math shows the item costs you $4.20. Now, if you want to maintain a food cost of 30 percent, where do you need to price the duck breast?

$4.20 (ingredient food cost) ÷ 0.30 (30% food cost) = $14.00 (selling price)

Overall food cost for an operation is shown on monthly income statements. This number will help you decide how well your operation is doing. A high food cost can be an indication of many things: the need for employee training, the need to adjust menu prices to reflect costs better, overpurchasing and waste, and theft, to name a few.

To determine the revenue you can make from an item, look at the cost, the menu price, and your sales history. If you divide the total income into the total cost of the item, you can determine food cost for a particular event. For example, if you catered an event for 200 people:

$840 (cost of $4.20 x 200) ÷ $2,800 (sold 200 at $14.00) = 30%

PRICING METHODS

Once you have costed out your goods, several pricing methods can be used. Unfortunately when it comes to pricing, you have to do math! The industry generally uses three different pricing methods. The pros and cons of each method are discussed below.

1. Food-cost percentage

2. Factoring

3. Actual cost

Food-Cost Percentage Pricing

This is probably the most widely used method of menu pricing, and more than likely it will be the way you price the majority of your menu items.

What you need to use it:

- Target food-cost percentage

- Actual item food cost

How it works. With the food cost percentage method, you determine what percentage of sales will be taken by overhead, labor, and food cost, and what percentage can be profit. Most operations want to realize a profit between 10 and 20 percent, but each business is different, so you'll need to determine what your actual and target percentages are.

To determine prices with this method you must know your actual food cost and your target food cost percentage.

Food cost ÷ target food cost percentage = menu price

Example:

Let's say you have a chicken Caesar salad on your menu. Its food cost is $1.84 and your target food-cost percentage is 35 percent. Therefore:

$1.84 ÷ 0.35 = $5.25

The price is actually $5.26, but as mentioned earlier, you will want to round to 5 or a 9 when setting your prices. You could also round up to $5.35, if you feel your customers will pay this amount for this item. Most caterers tend to round figures up.

Pros:

- It's an easy formula to use.

Cons:

- It does not take labor or other costs into consideration.

Factor Pricing

What you need to use it:

- Target food-cost percentage
- Actual item food cost

How it works. Factoring also uses your overall target food cost (as a percentage) and the particular item's food cost to determine price. This method, however, uses a factor that represents food-cost percentage. To determine prices with this method, the food cost is multiplied by the pricing factor. The factor will always be the percentage of your desired food cost divided by 100.

Let's say your target food cost is 35 percent. Divide 35 into 100, and you get 2.86 as your factor. By multiplying this number by your food cost, you come up with a price.

Example:

The food cost of a dish is $2.67

2.67 x 2.86 = $7.63 (round up to $7.65) (food cost x pricing factor = menu price)

Pros:

- It's an easy method.

Cons:

- Every individual item will not meet your overall target food cost. Some of your menu items will have a higher cost and some will have a lower cost.

Actual Cost Pricing

This method is used when the menu price is established before the food cost is known. By looking at all other costs, it determines what can be spent on food cost.

This method includes profit as part of the menu price. Catering operations use it when working with a customer who has a definite budget they have to meet. By working back from what the person can spend, you can determine what can be spent on food and, in turn, what kind of menu you can offer the client.

What you need to use it:

- Menu price

- Overhead costs (as a percentage)

- Labor costs (as a percentage)

- Desired profits (as a percentage)

How it works. First you need to determine what percentage of your costs are taken by overhead and labor and what percentage of sales need to go to profit. Since this equation is expressed as a percentage, overhead, labor, food cost and profit must equal 100 percent:

100 percent - labor % - overhead % - profit % = food cost %

Example:

By looking at your profit and loss statement you see that your labor is 30 percent of your sales, overhead is 20 percent, and you know you are aiming for a 15 percent profit.

100% - 30% - 20% - 15% = 35%

So, you can spend 35 percent of the price you establish on food cost.

Now, look at your sales history. Let's say you earned $100,000 in a 6-month period. Of that $100,000:

- $30,000 was spent on labor

- $20,000 was spent on overhead expenses

- $15,000 was allocated to profit

That leaves you $35,000 to spend on food.

Let's look at a specific menu item now. Your vegetable black bean lasagna sells for $11. Of that $11, $3.30 is spent on labor; $2.20 is spent on overhead, and $1.65 is profit. That leaves you $3.85 to spend on food.

Pros:

- It includes profit in the calculation of the price of each menu item.

Cons:

- You are working backward from menu price to food cost, so this method is not helpful if your goal is to come up with menu prices in the first place.

Two Other Methods

Method 1

Figure out the total cost, add 10 percent to cover unexpected expenses and divide by the number of guests.

Example:

Total cost of goods = $700

Number of guests = 40

Cost of goods + 10% ÷ number of guests = $19.25

Now add 15 percent for price and this will give you the per-person price for a menu item:

($19.25 x 0.15) + $19.25 = $22.14 (round off)

Pros:

- Very easy.

Cons:

- Very simplistic.

Method 2

A simpler way to determine pricing is to multiply the cost of food times three and then divide by the number of guests.

Example:

Assume the food for the party we costed above was $395:

$395 x 3 = $1,185

$1,185 ÷ 40 = $29.63 (round off)

Pros:

- Even easier.

Cons:

- Too simplistic for anything more than ballpark figuring.

DETERMINING REVENUE PERCENTAGE

To determine the revenue you can make from an event, you'll want to look at the cost, the event price, and your sales history. If you divide the total income into the total cost of the event, you can determine food cost for a particular period of time.

Example:

Suppose you run ran five events during a month:

$10,000 (cost of $200 multiplied by 5) ÷ $30,000 (sold 5 events at $600 each) = 33 percent

PRICING BUFFETS AND RECEPTIONS

For buffets, clients are generally charged per person. A plate count should be taken before and after the function to determine the number actually served. Buffets often have a guarantee and a set count, billed in the same manner as a seated function.

Determining A Per-Person Charge

Caterers often charge per person for an event. Rates vary considerably and are based on the type of event and food. For a luncheon, a price between $8 and $12 is an average range. Dinners may fall as low as $9, but they may also run as high as $40 per person.

As a caterer you must know what your overhead costs and break-even figures are, and you have to charge more than this figure. Logically then, the greater the number, the bigger the profit. This is why many large reception facilities have a "minimum" policy. For example, a facility may have determined it will take a minimum of 250 guests at $15 per person to meet overhead expenses and to allow for a modest profit.

The per-person rate of some caterers includes all or most of their costs, from food and beverages to china and table linens. Others restrict per-person fees to food and beverages alone, choosing to bill other expenses as individual line items each with its own profit margin. Regardless of your method, you must recoup costs with enough left over for a reasonable profit. The art of pricing is to charge enough to earn an overall profit, but not so much that most proposals are lost.

Don't forget that per-person charges also cover the cost of room rental. Clients don't like to see this as a line item, so work it into your overall costs instead.

Alcoholic beverages are, however, expected to be charged separately. Customers are usually required to pay on a consumption basis, with the options of an open or cash bar and house or premium brand spirits at different price points. Additional supplies should be billed as line items. Standard linens are part of the per-person price, but themed linens, chair covers, and other amenities are extra.

On top of the pricing decisions regarding rentals, markups, service charges, discounts and more, if you are an off-premise caterer, there are also transportation costs. Factor in gasoline, parking, tolls, insurance, parking tickets, and towing fees.

Disposables such as plastic wrap to cover pans, detergent for washing dishes, boxes, aluminum foil, plastic gloves, and hand wipes need to be considered as well.

Package Pricing

Depending on the type of catering you do, you may need to provide your clients with package pricing. Wedding functions are an example.

If you cater a wedding, you will likely be responsible for more than just one meal. You may be responsible for a cocktail hour, bride's brunch, sit-down dinner, wedding toasts, parking, the wedding cake, flowers, etc.

To create a package price, you must identify a per-person price for services beyond the food preparation and service. Let's say you are catering a wedding with 200 guests. Along with a buffet dinner, you are responsible for:

- Wedding cake
- Photographer
- Band for reception
- Limo service
- Flowers for the dining tables (ten centerpieces and three arrangements for the buffet tables)

The costs for these items are as follows:

- Wedding cake - $300
- Photographer - $1,000
- Band - $1,200
- Limo service - $300
- Flowers - $600
- **Total = $3,400**

Now divide that by 200 (# of guests) and you get a price of $17.

If your meal charges are $50 per person, you will need to add this $17 in order to come up with a full per-person price for all of the services you will be providing. To that figure you add your profit percentage. You may have different percentages for different functions.

Other Pricing Considerations

While costs are a main consideration when setting prices, remember that they are not the sole determining factors. Every catering event is a negotiation and a relationship. In order to make the most of your pricing potential, you first have to find out exactly what's important to your client.

Before setting prices you should take other factors into consideration.

- **Determine your pitch.** In order to come up with a realistic and profitable rate, you'll need to consider the rates for your area, the type of party being catered, whether you hope to get repeat business from the client, and the buoyancy of your current business.

- **Analyze the competition.** Understandably it's not as simple as adopting the competitors' prices; however, you'll get an idea of the cost range within which you can work. You can gather this information incognito by calling competitors and asking them to send you some sample menus. Many caters also have Web sites, so you may be able to find this information online as well.

- **Use your income statement (profit and loss).** It's a good idea to calculate an income statement for each party or function as if it was a one-time event. This way you have a profit margin that guarantees financial success for every event.

- **Certain events may warrant an additional charge.** Hosting a tent party in Chicago in October or an event on a boat in the middle of a lake requires more labor than a simple indoor banquet. Bill unusual events accordingly.

- **Place settings and pricing.** Never set a single setting more than the client has agreed to pay for. Remember that your service staff assignments and your kitchen are all tied into the set count. Just because you set a few extra tables doesn't mean the kitchen will have meals prepared, or, for that matter, that you'll have staff to service them. It will, however, give the client that impression. All clients have a vested interest in keeping the guarantee count as close to the actual count as possible.

- **Finalizing the deal.** Once prices have been agreed, ask your client to check and finalize the details of the event. Also, at this point, ask the client to sign off on the number of people to be served and the specific quantities of food and beverages you've agreed upon. This is your contract.

- **Guarantee.** Base the guarantee on the number of guests that the client has agreed to pay for—regardless of how many people actually eat. The contract generally covers a certain cushion beyond the guarantee (often 5 percent), which the caterer agrees to set and prepare for in the event that a few extra show up. Some caterers specify that any amendments to the guarantee, within 24 hours, automatically changes the guarantee count to the set count and that the client will be billed accordingly.

- **Gratuities.** Some caterers add gratuities for servers into the invoice while others don't. In general, gratuities usually are 15 to 25 percent of the total food and beverage cost.

Frequently you'll be asked to reduce quoted prices. A good philosophy is not to reduce a price without reducing something else in the event. You can work with a client who wants a reduction, but to accomplish this you may need to discuss limiting the buffet to two entrée choices rather than three, or perhaps switching out the seafood entrée for a less expensive item such as chicken.

Pricing is the backbone of your operation: You don't want to price yourself out of the market, but you don't want to be known as the bargain basement of caterers. Catering is perceived as an elite service, and bargain hunting is not a selling feature.

LOCATION: Nashville, Tennessee

SERVICES: Michael Attias operates a restaurant in Nashville, Tennessee, and helps restaurant owners add or expand a catering profit center through his company, The Results Group. You can download his FREE report: Tapping Into Your Hidden Catering Profit$ at www.ezRestaurantMarketing.com.

FINDING NEW CUSTOMERS By Michael Attias

I have a saying, "Your future customers resemble your current customers." It is the basis of down-and-dirty database analysis. Clusters, or niches, of your catering customers have something in common. They might be in the same industry, like pharmaceutical reps, or they might be throwing similar events, like holiday parties, corporate picnics or nonprofit fundraisers. By analyzing your customer list, you'll uncover significant variables that will lead you to niches to target.

For instance, you might look at your customer list and notice that you had four athletic banquets last year. Birds of a feather flock together, so if one school has a sports banquet, you can guarantee most of them do. You would then rent or assemble a list of all your local schools and target the athletic directors via mail or phone for more athletic banquets.

You also want to look at geographic targets and determine how far out you will travel to cater an event. Some people just want to cater in their neighborhood. If you're downtown, you may only want to cater a four-block radius. I'll travel two hours comfortably if a client has 500 to 1,000 people because it's profitable.

Once you've identified your geographic boundaries, you'll want to employ a marketing technique called farming. On a regular basis, mail out a letter, postcard or newsletter to business prospects. You want to be in front of them from four to twelve times a year. When a catering need arises, you want your name to be the first that comes to mind.

LOCATION: Tampa Bay

SERVICES: Robert Meli is in charge of a wedding and event consulting company serving the Tampa Bay area. He offers consulting, full planning and "day of" coordination services. He offers free consultations for any event. Visit www.bellaroseweddings.com or call 727-463-7673 for more information.

Robert believes that being a professional consultant helps people with many responsibilities it takes to get a job done. A consultant will play advisor, coordinator, negotiator, supervisor, financial planner, mediator, and friend. A wedding consultant should be part of your budget, not an extra expense. In fact, you often save money because a consultant suggests less expensive alternatives and can often obtain discounts from other bridal vendors.

He also feels that being a step ahead is always a good thing. "Always be ahead of your employees and have something for them to do. Whether it is a sit-down dinner or a buffet, the timing of the meal is everything. They should be served timely, so that the rest of the event can just flow."

Sanitation and Safety Procedures

Preventing food-borne illness is essential to the success of your business. An outbreak of illness would be catastrophic to your catering business. Anyone can fall a victim to food-borne illness, but some members of the population are more susceptible than others. These include pregnant women, the elderly, the very young, and people with impaired immune systems due to AIDS, cancer, diabetes, or medications that suppress their immune function. Whereas the general population may recover from an incident in a few days, people in this group are much more likely to die from a food-borne illness.

Food-Borne Illnesses

Food-borne illnesses are generally classified as food-borne infections, intoxication, or toxin-mediated infection. Infections are caused by eating food that contain living disease-causing organisms. Intoxication is caused by eating food that contains a harmful toxin or chemical produced by bacteria or another source. Toxin-mediated infection is caused by eating a food that contains harmful organisms that will produce a toxin once it has been consumed.

A food-borne hazard is a biological, chemical or physical hazard that can cause illness when it is consumed in food. The main symptoms of food-borne illness include the following:

- Headache
- Abdominal pain
- Diarrhea
- Fatigue

- Fever
- Vomiting
- Nausea
- Dehydration

Food hazards include:

Bacterial material

- Bacterial growth
- Bacterial toxin production
- Bacterial, parasitic, or viral cross-contamination
- Bacterial, parasitic, or viral contamination
- Bacterial, parasitic, or viral survival

Physical objects

- Stones
- Glass
- Metal fragments
- Packaging materials

Chemical contamination

- Dehydration—cleaning compounds
- Dehydration—food additives
- Dehydration—nonfood-grade lubricants
- Dehydration—insecticides

In a report from the Centers for Disease Control and Prevention (CDC) titled, "Surveillance for Food-Borne Disease Outbreaks—United States, 1988-1992", it is clear that bacterial agents are the leading cause of laboratory-confirmed outbreaks and that the main reasons for the outbreaks are improper holding temperatures, poor personal hygiene, improper cooking temperatures, foods from unsafe sources, and contaminated equipment.

BACTERIA

Bacteria are everywhere: in the air, in all areas of the kitchen and all over one's body. Most bacteria are microscopic and of no harm to people. Many forms of bacteria are actually beneficial, aiding in the production of such things as cheese, bread, butter, alcoholic beverages, etc. Only a small percentage of bacteria will cause food to spoil and can generate a form of food poisoning when consumed.

Bacteria exist in a vegetative state. The vegetative cells grow and reproduce like any other living organism. Some bacteria form "spores." The spores help the bacteria survive in less-than-ideal environments and temperatures that may not have enough food or moisture. This spore structure allows the bacteria to survive stresses such as cooking, freezing, and high-salt environments. In other words, cooking, freezing or curing will not kill these bacteria.

The spores themselves are not harmful except to babies. The spore Clostridium botuinlum, which can be found in honey, can cause infant botulism. However, if the environmental conditions become suitable for bacterial growth, the spore will turn into a vegetative cell, and this cell can multiply and cause illness.

Bacteria need several things in order to reproduce. Many food service managers refer to these items as F-A-T-T-O-M:

- Food
- Acid
- Temperature
- Time
- Oxygen
- Moisture

Food. Most bacteria prefer foods that are high in protein or carbohydrates, like meats, poultry, seafood, cooked potatoes, and dairy products.

Acid. Most foods have a pH less than 7.0. Very acidic food like limes and lemons normally do not support bacterial growth. While most bacteria prefer a neutral or slightly acidic environment, they are capable of growing in foods that have pHs between 4.5 and 9.0.

The quality known as "pH" indicates how acidic or alkaline ("basic") a food or other substance is. The pH scale ranges from 0.0 to 14.0—7.0 being exactly neutral. Distilled water, for example, has a neutral pH of 7.0. Bacteria grow best in foods that are neutral or slightly acidic, in the pH range of 4.6 to 7.0. Highly acidic foods, such as vinegar and most fresh fruits, inhibit bacterial growth. Meats and many other foods have an optimal pH for bacterial growth. On the other hand, some foods normally considered hazardous, such as mayonnaise and custard filling, can be safely stored at room temperature if their pH is below 4.6.

Lowering the pH of foods by adding acidic ingredients, such as making sauerkraut from cabbage or pickles from cucumbers, may render them non–potentially hazardous. This is not a foolproof prevention method, however. For example, although commercially prepared mayonnaise has a pH below 4.6, adding mayonnaise to a meat salad will not inhibit bacteria. The moisture in the meat and the meat's pH are likely to raise the pH of the salad to a point where bacteria can multiply.

ACIDITY VS. ALKALINITY — PH LEVELS OF SOME COMMON FOODS	
Vinegar	2.2
Lemons	2.2
Cola drinks	2.3
Commercial mayonnaise	3.0
Grapefruit	3.1
Dill pickles	3.2

ACIDITY VS. ALKALINITY — PH LEVELS OF SOME COMMON FOODS	
Orange juice	3.7
Pears	3.9
Tomatoes	4.2
Buttermilk	4.5
Carrots	5.0
White bread	5.1
Tuna	6.0
Green peas	6.0
Potatoes	6.1
Chicken	6.2
Corn	6.3
Steamed rice	6.4
Fresh meat	6.4
Milk	6.6

Temperature. Most disease-causing bacteria grow between the temperatures of 41°F and 140°F. This is called the temperature danger zone. Some bacteria like Listeria monocytogenes, a bacteria that is often the culprit in food-borne illness related to processed luncheon meats, can grow at temperatures below 41°F.

Time. Bacteria only need about four hours to reproduce enough cells to cause a food-borne illness. This time is the total time the food item spends in the temperature danger zone.

Oxygen. There are aerobic bacteria and anaerobic bacteria, and these two types have different oxygen requirements. Aerobic bacteria must have oxygen in order to grow; anaerobic bacteria do not. These bacteria grow well in vacuum packed or canned food items. Anaerobic conditions might also exist in the middle of large, cooked food masses such as a large stockpot of stew or the middle of a large roast.

Moisture. The amount of water in a food that is available to support bacterial growth is called water activity. It is measured on a scale between 0.0 and 1.0; water activity must be greater than 0.85 to support bacterial growth. Dairy products, meats, fish, shellfish, poultry, egg, cut melons, pasta, steamed rice, and sprouts all have water activity levels between 0.85 and 1.0.

Bacterial growth rate depends upon how favorable these six conditions are. Bacteria prefer to ingest moisture-saturated foods, such as meats, dairy products and produce. They will not grow as readily on dry foods such as cereals, sugar or flour.

The greatest problem in controlling bacteria is their rapid reproduction cycle. Approximately every 15 minutes the bacteria count will double under optimal conditions. The more bacteria present, the greater the chance of bacterial infection. This is why food products that must be subjected to conditions favorable to bacteria are done so for the shortest period possible.

An important consideration when handling food products is that bacteria need several hours to adjust to a new environment before they are able to begin rapidly multiplying. Thus, if you had removed a food product from the walk-in refrigerator and inadvertently introduced bacteria to it, advanced growth would not begin for several hours. If you had immediately placed the item back into the walk-in, the temperature would have killed the bacteria before it became established.

Bacterial forms do not have a means of transportation; they must be introduced to an area by some other vehicle. People are primarily responsible for transporting bacteria to new areas. The body temperature of 98.6°F is perfect for bacterial existence and proliferation.

A person coughing, sneezing or wiping their hands on a counter can introduce bacteria to an area. Bacteria may be transmitted also by insects, air, water, and items to which they have attached themselves, such as boxes, blades, knives, and cutting boards.

An important consideration when handling food products is that bacteria need several hours to adjust to a new environment before they are able to begin rapidly multiplying. Thus, if you had removed a food product from the walk-in refrigerator and had inadvertently introduced bacteria to it, advanced growth would not begin for several hours. If you had immediately placed the item back into the walk-in, the temperature would have killed the bacteria before it became established.

Dangerous Forms of Bacteria

An estimated 76 million cases of food-borne disease occur each year in the United States. The majority of these cases are mild and cause symptoms for only a day or two. Some cases are more serious, and the CDC estimates that there are 325,000 hospitalizations and 5,000 deaths related to food-borne diseases each year. The most severe cases tend to occur in the very old, the very young, those who have an illness already that reduces their immune system function, and in healthy people exposed to a very high dose of an organism.

Persons at particularly high risk should take more precautions. Pregnant women, the elderly, and those with weakened immune systems are at higher risk for severe infections such as Listeria and should be particularly careful not to consume undercooked animal products. They should avoid soft French-style cheeses, pâtés, uncooked hot dogs, and sliced deli meats, which have been sources of Listeria infections. Persons at high risk should also avoid alfalfa sprouts and unpasteurized juices. Persons with liver disease are susceptible to infections with a rare but dangerous microbe called Vibrio vulnificus, found in oysters.

There are a number of harmful bacteria that may be found in a catering operation. The technical names and jargon are given for your own information but the important points to retain are the causes and preventive actions for each.

Bacteria Commonly Found in Catering Operations

Clostridium perfringens. Clostridium perfringens is one of a group of bacterial infectious diseases that will cause a poisoning effect. These bacteria are extremely dangerous because they are tasteless, odorless and colorless, and therefore nearly impossible to detect.

Clostridium perfringens are usually found in meat or seafood that was previously cooked and then held at room temperature for a period of time. These perfringens are anaerobic; they do not need air in order to survive. They can thrive in masses of food or in canned foods in the form of botulism. In order to survive, the bacterium will form a spore and surround itself. The spore will protect the bacterium from exposure to the air and give it a much wider temperature range for survival than normal bacteria: 65°–120°F. These bacterial forms may survive through long periods of extreme temperature and then multiply when the conditions are more favorable.

Keeping cooked food consistently above 148°F or below 40°F eliminates clostridium perfringens bacteria.

Clostridium botulism. This is another of the poisoning forms of bacteria. Botulism is a rare infectious disease but it is far more lethal than the other types. Botulism exists only in an air-free environment like that of canned goods. These bacteria are most often found in home-canned goods; however, several national food packers have reported outbreaks in their operations.

Symptoms such as vomiting, double vision, abdominal pain and shock may occur anytime from three to four hours after ingestion to eight days later.

Examine all canned goods closely before using. Look for dented, leaking cans and swollen cans or jar tops.

Staphylococci poisoning. Staphylococci bacteria (Staph) are perhaps the most common cause of food poisoning. Staph bacteria can be found everywhere, particularly in the human nose. The bacteria by themselves are harmless. The problem arises when they are left uncontrolled to grow in food items. Food that has been left out, un-refrigerated, for just a few hours can produce the poisonous toxins of Staph bacteria.

Symptoms will appear two to six hours after consumption. Common symptoms are vomiting, muscle weakness, cramps and diarrhea. The sickness ranges from very severe cases—sometimes lethal—to a relatively mild illness. To prevent Staph poisoning, follow refrigeration procedures precisely. Only remove the refrigerated food items that you will be using right away.

Salmonella infection. The bacteria themselves directly cause salmonella infection after humans consume them. In certain cases, death has resulted. Usually Salmonella causes severe—but temporary—illness. Symptoms are vomiting, fever, abdominal pain and cramps. Symptoms usually show up 12 to 24 hours after consumption and may last for several days.

Salmonella are found in the intestinal tract of some animals. They have been discovered in some packaged foods, eggs, poultry, seafood and meat. Thorough cooking and following refrigeration procedures can keep Salmonella growth to a safe limit.

Hepatitis, Dysentery and Diphtheria are some of the other infectious diseases that are bacterially derived.

Here are a few Web sites that can provide you with more information on food-borne illnesses and allergies:

- Center for Disease Control: **www.cdc.gov**

- National Restaurant Association's Educational Foundation: **www.nraef.org**

- International Food Information Council: **www.ific.org**

- FDA: **www.cfsan.fda.gov**

Controlling Bacteria

According to the CDC, the most common reason food-borne illness occurs is because of food mishandling. This includes time and temperature abuse, poor personal hygiene, poor hand-washing technique, and cross contamination. According the CDC's Surveillance for Food-Borne Disease Outbreaks (1988-1992), the following are the major factors for outbreaks:

- Use of leftovers – 4%
- Improper Cleaning – 7%
- Cross-Contamination – 7%
- Contaminated raw food – 7%
- Inadequate reheating – 12%
- Improper hot storage – 16%
- Inadequate cooking – 16%
- Infected people touching food – 20%

- Time between preparing and serving – 21%
- Improper cooling of foods – 40%

The good news is that most bacteria can be controlled. Best practices include:

- Good personal hygiene.
- Eliminating cross-contamination.
- Monitoring time and temperature.
- Employing a sanitation program.

TIME AND TEMPERATURE CONTROL

One of the most critical things you can do to avoid contamination of food is to control time and temperature. Most disease-causing bacteria grows between 41°F and 140°F. By properly cooking and reheating foods and storing cold foods below 41°F and hot foods above 140°F, you can control the growth of bacteria on these foods.

As mentioned previously, bacteria's' growth rate is very quick. Bacteria can double in number every 15 minutes, generating over 1 million cells in just 5 hours. In the food service industry, the general principle is that bacteria need 4 hours to grow in high enough numbers to cause food-borne illnesses—this includes the total time the food is in the temperature danger zone. By practicing proper storage, you can help prevent this bacterial growth.

Food must be cooked, cooled, reheated and prepared. While engaged in these activities, you should try to minimize the time the foods are in the temperature danger zone. For example, while slicing deli meat, you shouldn't stop in the middle to take a break, unless you put the meat back in the refrigerator until you go back to work.

Temperature measurements. The temperature measurement is only as accurate as the device used. Regular calibration of the device is an important practice and a provision of the Food Code. Thermometers should have calibration instructions from the manufacturer and suggested calibration intervals.

Modern thermometers, which measure temperature electrically rather than the older bimetal types, which rely on thermal expansion of two different metals, are recommended. In these instruments, a sensor is used to detect the temperature and the signal is amplified and processed electronically. This device generally yields a faster response and provides greater overall accuracy because it does not drift out of calibration and is less likely to give variable readings.

HACCP

Hazard Analysis of Critical Control Points (HACCP) is a system for monitoring the food service process to reduce the risk of food-borne illness. You are responsible for protecting your customers by serving safe and wholesome food. To accomplish this, you need a systematic process for identifying potential hazards, for putting safety procedures in place, and for monitoring the success of your safety system on an ongoing basis. HACCP helps you do all of these things.

HACCP focuses on how food flows through the process—from purchasing to serving. At each step in the food-preparation process there are a variety of potential hazards. HACCP provides managers with a framework for implementing control procedures for each hazard. It does this through identifying critical control points (CCPs). These are points in the process where bacteria or other harmful organisms may grow or food may become contaminated.

Using HACCP, you can identify potentially hazardous foods and places in the food-preparation process where bacterial contamination, survival and growth can occur. Then you can take action to minimize the danger.

HACCP is based on this principle: If the raw ingredients are safe, and the process is safe, then the finished product is safe.

HACCP'S EIGHT KEY STEPS OF THE FOOD SERVICE PROCESS

In order, we'll look at:

1. Purchasing.
2. Receiving.
3. Storing
4. Preparing.

5. Cooking.
6. Serving and holding.
7. Cooling.
8. Reheating.

There are multiple hazards at, and specific preventative measures for, each step. Depending on the size of your catering operation, all these steps may not be applicable to your situation. Safe food preparation, however, is applicable to everyone!

HACCP Step 1: Purchasing

The goal of purchasing is to obtain wholesome, safe foods to meet your menu requirements. Safety at this step is primarily the responsibility of your vendors; it's your job to choose your vendors wisely. Suppliers must meet federal and state health standards. They should use the HACCP system in their operations and train their employees in sanitation.

Delivery trucks should have adequate refrigeration and freezer units, and foods should be packaged in protective, leakproof, durable packaging. Let vendors know up front what you expect from them. Put food-safety standards in your purchase specification agreements. Ask to see their most recent board of health sanitation reports, and tell them you will be inspecting trucks on a regular basis.

Good vendors will cooperate with your inspections and should adjust their delivery schedules to avoid your busy periods so that incoming foods can be received and inspected properly.

HACCP Step 2: Receiving

The goals of receiving are to make sure foods are fresh and safe when they enter your facility and to transfer them to proper storage as quickly as possible.

Let's look more closely at two important parts of receiving: 1) getting ready to receive food, and 2) inspecting the food when the delivery truck arrives.

There are several important guidelines to keep in mind and tasks to complete as you get ready to receive food:

- Make sure your receiving area is equipped with sanitary carts for transporting goods.

- Plan ahead for deliveries to ensure sufficient refrigerator and freezer space.

- Keep the receiving area well lit and clean to discourage pests.

- Remove empty containers and packing materials immediately to a separate trash area.

- Keep all flooring clean of food particles and debris.

- When the delivery truck arrives, make sure it looks and smells clean and is equipped with the proper food storage equipment.

Then inspect foods immediately:

- Check expiration dates of milk, eggs, and other perishable goods.

- Make sure shelf-life dates have not expired.

- Make sure frozen foods are in airtight, moisture-proof wrappings.

- Mark all items for storage with the date of arrival or the "use by" date.

- Reject foods that have been thawed and refrozen. Look for signs of thawing and refreezing such as large crystals, solid areas of ice, or excessive ice in containers.

- Reject cans that have any of the following: swollen sides or ends; flawed seals or seams; dents or rust. Also reject any cans whose contents are foamy or bad smelling.

- Check temperature of refrigerated and frozen foods, especially eggs and dairy products, fresh meat, and fish and poultry products.

- Look for content damage and insect infestations.

- Reject dairy, bakery, and other foods delivered in dirty flats or crates.

HACCP Step 3: Storing

In general, there are four possible ways to store food:

1. In dry storage, for longer holding of less perishable items.

2. In refrigeration, for short-term storage of perishable items.

3. In specially designed deep-chilling units for short periods.

4. In a freezer, for longer-term storage of perishable foods.

Each type of storage has its own sanitation and safety requirements.

Dry Storage

There are many items that can be safely held in a sanitary storeroom. These include, for example: canned goods, baking supplies (such as salt and sugar), grain products (such as rice and cereals), and other dry items. In addition, some fruits (such as bananas, avocados and pears) ripen best at room temperature. Some vegetables, such as onions, potatoes and tomatoes, also store best in dry storage. A dry-storage room should be clean and orderly, with good ventilation to control temperature and humidity and retard the growth of bacteria and mold. Keep in mind the following:

- For maximum shelf life, dry foods should be held at 50°F, but 60°–70°F is adequate for most products.

- Use a wall thermometer to check the temperature of your dry-storage facility regularly.

- To ensure freshness, store opened items in tightly covered containers. Use the FIFO rotation method, dating packages and placing incoming supplies in the back so that older supplies will be used first.

- To avoid pest infestation and cross-contamination, clean up all spills immediately, and do not store trash or garbage cans in food storage areas.

- Do not place any items—including paper products—on the floor. Make sure the bottom shelf of the dry-storage room is at least 6 inches above the ground.

- Never use or store cleaning materials or other chemicals where they might contaminate foods. Store them, labeled, in their own section in the storeroom away from all food supplies.

Refrigerated Storage

Keep fresh meat, poultry, seafood, dairy products, most fresh fruit and vegetables, and hot leftovers in the refrigerator at internal temperatures of below 40°F. Refrigeration increases the shelf life of most products. Refrigeration slows bacterial growth; the colder a food is, the safer it is.

Your refrigeration unit should contain open, slotted shelving to allow cold air to circulate around food. Do not line shelves with foil or paper. Do not overload the refrigerator, and be sure to leave space between items to further improve air circulation. All refrigerated foods should be dated and properly sealed. In addition:

- Use clean, nonabsorbent, covered containers that are approved for food storage.

- Store dairy products separately from foods with strong odors like onions, cabbage and seafood.

- To avoid cross-contamination, store raw or uncooked food away from and below prepared or ready-to-eat food.

- Never allow fluids from raw poultry, fish or meat to come into contact with other foods.

- Keeping perishable items at the proper temperature is a key factor in preventing food-borne illness. Check the temperature of your refrigeration unit regularly to make sure it stays below 40°F. Keep in mind that opening and closing the refrigerator door too often can affect temperature.

Many commercial refrigerators are equipped with externally mounted or built-in thermometers. These are convenient when they work, but it is important to have a backup. It's a good idea to have several thermometers in different parts of the refrigerator to ensure consistent temperature and accuracy of instruments. Record the temperature of each refrigerator on a chart, preferably once a day.

Deep Chilling

Deep or super chilling—that is, storing foods at temperatures between 26°F and 32°F—has been found to decrease bacterial growth. This method can be used to increase the shelf life of fresh foods, such as poultry, meat, seafood, and other protein items, without compromising their quality by freezing. You can deep-chill foods in specially designed units or in a refrigerator set to deep-chilling temperature.

Frozen Storage

Frozen meats, poultry, seafood, fruits and vegetables and some dairy products such as ice cream should be stored in a freezer at 0°F to keep them fresh and safe for an extended period of time.

As a rule, you should use your freezer primarily to store foods that are frozen when you receive them. Freezing refrigerated foods can damage the quality of perishable items. It's important to store frozen foods immediately. It's also important to remember that storing foods in the freezer for too long increases the likelihood of contamination and spoilage. Like your refrigeration unit, the freezer should allow cold air to circulate around foods easily.

- Store frozen foods in moisture-proof material or containers to minimize loss of flavor, as well as discoloration, dehydration and odor absorption.

- Monitor temperature regularly, using several thermometers to ensure accuracy and consistent temperatures. Record the temperature of each freezer on a chart.

- Frequently opening and closing the freezer can cause contamination and spoilage. Like your refrigeration unit, the freezer should allow cold air to circulate around foods easily.

- Minimize heat gain by opening freezer doors only when necessary and removing as many items at one time as possible. You can also use a freezer "cold curtain" to help guard against heat gain.

HACCP Step 4: Preparing

Thawing and Marinating

Freezing food keeps most bacteria from multiplying, but it does not kill them. Bacteria that are present when food is removed from the freezer may multiply rapidly if thawed at room temperature.

Thus, it is critical to thaw foods out of the temperature danger zone. Never thaw foods on a counter or in any other non-refrigerated area.

Some foods, such as frozen vegetables and pre-formed hamburger patties and chicken nuggets, can be cooked from the frozen state. It is important to note, however, that this method depends on the size of the item. For example, cooking from the frozen state is not recommended for large foods like a 20-pound turkey.

The two best methods for thawing foods are:

- In refrigeration at a temperature below 40°F, placed in a pan on the lowest shelf so juices cannot drip on other foods.

- Under clean, drinkable running water at a temperature of 70°F or less for no more than two hours, or just until the product is thawed.

Always marinate meat, fish and poultry in the refrigerator—never at room temperature. Never save and reuse marinade. With all methods, be careful not to cross-contaminate!

Cautions for Cold Foods

When you are preparing cold foods, you are at one of the most hazardous points in the food-preparation process. There are two key reasons for this:

1. Cold food preparation usually takes place at room temperature.

2. Cold food is one of the most common points of contamination and cross-contamination.

Chicken salad, tuna salad, potato salad with eggs, and other protein-rich salads are common sources of food-borne illness. Sandwiches prepared in advance and held un-refrigerated are also dangerous.

Because cold foods such as these receive no further cooking, it is essential that all ingredients used in them are properly cleaned, prepared and, where applicable, cooked. It is a good idea to chill meats and other ingredients and combine them while chilled.

Here are several other important precautions to keep in mind:

- Prepare foods no further in advance than necessary.

- Prepare foods in small batches and place in cold storage immediately; this will prevent holding food too long in the temperature danger zone.

- Always hold prepared cold foods below 40°F.

- Wash fresh fruits and vegetables with plain water to remove surface pesticide residues and other impurities, such as soil particles.

- Use a brush to scrub thick-skinned produce, if desired.

- Avoid cross-contamination:

    - Keep raw products separate from ready-to-serve foods.

    - Sanitize cutting boards, knives, and other food contact surfaces after each contact with a potentially hazardous food.

    - Discard any leftover batter, breading or marinade after it has been used with potentially hazardous foods.

HACCP Step 5: Cooking

Even when potentially hazardous foods are properly thawed, bacteria and other contaminants may still be present. Cooking foods to the proper internal temperature will kill any existing bacteria and make food safe.

Keep in mind the following "safe cooking" tips:

- Stir foods cooked in deep pots frequently to ensure thorough cooking.

- When deep-frying potentially hazardous foods, make sure fryers are not overloaded, and make sure the oil temperature returns to the required level before adding the next batch. Use a hot-oil thermometer designed for this special application.

- Regulate size and thickness of each portion to make cooking time predictable and uniform.

- Allow cooking equipment to heat up between batches.

- Never interrupt the cooking process. Partially cooking poultry or meat, for example, may produce conditions that encourage bacterial growth.

- Monitor the accuracy of heating equipment with each use by using thermometers. In addition, always use a thermometer to ensure food reaches the proper temperature during cooking. Use a sanitized metal-stemmed, numerically scaled thermometer (accurate to plus or minus 2°F) or a digital thermometer. Check food temperature in several places, especially in the thickest parts, to make sure the food is thoroughly cooked. To avoid getting a false reading, be careful not to touch the pan or bone with the thermometer.

HACCP Step 6: Serving and Holding

Food that has been cooked isn't necessarily safe. In fact, many outbreaks occur because improper procedures were used following cooking. Although it may be tempting to hold food at temperatures just hot enough to serve, it is essential to keep prepared foods out of the temperature danger zone. This means, specifically:

- Always keep hot foods in hot-holding equipment above 140°F.

- Always keep cold foods in a refrigeration unit or surrounded by ice below 40°F.

For safer serving and holding:

- Use hot-holding equipment, such as steam tables and hot-food carts, during service but never for reheating.

- Stir foods at reasonable intervals to ensure even heating.

- Check temperatures with a food thermometer every 30 minutes.

- Sanitize the thermometer before each use, or use a digital infrared thermometer that never touches the food.

- Cover hot-holding equipment to retain heat and to guard against contamination.

- Monitor the temperature of hot-holding equipment with each use.

- Discard any food held in the temperature danger zone for more than 4 hours!

- Never add fresh food to a serving pan containing foods that have already been out for serving.

SOME KEY POINTS
1. Always wash hands with soap and warm water for at least 20 seconds before serving food.
2. Use cleaned and sanitized long-handled ladles and spoons so bare hands do not touch food.

3. Never touch the parts of glasses, plates or tableware that will come into contact with food.

4. Never touch the parts of dishes that will come into contact with the customer's mouth.

5. Wear gloves if serving food by hand.

6. Cover cuts or infections with bandages, and if on hands, cover with gloves.

7. Discard gloves whenever they touch an unsanitary surface.

8. Use tongs or wear gloves to dispense rolls and bread.

9. Clean and sanitize equipment and utensils thoroughly after each use.

10. Use lids and sneeze guards to protect prepared food from contamination.

Always wash hands, utensils and other food-contact surfaces after contact with raw meat or poultry and before contact with cooked meat or poultry. For example, do not reuse a serving pan used to hold raw chicken to serve the same chicken after it's cooked, unless the pan has been thoroughly cleaned and sanitized.

Sanitary Self-Service

Like workers, customers can also act as a source of contamination. Unlike workers, customers—especially children—are generally not educated about food sanitation and may do the following unsanitary things:

- Use the same plate twice.

- Touch food with their hands.

- Touch the edges of serving dishes.

- Sneeze or cough onto food.

- Pick up foods, such as rolls or carrot sticks, with their fingers.

- Eat in the food line.

- Dip their fingers into foods to taste them.

- Return food items to avoid waste.

- Put their heads under sneeze guards to reach items in the back.

Be sure to observe customer behavior and remove any foods that may have been contaminated. Also, as a precautionary measure, serve sealed packages of crackers, breadsticks and condiments, and pre-wrap, date and label sandwiches if possible.

HACCP Step 7: Cooling

It is often necessary to prepare foods in advance or use leftover foods. Unfortunately, this can easily lead to problems unless proper precautions are taken. In fact, problems at this stage are the number-one cause of food-borne illness. The two key precautions for preventing food-borne illness at this point in the process are rapid cooling and protection from contamination.

Chilling It Quickly

All potentially hazardous, cooked leftovers should be chilled to an internal temperature of below 40°F. Quick-chill any leftovers larger than half a gallon or 2 pounds. Quick chilling involves five simple steps:

1. **Reduce food mass.** Smaller amounts of food will chill more quickly than larger amounts, so cut large items into pieces or divide food among several containers or shallow pans.

   Use shallow, pre-chilled pans (no more than 4 inches deep). Use stainless-steel containers when possible; stainless steel transfers heat better and cools faster than plastic.

2. **Chill.** Ideally, place food in an ice-water bath or quick-chill unit (26°–32°F) rather than a refrigerator. These options are best for two reasons:

   1. Water is a much better heat conductor than air. As a result, foods can cool much more quickly in an ice bath than they can in a refrigerator.

   2. Refrigeration units are designed to keep cold foods cold rather than to chill hot foods. They can take too long to cool foods to safe temperatures.

   Another option is to pre-chill foods in a freezer for about 30 minutes before refrigerating.

   Separate food items so air can flow freely around them. Do not stack shallow pans. Never cool at room temperature.

3. **Stir frequently.** Stirring accelerates cooling and helps to ensure that cold air reaches all parts of the food.

4. **Measure temperature periodically.** Food should reach a temperature of 70°F within 2 hours and 40°F within 4 hours. This time must be reduced if food has already spent time in the temperature danger zone at any other point in the preparation and serving process.

5. **Tightly cover and label cooled foods.** Include preparation dates and times on labels.

Be aware that although uncovered foods cool faster, they are at increased risk for cross-contamination. Be sure to store uncovered cooked and cooled foods on the upper shelves of the cooler, and cover them when they reach 45°F. Never store them beneath raw foods.

HACCP Step 8: Reheating

While assuming leftovers are safe might seem reasonable, it's not. In reheating and serving leftovers—just as in all phases of the food-preparation process—you must be careful to avoid contamination.

To safely reheat and serve leftovers, be sure to:

- Boil sauces, soups and gravies, and heat other foods to a minimum of 165°F, within 2 hours of taking the food out of the refrigerator.

- Never reheat food in hot-holding equipment.

- Never mix a leftover batch of food with a fresh batch of food.

- Never reheat food more than once.

The Difference Between Clean and Sanitary

Heat or chemicals can be used to reduce the number of bacteria to acceptable levels. They can also be used for certain other harmful microorganisms.

Heat sanitizing involves exposing equipment to high heat for an adequate length of time. This may be done manually by immersing equipment in water maintained at a temperature of 170°–195°F for at least 30 seconds, or in a dishwashing machine that washes at 150°F and rinses at 180°F.

For any method, it is important to check water temperature frequently. Thermometers and heat-sensitive tapes and labels are available for determining whether adequate sanitation temperatures have been achieved.

Chemical sanitizing can be accomplished by immersing an object in, or wiping it down with, bleach or sanitizing solution. For bleaching, use 1/2 ounce or 1 tablespoon of 5 percent bleach per gallon of water. For using commercial products, follow the manufacturers' instructions. Chemical sanitizers are regulated by the EPA, and manufacturers must follow strict labeling requirements regarding what concentrations to use, data on minimum effectiveness and warnings of possible health hazards.

Chemical test strips are available for testing the strength of the sanitizing solution. Because sanitizing agents become less effective as they kill bacteria and are exposed to air, it is important to test the sanitizing solution frequently.

SANITIZING PORTABLE EQUIPMENT

To properly clean and sanitize portable equipment, you must have a sink with three separate compartments: for cleaning, rinsing, and sanitizing. There should be a separate area for scraping and rinsing food and debris into a garbage container or disposer before washing, and separate drain boards for clean and soiled items.

To sanitize a piece of equipment, use the following procedure:

1. Clean and sanitize sinks and work surfaces.

2. Scrape and rinse food into garbage or disposal. Presoak items, such as silverware, as necessary.

3. In the first sink, immerse the equipment in a clean detergent solution at about 120°F. Use a brush or a cloth to loosen and remove any remaining visible soil.

4. Rinse in the second sink using clear, clean water between 120°F and 140°F to remove all traces of food, debris and detergent.

5. Sanitize in the third sink by immersing items in hot water at 170°F for 30 seconds or in a chemical sanitizing solution for one minute. Be sure to cover all surfaces of the equipment with hot water or the sanitizing solution and keep them in contact with it for the appropriate amount of time.

6. If soapsuds disappear in the first compartment or remain in the second, if the water temperature cools, or if water in any compartment becomes dirty and cloudy, empty the compartment and refill it.

7. Air-dry; wiping can re-contaminate equipment and can remove the sanitizing solution from the surfaces before it has finished working.

8. Make certain all equipment is dry before putting it into storage; moisture can foster bacterial growth.

SANITIZING IN-PLACE EQUIPMENT

Larger and immobile equipment should also be washed, rinsed and sanitized.

Use the following procedure:

- Unplug electrical equipment, such as meat slicers.

- Remove fallen food particles and scraps.

- Wash, rinse and sanitize any removable parts using the manual immersion method described..

- Wash the remaining food-contact surfaces and rinse with clean water. Wipe down with a chemical sanitizing solution mixed according to the manufacturer's directions.

- Wipe down all non-food-contact surfaces with a sanitized cloth, and allow all parts to air-dry before reassembling. Sanitize cloth before and during sanitizing by rinsing it in sanitizing solution.

- Resanitize the external food-contact surfaces of the parts that were handled during reassembling.

- Scrub wooden surfaces, such as cutting boards, with a detergent solution and a stiff-bristled nylon brush, then rinse in clear, clean water and wipe down with a sanitizing solution after every use.

MAINTAIN A FIRST-RATE FACILITY

Safe and sanitary food service begins with a facility that is clean and in good repair. The entire facility—work areas as well as equipment—should be designed for easy cleaning and maintenance.

It's important to eliminate hard-to-clean work areas as well as faulty or overloaded refrigerators or other equipment. Also get rid of dirty surroundings and any conditions that will attract pests.

Remember, the easier the workplace is to clean, the more likely it will stay clean.

Floors, Walls and Ceilings

Floors, walls and ceilings should be free of dirt, litter and moisture. Clean walls regularly by swabbing with a cleaning solution or by spraying with a pressure nozzle. Sweep floors, then clean them using a spray method or by mopping. Swab ceilings, instead of spraying them, to avoid soaking lights and ceiling fans. Don't forget corners and hard-to-reach places.

Ventilation

Good ventilation is a critical factor in maintaining a clean food service environment. Ventilation removes steam, smoke, grease and heat from food preparation areas and equipment. This helps maintain indoor air quality and reduces the possibility of fires from accumulated grease. In addition, good ventilation eliminates condensation and other airborne contaminants. It also reduces accumulation of dirt in the food preparation area, odors, gases and fumes, and mold growth by reducing humidity.

To ensure good ventilation:

- Use exhaust fans to remove odors and smoke.

- Use hoods over cooking areas and dishwashing equipment.

- Check exhaust fans and hoods regularly to make sure they are clean and operating properly.

- Clean hood filters routinely according to the instructions provided by the hood manufacturer.

Storerooms

Like all areas of the facility, storerooms must be kept clean and litter-free. To accomplish this, be sure to sweep and scrub walls, ceilings, floors, shelves, light fixtures and racks on a routine basis. Check all storage areas frequently—this includes your refrigerator and freezer as well as your dry-storage room. When checking storage areas:

- Look for damaged or spoiled foods, broken or torn packages, and bulging or leaking cans.

- Remove any potentially spoiled foods immediately, and clean the area thoroughly.

- Make sure foods and other supplies are stored at least 6 inches from the walls and above the floor.

Bugs, Insects and RODENTS

Bug and insect infestation in a food service establishment is the result of poor sanitation practices. Aside from being a nuisance, they are a threat to food safety. Flies, cockroaches, and other insects all carry bacteria, and many, because of where they get their food, carry disease. Bugs, insects and rodents require the same three basic necessities of life as bacteria do: food, water and warmth.

When bugs and insects are visible, this is an indicator that proper sanitation procedures have not been carried out. Eliminate the environment that these pests need to live, and you will be eliminating their existence. Combining proper sanitation practices with periodic extermination spraying will stop any problems before they start.

To prevent the spread of flies in your establishment, keep all doors, windows and screens closed at all times. Ensure that garbage is sealed in airtight containers and is picked up regularly. All trash must be cleaned off the ground; flies can deposit their eggs on the thinnest scrap of food. Dumpsters must be periodically steam cleaned and deodorized. They should never contain any decaying food scraps.

All doorjambs and building cracks, even the thinnest ones, must be sealed. Be cautious when receiving deliveries; bugs may be in the boxes or crates.

The greatest protection against cockroaches is your exterminator. Of course, the exterminator will be of little value if you do not already have good sanitary practices in place. Select an exterminator who is currently servicing other caterers. Chemicals sprayed in a food service operation must be of the nonresidual type. These are safe and approved for use in food service establishments.

Rodents are prolific breeders, producing as many as 50 offspring in a lifespan of one year. They tend to hide during the day, but they can be discovered by their telltale signs, including droppings, holes, nesting materials, gnawing, and tracks on dusty surfaces.

Pests, such as rats and mice, are a very serious problem for caterers and anyone in the food service industry. They are filthy animals that will eat any sort of garbage or decaying food available. Rats are infested with bacteria and often disease. They have been known to bite people, as have their fleas, which also spread their bacteria and disease. Rats and mice have evolved into creatures highly developed for survival. Once they have become settled in an area, they are very difficult to get rid of.

Rats and mice, like flies, are attracted to exposed garbage. They are extremely strong and can easily gain access to a building through a crack or hole no larger than a quarter. Ensure that your building's foundation is airtight. Keep all food products at least 6 inches off the floor; this enables the exterminator to get under the shelving to spray. Rat bait, a poisoning capsule resembling food, is particularly effective when spread around the building and dumpsters. As with any poison or chemical you use, make certain that it is labeled clearly and stored away from food storage areas.

Sanitation Inspections

Local and state boards of health make frequent and unannounced inspections at all food establishments. You cannot afford to let standards slip, even momentarily. Bear in mind the following:

- Foods must come from approved sources and be wholesome and unadulterated (legal and USDA-inspected). For more information on the USDA, visit **www.usda.gov**.

- Meat must be inspected by the USDA and carry a stamp of approval on the meat carcass or a tag on poultry.

- Fish and frozen foods must be certified by the U.S. Public Health Service (**www.hhs.gov/phs**). Fishing sources and fish processing must be certified by the U.S. Department of the Interior.

- Milk, eggs, fruits and vegetables should be inspected by the USDA.

- Food must be protected against all potentially hazardous agents and maintained in temperature-controlled areas during storage, preparation, service and transport.

- Personnel must wear clean clothes and effective hair restraints and practice good personal hygiene.

- Utensils and equipment must be kept clean; pots must be free of grease and carbon accumulation.

- With respect to garbage and rubbish storage and disposal, a number of covered, rodent-proof, clean containers should be available.

- Floors, walls and ceilings must be properly constructed and in good repair and drains must be in working order. Mats must be removable, clean and in good repair. Lighting must be adequate and fixtures must be clean. All rooms and equipment hoods must have ducts vented, as required.

- Clean and soiled laundry must be properly stored.

INFECTION-CONTROL SANITARY MAINTENANCE PRODUCTS

Transportation

Transporting food even short distances requires special attention and care. Food should be transported with covers in either heated or refrigerated containers.

Pre-chill foods that are to be served cold before you transport them to the venue. Keep these foods at a temperature of 45°F for both storage and service. Keep foods that are to be served hot at a temperature of 165°F or above. For off-premise caterers, it is very important to understand that during food transportation the risk of contamination is great. Carry all food, serving equipment and utensils in securely wrapped packages. Whether chilled or cooked, foods should be maintained in constant, controlled temperatures at all times.

Here are some other tips when transporting food:

- When unloading, unload food items first.

- Do not rely on winter weather to keep foods cold.

- Bring a thermometer and use it.

- Take extra precautions in hot weather.

- Make sure to keep the interiors of transportation vehicles clean.

- Do not pack food items too tightly in containers. Allow air to circulate between the items.

To ensure all equipment and food service areas are as clean as possible, it is important to use proper tools to maintain a sanitary environment. Tucel Industries, Inc., **www.tucel.com**, is a leading research-driven manufacturing corporation that manufactures and markets a broad range of hygienic cleaning tools:

- Food•Prep™ brushes are manufactured using FDA-approved raw materials to ensure that the brush cannot absorb any bacteria that could contaminate the food by direct contact.

- Equip•Clean patented brushes are manufactured in various designs and materials for the end user to remove grime and clean ergonomically without leaving bacteria on the sanitized surfaces.

- Special Equip brushes are manufactured for specific jobs for the end user to remove grime and clean ergonomically leaving bacteria free, sanitized surfaces.

- Floor & Wall brushes are manufactured using FDA-approved raw materials to ensure that the brush cannot absorb any bacteria that could contaminate any surface by direct contact.

- Sanitary•Maintenance brushes are manufactured using FDA-approved raw materials to ensure that the brush cannot absorb any bacteria which could cause cross-contamination during use.

- Kits•Handles are designed and manufactured using FDA-approved raw materials to ensure that the end-user's job is completed quickly and efficiently and bacteria-free surfaces result.

Personal Hygiene

Infected food employees are the source of contamination in approximately one in five food-borne disease outbreaks reported in the United States with a bacterial or viral cause. Most of these outbreaks involve enteric fecal-oral agents. Because of poor or nonexistent hand-washing procedures, workers spread these organisms to the food. In addition, infected cuts, burns or boils on hands can also result in contamination of food. Viral, bacterial and parasitic agents can be involved.

Personal hygiene is the best way to stop bacteria from contaminating and spreading into new areas. Hands are the greatest source of contamination. Hands must be washed constantly throughout the day. Every time an individual scratches her head or sneezes, she is exposing her hands to bacteria and will spread it to anything she touches, such as food, equipment and clothes. Hand and nailbrushes, antibacterial soaps and disposable gloves should be a part of every food service operation, even if not required by law. Proper training and management follow-up is also critical.

Every employee must follow basic hygiene practices:

- Short hair, and hair contained in a net.

- Clean shaven, or facial hair contained in a net.

- Clean clothes/uniforms.

- Clean hands and short nails.

- No unnecessary jewelry.

- A daily shower or bath.

- No smoking in or near the kitchen.

- Hand washing prior to starting work, periodically, and after handling any foreign object: head, face, ears, money, food, boxes or trash.

An employee who has the symptoms of the common cold or any open cuts or infections should not go to work. By simply breathing, he may be inadvertently exposing the environment to bacteria. Although it is rarely practiced in the food industry, all employees should be required to have a complete medical examination as a condition of employment. This should include blood and urine tests. A seemingly healthy individual may unknowingly be the carrier of a latent communicable disease.

Except when washing fruits and vegetables or when otherwise approved, employees may not contact exposed, ready-to-eat foods with their bare hands and shall use proper utensils such as deli tissue, spatulas, tongs, single-use gloves, or dispensing equipment.

HAND WASHING

Hand washing is perhaps the most critical aspect of good personal hygiene in food service.

Employees should wash their hands after the following activities:

- Smoking (hands come in contact with mouth)

- Eating (hands come in contact with mouth)

- Using the restroom

- Handling money

- Touching raw food (the raw food may contain bacteria)

- Touching or combing their hair

- Coughing, sneezing or blowing their nose

- Taking a break

- Handling anything dirty (touching a dirty apron or taking out the trash)

Employees must wash their hands using the proper techniques. Workers should wash their hands with soap and warm water for 20 seconds. When working with food, they should wash gloved hands as often as bare hands.

The proper hand-washing method is as follows:

- Remove any jewelry.

- Turn water on as hot as you can stand it.

- Moisten hands and forearms up to elbows.

- Lather them thoroughly with soap.

- Wash for at least 20 seconds, rub hands together, wash between fingers up to the elbows.

- Use a brush for under nails.

- Rinse hands and forearms with hot water.

- Dry hands and forearms with a paper towel.

Hand washing is such a simple yet very effective method for eliminating cross-contamination, you may want to use the following exercise in your training:

To show trainees the "invisible dirt" that may be hiding on their hands, use the Glo Germ Training Kit.

1. Have employees dip their hands in the fluorescent substance.

2. Tell employees to wash their hands.

3. Have employees hold their hands under the black light to see how much "dirt" is still there.

4. Explain proper hand-washing technique.

5. Have employees wash their hands again, this time using the proper hand-washing technique.

6. Have employees once again hold their hands under the black light.

Fingernails

Fingernails must be trimmed, filed and maintained. This is designed to address both the cleanability of areas beneath the fingernails and the possibility that fingernails or pieces of the fingernails may end up in the food due to breakage. Failure to remove fecal material from beneath the fingernails after defecation can be a major source of pathogenic organisms. Ragged fingernails present cleanability concerns and may harbor pathogenic organisms.

Jewelry

Jewelry, such as rings, bracelets and watches, may collect soil, and the construction of the jewelry may hinder routine cleaning. As a result, the jewelry may act as a reservoir of pathogenic organisms transmissible through food.

The term "jewelry" generally refers to the ornaments worn for personal adornment. Medical alert bracelets do not fit this definition; however, the wearing of such bracelets carries the same potential for transmitting disease-causing organisms to food. In the case of a food worker who wears a medical information or medical alert bracelet, the EEOC has agreed that this requirement can be met through reasonable accommodation in accordance with the Americans with Disabilities Act by the person in charge and the employee working out acceptable alternatives to the bracelet worn at the wrist. An example would be wearing the bracelet high on the arm or secured in a manner that does not pose a risk to the food but provides emergency medical information if it is needed.

An additional hazard associated with jewelry is the possibility that pieces of the item or the whole item itself may fall into the food being prepared. Hard foreign objects in food may cause medical problems for consumers, such as chipped and broken teeth and internal cuts and lesions.

Outer Clothing

Dirty clothing may harbor diseases that are transmissible through food. Food employees who inadvertently touch their dirty clothing may contaminate their hands. This could result in contamination of the food being prepared. Food may also be contaminated through direct contact with dirty clothing. In addition, wearing dirty clothes sends a negative message to consumers about the level of sanitation in the establishment.

Eating, Drinking, or Using Tobacco

Smoking or eating by employees in food preparation areas is prohibited because of the potential that the hands, food, and food-contact surfaces may become contaminated. Unsanitary personal practices such as scratching the head, placing the fingers in or about the mouth or nose, and indiscriminate and uncovered sneezing or coughing may result in food contamination. Poor hygienic practices by employees may also adversely affect consumer confidence in the establishment.

Food preparation areas such as hot grills may have elevated temperatures. The excessive heat in these areas may present a medical risk to the workers as a result of dehydration. Consequently, in these areas food, employees are allowed to drink from closed containers that are carefully handled.

Discharges from the Eyes, Nose and Mouth

Discharges from the eyes, nose or mouth through persistent sneezing or coughing by food employees can directly contaminate exposed food, equipment, utensils, linens, and single-service and single-use articles. When these poor hygienic practices cannot be controlled, the employee must be assigned to duties that minimize the potential for contaminating food and surrounding surfaces and objects or sent home.

Hair Restraints

Consumers are particularly sensitive to food contaminated by hair. Hair can be both a direct and indirect vehicle of contamination. Food employees may contaminate their hands when they touch their hair. A hair restraint keeps dislodged hair from ending up in the food and may deter employees from touching their hair.

Animals

Dogs and other animals, like humans, may harbor pathogens that are transmissible through food. Handling or caring for animals that may be legally present is prohibited because of the risk of contamination of food employee hands and clothing.

Handling Dishware

Even employees with clean hands need to follow certain procedures when handling food and dishware:

- Use tongs, scoops, or food-grade rubber gloves when picking up bread, butter pats, ice, or other ready-to-eat foods.

- Pick up glasses from the outside, not with fingers inside the glass or on the rims. Cups must be picked up by the handles or bottoms. Do not touch glass or cup rims with your bare hands.

- Pick up forks and spoons by the handles rather than the tines or bowls.

- Carry plates by the bottoms or edges; do not touch the eating surface.

- Do not stack dishes, cups and saucers in order to carry more.

- Wash your hands after handling soiled dishes.

- Wash your hands before you put on gloves. Also be aware that gloved hands become contaminated if a task is interrupted. Contaminated gloves should be removed, discarded, hands must be washed, and fresh gloves put on to resume the task.

- An employee may not use a utensil more than once to taste food that is to be sold or served.

Gloves

Multi-use gloves, especially when used repeatedly and soiled, can become breeding grounds for pathogens that could be transferred to food. Soiled gloves can directly contaminate food if stored with ready-to-eat food or may indirectly contaminate food if stored with articles that will be used in contact with food. Multi-use gloves must be washed, rinsed and sanitized between activities that contaminate the gloves. Hands must be washed before donning gloves. Gloves must be discarded when soil or other contaminants enter the inside of the glove.

Slash-resistant gloves are not easily cleaned and sanitized. Their use with ready-to-eat foods could contaminate the food.

Natural latex rubber (NRL) gloves have been reported to cause allergic reactions in some individuals who wear latex gloves during food preparation, and even in individuals eating food prepared by food employees wearing latex gloves. This information should be taken into consideration when deciding whether single-use gloves made of latex will be used during food preparation.

Training Your Staff

You must provide employees with the training, knowledge and tools that will enable them to establish and practice proper food handling and sanitation procedures. Each employee must be thoroughly familiar with basic food safety and sanitation practices in order to control food contamination, the spread of infectious diseases, and personal safety practices.

Under the guidance of your local health department, you and your staff can obtain training and knowledge. First, however, the business must be equipped with the proper tools, training and working conditions. Employees will never establish good sanitation procedures if they do not first have the proper environment in which to practice them.

Aside from what is required by law, you should provide training materials, proper training sessions or clinics, hand sinks at every station, hand and nailbrushes, labels for dating and rotation procedures, disposable towels, gloves, first-aid kits, germicidal hand soaps, employee bathrooms and lockers, uniforms, hairnets, thermometers, test kits, and quality, color-coded utensils.

There are many ways to train servers about food safety. While in-house training will go a long way in getting your employees off to a good start, you should consider enrolling them in the National Restaurant Association's ServSafe program or other similar programs at area colleges. This way your employees can become certified by the state.

- **The Education Foundation of the National Restaurant Association (NRA).** The NRA is the foremost training and testing leader for food service sanitation throughout the United States. Consult the NRA for information about its Applied Food Service Sanitation course. This course provides food service managers with basic sanitation principles, as well as methods for training and motivating employees to follow sound sanitation practices.

- **Culinary programs.** Check area colleges and vocational schools for culinary programs as well. These programs usually offer a course in food safety and sanitation. Upon passing the course, the individual will be certified in food safety and sanitation by the state.

- **Legislation.** Note that in Illinois and Florida, some form of sanitation certification is mandatory. Other states are in the process of enacting similar appropriate legislation.

KITCHEN SAFETY

By its nature, the food service environment is full of potential hazards to employees' safety. Knives, slicers, grinders, glass, hot surfaces, and wet or greasy floors are only a few of the hazards food service workers face every day. Fortunately, most accidents also involve human error and, therefore, can be prevented.

Don't leave anything to chance. Rules regarding safety procedures should be well documented and posted in a prominent position. Also, all employees must be 100 percent familiar with official procedures in the event of an emergency. Reassess and update ways in which you can reduce the risks of accident for both employees and clients alike. Make sure that the following safety measures are implemented and adhered to at all times:

- Keep floors clean, dry and in good repair. Use signs such as "Caution" and "Wet Floor" as appropriate.

- Install adequate lighting.

- Advise your employees to use extreme caution when working at off-premise sites.

- Only allow trained staff to operate specific equipment. Protective goggles and gloves should be worn while operating hazardous machinery. Also, only use equipment for its designated purpose.

- Keep your knives sharp. Blunt knives are a common cause of both minor and major injuries. When using a knife, cut foods with fingers curled under. Cut away from the body, and make sure all your kitchen employees know the proper way to handle knives.

- Train your employees in correct lifting and transporting methods. Teach your employees the correct procedures for carrying heavy items and trays.

- Keep beverages away from fryer stations. Cold beverages spilled into the hot fryer can cause major eruption of hot grease.

- All ovens, broilers and grills fueled by large tanks of propane should not be used indoors. Also, you may need a special permit from local authorities to use butane fuel indoors.

- The ultimate dread of any caterer is fire. Locate fire extinguishers strategically throughout the establishment. Make sure that an extinguisher is available near each potential fire source. Also, keep at least one fire extinguisher in each catering vehicle.

- First-aid kits should be located on your premises and in your transportation vehicles. Teach your employees the Heimlich Maneuver. Remember, choking can happen at any time, but particularly when a person who has had too much to drink or eats their food too quickly.

- Complete an accident report for all accidents, however major or minor. Forward a copy to your workers' compensation insurer, OSHA (**www.osha.gov**), and the insurance company providing business insurance.

- Post emergency first-aid information. Ensure managers are trained and certified in first-aid procedures.

Heat and Burns

There are many ways employees can get burned in a food service environment. Burns can result from contact with hot surfaces such as grills, ovens, burners, fryers, and other heating equipment. Burns can also be caused by escaping steam or by hot food or drinks that are splattered, splashed or spilled. To prevent burns:

- Use thick, dry potholders or mitts, and stir food with long-handled spoons or paddles.

- Turn on hot-water faucets cautiously. Wear insulated rubber gloves for rinse water that is 170°F. Follow instructions for the use of cooking equipment—particularly steam equipment. Be sure all steam is expelled from steamers before opening the doors.

- Lift cooking lids and similar equipment away from yourself to avoid burns from steam.

- To avoid splattering and splashing, don't fill kettles too full, and don't allow food to boil over.

- Remember that oil and water don't mix, so be sure food is dry before you place it in a fryer.

- Point pan handles away from foot traffic, but also within reach, to avoid knocking over other pans.

- Do not crowd cooking surfaces with hot pans. Remove cooked foods from cooking surfaces immediately.

- Allow oil to cool, and use extreme caution when cleaning fryers.

- Use caution when removing hot pans from the oven. Wear insulated gloves or mitts, and be certain no one is in the removal path.

- Do not wear clothing that may drape onto a hot spot and catch on fire.

Cuts

Food service workers need to be careful not to get cut. And it's not just knives that can cause trouble—workers can hurt themselves or their coworkers with the sharp edges of equipment and supplies or with broken glass. Nails and staples used in food packaging can also be dangerous. To prevent cuts, take the following precautions:

- Use appropriate tools (not bare hands) to pick up and dispose of broken glass. Immediately place broken glass into a separate, clearly marked garbage container.

- Take care when cutting rolls of kitchen wrap with the cutter.

- Be careful with can openers and the edges of open cans. Never use a knife to open cans or to pry items loose.

- Use a pusher to feed food into a grinder.

- Turn off and unplug slicers and grinders when removing food and cleaning.

- Use guards on grinders and slicers.

- Replace equipment blades as soon as they are cleaned.

- Be aware that left-handed people need to take extra care when working with slicers and similar equipment. This is because the safety features are usually designed for right-handed people.

- Keep knives sharp; dull blades are harder to work with and cause more cuts than sharp ones.

- Never leave knives or equipment blades in the bottom of a sink.

- Carry knives by the handle with the tip pointed away from you. Never try to catch a falling knife.

- Cut away from yourself on a cutting board.

- Slice, do not hack.

Also, when storing or cleaning equipment, be sure to:

- Store knives and other sharp tools in special places when not in use.

- Wash dishes and glasses separately to help prevent them from being crushed by heavier objects and breaking in the dishwasher or sink.

- Do not stack glasses or cups inside one another.

- Watch out for nails, staples, and protruding sharp edges while unpacking boxes and crates.

Electrical Shock

Because of the variety of electrical equipment used in food service, electrical shock is a common concern. To prevent electrical shock:

- Properly ground all electrical equipment.

- Ensure that employees can reach switches without touching metal tables or counters.

- Replace all worn or frayed electrical cords.

- Use electrical equipment only when hands are dry.

- Unplug equipment before cleaning.

- Locate electrical switches and breakers to permit rapid shutdown in an emergency.

Strains

Carrying equipment or food items that are too heavy can result in strains to the arms, legs or back. Below are some tips to help avoid strains:

- Store heavy items on lower shelves.

- Use dollies or carts when moving objects that are too heavy to carry.

- To move objects from one area to another, use carts with firm shelves and properly operating wheels or casters.

- Don't carry too many objects at one time; instead, use a cart.

- Don't try to lift large or heavy objects by yourself.

- Use proper lifting techniques. Remember to bend from your knees, not your back.

Slipping and Falling

Anyone who slips and falls onto the floor can be badly hurt. Be sure your facility does not have hazards that put workers at risk. Safety tips include:

- Clean up wet spots and spills immediately.

- Let people know when floors are wet. Use signs that signal caution, and prominently display them. Wear shoes that have non-slip soles.

- Do not stack boxes or other objects too high. They can fall and cause people to trip.

- Keep items such as boxes, ladders, step stools and carts out of the paths of foot traffic.

Fires

More fires occur in food service than in any other type of operation. Fire extinguishers should be available in all areas where fires are likely, especially in the kitchen near grills and deep fryers. But be careful: don't keep extinguishers so close to the equipment that they will be inaccessible in the event of a fire.

All employees should be trained in avoiding fires as well as in the use of fire extinguishers and in evacuation procedures. Remember, always call the fire department first, before using a fire extinguisher!

Choking

Anyone can choke on food if he or she is not careful. That's why an important part of food service safety is being alert to your customers. Here's what to look for and what to do:

- If a person has both hands to the throat and cannot speak or cough, it is likely he or she is choking.

- If this person can talk, cough or breathe, do not pat him or her on the back or interfere in any way.

- If this person cannot talk, cough or breathe, you will need to take action. Use the Heimlich maneuver, and call for help immediately.

All food service employees should be trained in the use of the Heimlich Maneuver, and posters with instructions on how to perform it should be posted near the employee dining area.

Exposure to Hazardous Chemicals

Improper exposure to cleaning agents, chemical pesticides and chemical sanitizers may cause injury to the skin or poisoning. To protect workers from exposure to hazardous materials, special precautions need to be taken, including certain steps that are required by law. For example, OSHA requires food service establishments to keep a current inventory of all hazardous materials.

Manufacturers are required to make sure hazardous chemicals are properly labeled and must supply a Material Safety Data Sheet (MSDS) to be kept on file at the food service facility. The MSDS provides the chemical name of the product and physical hazards, health hazards, and emergency procedures in case of exposure.

Information about each chemical—including its common name, when it is used, who is authorized to use it, and information from the MSDS—must also be provided to workers. To prevent improper exposure to hazardous materials, make sure:

- Only properly trained workers handle hazardous chemicals.

- Employees have safety equipment to use when working with hazardous chemicals.

- Employees wear nonporous gloves and eye goggles when working with sanitizing agents and other cleaners.

Improper handling of food products or neglecting sanitation and safety procedures will certainly lead to health problems and personal injury. A successful caterer must develop a reputation for serving quality food in a safe environment. Should there ever be a question in your customers' minds as to the wholesomeness or quality of a product, the business will quickly lose its hard-earned reputation. The sanitation and safety procedures described in this section are very simple to initiate, but management must follow up and enforce them.

CASE STUDY: WORD FROM THE EXPERTS

THE RESULTS GROUP

LOCATION: Nashville, Tennessee

SERVICES: Michael Attias operates a restaurant in Nashville, Tennessee, and helps restaurant owners add or expand a catering profit center through his company, The Results Group. You can download his FREE Report: Tapping Into Your Hidden Catering Profit$ at www.ezRestaurantMarketing.com.

WIN-WIN RELATIONSHIPS By Michael Attias

There is a marketing technique called the host beneficiary relationship. It's really what I call win-win marketing. Somebody's got what you want, and you've got what they want. We have some hotels around town that don't have kitchens, so they re-market our catering to their groups that come in, and we do drop-off for them. I am piggybacking off that relationship.

We've done a picnic open house with non-competing businesses. We had one that provided the inflatables, clowns and entertainment, and the other company had a really nice campground, so we did a joint open house. We booked about $20,000 worth of catering at our first joint open house. All the businesses won by bringing their contacts and expertise to the event.

If you start your business at home,

you'll eliminate approximately 75 percent

of the startup costs you would have

starting in an alternate location..

Equipment

There are a great number of items you need to run a successful catering operation. Some are obvious: commercial stove and refrigeration unit; and others not so obvious: cutting boards and scales. In addition to equipment, you need to meet certain facility requirements, and this part of the handbook is designed to be a general guideline for the things you will need to get started in the catering business.

Kitchen and Service Equipment

Kitchens must have the appropriate amount of space for food production and appropriate traffic flow patterns to make everyone's work easier. If you are considering starting a catering operation in your existing kitchen, take some time to consider its size and layout.

A restaurant designer or consultant may be brought in to analyze your setup. In order to design the most efficient system possible, this person will need to know everything about your equipment, staff, menu, preparation procedures and sales. This is why it might be advantageous to contact one of these individuals after you have been operating for a while and have made all necessary changes. However, a designer certainly would be valuable in the initial planning stage. The savings derived from the increase in productivity and in employee morale created by your new setup will offset the cost of this consultant.

Kitchens will be based on how and where food products are received, stored, prepared, served, cleaned up and disposed of. A basic kitchen will need the following:

- Separate work surfaces for food-contact and non-food-contact areas.

- Work sinks for preparation and cleanup.

- Enough cutting surfaces to prevent cross-contamination.

- Storage for:

  - Utensils and small equipment.

  - Cooking equipment.

  - Food products that have been prepared for service.

  - Unused food products.

- Adequate refrigeration and freezer storage.

- Garbage facilities.

You may need to make some adjustments before you begin. If you are starting fresh, here are some considerations to keep in mind when designing and building:

- **The type of operation.** Will you be catering large events or small events? What type of food will you be preparing?

- **Type of menu and food service** you will offer.

- **How food is received.** This is probably the most important area in your entire installation. In general, you'll need a counter scale with a 500-pound capacity, a portion scale, space for inspecting incoming products, a stand-up desk or shelf for checking packing slips, and a heavy-duty hand truck for moving goods.

- **Where will food be stored.**

- **How often food is received.**

- **Types and amounts of ingredients that need to be stored.** How much cold and dry storage will you need? The dry storage should be dry, well ventilated, and maintained at a temperature between 55 and 60 degrees Fahrenheit. A thermometer should be placed in a prominent position to prevent temperatures fluctuating outside this range.

  - Dry storage shelves ought to be at least 6 inches off the floor and should be convenient for FIFO rotation. Avoid high stacking of cereal, flour and sugar. For expensive foods and equipment, a lockable valuable-items cabinet should be available.

  - Depending on the size of your operation, you may need one or several refrigerated storage areas. Keep in mind, however, that unnecessarily large refrigerators and freezers waste energy, thus increasing operating costs. Greater refrigerated storage requirements may be justified when extra delivery charges are incurred for small quantities.

- **Anticipated volume of work.**

- **Access.** Avoid establishing a kitchen in a building where you must use an elevator, either to enter the kitchen or to pass from one department to another.

- **Lighting.** Install adequate lighting (both gas and 220-volt electric). Maximize on natural lighting.

- **Ventilation.** Organize kitchen layout so as to make the most of natural ventilation. Also, take the extra precaution of placing ovens, ranges and steam kettles so that the mechanical exhaust units above them can operate at peak efficiency. Exhaust hoods above cooking areas should include automatic fire-fighting equipment.

- **Open space.** The placement of equipment should allow for sufficient aisle space. For a commissary-style operation, you'll need extra space for counting, organizing, packing, storing and shipping. For off-premise catering, it's important that you include sufficient space for all these extra activities.

Before you design your kitchen and choose equipment, be sure to find out whether the location and layout meet with local zoning laws. Check the zoning laws and the local board of health to determine what type of permit you need to setup a commercial kitchen. What are the restrictions regarding hours of operation? Is the parking space adequate for deliveries from vendors or for your employees? Also, check out whether there are waste and septic systems in place.

Major Equipment

Every year new pieces of equipment, large and small, expensive and inexpensive, are introduced that will save time, labor and energy. Aside from saving additional labor costs, new mechanization will reduce product handling, eliminate work drudgery, and make each task—as well as the overall job— more enjoyable for the employee.

The large initial capital expenditure for new equipment can usually be financed over several years through either the manufacturer or distributor. The total cost may be depreciated over several years and written off as a business tax-deductible expense.

Heavy kitchen equipment is expensive and should last a long time. When you are purchasing items such as ovens, freezers and grills, be sure to do your homework so you get what you really need, not just what the salesperson wants to sell you.

Henny Penny is a manufacturer of food service equipment including pressure fryers, open fryers, rotisseries, heated merchandisers, island merchandisers, display counter warmers, SmartHold humidified holding cabinets, heated holding cabinets for floor or countertop, bun warmers, SmartCooking Systems™, combis, blast chillers/freezers, and breading systems. Visit **www.hennypenny.com** *for more information or call 800-417-8417.*

Ranges and Ovens

Commercial kitchens generally favor gas stoves, which may be expensive, but they can be purchased at second-hand stores or auctions.

It is quite possible to manage without a range for a long time. One low-cost solution is to be licensed as a "cold" kitchen. You could also start with a half-sized convection oven, which can handle three large turkeys. Convection ovens are light, portable and very convenient. But, be aware that domestic ovens are not allowed in commercial kitchens by the board of health. Also, because they tend to dry food out, caterers are increasingly opting for the new convection steam ovens that operate as pressure-less steamers—a high-humidity convection oven.

If you are buying a regular commercial oven, you can purchase a range oven combination, or there are stackable ovens as well. Stack ovens are good because you can buy one at a time and add as your business increases. They also take up less floor space.

Flat-top stoves are useful because you can fit any size pan on the burners. They come with four or six burners in the standards sizes. These stoves provide fast, high heat needed for items like omelets and for sautéing.

Griddle stoves are good for quickly sautéing small amounts of food, such as diced onions that you are going to put in another dish. These stoves can also be used to keep foods warm and as a griddle for items such as French toast and pancakes.

One of the latest trends in ovens is induction cooking. The induction cooktop is becoming increasingly popular with caterers. They come in a variety of forms, from full-sized ranges to portable hot plates. They cook food quickly, are easy to use, and easy to clean. Induction cooktops can be used with any type of food, and will cook as thoroughly and evenly as any electric or gas range. Induction cooking can be used with any type of cookware from frying pans to woks. However, it only works when used with magnetic-based materials, such as iron and steel, that will allow an induced current to flow within them.

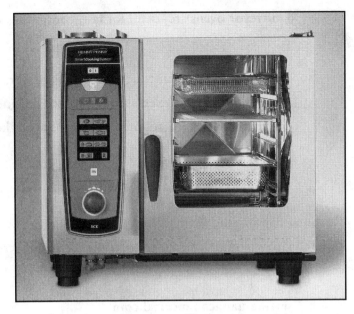

SmartCooking System™ from Henny Penny. Cooking a complete menu is simple. Press the SmartCooking Control™ key, and select the type of food. It cooks everything from roasts to fish to casseroles to pies, literally at the touch of a button. For greater control, simply press the moist heat or dry heat mode keys and set time, temperature, and special functions.

Combi ovens, also known as steamers, are a caterer's dream. These ovens combine the browning capacity of a regular oven with convection steam cooking, keeping meats moist and preventing cooking loss. They also cook 30 to 40 percent faster than conventional convection ovens. Roasting in combi mode reduces shrinkage 20 to 30 percent (and food cost), yielding a juicier product. Shellfish cook rapidly in steam mode without washing out flavors or dealing with heavy stockpots. Hot-air mode operates as a normal convection oven for baking cookies, cakes and flaky pastries. High-sugar recipes are less likely to scorch when using combi mode. Breads, pastries and other yeast-raised products bake up higher and lighter with combi mode.

*Blodett's Gas Boilerless Combination Oven/Steamer. To see a complete selection of Blodett's combi ovens, visit **www.blodgett.com** or call 800-331-5842.*

Other oven options include:

- **Deck ovens.** These horizontal ovens can be used for baking and roasting and usually have one shelf each.

- **Rotating ovens** have rotating shelves and are used as high-production ovens.

- **Conveyor ovens** are useful for fast, continuous production such as pizzas or steaks for large parties.

- **Roll-in ovens** are constructed so you can roll racks of food directly into the oven. These are great ovens for large events. Roll-in ovens designed for baking have steam injectors and some come equipped with automatic thermostats to keep the food at a desired temperature.

- **Low-temperature ovens** cook at a temperature so that a hood is not required. Like the combi oven, meat cooked in a low-temperature oven stays moist and shrinkage is minimal.

Restaurant shows and food service magazines are the best places to look for the announcement and review of new equipment. You can also visit manufacturer's Web sites or other sites that let you compare brands and prices, such as:

- **www.amanacommerical.com**

- **www.hennypenny.com**

- **http://Web1.panasonic.com/food_service/cmo**

- **www.ckitchen.com**

- **www.abestkitchen.com**

- **www.bevles.com**

- **www.horizonfoodequipment.com**

- **www.restaurantequipment.net**

- **www.hatcocorp.com**

- **www.blodgett.com**

- **www.business.com/directory/food_and_beverage/restaurants_and_foodservice/ equipment_and_supplies/cooking_and_baking/ovens**

GRILLS, SMOKERS AND ROTISSERIES

Grills provide a cooking source that gives food an attractive appearance. The grill marks on steaks or vegetables add to a winning plate presentation. For most catering operations, grills are used to mark food and to pre-cook it. Then the food is finished in the oven.

You can find gas, charcoal and electric grills. While charcoal grills are seldom used in a catering kitchen, you may want to add this or a wood stove if you are serving dishes that require a particular smoked flavor or are thinking of creating a signature dish. Gas grills have lava stones. The fat dripping onto the stones gives flavor to the meat.

If you will be catering specialty items, such as barbecue, you may be interested in a grill or rotisserie. There are numerous types and many manufacturers to choose from. Check out:

- **Big John Grills & Rotisseries** has designed, manufactured, packaged and distributed outdoor cooking equipment for over 42 years. The extensive product line includes gas grills, portable gas grills, smokers, roasters, portable griddles, steam tables, gas towables, utility stoves, smokers, portable fryers, countertop fryers, ovens and ranges, as well as countertop griddles, broilers and fryers. For more information, visit **www.bigjohngrills.com** or call 800-326-9575.

- **Belson Outdoors** also has a wide selection of portable grills including the PORTA-GRILL® Mobile Trailer Mounted Barbecue Grills, Pig Roaster Rotisserie for PORTA-GRILL® Commercial Barbecue Grills, Chicken & Rib Roaster Rotisserie for PORTA-GRILL®,

The E-Z Way Roaster is a product of Big John Grills & Rotisseries. You simply open the hood, place a pig inside, fill the smoking trough with wood chips, start the fuel-efficient 80,000 Btu gas burner, and walk away. Come back hours later to enjoy a delicious pig pickin' party. The entire process of preparing a moist, tender, flavorful pig roast is that easy.

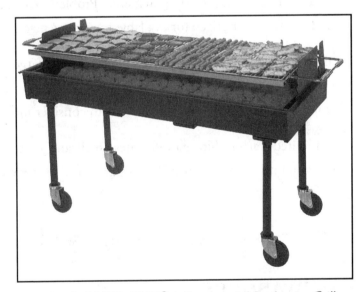

Belson's PORTA-GRILL® I Commercial Barbecue Grill. This charcoal-fired model is big enough to feed large gatherings, yet light enough to be transported without a trailer. It has casters for short trips and removable legs for long trips. With a sanitary nickel-plated cooking grate made from round steel bars, it easily adjusts to four different cooking heights. Patented flip-back grill feature allows for easy charcoal servicing and cleaning.

and PORTA-GRILL® Corn & Potato Roaster Barbecue Grills. Visit **www.belson.com** or call 800-323-5664.

- **Holstein Manufacturing.** Offering custom-built products, Holstein Manufacturing has numerous products popular with the catering industry including a six-foot towable barbecue grill, a corn roaster, a deep-fat fryer and portable concession trailer. For more information, visit **www.holsteinmfg.com** or call 800-368-4342.

- **Cookshack** offers state-of-the-art electric smoker ovens, such as the SmartSmoker with electronic controls, pre-programmed for brisket, ribs and chicken. It is available in four sizes and eight models to fit your needs. For more information, **visit www.cookshack.com** or call 1-800-423-0698.

Refrigerators and Freezers

At least one separate refrigerator and one large freezer are essential. As for their size, double the minimum capacity needed for your refrigerator to keep food for a good-sized event. Don't forget that you need space for usable leftovers as well. In addition, you'll need refrigerated space for deliveries such as dairy items, salads, vegetables, meats, fish and poultry. In general, a large commercial refrigerator will accommodate all these requirements. Problems can develop, however. It's a good idea to have a second freezer and refrigerator available for emergencies.

Walk-in freezers and refrigerators are used by most larger operations. These allow plenty of room to roll in carts of food as well as providing shelf space. You will also want smaller reach-in refrigeration to store small items, and you might want to consider mobile refrigerators for transporting food.

Leer Limited Partnership manufactures stock and custom walk-in coolers and freezers. They offer standard nominal sizes to special configurations. Visit **www.leerlp.com** to see their product line.

Other Kitchen Equipment

DISHWASHERS

Consider a commercial dishwasher with more than two racks. It saves time when storing glasses on dishwasher trays. Heat generated by dishwashers can be a problem. Solve the problem by installing a condenser over the dishwasher. Choose a dishwashing system that is engineered to meet your kitchen's requirements. Base your decision on such factors as the space available, layout, traffic flow, amount and type of food soil, and the hardness of the water.

WASHER AND DRYER

There will be aprons, towels, napkins and uniforms to clean regularly. Invest in a robust washer and dryer, from the start. Choose a large-capacity, heavy-duty model.

BRAISING PANS AND TILT KETTLES

These pans come in many sizes and can be used for soups, stocks, stews, and even frying. They should have a water spigot for cleaning and a deep trough on the floor to catch any liquid when the pan is titled. These are used in large commercial kitchens. Smaller catering operations will probably not have the space.

Blodett's Electric Tabletop Tilting Round Braising Pan.

Blodgett has long been recognized as a manufacturer of premium equipment for the food service industry. Available in electric or gas, Blodgett's braising pans have four different tilting mechanisms from which to choose: tabletop or floor model, manual, gearbox, power or hydraulic tilt.

STEAM KETTLES

Steam kettles are surrounded by jackets that have steam injected into them to heat the kettle. This piece of equipment is available in a variety of sizes from 5 gallons to 100 gallons. Like tilt frying pans, these should have a facet and a trough for draining.

Blodgett's Gas Quad-Leg Stationary Kettle.

Direct-steam kettles are available in a variety of sizes (from 6 to 100 gallons) for connection to an outside steam source, such as the Blodgett steam boiler cabinets.

SALAMANDER

This handy device is used as an overhead heat source to brown food. The Blodgett Infrared Salamander Broilers broil in half the time with a third less gas than ordinary broilers. The burners reach operating temperature in just 90 seconds, and their intense infrared energy quickly heats the food, not the surrounding air. The broiling grid adjusts to five heights, and rolls out for easy access. See **www.blodgett.com** for more details or call 800-331-5842.

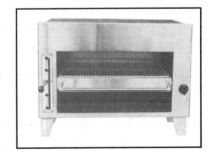

Blodgett's Infrared Salamander Broiler.

SLICER

A slicer should have a large blade, control handle, heavy body to prevent sliding when used, and a safety on/off switch.

Small Equipment

You should analyze a number of factors in order to determine your small-equipment needs. The number of guests that you intend to serve as well as the type of menu items are factors in what equipment you should purchase. For example, if you sell cold canapés, you'll need to invest in rolling racks and refrigerated storage; if you sell deep-fried hors d'oeuvres, you could store the raw product in plastic containers. Although the type of equipment needed is very specific to your type of operation, the following section contains a basic overview of what most operations will need.

The are a variety of sources for small equipment. It is a good idea to compare various sources for price and quality. Small equipment can also be very personal. Many chefs have a preferred brand or manufacturer.

Browne-Halco is a prime supplier of small equipment in the United States. They offer in excess of 3,000 smallwares products. Browne-Halco's objective is to provide food service operators with high-quality and cost-efficient smallwares products. For further details and to view the Browne-Halco product line, visit **www.halco.com**.

Franklin Machine Products is another leading supplier of parts and accessories for the food service industry. Their annual catalog is over 1,000 pages and offers an enormous selection of products. For further details and to view the FMP product line, visit **www.FMPonline.com**.

POTS AND PANS

The type, number and size of pots and pans you'll need is highly dependant on the menus you offer. Make sure to purchase plenty of hotel pans, half-hotel pans, sheet pans and half-sheet pans. You'll find a multitude of uses for these—cooking a chicken stew to baking cookies, transporting individual appetizers and using as shelves in cambros. Following are some sources for pots and pans:

Elegance Stainless Steel Cookware by Regal Ware.

*Elegance Stainless Steel Cookware
by Regal Ware.*

*Elegance Stainless Steel Cookware
by Regal Ware.*

Regal Ware Food Service, a division of Regal Ware Worldwide™, specializes in providing top-quality beverage and food preparation products to the food service industry. With craftsmanship dating back to 1945, Regal Ware Food Service offers a variety of products. Visit **www.regalwarefoodservice.com** or call 262-626-2121 for more information.

- **Sitram Cookware.** For more than 40 years, Sitram has supplied chefs across Europe with a comprehensive range of heavy-duty "Catering" cookware. Sitram's success is the result of the heavy copper bottom sandwiched between two layers of stainless steel. Copper is a good conductor of heat and guarantees fast, uniform heat distribution. Extremely durable, the cookware is also impervious to acidic foods: won't pit, discolor or alter the flavors of foods. It's dishwasher safe and carries a lifetime limited warranty. Visit **www.sitramcookware.com /catering** or call 800-515-8585 for more information.

Sitram's Catering (Inox) Collection.

- **Polar Ware Company.** Polar Ware has a wide selection of food preparation, serving and storage products—from heavy-duty mixing bowls to kitchen utensils and storage canisters. They also offer a wide variety of stainless steel and tri-ply stainless steel stock pots and matching covers. The aluminum cookware line is manufactured using deep draw techniques perfected by Polar Ware. Visit **www.polarware.com** or call 800-237-3655 for more information.

Polar Ware Aluminum Cookware.

- **Browne-Halco.** Browne-Halco offers an extensive line of high-quality cookware that is both durable and reliable. Eagleware® Cookware is their premier line of professional aluminum cookware. It features a thick bottom construction for even heat distribution as well as a heavy top with smooth rim. The beadless rim eliminates food traps and makes cleaning easier. Other product lines include Futura Stainless Steel Professional Cookware and Thermalloy Aluminum Cookware. To view the online catalog, visit **www.halco.com** or call 888-289-1005 for more information.

Bain-marie

A bain-marie is a water bath used to keep stocks and soups hot until service. The best height is 20 inches; this will provide depth, but also allow you to easily lift pans into and out of the water bath.

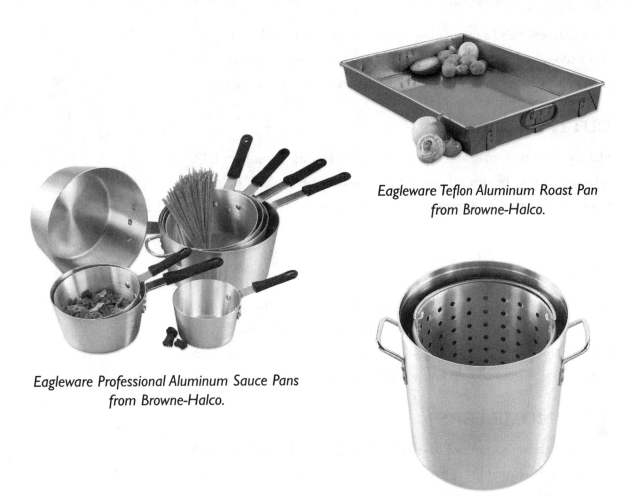

Eagleware Teflon Aluminum Roast Pan from Browne-Halco.

Eagleware Professional Aluminum Sauce Pans from Browne-Halco.

Eagleware Stock Pot, Lid and Aluminum Basket from Browne-Halco.

FOOD PROCESSING EQUIPMENT

Depending on your menus, you may want to consider purchasing the following items to use for food prep:

- Meat grinder
- Food processor
- Hand-held mixers
- Stand mixers
- Vacuum machine for vacuum packing food
- Immersion blender

KNIVES

Invest in the best chef's knife (sometimes called a French knife), carving knife (slicer), large serrated knife, and several smaller paring knives that the budget will allow. Complete the collection with a knife sharpener and a sharpening stone. For special purposes, you may also need a boner and a fillet knife. Learn how to sharpen and hone your knives. Hone them regularly and sharpen them about once a year.

CUTTINGBOARDS

Have at least two small and two large cutting boards. Look for HDP (plastic) cutting boards as opposed to wooden ones, as any odor or stain on polyethylene boards can easily be removed with a chlorine soak.

6" Portion-Control Scale from Browne-Halco.

SCALES

Have at least three scales: one so sensitive that it can weigh a cinnamon stick accurately; one less accurate that can weigh anything from 3 to 10 pounds; and a third larger scale that can weigh at least 25 pounds. They should also be used to help you accurately measure portions.

THERMOMETERS

Thermometers are critical to food safety. You will need to check temperature frequently to make sure you are preparing and holding food properly. There are a wide variety of thermometers available.

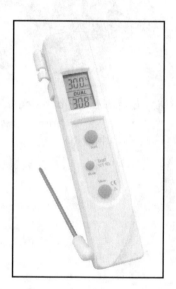

The ThermaTwin Infrared Thermometer.

FOOD WHIP

For delicate operations or desserts, whipped creams and sauces that need to be prepared at the last minute, you may want to have a food whip on hand. iSi NorthAmerica makes a variety of whippers. For more information, visit **www.isinorthamerica.com/foodservice** or call 800-447-2426.

Equipment for Serving Food

CHINA

If you are a smaller operation or home-based caterer, you may want to leave the china to the rental companies. It takes up a lot of storage space and is very heavy to move from location to location. When providing off-site catering, many of the locations you use may also have their own china sets, so you may not need to rent or buy; be sure to check when doing your

iSi Cream and Food Whipper.

pre-event work. Or, consider disposable options. See Chapter 12 for a listing a manufacturers who offer disposable flatware, serving and catering products.

If you do purchase china, at a minimum you should purchase the following types of dishes:

- Service plates
- Dinner plates
- Bread plates
- Luncheon plates
- Salad plates
- Soup bowls
- Cups and saucers

- Relish trays
- Platters
- Ramekins
- Ashtrays
- Sherbet/ice cream cups
- Dessert plates

How much of these you buy depends on the size of events you cater.

You may also want to consider:

- Champagne buckets and stands
- Compotes (footed candy/nut dishes)
- Creamer and sugar sets
- Salt and pepper sets
- Display trays

FLATWARE

Again, depending on the volume of work you do and the types of events you cater, you may want to consider renting rather than buying flatware. If you do purchase flatware, you'll want it to be an attractive pattern. Open stock designs are the least expensive to purchase. You basic flatware needs will be:

- Dinner fork
- Salad fork
- Fish fork
- Dessert fork
- Dinner knife

- Butter spreader
- Steak knife
- Soup spoon
- Teaspoon
- Iced tea spoon

You will also need serving pieces such as:

- Salad tongs
- Large serving forks

- Large serving spoon
- Cake knife and server

Browne-Halco carries many different lines of flatware suited to different tastes and budgets. Below are a few options. To view their online catalog, visit **www.halco.com** or call 888-289-1005 for more information.

Celine Pattern Flatware.

Dominion Pattern Flatware.

Elegance Pattern Flatware.

GLASSWARE

Glassware, like china and flatware, can either be purchased or rented. Dining room glasses should include:

- Fruit juice glass (5 ounces)

- Water tumbler (8 to10 ounces)

- General beverage glass (9 ounces)

- Iced tea glass (12 ounces)

If you serve alcohol, you will also need:

- Wineglasses (red and white)

- Beer mugs or glasses

- On-the-rocks glasses

COFFEE SERVICE

You will definitely want to purchase a good coffee urn. An urn is simply a large coffee pot with a spout. They typically come in 35-cup and 85-cup models. You can also purchase attractive serving containers for your servers to take around the dining room. Following are some coffee service manufacturers and options:

Zojirushi's Stainless Steel Lined Thermal Gravity Pot® (Coffee Server).

Zojirushi's Satellite Coffee Server.

Regal Ware 2.2 Liter, 2.5 Liter and 3
Liter Stainless Steel
Lever Air Pot.

Regal Ware 101 Cup Black Satin
Aluminum Coffee Urn.

Regal Ware Food Service offers a variety of commercial coffeemakers including stainless steel and aluminum. They also offer vacuum-insulated thermal carafes and vacuum-insulated airpots. Visit **www.regal- warefoodservice.com** or call 262-626-2121 for more information.

- **The Gravity Flow Beverage Dispensers by Zojirushi** provide an ideal way to keep coffee hot and fresh-tasting while using the force of gravity for quick and easy serving. These dispensers minimize the coffee's contact with air; the freshly brewed taste is sealed in. They also provide exceptional heat retention to ensure the coffee

Regal Ware 1.5 Liter, 2 Liter and 1 Liter
Stainless Steel Thermal Carafes.

remains hot until served. Products include the Satellite Coffee Servers, Thermal Gravity Pots®, Stainless Steel Lined Thermal Gravity Pots®, as well as carafes, air pots and servers. To learn more about the entire collection of serving products by Zojirushi, call 800-733-6270 or visit **www.zojirushi.com**.

- **ASTORIA espresso and cappuccino coffee machines by General Espresso Equipment** are available in a variety of commercial lines. The Astoria JADA Super Automatic is the most productive espresso and cappuccino machine in the world. Two independent brewing groups can dispense four espresso servings simultaneously. The JADA  is controlled by an advanced user-friendly micro-processor system with easy-to-read, easy-to-operate touch pads and an illuminated electronic functions display. The Astoria Sibilla is available in one, two or three brewing heads (groups) with six programmable/volumetric portion selections and an override semiautomatic button. It can produce up to 240 espresso servings per hour. For more information, visit **www.espressobrewer.com** or call 336-393-0224.

TRAYS

You'll need trays for all sorts of tasks in your business. Make sure to have a ready supply of waiter trays (22 by 22 inches), kitchen trays (15 by 20 inches) and bar trays (12 by 14 inches with a cork surface).

PLATTERS

In addition to trays, you will need serving platters. These can be used directly for service on a buffet or carried by waitstaff. Stock a variety of sizes or look into renting platters for larger occasions.

Browne-Halco carries stainless steel oval serving platters that range in size from 14" x 9" to 26" x 18". Round platters are also available.

BUSBOXES

These are used to carry dirty dishware from the dining room to the back kitchen area for washing. They are usually made of plastic and measure 12 by 18 inches to 18 by 24 inches.

TABLES

You can never have too much work space when preparing catered events. Purchase stainless steel worktables that have shelves to store equipment. Make sure tables are placed close to electrical outlets so you can use slicers, mixers, blenders, etc. You may also want to purchase mobile worktables.

Depending on your menu and the locations you cater, you may find the need to cook some things on-site. If you do, make sure this equipment is portable. Some items that many caterers find useful to include in the pantry are:

- Electric frying pan
- Hot plate
- Small microwave
- Crock pot

CHAFING DISHES AND STEAM PANS

You'll also want to invest in two or three chafing dishes or steam pans to use for buffet services. These dishes are used on buffets to keep dishes hot. They usually are silver pans with a cover that sit in a stand. A heat source is placed under the dish to keep food items warm during service. They are

Deluxe Full-Size Chafer.

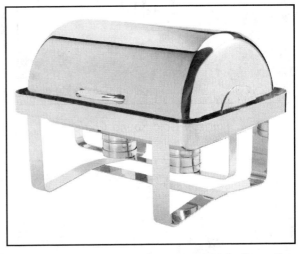

Deluxe Heavyweight Chafer with 180° Rolltop Cover.

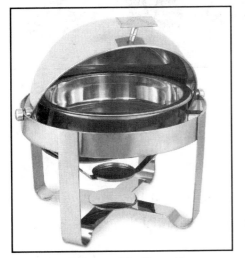

Deluxe Round Rolltop Cover.

Economy Chafer.

generally available in 2-, 4-, and 8-quart sizes. There are a variety of chafers available and range from utilitarian to artistic display pieces. Following are some options:

- **Browne-Halco** offers a full line of chafers and buffet servingware. Below are a few options. To view their online catalog, visit **www.halco.com** or call 888-289-1005 for more information.

- **Polar Ware Company.** Polar Ware has a wide selection of chafers, components, accessories and serving utensils. Below are a few options. Visit **www.polarware.com** or call 800-237-3655 for more information.

Horizon Gold Round Chafer.

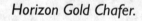

Horizon Gold Chafer.

Economy Chafer.

Sierra Chafer.

WARMERS

In addition to steam pans and chafers, there are other types of warmers available, usually specific to certain types of foods. For example, if you cater numerous soup and sandwich luncheons, you may want to look into a soup warmer.

- **Micom Soup Warmer.** A free-standing appliance with five keep-warm temperature settings, this warmer keeps soup at the perfect serving temperature. It also works for keeping chili, nacho cheese dip, and other items hot and ready to serve. It also features a dry-type keep-warm operation that requires no water for keeping the inner pan warm. Select the desired temperature setting and the unit's direct thermal sensor system will automatically regulate the heating elements around the inner pan to ensure the selected temperature is maintained. It has a two-gallon capacity, and the stainless steel inner pan can be used directly on a stovetop burner to prepare

soups of many varieties—this eliminates the need to use and clean an extra stockpot when preparing soup. For more information on the Micom Soup Warmer and other products by Zojirushi, call 800-733-6270 or visit **www.zojirushi.com**.

COOLING EQUIPMENT

Many dishes need to be held and served cold. There are a variety of products that make this simple:

- **FILL 'N CHILL™ Party Table** from Chillin' Products. Place this table in any convenient location, load it with 75 pounds of ice, and fill it with food and drink. It features rugged yet lightweight construction and has a durable, easy-to-clean, one-piece, FDA-approved, polyethylene top. The bottom is tapered with a centrally located drain. It is easy to transport and store. The steel legs are collapsible. For more information visit **www.chillinproducts. com** or call 866-932-4455.

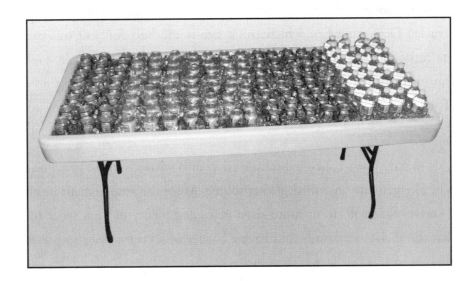

- **Satellite Cold Buffet System.** The patented Satellite Cooling System is the chef-designed innovative solution for food safety, presentation and mobility. It solves the problem of how to keep buffet appetizers, entrées and desserts cold at a consistent, regulated temperature while maintaining a fresh, attractive appearance. It eliminates ice and decreases labor costs and food waste. The Satellite Cooling System is NSF approved, can be setup virtually anywhere, and is completely mobile. For more information, visit **www.satellitecool.com** or call 888-356-2665.

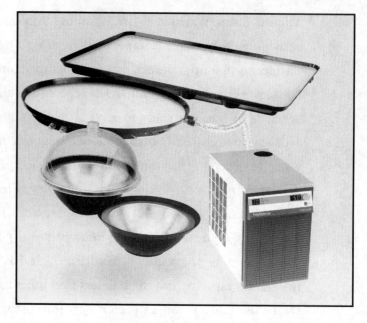

Equipment for Transporting Food

Caterers, unlike restaurants, need equipment to use for transporting food. On-site caterers will need to get food from the kitchen to event rooms that may be on the other end of the building, and off-site caterers often will need to transport food across town.

TRUCK OR VAN

You will need at least one vehicle for transporting food and supplies to the event location. Commit yourself to a professional-looking and practical vehicle. Larger operations, however, will need refrigerated trucks. Determine first which truck size is the best for you (no matter what amount you anticipate carrying, your vehicle is always too small). Vans, for example, are practical and very economical for off-premise caterers that rent tables and chairs for events, instead of supplying them themselves. Trucks, on the other hand, are expensive and you may find it's more cost-effective to rent them.

You may decide to have a self-contained refrigeration unit with a built-in generator, or a refrigeration unit that can be plugged into an outside power source. As for the arrangement inside, you should have a set of fixed shelves for small- to medium-sized items and plenty of floor space for large equipment. Make sure that the shelves are sturdy and have a barrier of several inches to prevent slippage during transportation.

If you don't own a large vehicle, check into renting one. Compare rates when you call, and make sure the rental company knows you are a business. If you do use rental vehicles, make sure to include the cost in your estimates.

CARRYING CASES

Make sure you have carrying cases for all your equipment needs:

- Glass boxes for glassware such as wineglasses, iced tea glasses, and water tumblers.

- Boxes for your chafing dishes.

- Plastic containers for flatware, linens, kitchen utensils, serving utensils, pitchers, etc.

- Boxes and packing material for any platters you take.

- Boxes for china and coffee cups.

You can find a wide selection of food transport items at **www.cambro.com**.

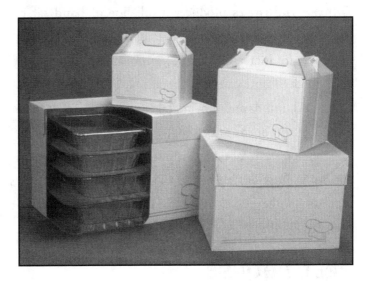

Wes-Pak offers pop-up food service carriers, which are an affordable alternative. Perfect for one-time, temporary use, no assembly is required. The Pop-Up Carriers are quick and easy to load. They are lightweight yet durable, and with their leak-proof liners, these carriers are great for cooling drinks and storing ice and they handle hot food pans with ease. Once the food is unloaded, disposal is easy—simply flatten them with a quick push and place them in the recycling bin. No assembly, no retrieval, no cleaning necessary. For more information, visit **www.wespakinc.com** or call 800-493-7725.

HOLDING OVEN

During transportation and setup, a holding oven is usually required to keep food hot. These are used to keep dinner rolls, roasts, turkeys, chicken breasts, and all other hot food at the right temperature when you are transporting to the site.

ICE CHESTS

It's also a good idea to invest in some large ice chests. You will have drinks, fruit, vegetables, and dairy products you will want to keep cool during transport.

ROLLING RACKS

If you are an on-premise caterer or working a large event, rolling racks can hold a lot of food in a small space. These racks can hold sheet trays of prepared foods or raw foods that can then be placed in the oven to cook.

KITCHEN GRIPS AND MITTS

You will need these when transporting hot dishes. It is a good idea to invest in quality mitts with a good grip. You don't want to have food loss due to dropping and spilling.

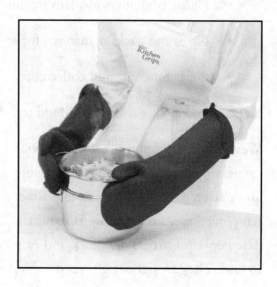

Duncan Industries produces a full line of hand safety products including oven mitts and hot pads. They are designed to increase safety, hygiene and sanitation in your kitchen and catering operation. They repel water, steam and liquids and provide maximum protection from painful steam burns caused by wet protection equipment. Textured crosscut fabric provides a safer grip and increased control in busy operations. They are dishwasher safe and stain resistant. They are also sub-zero safe, so you can handle freezer foods, even dry ice. For more information, visit **www.kitchengrips.com** or call 800-785-4449.

CELL PHONES

Cell phones are great investments. Sending cell phones with your crew to event sites lets them stay in contact with you if things go wrong or if they forget something and need to send someone back. It's also a good safety measure in case the crew has vehicle trouble along the way.

Additional Equipment

EMPLOYEE UNIFORMS

How you and your employees present themselves can be as important as the food presentation. If you wear uniforms, make sure they are clean and neat. Have aprons available for staff. Many linen rental companies will supply items such as jackets for cooks and waiters. or you may want to invest in chef's coats and hats. Following are some sources:

Dickies Chef. Since 1922 Dickies has stood for the quality, toughness and pride that embodies the spirit of the American worker. Dickies and Selecta Corp, LLC are proud to present the Chef Collection. It offers a wide selection of shirts, coats, pants, aprons and hats with the same quality and durability of the Dickies brand. To view the collection online, visit **www .dickieschef.com** or call 866-262-6288 to order a catalog.

Dickies Floppy Print Hat, Pepper Row Pattern.

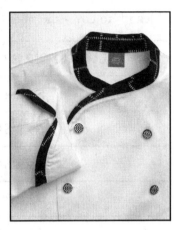

Detail of one of Dickies Chef's Coats.

Dickies Skull Cap, Chef's Coat and Pants.

Aprons, Etc. If you are looking for an apron, smock or vest with your logo printed on it, Aprons, Etc. is an excellent source. They have a huge selection of fabrics, colors and styles from which to choose. They also supply restaurant, chef,

Chef's Hats and Attire from Aprons, Etc.

Tuxedo-Style Apron from Aprons, Etc.

waitstaff and bar apparel. Visit **www.apronsetc.com**. to view the collection online and find a distributor in your area.

LINEN

Linen is another item you can purchase or rent. While most rental companies do offer more unusual colors and patterns, for the most part these are more expensive and they have fewer in stock. If you expect that you'll need these types of linens often, you might want to consider purchasing them. Remember, however, if you do purchase linens, you also have to launder and iron them after every use!

Whether you rent or buy, your tablecloths will need to cover buffet and dining tables and have plenty of length to cover the sides. The following chart provides standard linen sizes.

LINEN SIZE (INCHES)	TABLE SIZE
44 x 44	32 inch
54 x 54	48- to 50-inch round
64 x 64	60-inch round
72 x 72	68-inch round
81 x 81	77-inch round
90 x 90	84-inch round
44 x 64	5-foot rectangular
54 x 72	5-foot rectangular
54 x 96	7-foot rectangular
54 x 120	8-foot rectangular
54 x 144	8-foot rectangular
72 x 144	10-foot rectangular
80 x 120	8-foot rectangular
80 x 144	10-foot rectangular

DINNER NAPKINS

Dinner napkins are 20 inches by 20 inches, and lunch napkins are 18 inches by 18 inches.

The colors most frequently used on buffet tables are white, pale yellow, pale pink, blue (medium and light), and red, and bright colors such as yellow, green and orange for informal events.

In addition to dining room linen, you will need kitchen cloth items as well. Make sure your cooks also have an ample supply of potholders, dish towels, hand towels, bar rags, and mop-up rags.

PAPER GOODS

If you cater informal events, you will want to have a supply of paper plates and napkins and plastic cups and flatware. You can purchase these items in bulk at stores such as Gordon's Food Service or Sam's Club. Chapter 12 also has a listing of manufacturers and resources for disposable items.

You'll also want a supply of various sizes of doilies for dessert and appetizer trays as well as paper cocktail napkins for bar service.

THE SMALL STUFF

Make sure your crews always go out with the following items:

- Dish towels
- Plastic storage bags
- Garbage bags
- A first-aid kit

Logos. If you want to have your logo inscribed on your china and glassware, be discreet; you do not want to appear to be advertising. Offer individual house drinks and special desserts in large footed hurricane glasses, or oversized parfait glasses, etched or imprinted with your business name.

Decorative items. Ranging from tiny to huge, you can find inexpensive baskets from various sources. In addition, you'll need attractive candleholders, vases, and other décorative table pieces. Start a collection of special items for specific events. Let the client think that the preparation was designed personally for them.

Additional Resources to Find Equipment

Now that you know what you need for your operation, how do you find it? We have listed many manufacturers in this chapter from which you can purchase directly. There are also many other avenues to try when searching for equipment. Make sure you're creative when looking for the larger items; you are likely to save some money.

- **Restaurant equipment stores** are a good place to start. Make sure to check the Yellow Pages for second-hand stores. It may also be worth a trip to the National Restaurant Show held each May in Chicago. Major areas of focus include food, beverage, equipment, apparel, furnishings, and design. You can get information about the show from the National Restaurant Association.

- **Retail stores** such as Homegoods and T.J. Maxx are a good option for china and hotel-quality pans. These types of stores are often hit or miss, but if you can find what you are looking for, the price is usually right.

- **Networking** is also a way to find equipment. You should talk to friends in the business. If they are catering part time, you may be able to borrow equipment or split the cost and use of new equipment.

- **Restaurant equipment auctions** are a good place to look for the large and small items. You can find everything from ovens to rolling racks to boxes of flatware. Since these are usually going-out-of-business sales, the prices tend to be pretty attractive.

Here are some additional ideas for where to find equipment:

- **www.chefscatalog.com** and **www.chefswear.com.** These aren't the most cost effective sources for equipment and uniforms, but they are convenient!

- **Online auctions.** This is another hit-or-miss source, but it's worth pursuing. Log on and register at **www.ebay.com**.

- **Institution sales.** Some colleges make their old equipment available to the public at dirt-cheap prices. The items for sale can include desks, fluorescent lighting, industrial fryers, and steam tables. Call around to your area colleges and universities to see if such a program exists.

Equipment is an area where you don't want to scrimp. Spend the money up front for quality items and avoid the hassle and expense of having to replace pieces only months later.

Recordkeeping

A record system is an important part of your business management system. To be successful, it should be disciplined, current, and regularly reconciled. With up-to-date bookkeeping you'll know whether you are making a profit, barely breaking even, or in real financial trouble.

Your records system and bookkeeping activities provide a steady flow of information about the state of your business. They are a quick and accurate means to compile, record and analyze your business activity.

Information from your business records will help you avoid potentially damaging mistakes, such as investing or spending too much, setting incorrect prices, or not accruing enough to pay your yearly income taxes.

Setting Up a Records System

Before you spend any money on your business, setup a record system using the accounts we discussed in the Business Plan chapter. In your record of startup expenditures, include both operating expenses and capital purchases prior to the business opening. Typical expenditure categories include legal and accounting services; remodeling and painting; utilities (heating, water, electricity); vehicle mileage; and the variety of supplies and other expense items unique to your business. Be sure to keep accurate records of your start-up inventory.

After your business opens, your business records will document all operating costs; the gross and net costs of additions to inventory; the dates and dollar value of all sales; and, if you have employees, the hiring and tax status for each as required by Internal Revenue Service and Immigration and Naturalization Service regulations. Under these agencies you must keep records for each employee indicating hours worked, wages, and payroll taxes withheld and deposited in accordance with applicable rules and regulations.

Your records system provides the framework for your bookkeeping activities. If you are not familiar with bookkeeping principles, it is best to have a professional setup your system for you. Whether you setup a paper system or computer system depends on the level of your computer skills, your recordkeeping experience, and the nature of your business.

If your business is small and you're not computer proficient, it is best to keep track of your records manually. If you are comfortable with computers and have access to one, then a computerized system makes sense as there are many inexpensive options from which to choose.

You must also decide if you will use single-entry or double-entry record system. In double-entry systems, all business transactions are entered in a journal and then posted to accounts using procedures that allow excellent control of errors. Single-entry systems are less controlled but much more efficient. In fact, most computerized systems use the single-entry method.

ESSENTIAL RECORDS

The principle categories of records that you need are the ones that provide the basis for income tax preparation and management decision-making purposes.

Capital Assets Account – This is a cumulative listing of purchases, sales/exchanges, and annual depreciation of all capital items.

Inventory Account – This is your record of goods or products held for sale by your business. Inventory entries usually contain a count of items (physical inventory) and the dollar cost (inventory value) of those items. Purchases and sales are the primary entries.

Sales Ledger – When you sell services, the ledger is your record by customer (client) and by service you've provided, charges and payments for those services, and any refunds you've made.

Checking Account Ledger – If your business is small, this ledger may be the check register for your business checkbook. As your business grows, or as information needs grow, you may want to keep a separate ledger and more complete information (possibly with voucher copies) for each check and deposit.

Business Files – This is the filing system for all of the deeds, licenses, permits, contracts, leases, agreements, insurance policies, personnel records, and other documents making up the legal foundation of your business operation. You need to be able to refer to these whenever needed, and to have easy access to the amounts and due dates of payments.

Bookkeeping is one of the more tedious but absolutely essential responsibilities of owning a business. When you books are setup correctly, though, the information you can glean from them far outweighs the time spent keeping them up to date.

DEFINING THE ACCOUNTING PERIOD

It is imperative that all expenses be entered into the purchase ledger for the month in which they were received. The expenses must be entered in this manner regardless of when you are billed for the items, when they are actually paid for, or when the items are actually used.

Adjustments will be necessary to accurately record prepaid accounts—such as insurances and magazine subscriptions—to ensure the expense is entered into the budget during the month the expense is incurred. Most of these adjustments may be computed during the budgeting process.

Certain **expenditures**, such as the telephone and utilities bills, might not be received until five to six working days after the end of the month. Since the bank statement and suppliers' monthly statements will arrive during the first week of the month, it is recommended that the final profit and loss statement not be prepared until the 7th or 15th of the following month. This will allow time for the bank statement to be reconciled, unrecorded expenses to be entered into the purchase ledger, and any necessary final adjustments to be included. Although the profit and loss statement will not be published until the middle of the next month, the ending inventories and most costs will be projected on the first of the month, prior to opening.

Audit Procedures

Auditing is the process whereby you confirm that your controls are working and that the information you have in your business records is accurate and up to date. Effective audits are done to keep them accurate and manageable. By auditing your inventory, labor expenses, purchases, etc., you can be much more confident that your financial statements are a fair and accurate representation of your financial position. It is critically important to have this kind of accurate information when making day-to-day management decisions as well as long-term strategic planning.

On the last day of the month:

- Gather your inventory records for food, liquor, wine and operational supplies.

- Using current invoices and past inventories, cost out the inventory. The unit cost (or price) must correspond to the item and unit in the actual inventory.

- Correct prices are ensured by continual evaluation of invoices and contact with the suppliers.

- Ensure that the employees organize and clean the storage areas and walk-ins so that the ending inventory may easily be taken the following morning.

- Combine all containers and bottles. Organize and label all shelves.

- Schedule the bookkeeper and the employees involved in taking the physical inventory—the assistant manager, kitchen director, bar manager and general manager—to arrive early in the morning prior to the start of business on the first of the month.

- Schedule the preparation cooks to arrive an hour after the inventory crew so that you may inventory the food areas without disturbing them.

On the following morning, the first day of the next month, the bookkeeper should:

- Arrive as early as possible in order to complete all of his or her work prior to management's completion of the inventory.

- Reconcile and record all the transactions from the previous day, as usual.

- Enter the daily sales information.

- From the employee time cards, complete, total, double-check and verify the labor expense recorded.

- Ensure that all purchases are recorded in the purchase ledger.

- Complete, total, double-check and verify the purchase ledger.

- Total the purchases in each expenditure category: food, liquor, wine, and each individual operational category.

By completing a regular audit process according to prescribed standards, you can be sure that you will catch discrepancies quickly and that you are working from the most accurate information possible.

Budgeting and Profit Planning

Setting up records allows you to gain control over the financial health of your company. Establishing and following a budget is one of the methods for tracking your financial position and making adjustments to ensure good financial health.

BUDGETING

All caterers are in business to make a profit. In order to plan financially, you must first setup a long-range plan detailing how much money you need the to make and when. This financial plan is the restaurant's budget. Aside from being the restaurant's financial plan, the budget is also used to control costs and account for sales and products.

Budgeting is an accounting record and a tool used to evaluate how effectively the restaurant, management and employees operated during the month. Based on this information, management can then recognize any cost problems and plan to fix them accordingly.

Even if your catering business is still in the pre-opening stage, it is imperative that you start to develop an operating budget now. As soon as the budget is prepared, you will possess the control for guiding the business towards your financial goals.

Your budget is never completely accurate—there are always circumstances you can't predict or plan for, but the process of budgeting allows you to start gaining control over your costs, rather than letting them control you.

The benefits of budgeting include:

- You and your employees will develop an increased awareness and concern about the operation's costs.

- A well-structured, defined budget and orderly financial records will aid you greatly in obtaining loans and developing future plans.

- Cost problems can be easily pinpointed once the expense categories are broken down.

- You will become a better manager as your financial decisions and forecasts will become increasingly consistent and accurate.

Essentially budgeting changes the focus from reacting to symptoms and problems to looking at ways to prevent the problems from occurring in the first place. Operational budgets are typically broken down into sales, material costs, labor costs, operating expenses, and general expenses.

Total Sales

Projecting total sales is the most crucial and difficult aspect of budgeting. It is impossible to know how business will be from day to day or month to month, which makes budgeting total sales a perplexing task. Many costs are directly related to sales and it becomes very confusing. With some guidance and practice, though, you can master this important financial tool.

Remember that your initial budgets may be based on unrealistic expectations. Sales will probably be lower than you thought, and operating costs will be higher. Labor costs will be inordinately high due to training and getting to know how things work. Don't get discouraged. Use this time to perfect your product. Your intention is to be in business for a long time so you need to allocate sufficient funds now to make sure the business gets off on the right foot in order to guarantee profits for many years to come. Once you have a solid reputation for service excellence, the budget and profits will fall into place.

Projecting Total Sales

If you are just starting out, use information gained from catering organizations and competitions during your planning to form a basic sales number. Break it down into a monthly amount and allow for seasonality. Think about the following:

- How many contracts on average do catering companies of your size secure in a year?

- How many catering contracts do you reasonably expect to secure in the year?

- Of that yearly total, how many contracts do you anticipate to get each month?

- What is the average revenue of a catered event?

- Where does your catering revenue come from? Are there different average contracts for different sectors of the industry (social, corporate, wedding, etc.)?

- What effect does the season have on average revenue?

- How much (if any) of each contract to you intend to subcontract?

If you are already in business, review and analyze the growth in contracts during the past year, current year, and current month. Anticipate a growth or decline in your future business based on this evidence. Multiply the percentage of growth or decline by the total sales projection.

Material Costs

Material costs are those that go directly to your costs of sales. Things like the food and liquor you purchase vary directly with the number of catering events you manage. Here you are not concerned with the actual costs but the percentage of cost, or the cost-of-sales percentage.

To calculate the cost-of-sales percentage, divide the actual cost of the sale by the total sales. You should break down your cost-of-sales percentages into the different types of materials that go into the delivery of your service: food and liquor, for instance.

If you know from historical evidence or industry averages that the cost-of-sales percentage for food is 40 percent, and you have projected $400,000 in sales for the year, then your total food costs are budgeted at $160,000.

If you cater many different type of events, you should consider projecting and tracking the revenue and expense created from each. For instance, corporate, social, buffet, sit-down, lunch, dinner, etc., will all generate different cost-of-sales due to difference in the volume of direct materials used to hold the event. The more detail in your budget, the more accurate your budgeted amounts will be.

This formula will present an accurate indication of the material costs, as the cost of sales are proportionate to each other.

Labor Costs

Owner/Manager salary. Your salary and those of your managers should be a fixed monthly cost. Break down this total into a monthly amount and enter that into your total budget.

Employees' salary. Your employee salary expense is a semi-variable cost that will fluctuate directly with total sales. Total labor cost is a mix of the minimum amount of labor you employ to operate your business plus the labor costs associated with contract/on-call employees who work only to prepare for and serve events.

Calculate your fixed monthly employee cost: employee rate x hours worked.

Calculate your average variable labor cost the same way by analyzing the amount of contract labor you typically employ per event and then by your total sales projection. Again, you may choose to break this down further by event type.

Fixed labor. You employ one full-time office coordinator, one full-time food preparer, and one part-time bookkeeper:

EMPLOYEE	HOURS PER WEEK	RATE PER HOUR	TOTAL PER YEAR	TOTAL PER MONTH
Office Coordinator	35	$24	$43,680	$3,612
Food Prep	35	$12	$21,840	$1,806
Bookkeeper	10	$15	$7,800	$645
			TOTAL	$6,063

Variable labor. You project that you will cater 25 events this year, and each event typically uses 50 extra hours of food prep, 16 hours of set-up labor, and 80 hours of service staff labor.

EMPLOYEE	HOURS PER EVENT	RATE PER HOUR	TOTAL PER EVENT	TOTAL PER YEAR	TOTAL PER MONTH
Food Prep	50	$12	$600	$15,000	$1,250
Set-Up Labor	16	$10	$160	$4,000	$333
Service Staff	80	$15	$1,200	$30,000	$2,500
				TOTAL	$4,083

- Fixed labor = $6,063

- Variable labor = $4,083

- Total labor cost per month = $10,146

- Total labor cost per year = $122,320

Assume the same total projected sales figure as above at $400,000 and your labor cost percentage is 25 percent. This is a very simple example as it does not take into account the other expenses related to labor, such as unemployment insurance, vacation, and benefits.

If your business is highly seasonal, you should calculate these costs on a monthly basis using your monthly sales projection rather than an average based on yearly totals.

Overtime. Overtime should be nonexistent—or at least kept to an absolute minimum. No amount should be budgeted for overtime. Money spent on overtime usually indicates poor management and inefficiency. Bookkeepers should be on the lookout for employees approaching 40 hours of work near the end of the week. Carefully prepared schedules will eliminate 98 percent of all overtime work and pay. Employees who wish to switch their schedules around should only be allowed to do so after approval from the manager.

Controllable Operational Costs

The operating costs that you control can be fixed, variable, and semi-variable. The general rules for the category of cost are as follows:

Variable costs. The costs that change in direct proportion to a change in the level of sales or production. Examples of variable costs include the following:

- Food
- China
- Utensils
- Bar supplies
- Dining room supplies
- Laundry cleaning

- Glassware
- Kitchen supplies
- Legal

Fixed costs. The costs that remain the same regardless of a change in sales or production. Examples of fixed costs include the following:

- Depreciation
- Insurance
- Property taxes
- Office supplies
- Laundry and linen
- Uniforms
- Accounting (may have a slight variation for year-end or audits)
- Maintenance

Semi-variable costs. The costs that contain both properties of fixed and variable costs. A good example of a semi-variable cost would be the telephone expense. A fixed monthly service charge will be billed to the restaurant regardless of use. When sales are increased, more long-distance phone calls will be made to suppliers. This additional use of the telephone for toll charges is the variable cost. Variable costs include:

- Payroll
- Water
- Telephone
- Electricity
- Heat (may be included in rent)
- Gas (depends on what you use for appliances and heating)

General Operating Costs

Payroll and labor taxes. This is the tax amount the employer is required to contribute to the state and federal government. A separate tax account should be setup with your bank to keep all the tax money separate. Labor taxes include Social Security, Medicare tax, federal unemployment tax, and state unemployment tax.

Other taxes. This includes all miscellaneous taxes, such as local taxes, and sales tax paid on purchases. This column is for any tax the business pays for goods and services. It is not for sales tax or other taxes the business collects, as they are not expenditures. Federal income tax is not a deductible expenditure and should not be listed here either.

Equipment repairs and maintenance. This includes the cost of scheduled and emergency repairs and maintenance to all equipment. Always budget a base amount for normal service. Adjust this figure if major repairs or overhauls are anticipated.

Building repairs and maintenance. This includes the cost of minor scheduled and emergency repairs and maintenance to the building. Always budget a base amount for normal repairs and maintenance. Large remodeling or rebuilding projects should be budgeted as a separate expenditure and depreciated.

Entertainment. Entertainment includes bands, music, entertainers, and so forth.

Advertising. Advertising includes all the costs of advertising the business, including television, radio, mailing circulars, newspapers, etc.

Promotional expense. This is the expense of promotional items: key chains, calendars, pens, free dinners, T-shirts, sponsorship of sporting events, etc.

Equipment rental. This cost is the expense of either short- or long-term renting of pieces of equipment or machinery.

Postage. The cost of postage and shipping/freight expenses.

Trade dues. This includes dues paid to professional organizations, such as the National Restaurant Association. Trade magazine subscriptions should also be entered in this category. This expense should be divided by 12 to apportion the cost from the month in which it occurs.

Licenses. This is the expense of all business and government licenses: operating licenses, a health permit, liquor licenses, etc. This expense should also be divided by 12 to apportion the cost from the month in which it occurs.

Credit card expense. Credit card expense can be computed by multiplying the service charge cost-of-sales percentage by the total projected credit card sales volume.

Travel/Automotive. Travel includes the expense of ordinary and necessary travel for business purposes for yourself and your employees. For off-premise catering, you may have company vehicles for employees to use or they may be required to transport items on their own vehicles.

Bad debt. This expense should be nonexistent if the proper procedures for handling credit cards and checks are enforced. Normally, the full amount of a bad debt is a tax-deductible expense. However, you must prove the debt is worthless and un-collectable.

Use the following Operational Budget Worksheet to begin planning your own budget. You may need to add, delete or modify category titles to best reflect your own business operations.

OPERATIONAL BUDGET WORKSHEET

ITEM	BUDGETED	PERCENT	ACTUAL	PERCENT
SALES				
Social				
Corporate				
Wedding				
TOTAL SALES				
MATERIALS				
Food Costs				
Liquor Costs				
Wine Costs				
TOTAL COSTS				
GROSS PROFIT				
LABOR				
Manager Salary				
Employee				
Overtime				
TOTAL LABOR COSTS				
TOTAL THIS PAGE				
Controlled Oper. Costs				
China and Utensils				
Glassware				
Kitchen Supplies				
Bar Supplies				
Dining Room Supplies				
Uniforms				
Laundry/Linen				
Services				
Trash Pick-Up				
Laundry Cleaning				

OPERATIONAL BUDGET WORKSHEET

ITEM	BUDGETED	PERCENT	ACTUAL	PERCENT
Protection				
Freight				
Accounting				
Maintenance				
Payroll				
Utilities				
Phone				
Water				
Gas				
Electricity				
Heat				
Fixed Operating Costs				
Rent				
Insurance				
TOTAL THIS PAGE				
Property Taxes				
Depreciation				
General Operating Costs				
Labor Taxes				
Other Taxes				
Repairs-Equipment				
Repairs-Building				
Entertainment				
Advertising				
Promotion				
Equipment Rental				
Postage				

OPERATIONAL BUDGET WORKSHEET

ITEM	BUDGETED	PERCENT	ACTUAL	PERCENT
Contributions				
Trade Dues, etc.				
Licences				
Credit Card Expense				
Travel				
Bad Debt				
TOTAL THIS PAGE				
TOTAL EXPENDITURES				
TOTAL NET PROFIT				

Budgeted total net profit. To figure your net profit, add the total budgeted expenditures and subtract that number from total budgeted dales.

The result is the total net profit, or pre-tax profit. Your pre-tax net profit percentage is found by dividing the total net projected profit by projected total sales. Total projected sales minus total material costs will equal the gross profit amount.

DEPRECIATION

Depreciation may be defined as the expense derived from the expiration of a capital asset's quantity of usefulness over the life of the property. Capital assets are those assets that have utility or usefulness of more than one year.

Since a capital asset will provide utility over several years, the deductible cost of the asset must be spread out over its useful life—over a specified recovery period. Each year a portion of the asset's cost may be deducted as an expense.

Some examples of depreciable items commonly found in a catering business include:

- Office equipment
- The building (if owned)
- Kitchen equipment
- Display items

Items like light bulbs, china, stationery, and merchandise inventories may not be depreciated. The IRS publishes guidelines for the number of years to be used for computing an asset's useful life. The following are depreciation worksheets for you to use and modify as necessary.

DEPRECIATION WORKSHEET AND RECORD								
DATE	DESCRIPTION	METH	LIFE	NEW/ USED	AC RS	COST	SALVAGE	ADDIT 1st YR

BALANCE	DEPREC 20	BALANCE	DEPREC 20	BALANCE

You're in business to make money, therefore you need to do more than just cover your expenses each month. To plan for profit, you should determine at what point your expenses are covered—from that you will know if and when your company is generating a return for you and, if applicable, your investors. The easiest way to accomplish this is through a break-even analysis.

Break-Even Analysis

A break-even analysis is a simple yet very important and useful accounting tool for caterers. An understanding of break-even analysis will aid your budgeting, profit planning, and pricing decisions. Break-even analysis is concerned with the break-even point, which is defined as the point or level of operations where neither a profit nor loss is incurred. Break-even is the point where total sales minus total costs equal zero.

The first step in computing the break-even point is to separate the semi-variable cost into its two components: fixed and variable expenses. Next you must figure your variable unit cost. This is the amount of variable cost that is attributed to an average sale. Once you have done that, use the break-even equation to figure your break-even point:

Break-even = fixed cost / (unit price - variable unit cost)

Example:

Fixed costs = $18,000

Variable Costs = $22,000

Projected units/sales contracts = 10

Variable cost per unit = $2,200

Unit Price = $8,000 (average catering contract)

BE = $18,000 / ($8,000 - $2200) = $18,000 / $5,800 = 3.1

In order to break even you would need to secure more than 3 contracts. Or, in this case, have total revenue of more than $24,000.

Thoroughly understanding break-even analysis will aid the catering manager in the following situations:

- When determining how many contracts must be fulfilled in a specific time period before a profit is realized.

- When analyzing remodeling or rebuilding plans to see how long the cost of the project can be recovered and how many additional events must be catered in order to make the project profitable.

- When evaluating menu prices and net pre-tax profit margins, and what additional profits could be realized from a menu price increase.

All of these situations are common problems faced by catering businesses and all can be easily solved through the understanding and application of break-even analysis and one of the formulas used to compute the break-even point.

There are certain assumptions made in projecting break-even analysis that may not always hold true, and should be pointed out. The most common assumption is that the menu or selling price and costs will remain constant over a long period of time. This, of course, may not be the case, as no one can accurately foresee the future. A change in the product mix will have an effect on the break-even point.

Break-even analysis will provide you with a valuable tool in analyzing the relationships between volume, selling prices, and expenses. Furthermore, break-even analysis will enable you to effectively prepare long-range budgets and provide essential information relating to price levels, expansion possibilities, and past operational performances.

LOCATION: Nashville, Tennessee

SERVICES: Michael Attias operates a restaurant in Nashville, Tennessee, and helps restaurant owners add or expand a catering profit center through his company, The Results Group. You can download his FREE Report: Tapping Into Your Hidden Catering Profit$ at www.ezRestaurantMarketing.com.

FINDING YOUR NICHE By Michael Attias

Let's think about doctors. The more specialized their practice is, the more money they make. The same thing can be said of catering. When you specialize in a catering niche or you go after niches, then you can make more money and you will stand out.

I want to share a few niches that have been really profitable. One of them is going after nonprofits. You can either do fundraisers for them or social functions. Another niche is hospitals. There's a thing called Hospital Week. I don't know if you've ever heard of it, but they celebrate the fact that their employees do a great job every spring. We invested about $20 mailing out about 20 letters to hospitals. We booked around $17,000 worth of business going after that niche.

Targeting retailers the day after Thanksgiving, the busiest shopping day, is another profitable niche. Everybody wants to keep their employees in the store. They want to keep them happy. They want to give them a lunch half-hour instead of a lunch hour, so they bring in lunch. The first year we targeted this niche, we spent $45 and catered around $6,000 worth of events.

There are over 30 niches you can go after. If one of them doesn't fit you, there are other niches you can go after. If you want the greatest sales and marketing advantage, then you need to market to the niches.

Home-Based Catering

Most people who start out in the catering business start small, and many, when health department codes allow it, will start in their own home kitchens. While this is an easy way to get your feet wet in the business, think about the type of catering you want to do before you go this route. While it is cheaper and more convenient, if you want to cater large parties, you might want to take the plunge and find a commercial kitchen— it's not easy to cook brunch for 300 on a standard-issue stove.

If you do decide to start out from home, there are advantages. If you start your business at home, you'll eliminate approximately 75 percent of the startup costs you would have starting in an alternate location since you are already paying your rent or mortgage as well as your phone, utilities, and insurance. You'll also be able to start work as soon as you want. You'll have comfortable working conditions, no commute, flexibility, tax benefit and no office politics! Perhaps most important, starting a catering business at home lets you test the waters with little financial risk.

Disadvantages include isolation, limited workspace, zoning restrictions, and difficulty in establishing solid work habits.

If you do decide to start your business in your home, everything in this book applies to you, but there are some additional factors you should consider.

By definition, catering is the act of providing food and services. Today catering involves so many aspects, whether the enterprise is home-based or a large-scale operation. In many instances, home-based caterers tend to have limited experience, smaller insurance policies, and less knowledge about proper sanitation. In fact, these caterers are sometimes viewed as unfair competition to a licensed caterer because the home-based caterer does not incur the same expenses, has low overhead, and is able to price a lower cost-per-plate than the licensed caterer. If you're thinking of testing the waters with a small-scale, home-based business, you'll need to consider the following issues.

Health department regulations. If you decided to set up your catering service in your own home, using a spare bedroom as your office and using your own kitchen, you'll first need to check out the health department regulations that govern the catering trade. Make no assumptions; if you overlook the smallest detail regarding health regulations, you could be put out of business. Be sure to obtain the proper licenses.

Think about limiting your events to those in equipped kitchens. If you cannot find a kitchen to work in, you should consider limiting your events to those in venues that come equipped. While it may cramp your style in the beginning, it could provide you with the capital you need to purchase a site and equipment at a later date.

Small business incubators. Many areas have small business incubator programs. These programs provide entrepreneurs with networking opportunities and resources. Some of these incubators have kitchens available for a rental fee. To find out more about the business incubator program, log on to **www.nbia.org**.

Tableware and the home-based setup. Even if you decide to use your own kitchen and cooking equipment, you may be better off renting the necessary tableware, etc. In the catering trade, there are very few items you can't rent for the day, including china, flatware, glasses, tents and more. Places to rent this type of equipment will be listed under "party supplies" in your local phone directory.

Personal touches. Just because you're home based, doesn't mean that you cannot provide the same wide range of products and services as a large-scale caterer. In fact, smaller operations are better able to add those individual touches to their presentation and services. In addition to the food, think about including table and chair setup, napkins and eating utensils, and even complete cleanup services.

Attentive service is just as important as delicious food. Don't take on jobs that are too big for your operation. The quality of service will suffer and so will your reputation. A typical home-based business is better off concentrating on food quality and personal service rather than quantity. Aim for jobs that involve between 20 to 100 guests.

This size of event should not overtax you and your staff. If you do take on a larger party, think about using some convenience products rather than trying to make every menu item from scratch. For example, you may want to buy ravioli from a store that makes these rather than making them yourself. You also have the option of hiring additional staff if you need to.

Finally, pay attention to your menu choices if you are going to take on a large event. If you are doing a cocktail reception for 20, it's easy to make items such as shrimp mousse on cucumber rounds, stuffed grape leaves, and raspberry and brie tartlets. If you are catering a reception for 100, however, you will want to stay away from the labor-intensive appetizers. For this size of party you should consider serving dips such as humus or guacamole and have displays such as a cheese board or shrimp cocktail.

Health Department Regulations and Finding a Home

If you want to be a home-based caterer and your local health department does not allow it, you do have a couple of options: You could move or you could look into renting space.

Caterers who are just starting out typically can't afford to outfit a brand new commercial kitchen space. One alternative you might want to consider is renting a facility from other caterers, churches, charitable organizations, etc. This will allow you to prepare in a fully licensed and certified kitchen.

When looking for kitchen space to rent, be sure to consider the following:

- Only rent space in established, licensed commercial facilities like community hall kitchens, restaurants and bakeries.

- Make sure the kitchen is appropriate for you and your product by contacting your local health department.

- Ask to see the premises, go in and ask questions.

- Get references if other people are renting the same facility.

- Find out if you can use the refrigerators and storage space.

- Check on insurance and find out the last time the kitchen was inspected by the health department.

Rent or Purchase?

As a home-based caterer you must decide if you will purchase your preparation equipment. The general consensus in the catering trade that is that if you will use a piece of equipment six or more times per year, buy it.

RENT

If you rent equipment, you have access to a wider variety of items and can choose which items are necessary of each catered event. However, being dependent on a rental company can be inconvenient. You may need to pick up smaller orders or be reliant on the company's delivery schedule.

Extra care must be taken in counting and handling rental equipment. Rental companies bill at a replacement cost, normally higher than the actual cost for lost and damaged items.

Purchasing Food

Shopping for food can be a particular tricky task for home caterers. Suppliers generally won't deliver to small accounts, so you'll be doing most of the legwork for this task. If you organize yourself before shopping, you'll make the best use of your time. Make sure to create and use shopping lists for all your events.

You'll want to find as many wholesale food sources as possible because this will be less costly than simply going to your local grocer. The larger stores, such as Meijers and Biggs, Costco and Sam's Club are good options. You may also be able to set up accounts with large local food distributors and have them pull your order for will call. This means that they will supply you with the product, but you'll need to pick up the order. Some of these distributors may only let smaller accounts pay with cash, but see if you can get an account set up with them.

When dealing with wholesalers:

- Have your order written down and ready when you call.

- Don't hesitate to call somewhere else if prices seem too high.

- Get a guaranteed delivery or will call time.

- When the order arrives or you pick up the order, make sure to check that each item is there and check the quality of each item.

If you live in area where there are local farmers, check out the farmers' market. Produce will be fresh and local. This could be a good marketing tool. You might even find that some of the farmers are willing to set up accounts and deliver orders to you during the week.

Storage is another issue when procuring goods for your event. If you cater from your home, you'll only have so much space for raw product and finished goods. Invest in a second refrigerator and freezer for your basement or garage. This will be one of the best equipment investments you make for your business.

If you have an area appropriate for dry food storage, you'll also want to set up shelves to hold dry items so you can buy cheaper in bulk. Before building, however, make sure to check with local health department codes regarding inventory and storage.

Foods with a long shelf life include:

- Canned tomatoes
- Tomato paste
- Olives
- Pickles
- Canned broth

- Mustard
- Soy sauce
- Mayonnaise
- Ketchup

Foods that will hold three to six months include flour, sugar and dried pasta.

Foods that can be frozen for up to three months include:

- Chicken
- Beef
- Poultry
- Lamb

- Puff pastry
- Phyllo dough
- Berries
- Butter

Specializing and Sidelines

Don't limit your options—be creative! There are a number of sidelines that naturally spring from the catering business. For example, you can act as a coordinator for flowers, ice sculptures, photography, party locations, or themes. At the same time, remember that if people wanted to stick to a set menu, they could go to a restaurant, so be flexible.

In many catering establishments, this may not be an option. In hotel catering, for instance, there is not much room for flexibility. If you are marketing to smaller events or have the resources to be flexible, let your menu suggestions be just that. These can be a starting point, but let the client be your guide. Don't miss opportunities to turn a modest affair into a major profit-making event. Also, don't hesitate when you see an opportunity to bump up the bottom line of an event. You may be able to turn a barbecue into a Hawaiian luau, complete with roast pig.

KOSHER COOKING

Looking for a niche that separates you from the crowd? Consider kosher catering. Kosher means that food is properly prepared relative to Jewish dietary laws. These laws are regulated by Rabbis. This specialty area is quite complex, so you may want to consider working with a Rabbi to learn the ins and outs before undertaking kosher catering as a specialty area.

If this is a specialty area you'd like to focus on, be sure to do some research in the community to make sure it is something the public wants. If there is no public need, creating your own niche is meaningless because it will not bring you any business.

In kosher cooking, all preparations must be supervised or condoned by a Rabbi. Kosher foods are defined in two ways. First, a particular type of food may or may not be kosher. For example, pork products are prohibited. The only meat that is kosher is from mammals that chew their cud and are cloven-hoofed (cattle, deer, sheep and goats). Kosher cooking also refers to specific regulations concerning how different foods can be combined and prepared.

In addition to only certain animals being eaten, kosher cooking requires that meat cut from the hindquarters of an animal is not used. Furthermore, animals used in kosher cooking must be slaughtered in a proscribed humane and painless way, immediately drained of all blood, then soaked in cold water and salted by a kosher butcher before the meat can be used.

According to Jewish law, there are three classes of food: meat, dairy, and "pareve" foods, which basically encompass all the other foods such as grains, eggs, fruits, sugar, oil and seasonings. Food items for the meat and dairy groups can never be combined in the same dish or the same meal. Pareve items can be mixed with either of the other two groups.

Obviously all these rules will make for some creative menu planning. If you are serving meat as an entrée, for example, none of the rest of the meal can include dairy, including desserts. Nor can you use a cream-based sauce for the meat or serve a cream-based soup at the beginning of the meal.

If you specialize in this area, you will also need to be aware that certain items require special cleaning if they are also used to produce non-kosher foods. You'll need to set aside a complete set of dishes, knives, cutting boards, and cooking pots for your kosher meals.

To help get you started in your kosher menu planning, here are a couple of sample menus:

MENU 1
Gazpacho
Grilled Chicken with Madeira Sauce
Potato Latkes
Snow Peas and Red Pepper
Challah and Assorted Rolls with Margarine
Apple Strudel

```
+--------------------------------------------------+
|                     MENU 2                       |
+--------------------------------------------------+
|                                                  |
|                 Poached Salmon                   |
|                                                  |
|               Glazed Rack of Lamb                |
|                                                  |
|           Rosemary Roasted New Potatoes          |
|                                                  |
|                   Rice Pilaf                     |
|                                                  |
|                  Haricot Vert                    |
|                                                  |
|                  Fresh Fruit                     |
|                                                  |
|                Assorted Cookies                  |
|                                                  |
+--------------------------------------------------+
```

HOME CHEFS

With so many people working longer hours these days, the home chef business is taking off. One of the great things about the home chef business is that you don't have to worry about the health regulations concerning commercial catering operations. You will, however, probably want to be bonded since you will be working in other people's homes and will want to ensure them they are covered for any liability.

According to the American Personal Chef Institute and Association, **www.personalchef.com**, there are currently about 9,000 personal chefs in the United States serving 72,000 clients. These clients include two-income families; young, single professionals; people with restricted diets; and senior citizens. Over the next five years, some 300,000 clients of 20,000 chefs are expected to pay $1.2 billion for in-home meals.

As with any catering job, the first thing you'll do with a potential client is to meet with them to discuss the type of service they are looking for, food likes and dislikes, allergies, and any special dietary requirements.

Unlike a regular caterer, however, you will not be cooking for a single event. You will likely be cooking all the meals for a week in one day. You will want to discuss how many meals the client needs and any package deals you can provide. For example, many home chefs offer a "five by four"—four portions of five entrées and side dishes. This will provide 20 dinner-size servings. You can also provide a "five by two"—two portions of five entrées.

For a typical "five by four," most home chefs charge between $350 and $400, including groceries ($17.50 to $20 per person). A "five by two" usually costs $285 to $325, or around $30 per person.

If you do work as a home chef, you will likely provide shopping services as well as cooking. And if you service clients with dietary restrictions, which is a booming area in the home-chef industry, you will need to provide a nutritional breakdown for each meal. A nice way to present this information is to print out labels you can adhere to the containers (see the sections on Nutrition in the Menu Planning chapter).

As a home chef you are likely to need the following list of items for your cooking days.

- 2 skillets, large and small
- Spices
- Knife set
- Cutting boards
- Towels
- Paper towels
- Garbage bags

- 2-3 saucepans of varying sizes
- Dish soap and sponge
- Immersion blender
- Can opener
- Corkscrew
- Wooden spoons
- Spatulas

Whatever area you choose to focus on or specialize in, make sure that every event is a party to remember.

RULES FOR HOME-BASED CATERERS

1. **Don't act like an amateur.** Be professional, courteous, ethical and customer-focused in your dealings with clients. Maintain truth in your menu. Do not engage in misleading advertising or unexpected and unjustified last-minute add-ons to the price. Also, do not underbid a competitor when the client discloses your competitor's price.

2. **Separate yourself from the competition.** Do not copy the competition. Offer a unique menu, a unique service, or perhaps a unique location. Focus on what you do best. If you make exceptional vegetarian dishes, for example, be sure to include one on your menus whenever possible.

Adding Catering to a Restaurant

*I*f you already own a full-service restaurant, you might want to consider adding catering as one of your services. Before doing so, however, you should consider these factors:

- Location
- Customer profile
- Restaurant style/ concept
- Staffing capabilities
- Physical layout of building
- Cuisine and menu offerings

The proximity of your restaurant to other businesses will help determine where to focus your catering arm. If you are in an area heavily populated with offices, universities or hospitals, you may be able to incorporate business catering into your exiting business fairly easily. If you are currently only open for dinner, this would be an excellent opportunity. You could cater corporate lunches and increase the earning power of your restaurant without worrying about interrupting existing business.

You can also consider social catering. Many restaurants close on Mondays and Tuesdays because these nights tend to be slow and it would cost more to operate on those evenings than the restaurant would see in sales. Use those nights for catered events. For a small increase in food and labor cost, you can make a significant increase in sales for the week on the nights you cater social or business events.

Since you already have a built-in customer base, you may be able to get catering business from your existing customers. Be sure to let regular diners know about your catering service using signs, tables tents and text within your menu.

Make sure when considering adding catering to your services that you consider the size of your facility and the type of food you serve. Is your building big enough to handle the extra production work? Do you have space for on-site catering? Do you serve formal dinners or lunch sandwiches? How much storage space is available for catering food prep and supplies?

You may find that your space and menu limit you in some areas but not others. Use what you have. If you don't have space for on-premise catering, you can think about gourmet to-go dinners or another type of take-out service.

THE BEST OF BOTH WORLDS

Many restaurateurs cater on-premise special events and also pursue off-premise opportunities. Dual restaurant catering is advantageous because restaurateurs have invested in professional production equipment. By serving both markets you can lower the overall fixed costs of your operation while increasing, incrementally, gross sales. This increase in sales can be achieved without having to spend money on expanding the dining room or kitchen area. When in the pursuit of both types of business, aim to achieve the following:

Maximize on flexibility. Take advantage of the flexibility offered by a combination of on-premise/ off-premise catering. By blending both types of catering, dual restaurant-catering operations enjoy the freedom to prepare their foods within their own facility, while at the same time employing outside labor.

Maximize on expertise. Because of the flexibility offered by dual catering operations, you can draw on a greater pool of specialized expertise. This means that you will be in greater demand for a wider range of significant events.

Maximize on exclusivity. Define your exclusive target market. Determine, in advance, the specific clientele for your business. Securing exclusive clients is a definite advantage for a caterer; it will give you a strategic advantage over many other caterers in the market. Work towards exceeding your clients' needs. It will bring you recognition and market dominance in an exclusive area of the catering trade.

Develop a seasonal niche. The dual caterer should be aware of certain special annual events. These events involve preparation of the food on your own premises, while serving off-premises. The advantage of off-premise catering is that you can serve a greater number of people than at your own premises. Understand that the design of your kitchen will determine your capacity to cater off-premises.

Here are some suggestions for developing a catering business that serves up big profits:

- Decide early whether your restaurant's catering operation will be in-house or off-premises. An in-house operation will let you to use your own kitchen and equipment but it also may limit the size of events. Off-premise catering offers an opportunity for greater exposure, multiple daily events, and more revenue, but you also will have to abide by the rules of each particular venue.

- Staff smartly. You can use a culinary-staffing service to supplement your restaurant's regular staff during catered events, but pull from your existing staff for smaller events. Your employees will appreciate making the extra money.

- Remember, you don't have to reinvent the wheel. You don't have to create a whole new menu for catered events. Look at what you have on your existing menu and see which items are cater-friendly. If you cater off premises, be sure to choose items that can hold their temperature during transport and can be partially cooked ahead of time.

- Transporting food requires an even closer eye to food safety. Train your staff on the additional guidelines they will need to live by to handle transported food properly to prevent food-borne-illness outbreaks.

- Unless you cater on a daily basis, you may want to rent equipment for off-premise catering, such as stoves and hot boxes.

- Create lists of food items, job duties and equipment.

- Know when to say no. Don't let your regular restaurant business suffer for your new catering business. If you try to do too much, quality will decrease and both businesses will suffer. Know your limits and live by them.

STAFFING

If you are only adding a small catering component to your restaurant, you will probably not need much in the way of additional staff. If you plan to expand, you might need to staff catering as a separate department. In a large catering facility, typical positions include:

- **Director of Catering** – Assigns and oversees all functions and marketing efforts. Interacts with clients, coordinates sales staff, creates menus in coordination with chef.

- **Assistant Catering Director** – Services accounts, assists with marketing.

- **Catering Manager** – Services accounts and maintains client contacts.

- **Catering Sales Manager** – Oversees sales office and sales staff.

- **Catering Sales Representative** – Handles outside and inside sales.

- **Convention/Conference Service Managers** – Handles meeting and convention business and room setup (usually a position found in hotels).

- **Banquet Manager** – Oversees captains, supervises all functions in progress, schedules front-of-the-house staff, acts as operations director.

- **Assistant Banquet Manager** – Reports to Banquet Manager. Supervises table settings and décor.

- **Banquet Setup Manager** – Supervises banquet setup crew, orders tables and chairs and other equipment, supervises teardown of the event.

- **Scheduler** – Enters bookings in a master log, oversees timing of functions. Scheduled meeting rooms and other meal function rooms, keeps appropriate records to ensure there is no overbooking or double booking, communicates information to relevant departments.

- **Maitre d'Hotel** – The floor manager in charge of all service personnel and all aspects of guest service during the meal function.

- **Captain** – Oversees the activity of a meal function and the service personnel.

- **Server** – Food servers and cocktail servers work the event, handling and serving food and beverages to guests.

- **Bartender** – Serves drinks during events and restocks bar inventory. May also need to keep track of drinks for pricing information for the event.

- **Sommelier** – Wine steward.

- **Houseman** – Physically set up the tables, chairs, dance floor, stage, etc., for an event.

- **Attendant** – Refreshes meeting rooms. Does spot cleaning and trash removal.

- **Clerical staff** – Handles routine correspondence such as typing Banquet Event Order forms (BEOs), contracts, and handling and routing phone messages.

- **Engineer** – Provides utilities services and maintains catering equipment. May also handle audio-visual or lighting installation.

- **Cashier** – Collects money at cash bars, sells drink tickets and meal tickets if event has them.

- **Ticket Taker** – Collects tickets from guest before they are allowed to enter an event.

- **Steward** – Delivers requisitioned china, flatware, linen, etc.

- **Cook/Food Handler** – Prepares the finished food product according to the Banquet Event Order form (BEO).

You may also need to consider hiring temporary help for staffing large events. Check with your staff or other area caterers. There is usually a large pool of people that work temporary catering jobs, and they tend to work for several companies at once.

Remember, you'll be paying your catering staff per event, even if some of the help comes from your regular employees. If your regular employees work an event they should be paid in the same fashion as a temporary worker. Generally, for catered events, servers and bartenders are paid $95 to $120 for four hours (this does not include a tip the host or hostess might include). After four hours, the client is charged $15 to $20 per half hour. Kitchen staff is generally still paid a per-hour rate or flat rate per event. Per-hour rates generally fall between $15 and $25.

EQUIPMENT

Catering operations, much like restaurants, are production facilities. Unlike restaurants, which are designed to produce food in individual servings for individual diners, a catering kitchen must be able to serve many people the same food at the same time.

While you will have most of the equipment you need already, you will want to invest in additional flatware, china and linens, as well as the items listed in the "Equipment for Transporting Food" section of this handbook.

MENUS

When creating your catering menus, consider the following:

- Which items on your restaurant menu do well.

- What products you already order and have on hand.

- Which items on your menu would hold well.

- Which items could be mass produced easily.

- How much storage space you have available.

You don't have to start from scratch. If there are items you already sell that could hold and be produced in quantity, include these on your catering menus. Use your menu sales analysis and sales history to determine popular and cost-effective recipes you might want to include in your catering operation.

Menu sales analyses, or menu scores, track each menu item that is sold. Many restaurants have computerized cash registers, so getting a report on what items sold nightly, weekly or monthly is easy. If your restaurant does not have a computerized register, you can track a period of time (a month) and get this information from guest checks.

Cost can easily be pulled from your standardized recipes or cost sheets and your sales history can be pulled from a daily log that records customer counts, daily sales, daily costs.

A menu item's profit margin, what the item contributes to the overall profit of a restaurant, is the difference between the menu price and the item's food cost. To determine this, you will need to look at monthly financial statements. Subtract your total food-costs from your total sales.

You should also consider creating catering menus that allow you to use product already on hand. When creating a catering menu, take the opportunity to include items that will allow you to use leftover inventory. For a complete discussion, see the "Menu Planning" section of the handbook.

MARKETING

Just like your restaurant, you'll need to market your catering operation. However, since you already have a customer base, you already have a leg up in marketing your catering business. Take advantage of your existing customer base and do some internal marketing.

Internal marketing refers to techniques used once the customer is inside your restaurant. This type of marketing tool can be a great way to build business for the catering side of your operation. Here are some internal marketing ideas.

- The restaurant menu itself is an important internal marketing tool. The menu and quality of food will help entice your customers to use your facility for special events.

- Set up table tents or signs that let your customers know you cater.

- Provide carry-out catering menus at the cashier or hostess station as well as brochures and business cards.

- Have one of your servers take a tray of appetizers you use for your catering menu into your front area and serve the customers waiting to be seated.

- Have people drop business cards into a fishbowl and hold a drawing once a week. The winner receives a free catered lunch for himself and three friends.

- Use these business cards to create an e-mail list. Send out e-mails to promote your catering business.

- Create T-shirts with your logo and catering information, and sell these at the hostess stand.

- Give your servers buttons to wear that say "Ask me!" When customers ask, the servers can tell the customer about your new catering business and give them a brochure.

For external promotions, make sure you know exactly what needs promoting before spending your revenue on advertising. Advertising is expensive, and there's no guarantee it will succeed. Do your homework before you spend your money. Here are some ideas for external promotion of your catering arm.

- Donate food to a local public radio fund drive. This will give you free advertising on the station when they thank the people who donated food.

- Visit your local chamber of commerce. All cities have festivals, parades, and other events. See how you can involve your restaurant's catering operation.

- If you have the advertising budget, place ads in newspapers, on the radio, or on television.

- Set up cooking demonstrations at a local mall.

- Talk to area schools about a conducting a tour of your facility as a class field trip.

- Use a rubber stamp on outgoing mail saying "We cater!"

- Another possible marketing strategy is to offer cooking classes. You may be interested in doing a class at your facility or just doing a demo at a mall kiosk to increase your public exposure.

BOOKING AND PRICING

Booking an event is different from taking a reservation. While the same basic principles apply, booking an event involves a greater amount of detail. When taking a restaurant reservation, you will normally talk to your customer over the phone, asking for the date, time and number of guests in the party, and perhaps whether the guest prefers smoking or non-smoking.

When working with catering clients, however, you will meet with the client face to face and spend much more time discussing preferences. You will need to talk about what the event is for, how many people are expected, the budget, décor needs, menu preferences, dietary restrictions guests might have, entertainment and floral needs, and service style.

In many restaurants, finding a quiet, neat place for this discussion can be difficult. If you are adding catering to your restaurant, consider creating a new, enclosed office space to meet with potential clients or meet with them in your dining room during off hours when things are quiet.

CONCLUSION

Catering is a complex and exciting area within the food services industry. There are many factors to consider before deciding to open your own business, but if you decide to take the plunge, the rewards can be considerable.

By reading this handbook you have been exposed to the myriad of planning and organization details that need to be attended to before and after opening your business. It is our hope that the magnitude of information presented is not a deterrent but rather an enticement to enter this rich and creative profession.

For those drawn to the catering field, it offers an excellent and varied way to express your creativity, serve people, and continually challenge yourself to organize events that are truly memorable for your clients and you.

Don't forget to check out the CD-ROM for forms and a sample business plan!

CASE STUDY: WORD FROM THE EXPERTS

SUSAN CALLAHAN

LOCATION: Washington, D.C.

SERVICES: Susan Callahan is a chef and caterer in Washington, D.C. She is a member of Les Dames D'Escofier. She works now as a private chef, but has worked for many small and large catering businesses in D.C. She managed a nonprofit catering business that hired formally homeless men and women. Susan believes that the small things, whether with food, employees, or guests, matter the most in her business.

I am a strong advocate of food recycling programs. Every city has a kitchen that re-prepares usable food into food for the homeless or needy. Also, I like to feed the support staff when I do events; feed the superintendent and you will always have a friend!

I once had to re-decorate a wedding cake when the family could not be at the reception at the same time, so the bride and groom had two cake-cutting ceremonies. I had to remove a layer, re-frost and re-decorate a cake for the second cake-cutting ceremony.

I always apologize when the guest is unhappy. Let the person say what they want, don't interrupt. Then ask what you can do to make the person feel better. It doesn't always help, but it is an attempt. Never argue with the customer; it is not worth it.

Glossary

A

A LA BROCHE – Cooked over a flame on a skewer.

A LA CARTE – A list of individually priced and sold items.

A LA MINUTE – A style of cooking that is usually done in front of the guests and made to order.

A LA MODE – A dessert that includes pie with ice cream on top.

ACF – American Culinary Federation.

ACTION STATION – The location on a buffet table where a chef will prepare food made to order in front of the customers.

ADAPTIVE FIRM – A business that is able to evolve continuously to suit the era.

ADVERTISING – Purchase of space, time or printed matter for the purpose of increasing sales.

AGREEMENT – A contract between two or more people guaranteeing each party something from the other party.

AL DENTE – An Italian term usually referring to pasta; used to describe the texture when bitten.

ALE – Alcoholic beverage brewed from top-fermenting yeast.

AMBIANCE – Sounds, sights, smells and attitude of an operation.

APERITIF – An alcoholic drink taken before a meal to stimulate the appetite.

APPELLATION – A protected name under which a wine may be sold, indicating the grapes used are from a specific area.

AU GRATIN – Food that is topped with cheese or bread crumbs and then broiled until brown and crisp.

AU JUS – Served with the natural juices or gravy.

AU NATUREL – Plainly cooked food, prepared to resemble its natural state.

ℬ

BAGUETTE – A long, narrow loaf of French bread.

BAILY – A chewy roll that is round and flat with a depression in the center with sautéed chopped onions sprinkled on top of it before baking.

BAKED ALASKA – A meringue-covered dessert with a layer of sponge cake underneath ice cream.

BATCHING – An amount produced at one baking.

BITTERS – Alcohol flavored with bitter herbs and roots.

BLEND – A potable created from two or more whiskeys.

BOXED – A tablecloth pinned and creased at the corners.

BRAISE – Cooking method where food is browned in oil, then cooked slowly in a liquid in a covered container.

BREADING – The process of placing an item in flour, an egg wash (egg and milk), and then bread crumbs before frying or baking.

BRÛLÉE – Finishing method applied to dishes such as cream custards; can be done with torch or under broiler.

BRUNCH – A late breakfast.

BUFFET – A type of meal where guests help themselves to a variety of dishes displayed on a table.

BUTLERED SERVICE – Service when servers walk amongst the guests with drinks and hors d'oeuvres.

BYPRODUCT – Item or items that are made in the course of producing or preparing other items.

$\mathcal{C}$

CAJUN – A style of cuisine from the French-American area of Louisiana; traits include dark rouxs and spices like cumin, chili powder and ground coriander.

CAPITAL – Any cash, funds, assets and accounts that the business currently possesses.

CAPTIAN – Leader who oversees a particular section of the dining room.

CARAFE – A container used to serve house wine at the table.

CARBONATED – A beverage that has been charged with carbon dioxide gas.

CARVER – A chef that carves meat during the meal.

CASH BAR – A bar at a large party where drinks are purchased by the glass.

CATERER – A professional who is hired to provide the food and beverage at an event.

CENTERPIECE – A decoration placed in the middle of the table.

CHILL – To keep cold.

CLEAR – To clean the table after a meal.

CLIENT – The party for which professional services are rendered.

CMAA – Club Managers Association of America.

COCKTAIL – Any alcoholic beverage that mixes two or more ingredients.

COMMISSION – An individual's pay based on the amount of sales personally derived.

COMPLIMENTS OF THE HOUSE – An item that is free for the customer.

CONDIMENTS – A substance, such as mustard, used to flavor or complement food.

CONSUMPTION BAR – A type of bar where the bartender keeps a running tab and the host pays based on the total amount of beverages served.

CONTINENTAL BREAKFAST – A light breakfast consisting of fruit, pastries, coffee and juices.

CONTRACT – An arrangement between two or more parties, enforceable by law.

COOLER – A container used to keep items cool.

CORDIAL – A liqueur; a tonic.

COST – The amount paid to acquire or produce an item.

COUNT – The number of units or items.

COVER – A setting at the table for one person.

CROUTONS – Cubes of deep-fried or toasted bread.

CRUET – A container used to hold condiments.

CUSTOMER – One that buys goods or services.

DASH – Approximately 1/16 teaspoon.

DEFAULT – A breach of contract; failure to pay on a promissory note when due.

DESSERT – A sweet course that is served after the main meal.

DESSERT SPOON – A spoon larger than a teaspoon and smaller than a tablespoon.

DINER – A person eating a meal, especially at a restaurant.

DINING AREA – The area in the restaurant for the customers to eat.

DINNER PLATE – A plate used for the main dish.

DISTILL – To increase the concentration of and separate through the process of distillation.

DOUBLE – A drink with two measures of alcohol.

DRAFT – Distribute beer from a keg.

DRY – A wine that is not sweet.

E-COMMERCE – The way business is done online, by selling and receiving products on the Internet.

ENTRÉE – The main dish of a meal.

EXPENDITURE – Amount spent on goods and services.

FAMILY STYLE – Food served at the table on a large plate from which the customers serve themselves.

FOOD COST – The cost of food items purchased for resale.

FOOD STATIONS – A buffet set up into different, specific food sections.

FREEZER BURN – Loss of moisture in frozen food, evidenced by a dry, discolored surface.

FRENCH SERVICE – A type of service where a waiter or waitress serves each guest individually from a tray.

G

GARNISH – To decorate.

GENERAL PARTNERSHIP – A partnership in which each of the partners is liable for all of the business's debt.

GOURMET – A lover of fine foods and drinks.

GRATUITY/TIP – A gift or money given in return for a service.

GRAZING – The unauthorized consumption of food by employees.

GREET – To welcome customers.

GROSS COST – The total cost of food consumed.

GROSS PAY – Money earned before deductions are subtracted.

H

HORS D'OEUVRES – An appetizer served before a meal.

HOUSE WINE – Wine that is less expensive than brand-name wine.

I

INVOICE – Shows prices and amount of goods sent to a purchaser for payment.

ITEMIZE – To list the items, as in an itemized expense account.

J

JOB ANALYSIS – The study of a job description and specifications required for successful performance.

JOB SPECIFICATIONS – The qualifications needed to hold a job; includes educational, physical, mental and age requirements.

LAGER – Beer produced with bottom-fermenting yeast; fermented at much colder temperatures than top-fermenting beers.

LICENSE – Legal document giving official permission to do something.

LIQUEUR – Alcoholic beverage with a sweet taste made by flavored ingredients and a spirit.

LIQUOR – An alcoholic beverage made by distillation rather than by fermentation.

MAIN COURSE – The primary dish after the appetizer.

MAITRE D' – Person in charge of assigning customers to tables.

MANICOTTI – Noodles that are usually stuffed with a meat or cheese mixture.

MEASURE – A set amount.

MENU – A list of dishes available for a meal.

MIXED DRINK – A drink with more than one kind of liquor.

MIXER – Any nonalcoholic liquid added to a drink containing alcohol.

N

NAPKIN – A piece of cloth or absorbent paper used to protect clothes or wipe lips and fingers.

NEAT – A spirit drunk without ice, water or mixers.

OCCUPATIONAL SAFETY AND HEALTH ADMINISTRATION (OSHA) – The agency created within the Department of Labor to set safety and health standards for all workers in the United States.

ON-SITE LOCATION – A location that offers everything needed for a meal for a large quantity of people.

ON-THE-JOB TRAINING (OJT) – Instruction that allows an employee to acquire the needed knowledge and skills while on the job.

OPEN BAR – Practice at banquet functions whereby customers are not charged individually for the drinks they consume. The host pays for banquet-goers' beverages.

OPERATING BUDGET – Detailed revenue and expense plan for a determined period.

ORDER PAD – A pad used to take orders by the server.

OUTSOURCING – The procuring of services or products from an outside supplier or manufacturer in order to cut costs.

OVERTIME – Time worked exceeding regular hours.

P

PLACE SETTING – A setting that includes silverware, plates and glassware for one person; a cover.

PLATED SERVICE – A service where food is arranged artfully on the plate before being taken to the guest.

PORTION – One serving.

PORTION CONTROL – Ensures that the correct amount is being served each time.

PORTION COST – The cost of preparing one serving.

PORTION SIZE – A specific portion amount.

POURED DRINKS – Drinks requiring no stirring and contain only one ingredient.

PPBSE – Planning, programming, budgeting, staffing and evaluating.

PREMIUM BRANDS – Top-shelf liquor.

Q

QUALITY CONTROL – Ensuring the execution of tasks and responsibilities according to established standards.

R

RAMEKIN – A small dish used for baking and serving.

RECEIPT – A written acknowledgment that something has been received.

ROTATING MENU – A menu that alternates in a series; usually set up on a yearly basis.

ROUND – A serving to each of a group.

RSVP – Répondez s'il vous plait; an abbreviation on an invitation requesting a reply.

RUSSIAN SERVICE – Service when the waiter holds a tray in one hand and serves the guest with the other.

S

S.C.O.R.E. – Service Corps of Retired Executives; a nonprofit organization that provides small business counseling.

SALAD SERVERS – A pair of tongs used to serve salad.

SALES MIX – The proportion of sales coming from different products or services.

SERVICE AREA – The area where servers have all of their needed supplies.

SHAKE – To mix.

SHAKER – A container used to mix drinks.

SHRINKAGE – Inventory loss not affiliated with sales.

SIDE DISH – A dish that is served with the main course.

SIDE PLATE – A plate set to the side of the place setting.

SILVER SERVICE – Type of service where a server puts more food on a customer's plate from a serving dish.

SOFT DRINK – A carbonated drink that contains no alcohol.

SOUP PLATE – A shallow bowl used to serve soup.

SOUP SPOON – A spoon used for eating soup.

SPILLAGE – The alcohol lost during the drink-making process.

SPIRITS – A general term for an alcoholic beverage.

SPOILAGE – Loss due to poor food control and handling.

STAGGERED STAFFING – Employees are staffed according to business volume.

STARTER – An appetizer.

STATIC MENU – A menu that rarely changes.

STIR – To mix ingredients together.

STRAINER – Used to pour liquid through to filter larger items.

TABLE D'HOTE – A complete meal at a set price.

TACTICS – The means a company would use to accomplish a strategy.

TAX NUMBER – The number assigned to businesses by a state revenue department that enables the business to buy wholesale without paying sales taxes.

TEASPOON – A small spoon used to stir liquids.

TIP – A small amount of money given to someone for performing a service.

TREND ANALYSIS – Study of a company's past employment needs over a period of years to predict future needs.

UNIT COST – The purchase price divided by the applicable unit.

USABLE PORTION – The part of a fabricated product that has value.

W

WAGES – The amount paid or received for work.

WATER STATION – A service table that holds glasses and water.

WINE LIST – The list of wines available.

DID YOU BORROW THIS COPY?

Have you been borrowing a copy of *The Professional Caterer's Handbook* from a friend, colleague or library? Wouldn't you like your own copy for quick and easy reference? To order, photocopy the form below and send to:

Atlantic Publishing Company
1405 SW 6th Ave • Ocala, FL 34471

DID YOU BORROW THIS COPY?

Have you been borrowing a copy of *The Professional Caterer's Handbook* from a friend, colleague or library? Wouldn't you like your own copy for quick and easy reference? To order, photocopy the form below and send to:

Atlantic Publishing Company
1405 SW 6th Ave • Ocala, FL 34471

YES!

Send me_____copy(ies) of *The Professional Caterer's Handbook* (ISBN# 978-091062-760-3) for $79.95 + $5.00 for USPS shipping and handling.

Atlantic Publishing Company
1405 SW 6th Ave
Ocala, FL 34471

Add $5.00 for USPS shipping and handling. For Florida residents PLEASE add the appropriate sales tax for your county.

Please Print

_____
Name

_____
Organization Name

_____
Address

_____
City, State, Zip

❑ My check or money order is enclosed. *Please make checks payable to Atlantic Publishing Company.*

❑ My purchase order is attached. *PO #* _____

Order toll-free
800-814-1132
FAX 352-622-5836

www.atlantic-pub.com • e-mail: sales@atlantic-pub.com

State Restaurant Associations

Offices outside of the U.S are located at the end of the list.

ALABAMA

Alabama Restaurant and Foodservice
Association
P.O. Box 230207
Montgomery, AL 36123-
334-244-1320
FAX: 334-271-4621

Physical Address:
2000 Interstate Park Dr., Suite 402
Montgomery, AL 36109

ALASKA

Alaska Cabaret, Hotel and Restaurant
Association
341 East 56th Avenue
Anchorage, AK 99518
901-563-8133
FAX: 907-563-8640

ARIZONA

Arizona Restaurant Association
2701 N 16th Street, Suite 221
Phoenix, AZ 85006
602-234-0701
FAX: 602-266-6043

ARKANSAS

Arkansas Hospitality Association
603 Pulaski Street
P.O. Box 3866
LIttle Rock, AR 72203-
501-376-2323
FAX: 501-376-6517

CALIFORNIA

California Restaurant Association
3435 Wilshire Blvd., Suite 2230
Los Angeles, CA 90010
213-384-1200
800-794-4272
FAX: 213-384-1623

California Restaurant Association,
Government Affairs
980 9th Street, Suite 1480
Sacramento, CA 95814
916-447-5793
800-765-4842 (in CA)
FAX: 916-447-6182

Golden Gate Restaurant Association
415-781-5348

State Restaurant Association of
California (CALSRA)
P.O. Box 418446
Sacramento, CA 95841
888-994-2257
FAX: 888-993-2922

Western Restaurant Association
(CALSRA)
P.O. Box 418446
Sacramento, CA 95841
888-994-2257 • 888-994-2257
FAX: 888-993-2922

American Restaurant Association
(CALSRA)
P.O. Box 418446

Sacramento, CA 95841

888-994-2257

FAX: 888-993-2922

COLORADO

Colorado Restaurant Association

899 Logan St., Suite 300

Denver, CO 80203

303-830-2972

FAX: 303-830-2973

CONNECTICUT

Connecticut Restaurant Association

731 Hebron Avenue

Glastonbury, CT 06033

203-633-5484

FAX: 203-657-8241

DELAWARE

Delaware Restaurant Association

P.O. Box 7838

Newark, DE 19714-7838

302-366-8565

FAX: 302-738-8865

Physical Address:

Five Embry Court

Drummond North

Newark, DE 19711

DISTRICT OF COLUMBIA

Restaurant Association of Metropolitan

Washington, Inc.

7926 Jones Branch Dr., Suite 530

McLean, VA 22102-3303

703-356-1315

FAX: 703-893-4926

FLORIDA

Florida Restaurant Association

200 West College Avenue

Tallahassee, FL 32301

904-224-2250

FAX: 904-222-9213

GEORGIA

Georgia Hospitality & Travel Association

600 W Peachtree St., Suite 1500

Atlanta, GA 30308

404-873-4482

FAX: 404-874-5742

HAWAII

Hawaii Restaurant Association

1188 Bishop Street, Suite 1507

Honolulu, HI 96813

808-536-9105

FAX: 808-534-0117

IDAHO

Idaho Hospitality & Travel Association, Inc.

P.O. Box 7587

Boise, ID 83707

208-362-2637 • 800-959-2637 (in ID)

FAX: 208-362-0855

Physical Address

4930 Umarilla • Boise, ID 83709

ILLINOIS

Illinois Restaurant Association

350 W Ontario

Chicago, IL 60610

312-787-4000

FAX: 312-787-4792

INDIANA

Restaurant and Hospitality Association
of Indiana
115 W Washington St., Suite 11655
Indianapolis, IN 46204
317-673-4211
FAX: 317-673-4210

IOWA

Iowa Hospitality Association
606 Merle Hay Tower
Des Moines, IA 50310
515-276-1454
FAX: 515-276-3660

KANSAS

Kansas Restaurant and Hospitality
Association
359 S Hydraulic
Wichita, KS 67211
316-267-8383
FAX: 316-267-8400

KENTUCKY

Kentucky Restaurant Association
422 Executive Park
Louisville, KY 40207
502-896-0464
FAX: 502-896-0465

LOUISIANA

Louisiana Restaurant Association
2700 N Arnoult
Metairie, LA 70002
504-454-2277
FAX: 504-454-2299

MAINE

Maine Restaurant Association
Five Wade Street
P.O. Box 5060
Augusta, ME 04330
207-623-2178
FAX: 207-623-8377

MARYLAND

Restaurant Association of Maryland, Inc.
7113 Ambassador Road
Baltimore, MD 21244
410-298-0011
FAX: 410-298-0299

MASSACHUSETTS

Massachusetts Restaurant Association
95-A Turnpike Road
Westborough, MA 01581
508-366-4144
800-852-3042 (in MA)
FAX: 508-366-4614

Massachusetts Restaurant Association,
Government Affairs
141 Tremont St., 6th Fl.
Boston, MA 02111
617-426-1081
FAX: 617-426-8564

MICHIGAN

Michigan Restaurant Association
225 W Washtenaw Street
Lansing, MI 48933
800-968-9668

MINNESOTA

Minnesota Restaurant Association
871 Jefferson Avenue
Street Paul, MN 55102
612-222-7401
FAX: 612-222-7347

MISSISSIPPI

Mississippi Restaurant Association
P.O. Box 16395
Jackson, MS 39236
601-982-4281
FAX: 601-982-0062

MISSOURI

Missouri Restaurant Association
P.O. Box 10277
Kansas City, MO 64171
816-753-5222
FAX: 816-753-6993

Physical Address:
4049 Pennsylvania Ave., Suite 201
Kansas City, MO 64111

MONTANA

Montana Restaurant Association
1537 Avenue D, #320
Billings, MT 59102
406-256-1105
FAX: 406-256-0785

Physical Address:
3495 W Broadway
Missoula, MT 59802

NEBRASKA

Nebraska Restaurant Association
5625 "O" St. Building, Suite 7
Lincoln, NE 68510
402-483-2630
FAX: 402-483-2746

NEVADA

Nevada Restaurant Association
4820 Alpine Place, Suite B202
Las Vegas, NV 89107
702-878-2313
FAX: 702-878-5009

NEW HAMPSHIRE

New Hampshire Lodging and Restaurant
Association
4 Park Street, Suite 413
P.O. Box 1175
Concord, NH 03301
603-228-9585
FAX: 603-226-1829

NEW JERSEY

New Jersey Restaurant Association
One Executive Drive, Suite 100
Somerset, NJ 08873
908-302-1800
FAX: 908-302-1804

NEW MEXICO

New Mexico Restaurant Association
7800 Marble NE, Suite 4
Albuquerque, NM 87110
505-268-2474
FAX: 505-268-5848

NEW YORK

New York State Restaurant Association
505 Eighth Avenue, 7th Floor
New York, NY 10018
212-714-1330
FAX: 212-643-2962

New York State Restaurant Association
455 New Karner Road
Albany, NY 12205
800-452-5212
FAX: 518-452-4497

NORTH CAROLINA

North Carolina Restaurant Association
P.O. Box 6528
Raleigh, NC 27628
919-782-5022
FAX: 919-782-7251

Physical Address:
3105 Charles B. Root Wynd
Raleigh, NC 27612

NORTH DAKOTA

North Dakota State
Hospitality Association
P.O. Box 428
Bismarck, ND 58502
701-223-3313
FAX: 701-223-0215

Physical Address:
919 S. 7th St., Suite 601
Bismarck, ND 58504

OHIO

Ohio Restaurant Association
1525 Bethel Road, Suite 301
Columbus, OH 43215
614-442-3535 • 800-282-9049
FAX: 614-442-3550

OKLAHOMA

Oklahoma Restaurant Association
3800 N Portland
Oklahoma City, OK 73112
405-942-8181
FAX: 405-942-0541

OREGON

Oregon Restaurant Association
8565 SW Salish Lane, Suite 120
Wilsonville, OR 97070
503-682-4422
FAX: 503-682-4455

PENNSYLVANIA

Pennsylvania Restaurant Association
100 State Street
Harrisburg, PA 17101-
717-232-4433
800-346-7767
FAX: 717-236-1202

RHODE ISLAND

Rhode Island Hospitality Association
P.O. Box 6208
Providence, RI 02940
401-732-4881
FAX: 401-732-4883

Physical Address:
1206 Jefferson Blvd.
Warwick, RI 02886

SOUTH CAROLINA

South Carolina Restaurant Association
Barringer Building, Suite 505
1338 Main Street
Columbia, SC 29201
803-765-9000
FAX: 803-252-7136

SOUTH DAKOTA

South Dakota Restaurant Association
P.O. Box 638
Pierre, SD 57501
605-224-5050
FAX: 605-224-2059

Physical Address:
320 E Capitol
Pierre, SD 57501

TENNESSEE

Tennessee Restaurant Association
P.O. Box 681207
Franklin, TN 37068
615-790-2703
FAX: 615-790-2768

Physical Address:
1224-A Lakeview Drive
Franklin, TN 37064

TEXAS

Texas Restaurant Association
P.O. Box 1429
Austin, TX 78767

512-472-3666
FAX: 512-472-2777

Physical Address
1400 Lavaca
Austin, TX 78701

UTAH

Utah Restaurant Association
1555 E Stratford Street, #100
Salt Lake City, UT 84115
801-487-4821
FAX: 801-467-5170

VERMONT

Vermont Lodging and Restaurant
Association
Route 100 N R1, #1522
Waterbury, VT 05676
802-244-1344
FAX: 802-244-1342

VIRGINIA

Virginia Hospitality and Travel
Association-Restaurant Division
2101 Libbie Avenue
Richmond, VA 23230
804-288-3065
FAX: 804-285-3093

WASHINGTON

Restaurant Association of the State of
Washington, Inc.
2405 Evergreen Park Drive SW Suite A2
Olympia, WA 98502
360-956-7279
FAX: 360-357-9232

WEST VIRGINIA

West Virginia Hospitality and Travel
Association
P.O. Box 2391
Charleston, WV 25328
304-342-6511
FAX: 304-345-1538

Physical Address:
20003 Quarrier Street
Charleston, WV 25311

WISCONSIN

Wisconsin Restaurant Association
2801 Fish Hatchery Road
Madison, WI 53713
608-270-9950 • 800-589-3211
FAX: 608-270-9960
http://www.wirestaurant.org

WYOMING

Wyoming Lodging & Restaurant
Association
P.O. Box 1003
Cheyenne, WY 82003
307-634-8816
FAX: 307-632-0249

Physical Address:
211 W 19th, Suite 201
Cheyenne, WY 82001

OUTSIDE OF U.S.

CANADA

Canadian Restaurant & Foodservices
Association
316 Bloor Street W
Toronto, Ontario Canada
M5S 1W5
416-923-1450
FAX: 416-923-1450

ONTARIO

Ontario Restaurant Association
121 Richmond Street W
Suite 1201
Toronto, Ontario Canada M6S 2P2
416-359-0533
FAX: 416-359-0531

U.S. VIRGIN ISLANDS

Virgin Islands Restaurant & Bar
Association
c/o Virgin Rhythms Public Relations
P.O. Box 12048
St. Thomas, VI 00801
809-777-6161
FAX: 809-777-6036

PUERTO RICO

Puerto Rico Hotel and Tourism Association
954 Ponce de Leon Avenue, Suite 703
San Juan, PR 00907-3605
805-725-2901

Journals and Trade Publications

Bar & Beverage Business Magazine
Mercury Publications
1839 Inkster Blvd.
Winnipeg, Manitoba R2X 1R3

Bartender Magazine
Foley Publishing Corp.
P.O. Box 158
Liberty Corner, NJ 07938

Beer, Wine & Spirits Beverage Retailer
Oxford Publishing
307 W Jackson Avenue
Oxford, MS 38655

Beverage & Food Dynamics
Adams Business Media
1180 Avenue of the Americas, 11th Floor
New York, NY 10036

Beverage Bulletin
6310 San Vicente Blvd., Suite 530 Los
Angeles, CA 90048

Beverage World Periscope
Keller International Publishing
Corporation
150 Great Neck Road
Great Neck, NY 11021

Center of the Plate
American Culinary Foundation
10 San Bartola Drive
St. Augustine, FL 32086-5766

Cheers
Adams Business Media
50 Washington Street, 10th Floor
Norwalk, CT 06854

Chef
Talcott Communication Corp.
20 N Wacker Drive, #1865
Chicago, IL 60606-2905

Coffee & Cuisine
1218 3rd Avenue, #1315
Seattle, WA 98101-3021

Consultant
Foodservice Consultants Society
International
304 W Liberty, Suite 201
Louisville, KY 40202-3011

Cooking For Profit
CP Publishing
P.O. Box 267
Fond du Lac, WI 54936-0267

Correction Foodservice
International Publishing Company of America
665 La Villa Drive
Miami, FL 33166-6095

**Council on Hotel, Restaurant & Institutional
Education Communique**
Council on Hotel, Restaurant &
Institutional Education

3205 Skipwith Road
Richmond, VA 23294

P.O. Box 416
Denver, CO 80201-0416

Culinary Trends
Culinary Trends Publications
6285 Spring Street, 107
Long Beach, CA 90808

Food Channel
Noble & Associates
515 N State St., 29th Floor
Chicago, IL 60610-4325

El Restaurante Mexicano
Maiden Name Press
P.O. Box 2249
Oak Park, IL 60303-2249

Food Distribution Research Society News
Silesia Companies
P.O. Box 441110
Fort Washington, MD 20749-1110

Fancy Foods & Culinary Products
Talcott Communication Corporation
20 N Wacker Drive, #1865
Chicago, IL 60606-2905

Food Distributors International
201 Park Washington Court
Falls Church, VA 22046

FEDA News & Views
Foodservice Equipment Distributors
Association
223 W Jackson Blvd., #620
Chicago, IL 60606-6911

Food Management
Donohue/Meehan Publishing
The Penton Media Building
1300 E 9th Street
Cleveland, OH 44114

Food & Beverage News
886 W Bay Drive, #E6
Largo, FL 33770-3017

*Food Service Equipment and Supplies
Specialist*
Cahners Business Information
2000 Clearwater Drive
Oak Brook, IL 60523

Food Arts Magazine
M Shanken Communications
387 Park Ave. S, 8th Floor
New York, NY 10016-8872

FoodService and Hospitality
23 Lesmill Rd., Suite 101
Toronto, Ontario M3B 3P6

*Food Businesses: Snack Shops, Speciality Food
Restaurants & Other Ideas*
Prosperity & Profits Unlimited

Foodservice Equipment and Supplies
Cahners Business Information
1350 East Touhy Avenue
Des Plaines, IL 60018

FoodTalk
Pike & Fischer
1010 Wayne Ave., #1400
Silver Springs, MD 20910

Fresh Cup Magazine
P.O. Box 14827
Portland, OR 97293-0827

Frozen Food Executive
National Frozen Food Association
4755 Linglestown Road, Suite 300
Harrisburg, PA 17112

Healthcare Foodservice
International Publishing Company of
America
665 La Villa Drive
Miami, FL 33166-6095

Hotel, Restaurant, Institutional Buyers Guide
Urner Barry Publications
P.O. Box 389
Toms River, NJ 08754

*International Association of Food Industry
Suppliers*
1451 Dolly Madison Boulevard
McLean, VA 22101

Journal of Food Protection
International Association for Food
Protection
6200 Aurora Avenue, Suite 200W
Des Moines, IA 50322

*Journal of Restaurant and Foodservice
Marketing*
Haworth Press
21 E Broad Street
West Hazelton, PA 18201

Midwest Foodservice News
Pinnacle Publishing
2736 Sawbury Blvd.
Columbus, OH 43235

National Association of Concessionaries
35 E Wacker Drive, Suite 1816
Chicago, IL 60601-2270

National Culinary Review
American Culinary Federation
10 San Bartola Drive
St. Augustine, FL 32086

National Dipper
US Exposition Corp.
1841 Hicks Road, #C
Rolling Meadows, IL 60008

Nation's Restaurant News
Lebhar Friedman
425 Park Avenue
New York, NY 10022-3506

Nightclub & Bar Magazine
Oxford Publishing
307 W Jackson Avenue
Oxford, MS 38655

On Campus Hospitality
Executive Business Media
825 Old Country Road
P.O. Box 1500
Westbury, NY 11590

Onboard Services
International Publishing Company of
America
665 La Villa Drive
Miami, FL 33166-6095

OnSite
Nation's Restaurant News
3922 Coconut Palm Drive
Tampa, FL 33619-8321

Prepared Foods
Cahners Business Information 2000
Clearwater Drive
Oak Brook, IL 60523

Restaurant Business
Bill Communications
353 Park Avenue S
New York, NY 10010-1706

Restaurant Digest
Panagos Publishing
3930 Knowles Avenue, #305
Kensington, MD 20895

Restaurant Hospitality
Penton Media
The Penton Media Building
1300 East 9th Street
Cleveland, OH 44114-1503

Restaurant Management Today
Atcom
1541 Morris Avenue
Bronx, NY 10457-8702

Restaurant Marketing
Oxford Publishing
307 W Jackson Avenue
Oxford, MS 38655

Restaurant Wine
Wine Profits
P.O. Box 222
Napa, CA 94559-0222

Restaurants & Institutions
Cahners Business Information
1350 East Touhy Avenue
Des Plaines, IL 60018

Restaurants USA
National Restaurant Association
1200 17th Street NW
Washington, D.C. 20036-3006

Restaurants, Resorts & Hotels
Publishing Group
P.O. Box 318
Trumbull, CT 06611-0318

Showcase Magazine
National Association for the Specialty
Food Trade
120 Wall Street, 27th Floor
New York, NY 10005-40001

Southern Beverage Journal
14337 SW 119th Avenue
Miami, FL 33186-6006

Wine on Line Food and Wine Review
Enterprise Publishing
138 N 16th Street
Blair, NE 68008

Yankee Food Service
Griffin Publishing Company
616 Main Street
Dennis, MA 02638

Manufacturers Reference

The following manufacturers submitted photos and information to be used as references in *The Professional Caterer's Handbook*.

Accardis Systems, Inc.
20061 Doolittle Street
Montgomery Village, MD 20886
1-800-852-1992
www.accardis.com

Accubar
9457 S University Blvd
#261
Highlands Ranch, CO 80126
1-800-806-3922
www.accubar.com

Amana Commercial Products
2800 220th Trail
Amana, IA 52204
1-888-262-6271
www.amanacommercial.com

America Corporation
PO Box 91
13686 Red Arrow Highway
Harbert, MI 49115
1-800-621-5075
www.america-americabirchtrays.com

Aprons, Etc.
PO Box 1132
9 Ellwood Court
Mauldin, SC 29662
1-800-460-7836
www.apronsetc.com

Belson Outdoors, Inc
111 North River Rd
North Aurora, IL 60542
1-630-897-8489
www.belson.com

Big John Grills & Rotisseries
770 W College Ave
Pleasant Gap, PA 16823
1-800-326-9575
www.bigjohngrills.com

Biocorp
15301 140th Ave
Becker, MN 55308
1-866-348-8348
www.biocorpaavc.com

Blodgett
44 Lakeside Avenue
Burlington, VT 05401
1-800-331-5842
www.blodgett.com

Browne-Halco, Inc.
2840 Morris Ave
Union, NJ 07083
1-888-289-1005
www.halco.com

Buffet Enhancements International
PO Box 1000
Point Clear, AL 36564
1-800-990-0990
www.buffetenhancements.com

Caterease Software
1020 Goodlette Road N
Naples, FL 34102
1-800-863-1616
www.caterease.com

Chillin' Products, Inc.
1039 Railroad Street
Rockdale, IL 60436
1-866-932-4455
www.chillinproducts.com

CommLog
2509 E Darrel Rd
Phoenix, AZ 85042
1-800-962-6564
www.commlog.com

Cookshack, Inc.
2304 N Ash St
Ponca City, OK 74601
1-800-423-0698
www.cookshack.com

DayMark Food Safety Systems
12830 South Dixie Highway
Bowling Green, OH 43402
1-800-847-0101
www.daymark.biz

Duncan Industries
PO Box 802822
Santa Clarita, CA 91380
1-800-785-4449
www.kitchengrips.com

**EasyBar Beverage
Management Systems**
19799 SW 95th Ave, Suite A
Tualatin, OR 97062
1-503-624-6744
www.easybar.com

Franklin Machine Products
101 Mt. Holly Bypass
Lumberton, NJ 08048
1-800-257-7737
www.fmponline.com

**General Espresso Equipment
Corporation**
7912 Industrial Village Road
Greensboro, NC 27409
1-336-393-0224
www.geec.com

Genpak
PO Box 727
Glen Falls, NY 12801
1-518-798-9511
www.genpak.com

Gourmet Display
6040 South 194th, Ste #102
Kent, WA 98032
1-206-767-4711
www.gourmetdisplay.com

Henny Penny Corporation
1219 U.S. 35 West
Eaton, OH 45320
1-800-417-8417
www.hennypenny.com

Holstein Manufacturing
5368 110th St
Holstein, IA 51025
1-800-368-4342
www.holsteinmfg.com

iSi North America, Inc.
175 Rt 46 West
Fairfield, NJ 07004
1-800-447-2426
www.isinorthamerica.com

Motoman Inc.
805 Liberty Lane
West Carrollton, OH 45449
1-937-847-6200
www.motoman.com

OZEM Corp.
832 Harvard Dr
Holland, MI 49423
1-866-617-3345
www.ozwinebars.com

Polar Ware Company
2806 North 15th St
Sheboygan, WI 53083
1-800-237-3655
www.polarware.com

Precision Pours, Inc.
12837 Industrial Park Blvd
Plymouth, MN 55441
1-800-549-4491
www.precisionpours.com

Regal Ware, Inc.
1675 Reigle Dr
Kewaskum, WI 53040
1-262-626-2121
www.regalwarefoodservice.com

Sabert
879-899 Main St
Sayreville, NJ 08872
1-800-722-3781
www.sabert.com

Satellite Cooling
308 Washington Blvd, Ste
A-105
Mundelein, IL 60060
1-888-356-2665
www.satellitecool.com

Scannabar
101 Federal Street, Suite 1900
Boston, MA 02110
1-888-666-0736
www.scannabar.com

Sitram USA
4081 Calle Tesoro, Ste G
Camarillo, CA 93012
1-800-515-8585
www.sitramcookware.com

Slecta Corp dba Dickies Chef
13780 Benchmark Dr.
Farmers Branch, TX 75234
1-866-262-6288
www.dickiechef.com

Sunkist Foodservice Eq.
720 E Sunkist St
Ontario, CA 91761
1-800-383-7141
www.sunkistfs.com/equipment

Tucel Industries
2014 Forestdale Road
Forestdale, VT 05745
1-800-558-8235
www.tucel.com

Vinotemp International
17621 S Susanna Rd
Rancho Dominguez, CA 90221
1-310-886-3332
www.vinotemp.com

WNA Comet
6 Stuart Road
Chelmsford, MA 01824
1-888-962-2877
www.wna-inc.com

Wes-Pak, Inc.
9100 Frazier Pike
Little Rock, AR 72206
1-800-493-7725
www.wespakinc.com

Zing Zang Inc
950 Milwaukee Ave
Glenview, IL 60025
1-888-891-7489
www.zingzang.com

Winekeeper
625 E Haley St
Santa Barbabra, CA 93103
1-805-963-3451
www.winekeeper.com

Zojirushi America Corp
6259 Bandini Blvd
Commerce, CA 90040
1-800-733-6270
www.zojirushi.com

Index

T

References

Bode, Sony. *The Food Service Professional's Guide to Successful Catering: Managing the Catering Operation for Maximum Profit.* Ocala, FL: Atlantic Publishing, 2003.

Brown, Douglas R. *The Restaurant Manager's Handbook, 3rd Edition.* Ocala, FL: Atlantic Publishing, 2003.

Pavesic, David V. and Magnant, Paul F. *Fundamental Principles of Restaurant Cost Control.* Engelwood Cliffs, NJ: Prentice Hall, 2004

Pavesic, David V. *Cost Controls: 25 Keys to Profitable Success; Restaurant Manager's Pocket Handbook Series.* New York, NY: Lebhar-Friedman Books, 1999.

Pavesic, David V. *Food Cost: 25 Keys to Profitable Success; Restaurant Manager's Pocket Handbook Series.* New York, NY: Lebhar-Friedman Books, 1999.

Pavesic, David V. *Labor Cost: 25 Keys to Profitable Success; Restaurant Manager's Pocket Handbook Series.* New York, NY: Lebhar-Friedman Books, 1999.

Pavesic, David V. *Menu Pricing: 25 Keys to Profitable Success; Restaurant Manager's Pocket Handbook Series.* New York, NY: Lebhar-Friedman Books, 1999.

Pavesic, David V. *Purchasing and Inventory: 25 Keys to Profitable Success; Restaurant Manager's Pocket Handbook Series.* New York, NY: Lebhar-Friedman Books, 1999.

HACCP & Sanitation in Restaurants and Food Service Operations: A Practical Guide Based on the FDA Food Code

According to the FDA, it is estimated that up to 76 million people get a food-borne illness each year. Since people don't go to the doctor for mild symptoms, the actual number of illnesses can't be known, but 5,000 people a year die from food-borne illness in the United States, and many others suffer long-term effects.

Most all of this sickness and death could have been prevented with the proper procedures that are taught in this comprehensive book. If these numbers don't upset you, realize that a food-borne outbreak in your establishment can put you out of business, and if the business survives, it will certainly be severely damaged; this, of course, after the lawsuits are resolved. If you do not have proper sanitation methods and a HACCP program in place, you need them today.

This book is based on the FDA Food Code and will teach the food service manager and employees every aspect of food safety, HACCP and sanitation, from purchasing and receiving food to properly washing dishes. They will learn:

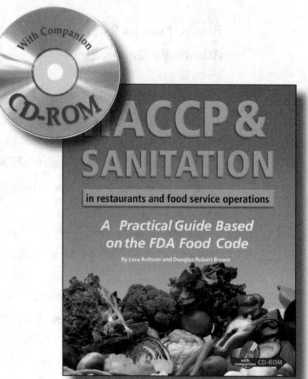

- Time and temperature abuses

- Cross-contamination

- Personal hygiene practices

- Biological, chemical and physical hazards

- Proper cleaning and sanitizing

- Waste and pest management

- Basic principles of HACCP

- Bacteria, viruses, fungi and parasites

- Various food-borne illnesses

- Safe food-handling techniques

- Purchasing, receiving and food storage

- Food preparation and serving

- Sanitary equipment and facilities

- Explain what safe food is and how to provide it

- Cleaning and sanitizing of equipment and facilities

- Accident prevention and crisis management

- Food safety and sanitation laws

The companion CD-ROM contains all the forms and posters needed to establish your HACCP and food-safety program.

ISBN# 978-091062-735-1 • $79.95
600 Pages Hardbound
ISBN 0910627-35-5

**To order call toll-free
800-814-1132 or visit
www.atlantic-pub.com**

The COMPLETE WAITSTAFF TRAINING COURSE Video
VHS & DVD IN ENGLISH OR SPANISH

In this new 53-minute, high-quality waitstaff training video, your staff will learn how to consistently deliver the quality service that makes customers not only come back, but tell others about their memorable experience. This training tape is ideal as a backbone in your training program for experienced waitstaff who are always looking to learn more or for people who have never waited tables and would like to learn the basics. Study guide and tests are included. A certificate of completion is available. Available in VHS, DVD, PAL English or Spanish. Topics covered include:

- Alcohol sales and wine service.
- Taking beverage orders.
- Correct service procedures.
- Placing the order.
- Serving food.

- Preparing for service.
- Hosting and greeting guests.
- Taking the food order.
- Picking up the order.
- Completing the service.

English VHS Video Item # CWS-EN $149.95
Distributor Price $74.98
ISBN 0910627-40-1

English PAL Video Item # CWS-ENPAL $149.95
Distributor Price $74.98
ISBN 0910627-42-8

English DVD Item # CWS-ENDVD-02 $149.95
Distributor Price $74.98
ISBN 0910627-44-4

English Certificate of Completion
Item # CWS-CREN $9.95
Distributor Price $4.98

Spanish VHS Video Item # CWS-SP $149.95
Distributor Price $74.98
ISBN 0910627-41-X

Spanish PAL Video Item # CWS-SPPAL $149.95
Distributor Price $74.98
ISBN 0910627-43-6

Spanish DVD Item # CWS-SPDVD $149.95
Distributor Price $74.98
ISBN 0910627-45-2

Spanish Certificate of Completion
Item # CWS-CRSP $9.95
Distributor Price $4.98

To order call toll-free 800-814-1132
or visit www.atlantic-pub.com